COLLINS FIELD GUIDE

BIRDS OF WEST AFRICA

COLLINS FIELD GUIDE

BIRDS OF WEST AFRICA

W. Serle, G.J. Morel

W. Hartwig

HarperCollins*Publishers*

HarperCollins*Publishers*

First published 1977 by
William Collins Sons & Co Ltd.
London · Glasgow · Sydney · Auckland
Toronto · Johannesburg

ISBN 0 00 219204 7

Reprinted 1979
Reprinted 1983
Reprinted 1984
Reprinted 1986
Reprinted 1988
Reprinted 1990
Reprinted 1992
Reprinted 1995

Produced by HarperCollins Hong Kong

PREFACE

The text of this book is the combined work of both authors, who have freely exchanged ideas and criticisms at all stages during its preparation. Dr William Serle, late of the Colonial Medical Service, was in West Africa for over twenty years – mainly in Nigeria and the Cameroons. In this guide he is mainly concerned with the birds of the rain forest and adjoining moist savanna and the montane areas, and has revised the whole text and compiled the Checklist of species (p. 263). Dr Gérard J. Morel has been stationed in West Africa – in Senegal – for some twenty years, engaged in ornithological research under the auspices of the Office de la Recherche Scientifique et Technique Outre-Mer (ORSTOM). In this book he is mainly concerned with the birds of the dry savanna in the thorn scrub and sub-desert zones.

The plates have been specially painted by Wolfgang Hartwig, who has considerable knowledge of West African birds both in the field and in the hand.

We have gratefully plundered the stores of factual information in the ornithological literature of Africa, especially the regional works of Bannerman – *The Birds of Tropical West Africa* (1930–1951); and Etchécopar and Hüe – *Birds of North Africa* (1967). The French bird names are primarily those of Dekeyser and Derivot – *Les Oiseaux de l'Ouest Africain* (1967). We are extremely grateful to Dr Wolters and Dr Bernis for so kindly supplying the German and Spanish vernacular names given in the section on pp. 295–335. The general layout of the book follows the pattern first established by R. T. Peterson.

William Serle,
The Manse, Drumoak,
Aberdeenshire, Scotland

Gérard J. Morel,
Office de la Recherche Scientifique et
   Technique Outre-Mer,
Richard-Toll, Senegal

CONTENTS

CONTENTS

ILLUSTRATIONS

INTRODUCTION

Territory. For the purpose of this field guide, West Africa comprises the following political divisions: southern Mauritania, Senegal, Gambia, Portuguese Guinea, Guinea, Sierra Leone, Liberia, Mali, Ivory Coast, Upper Volta, Niger, Ghana, Togo, Dahomey, Nigeria, Cameroons, Rio Muni, Gaboon, Congo, Central African Republic and Chad. The Cape Verde Islands are included and also the Gulf of Guinea islands of Fernando Po, Principe, Sao Tome and Annobon.

Coverage. It is difficult to produce a concise yet comprehensive guide to a wide geographical area as rich in bird species as West Africa. We have used our judgement in selecting certain species for extended and others for only brief treatment. We are aware of the defects arising from this need for selectivity and conciseness.

Of the 1097 birds recorded from the area, 726 are dealt with in the body of the text. Of these 726, some are fully treated and all those so treated are illustrated. The rest are termed *allied species* and they are dealt with more briefly and are not illustrated. The remaining 371 species (uncommon and/or local in West Africa) which occur in the area but which, for reasons of space are not dealt with in the body of the text, are included with brief status notes in the Checklist of species on pp. 263–94. This Checklist should go some way towards meeting the criticisms of incompleteness and unreliability often levelled against selective field guides. The book thus covers all the birds known to occur in West Africa.

Scientific names. The order of families and the nomenclature follow fairly closely, though not entirely, White's *Revised Check-list of African Birds* (1961–1965). Many West African ornithologists are more familiar with the nomenclature of Bannerman's *Birds of West and Equatorial Africa* (1953). Bannerman recognized many more genera than does White and gave specific status to many forms which in White are reduced to the status of subspecies. As a result the 'old' scientific names of Bannerman often differ from the 'new' scientific names of White. To help those perplexed by the many changes, Bannerman's name or names, when they differ from White's, are given in brackets after White's names both in the body of the text and in the Checklist. In the index also Bannerman's old generic names, when they differ from White's, are given in brackets after the new generic name.

Identification. The book is primarily concerned with species, although a few well-marked races, capable of identification in the field, are also mentioned. With those species which have extra-limital races, it is the West African race which is described and illustrated. The figure at the beginning of the description is the average length in inches from the tip of the bill to the tip of the tail.

In the paragraph on distribution and habitat, the range given is the range of the species within West Africa, and account has been taken of all important distributional papers published before the end of 1971. In this paragraph it has been possible to mention only very briefly the movements of the many migratory Palaearctic and Ethiopian forms.

A short paragraph on nest and eggs is included for those species which are breeding residents. In a few cases in which information was lacking from West Africa, data from other parts of Africa has been used for the completion of this paragraph and this fact is mentioned in the text in each such case. A description of the nest and eggs is of intrinsic interest and also is sometimes a useful aid to identification of the parent bird.

The **caption page** opposite each plate has the names of the birds, notes on important field characters, and page references to the main text.

TOPOGRAPHY, CLIMATE AND VEGETATION

The area covered by the Guide is bounded on the north by the Sahara along the line of the Ethiopian-Palaearctic divide (roughly 18°N–20°N); on the east by the watershed that separates the streams flowing eastwards to the White Nile from the streams flowing westwards to the Chari and the Oubangui; on the south-east by the Congo and its tributary the Oubangui, and on the south and west by the Atlantic Ocean. Northwards it includes the mountains of Air, Tibesti, and Ennedi but excludes the Ahaggar Plateau.

The main orographical feature of the area is the chain of mountains and hills collectively called the Cameroon highlands. From their highest point, the 13,000 foot high Cameroon Mountain rising from the sea at the head of the Bight of Biafra, the highlands penetrate the continent for several hundred miles in a north-easterly direction. The mountainous islands of Fernando Po, Principe, Sao Tome, and Annobon in the Gulf of Guinea are outliers of the same mountain system.

The Cameroon highlands are of great ornithological interest because the montane forests found on some of their higher slopes support a distinctive montane bird fauna most of whose species are absent from the lowland forests but often reappear in identical or closely allied forms in the montane districts of East and Central Africa.

Except for the Cameroon highlands the land surface of West Africa is generally flat and featureless. In places the monotony is relieved by rocky outcrops or mountains and hills of which the most notable are the Fouta Djallon in Guinea, the Loma Mountains in Sierra Leone, Mount Nimba in Liberia, the Jos Plateau in Nigeria, and the Air, Tibesti, and Ennedi Mountains in the northern desert region.

The river Niger, 2600 miles long, drains the greater part of West Africa west of the Cameroons. Its banks, islands, and associated flood plains and marshes provide feeding and breeding grounds for many aquatic birds.

The entire region lies within the tropics, and day and night temperatures are generally high except in a few mountainous localities. The most important element in the climate as far as bird life is concerned is the rainfall. It is the rainfall that mainly determines the type of vegetation at a particular locality and usually the type of vegetation is the most important element in the habitat to which a particular bird species is adapted.

There is great geographical variation in the rainfall. In the north – in the desert and its borders from Mauritania in the west to northern Chad in the east – the rainfall is very low, in some stations less than one inch in a year, and the sandy or rocky ground is barren or supports a sparse, mainly herbaceous vegetation. In the south – in the vicinity of the climatic equator from coastal

Sierra Leone and Liberia in the west to Gaboon and Congo in the east – the rainfall is high, often over a hundred inches in a year, and the rainy season is prolonged, and the vegetation takes the form of tropical rain forest. Between these extremes there is a gradual transition in climate as one travels equatorwards from the dry, arid north to the wet, lush south.

The region lies almost entirely north of the equator and the rainy season coincides with the Northern Hemisphere summer. Generally speaking the higher the annual precipitation the longer the wet season, and the lower the annual precipitation the shorter the wet season. Although the rainfall at any point on the map of West Africa is determined usually by its nearness to the climatic equator there are important local exceptions due to such factors as the orientation of the coast-line, the proximity of cold ocean currents, or the presence of mountains especially when these lie across the paths of rainbearing winds. For example the dry savanna coastlands of eastern Ghana, Togo, and Dahomey, which are bounded on the east and the west by tropical rain forest, probably owe their low rainfall and savanna-type vegetation to the orientation of the coastline which runs parallel to the prevailing winds, and to the proximity of an offshoot of the cold Benguella Current.

The two principal sorts of vegetation are forest and savanna. Each possesses its own bird fauna. Few forest species are found in the savanna and few savanna species are found in the forest. Forest occurs in areas of high rainfall. It is characterized by a preponderance of evergreen trees and a virtual absence of grass. Its appearance changes little with the seasons. Savanna occurs in areas of lower rainfall. Its appearance varies locally and seasonally. Essentially it is grassland but trees and shrubs are also usually a feature of the savanna landscape, scattered over it or concentrated in woodland or thickets. In the moister savanna the grass is tall and thick and the trees and shrubs are soft-leaved. In the drier savanna the grass is shorter and less rank and the trees and shrubs are thorny.

Each dry season the savanna is swept by grass fires which leave the ground bare and black and the trees within reach of the flames charred and leafless but still alive. At the end of the dry season and before the rains the new green grass and fresh foliage appears. The savanna grass fires extend right to the forest edge but cannot penetrate the forest because the forest floor has no herbaceous covering. Hence the transition from savanna to forest is abrupt and complete and it constitutes an effective ecological barrier to the passage of true savanna species into the forest and the passage of true forest species into the savanna. On the other hand, within the savanna the transition from one type of savanna vegetation to another type of savanna vegetation is usually gradual and the change in bird life as one passes from one type of vegetation to another is likewise gradual.

In West Africa vast areas of the forest and savanna have been cleared for cultivation. Clearing alters the composition of the bird life. In primary forest the felled area, if left to regenerate, is soon covered with dense second-growth trees and shrubs. This second-growth, though ecologically suited to certain species of forest birds, is unsuited to others and the latter disappear. If the felled area is cultivated and kept from regenerating, grass appears on the cropped land, many of the second-growth forest birds are repelled and there is an invasion of savanna species. In a forest zone locality, therefore, with primary forest, secondary forest, and cultivation clearing one encounters three quite dissimilar bird populations, geographically in close proximity but ecologically separated.

The changes caused by cultivation in the savanna are usually less marked. Many of the original trees and herbs are spared, most of the original savanna bird species adapt themselves to the changes, and there is no invasion of forest species.

TOPOGRAPHY OF A BIRD

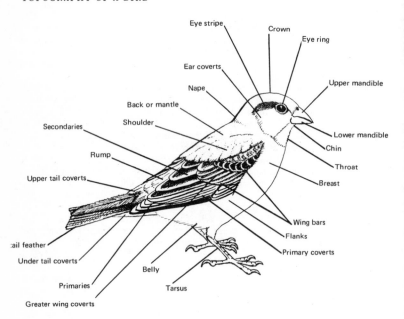

PLACE NAMES

Since this book was written some place names have been changed, notably Portuguese Guinea has become Guinea-Bissau and Congo has become Zaïre.

OSTRICHES: Struthionidae

OSTRICH *Struthio camelus*
Identification: 6–8′. Male much larger than female. Distinguished by its great size, long legs, and long neck. Male has black body plumage, white wings and tail, and pinkish unfeathered neck. Female and immature are greyish-brown. Terrestrial, swift, wary. Usually in small parties.
Voice: Male has a deep booming call.
Distribution and Habitat: The desert and open thorn scrub from southern Mauritania and Senegal east through Mali and Niger to north-eastern Nigeria and Chad.
Nesting: Nest a scrape in the ground. Eggs 10–20, cream-coloured with a glossy pitted surface.

GREBES: Podicipedidae

DABCHICK *Podiceps ruficollis (Poliocephalus ruficollis)* **Pl. 3**
Identification: 6″. Sexes similar. A small plump Grebe with no apparent tail. Short, straight, pointed bill. Conspicuous light spot at gape. Bright chestnut neck and cheeks; upperparts grey-brown with an oily gloss. Immature birds lack the chestnut. Conspicuous white wing patch in flight. Frequently dives and escapes more often thus than by flying. Characteristically runs along the surface of the water before taking off or settling. Chicks ride on parent's back.
Voice: During the breeding season a resounding trill.
Distribution and Habitat: Widespread and locally common in savanna and forest from Senegal and Gambia east to Chad and the Central African Republic and south to Gaboon and Congo, frequenting lakes, reservoirs, the backwaters of rivers, and rice fields.
Nesting: Nest a floating mass of water weeds anchored amongst reeds or open aquatic plants near the margin of a lake or backwater. Eggs 3–5, chalky-white and usually discoloured by buffish-brown nest stains.

PELICANS: Pelecanidae

Large aquatic birds with long flattened bills and a characteristic loose, capacious pouch hanging from the lower mandible and upper throat. Head withdrawn in flight like Herons.

PINK-BACKED OR GREY PELICAN *Pelecanus rufescens* **Pl. 2**
Identification: 54″. Sexes similar. Pale grey with a vinous-pink back, which however is plainly visible only in flight. Nape crested. Immature plumage brownish. Small size and greyer colour distinguish it from the White Pelican. At close range the character of the front edge of the feathering of the forehead is diagnostic; in the Pink-backed Pelican it forms a concave line, in the White Pelican it is pointed.
Voice: Usually silent. Gruntings and clacking recorded.
Distribution and Habitat: Widespread and locally abundant from Senegal

16

Plate 1

HERONS AND EGRETS

Plate 2

HERONS, HAMMERKOP, FLAMINGOES AND PELICAN

1. **NIGHT HERON** *Nycticorax nycticorax* page 19
Black crown and back.

2. **TIGER BITTERN** *Tigriornis leucolopha* 19
Barred upperparts; streaked underparts.

3. **LITTLE BITTERN** *Ixobrychus minutus* 19
Dark back; large cream-coloured wing-patch.

4. **HAMMERKOP** *Scopus umbretta* 23
Anvil-shaped head.

5. **SQUACCO HERON** *Ardeola ralloides* 20
Yellowish when settled; mainly white in flight.

6. **CATTLE EGRET** *Ardeola ibis* 20
Rufous-cinnamon plumes on crown, back, and breast.

7. **GREATER FLAMINGO** *Phoenicopterus ruber* 27
Bill mainly pale pink.

8. **LESSER FLAMINGO** *Phoenicopterus minor* 27
Bill mainly dark red.

9. **PINK-BACKED PELICAN** *Pelecanus rufescens* 15
Mainly pale grey; front edge of forehead feathering forms concave line.

and Gambia east to Chad and south to Gaboon where there are large rivers, lakes, and lagoons, but especially in the open country north of the forest.

Nesting: Breeds in colonies usually in high trees and often in company with Stork species. Nest a slight, crude platform of sticks. Eggs 2, white and chalky.

Allied species: The White Pelican (*Pelecanus onocrotalus*), 65″, is distinguished from the Pink-backed Pelican by its larger size and pinkish-white plumage and at close range by the feathering of the forehead. It occurs widely but sparingly in West Africa, especially in the arid parts and nests colonially (usually on rocky peaks) in Mauritania, northern Nigeria, northern Cameroons, and Chad. The resident population is probably increased by Palaearctic migrants.

CORMORANTS AND DARTERS: Phalacrocoracidae

Medium-sized water birds with dark plumage, hooked bills (except the Darters), and webbed feet with four toes. Neck extended in flight. Distinguished from Ducks by their long tails. Often seen perched, drying their wings in a 'heraldic' position. Dive and swim under water.

LONG-TAILED SHAG *Phalacrocorax africanus*   **Pl. 3**

Identification: 22″. Sexes similar. Black, with a sheen on the upperparts. Bare skin of face orange. Immature birds are brownish above and whitish below. Given to perching with wings open. Swims low in the water with neck only showing.

Voice: Silent except at the nest.

Distribution and Habitat: Widely and commonly distributed throughout our area. Resident. Frequents lakes, rivers, swamps, rice fields, tidal estuaries, and mangrove creeks.

Nesting: Breeds in colonies in trees and sometimes also on the ground. Nest of sticks and water weeds. Eggs 3–5, chalky-white with a greenish tinge.

Allied species: The White-breasted Cormorant (*Phalacrocorax carbo lucidus*), **Pl. 3**, 35″, is easily distinguished from the Long-tailed Shag by its larger size. Plumage black, but cheeks, throat, and upper breast white. Immature plumage mainly white below. A breeding resident on the coastal islands and deltas from Mauritania to Portuguese Guinea and occurs inland at Lake Chad and other lakes in Chad. Doubtful if it now occurs in the Cape Verde Islands.

AFRICAN DARTER *Anhinga rufa*   **Pl. 3**

Identification: 31″. A large aquatic bird with the build of a Cormorant but slimmer. Neck very long, sinuous, with a characteristic kink; bill thin and pointed; tail long and stiff. Male glossy black but head and neck mainly chestnut; a conspicuous white stripe on the side of the face and neck. Female and immature plumage mainly brown and fawn. Habits and habitat similar to those of Cormorants.

Voice: Rather silent. Harsh croakings at nest.

Distribution and Habitat: Widely and commonly distributed throughout our area frequenting mangrove creeks, tidal estuaries, the open sea-shore, and inland rivers and lakes.

Nesting: Breeds in colonies in trees, generally in company with Cormorant and Heron species. Nest a platform of sticks. Eggs 3–5, chalky-white with a green tinge.

HERONS AND EGRETS: Ardeidae

Tall, slim, long-legged wading birds with long pointed bills and broad wings. Slow wing beats. Head retracted in flight.

LITTLE BITTERN *Ixobrychus minutus* **Pl. 2**
Identification: 14″. A very small secretive Heron occasionally seen in laboured flight low over the reed beds when the large cream patch on the wing stands out clearly against the dark back and flight feathers. Upperparts (except neck) blackish in the male and brownish in the female. Underparts buff. In the adult male the neck is bright rufous in the resident African race (*I. m. payesii*) and buff-grey in the migratory European race (*I. m. minutus*). The female and immature plumages of the races are indistinguishable in the field.
Voice: A sharp 'kekekekec'.
Distribution and Habitat: Widely distributed throughout the region where there is suitable habitat in the form of lake, river, or marsh with reed beds or other thick cover. The resident population is augmented by Palaearctic migrants, the latter occurring mainly north of 12° N.
Nesting: Nest a small platform of roots and twigs amongst reeds above the water. Eggs 3–4, white.
Allied species: The Dwarf Bittern (*Ixobrychus sturmii*), 14″, is distinguished by its dark grey upperparts and pale buff underparts heavily streaked with black. At rest it assumes the typical upright Bittern stance. Widely but sparingly distributed in our area frequenting the thick foliage or herbage bordering streams and pools. A local migrant.

TIGER BITTERN *Tigriornis leucolopha* **Pl. 2**
Identification: 30″. Upperparts except for black crown conspicuously barred black and buff; underparts streaked brown and white. In the female the barring on the upperparts is narrower and less conspicuous. Shy, elusive, and solitary.
Voice: The call, which is mainly nocturnal, is described as a loud hollow-sounding note or two notes repeated slowly and regularly for three or four minutes.
Distribution and Habitat: Resident. Confined to the forest showing a preference for the smaller deeply shaded streams. Also in mangrove swamp. The range extends from Sierra Leone east to the Central African Republic and south to Gaboon and Congo.
Nesting: A solitary breeder. A slender platform of twigs hidden in the branches overhanging a sluggish waterway in the primary forest. The single egg is yellowish-buff with scattered reddish-brown spots and obscure greyish-violet secondary blotches

NIGHT HERON *Nycticorax nycticorax* **Pl. 2**
Identification: 22″. Sexes similar. A thick-set Heron with broad, rounded wings and silent, buoyant, owl-like flight. Unobtrusive, resting by day in thickly foliaged trees or shrubs, and fishing by night. Usually encountered at dawn or dusk flighting between roosting and feeding grounds. The shiny black crown and back contrast with the rest of the upperparts, which are pale

grey and with the white underparts. Two long white plumes rise from the nape. The immature plumage is grey-brown blotched and spotted with creamy-white.

Voice: A harsh bark or croak frequently uttered at night in flight.

Distribution and Habitat: Widespread in the region from Senegal and Gambia to Chad, the Central African Republic, Gaboon, and Congo, locally common, but restricted by its requirements of water for fishing and thick foliage for roosting. The resident population is augmented by Palaearctic migrants.

Nesting: Breeds in colonies, often with other Heron species, in reed beds or in trees on dry or flooded ground. Eggs 3, pale blue-green.

Allied species: In flight the White-backed Night Heron (*Nycticorax leuconotus*), 18″, has the same broad rounded wings and stumpy appearance as the Night Heron (*N. nycticorax*). At rest at close range the bright chestnut neck distinguishes it. Resident and widely dispersed in West Africa in the forest and its gallery extensions from Senegal and Gambia to Gaboon and Congo. It frequents wooded rivers, streams, swamp forest, and mangroves. Mainly crepuscular and nocturnal, hiding by day in thick vegetation.

SQUACCO HERON   *Ardeola ralloides*   Pl. 2

Identification: 17″. Sexes similar. Appears yellowish when settled and white when it takes flight. Body plumage yellowish to rufous; a cinnamon-brown patch on the back with buff plumes extending to the tip of the tail. Long black and white plumes on the nape. Rump, tail, belly, and wings white. In immature dress the neck is streaked, the back earth-brown, the wings white, the underparts dirty, and the plumes on nape and back are absent. Quiet, very inconspicuous, and usually solitary, standing hunched-up and immobile on a grassy river bank or at the side of a swamp or lake with rank marsh vegetation.

Voice: A harsh croak, higher pitched than that of *Ardea cinerea*.

Distribution and Habitat: Widely distributed throughout the area where there are lakes and sluggish streams and backwaters with abundant aquatic vegetation. A vagrant to the Cape Verde Islands. Numbers augmented by migrants from the Palaearctic Region during the northern winter.

Nesting: Breeds in colonies with other Heron species in low trees or bushes over water and often well concealed in the foliage. Eggs 2–4, blue-green, immaculate.

CATTLE EGRET   *Ardeola ibis* (*Bubulcus ibis*)   Pl. 2

Identification: 21″. Sexes similar. In nuptial plumage white but cap and plumes on back and breast rufous-cinnamon; bill and legs orange or red. In eclipse plumage white except for faint cinnamon cap, bill and legs yellow. At a distance appears totally white. Closely resembles the Little Egret but the latter is more slender, has black legs, and is strictly aquatic. The Cattle Egret is gregarious, tame, and often follows cattle or large ungulates for the insects they disturb. Usually on dry (often cultivated) ground but occasionally in swamps or rice fields.

Voice: Harsh croakings at the nest.

Distribution and Habitat: Widespread and abundant throughout the region except in closed forest. Breeds commonly in the semi-arid belt during the rains at which season it is mainly or entirely absent from the forest clearings and moist savanna.

Nesting: Breeds colonially in trees near or over water or on dry ground; sometimes in the vicinity of villages. Nest a platform of twigs. Eggs 3–5, very pale blue.

GREEN-BACKED HERON   *Butorides striatus*   Pl. 1
Identification: 16″. Sexes similar. A small Heron, often solitary, and usually discovered in undergrowth near water, quietly perched in typical hunched-up attitude. Progresses with body held almost horizontal and legs bent. In flight somewhat resembles the Giant Kingfisher. Crown dark green, back grey-green, underparts grey. Immature plumage mainly brown, heavily streaked with whitish and buff below.
Voice: Usually silent. Occasionally a low-pitched 'pruk' or sharp 'kia-kia-kia-kia'.
Distribution and Habitat: Widely and commonly distributed throughout the region south of 17° N. but never far from rivers, pools, or marshes, with wooded banks or shores. Also mangrove swamps.
Nesting: Breeds singly or in small colonies. Nest of small sticks placed in bushes or on mangrove stumps a few feet above the water. Eggs 3–4, pale greenish-blue.

GREAT WHITE EGRET   *Egretta alba* (*Casmerodius albus*)   Pl. 1
Identification: 35″. Sexes similar. The largest of the white Egrets. Plumage entirely white at all ages. Long nuptial plumes on back at breeding season. Bill long and strong, black when breeding, yellow at other times. Legs and feet black. Movements deliberate and sedate. Gregarious at roosting and breeding places but usually fishes solitarily.
Voice: A harsh croak, rarely heard outside of the breeding season.
Distribution and Habitat: Widespread and fairly common in our area including the Cape Verde Islands where it nests on the ledges of cliffs. Usually on the larger rivers, lakes, and swamps where there are expanses of open water. Common in the mangrove creeks.
Nesting: Breeds in colonies, often in the company of other Herons, usually in trees or reed beds. Substantial nest of sticks and reeds. Eggs 3–4, pale blue.
Allied species: The Yellow-billed Egret (*Egretta intermedia*), 26″, somewhat resembles the Great White Egret, but is considerably smaller and has a short, more stumpy yellow bill. Legs black, but tibiae yellowish in breeding season. Fairly widespread but local in our area mainly between 12° N. and 17° N. The Black Heron (*Egretta ardesiaca*) is about the same size as the familiar Little Egret. Entire plumage slaty-black. Bill and feet black, toes yellow. Gregarious. Often when fishing in the open both wings are extended, spread, and arched so as to cast a shadow on the water. Widespread but local in our region, both on the coast and inland, showing a preference for open lagoons, lakes, rice fields, and sluggish rivers.

LITTLE EGRET   *Egretta garzetta*   Pl. 1
Identification: 24″. Sexes similar. The smallest of the Egrets. Plumage entirely white at all ages. In nuptial dress two long plumes on nape; back also plumed. Distinguished from the Yellow-billed Egret by its black bill and from the Cattle Egret by its black legs and bill and absence of cinnamon cap. Gregarious at roost and breeding place but usually feeds singly, wading in the shallows and nimbly pursuing fish or water insects.

Voice: A short croak.

Distribution and Habitat: Where there is suitable habitat widespread and common throughout our area including the Cape Verde Islands, where it is resident. Numbers swelled by Palaearctic immigrants during the northern winter. Frequents lakes, sluggish rivers, dams, estuaries, and mangrove creeks.

Nesting: In colonies in trees over or near water or on sea cliffs. Nest a platform of sticks. Eggs 2, pale blue-green.

REEF HERON   *Egretta gularis (Demigretta gularis)*   **Pl. 1**

Identification: 24″. Sexes similar. In appearance and habits resembles the Little Egret but slate-grey with throat white and usually a white patch of varying extent on the wings. White phase Reef Heron closely resembles the Little Egret but the bill is heavier and is brown not black. Maritime habitat an aid to identification. Agile in pursuit of fish. Occurs singly or in small parties.

Voice: A short croak.

Distribution and Habitat: Mainly a bird of the sea coast affecting mangrove creeks, islands, sandy shore, and rocky shore. Occasionally occurs on inland waters.

Nesting: Breeds in colonies (often mixed) in trees near or over water or on low maritime plants. Nest a platform of twigs. Eggs 2–3, pale blue.

GREY HERON   *Ardea cinerea*   **Pl. 1**

Identification: 40″. Sexes similar. A large grey Heron with white forehead, cheeks, and neck, and black cap, wing tips, and underwings, this last character distinguishing it clearly in flight from the Black-headed Heron. Solitary. Flight is slow. Often perches in trees. Usually feeds wading in shallow water.

Voice: A guttural 'Kreek'. At the nest various harsh croaking sounds.

Distribution and Habitat: Widely distributed in our area where there is open shallow fresh or brackish water. Occasionally feeds in dry places. In that part of its range bordering the Sahara and in the Cape Verde Islands its status is probably that of winter visitor from the Palaearctic.

Nesting: Colonial, breeding in the crown of tall trees and making a large nest of sticks. Eggs 3–4, pale blue.

BLACK-HEADED HERON   *Ardea melanocephala*   **Pl. 1**

Identification: 38″. Sexes similar. In general appearance like the Grey Heron but head and neck black and underwings white not grey. Also in the main a dry-country species. Solitary except when breeding.

Voice: A guttural croak.

Distribution and Habitat: Widely and commonly distributed throughout the area except in closed forest. Partial to open grassy or cultivated ground in the savanna, including the Cameroon highlands, and in large forest clearings. Less often near water.

Nesting: Colonial. In the tops of high trees. Often in a village and sometimes alongside Egrets and Ibises. Nest a bulky platform of sticks lined with twigs and grass stems. Eggs 3–4, blue or blue tinged with green.

GOLIATH HERON   *Ardea goliath (Typhon goliath)*   **Pl. 1**

Identification: 55″. Sexes similar. Rather like the Purple Heron having grey upperparts and chestnut underparts, but the chestnut not black crown dis-

tinguishes it. Immature plumage paler and browner. The best character is the very large size. Flight slow and deliberate. Usually solitary or in pairs.
Voice: A hoarse bark.
Distribution and Habitat: Widely distributed, yet never common, the range extending from Senegal (16° N.) to Chad and the Central African Republic and south to Gaboon and Congo. Swamps, the sandbanks of large rivers, estuaries, and mangrove creeks attract it.
Nesting: Solitary. A large platform of sticks built among reeds or in a low tree. Eggs 3–4, pale blue.

PURPLE HERON *Ardea purpurea (Pyrrherodia purpurea)* **Pl. 1**
Identification: 35″. Sexes similar. At a distance in flight appears dark brown. At close range greyish above with rufous plumes on the back; bright chestnut below with long whitish plumes on the chest; crown black; neck rufous with long bold streaks of blackish on back and sides. Immature plumage mottled brown and pale rufous. Usually solitary but gregarious at roost and when breeding. Seldom perches in trees. Keeps more hidden than most other Heron species.
Voice: A guttural croak.
Distribution and Habitat: Widely distributed in our area in all zones where there is suitable habitat, its numbers being augmented by migrants during the northern winter. Swamps, reed beds, mangrove creeks, and irrigation canals in rice fields attract it.
Nesting: Colonial. Nests built in mangroves a few metres up, or (in the Cape Verde Islands) in the upper branches of tall mangos. Nest a bulky platform of sticks and twigs. Eggs 3–4, pale blue-green.

HAMMERKOP: Scopidae

HAMMERKOP *Scopus umbretta* **Pl. 2**
Identification: 22″. Sexes similar. Unmistakable. Dull brown all over, with a curious large thick crest which together with the stout bill give the head the shape of an anvil. Legs short. Flight buoyant. Aquatic. Solitary. Not shy.
Voice: A distinctive high-pitched noisy cackling.
Distribution and Habitat: Widely distributed wherever there is suitable habitat from Senegal and Gambia east to Chad and the Central African Republic and south to Gaboon and Congo. Frequents swamps, rice fields, ponds, pools on the course of rivers and streams, and especially estuaries and mangrove creeks.
Nesting: A massive roofed structure of sticks, grass, and mud, about four feet cube, built in the fork of a tree, normally over water. Usually in an open situation and visible from a great distance. Eggs 4–5, white.

STORKS: Ciconiidae

Large birds with strong, long, usually straight bills, long necks, and long bare legs. Fly with neck fully outstretched.

ABDIM'S STORK   *Ciconia abdimii (Sphenorynchus abdimii)*   **Pl. 4**
Identification: 30". Sexes similar. A medium-sized Stork, glossy black but with white underparts below the breast and a conspicuous white rump. White-necked Stork is distinguished from it by its white neck, and the European Black Stork (*Ciconia nigra*) by its bright red bill and legs and dark rump. Frequents towns and villages. Tame, sociable. Fond of cultivated or other open dry ground.
Voice: Usually silent. At the nest a feeble high-pitched 'peep peep peep' and clacking of the bill.
Distribution and Habitat: In the wet season resident and widely distributed in the drier savanna from Senegal to Chad and the Central African Republic and from about 9° N. in the south to the edge of the desert in the north. In the forest and adjoining savanna on passage only. Non-breeding season spent south of the equator.
Nesting: Nests gregariously in towns and villages. Nest of sticks lined with grass, built on low baobab or thorn trees or on buildings. Eggs 2–4, occasionally 5, chalky-white.

WHITE-NECKED STORK   *Ciconia episcopus (Dissoura episcopus)* **Pl. 4**
Identification: 34". Sexes similar. Glossy black but neck, belly, and undertail-coverts white. Perched the woolly white neck contrasts with the black body; in flight the white under the tail contrasts with the black wings. Immature plumage like adult but browner.
Voice: Usually silent. A harsh raucous cry.
Distribution and Habitat: Widely but thinly distributed throughout our area from Senegal and Gambia east to Chad and the Central African Republic and south to Gaboon and Congo. Frequents dry ground in the forest clearings and savanna, and also streams, water-holes, river banks, and coastal lagoons.
Nesting: Solitary. Nest of sticks built in a tree. Eggs 3, white.
Allied species: The White Stork (*Ciconia ciconia*), 46", sexes similar, is white or whitish with black flight feathers and bright red bill and legs. Its white tail and red bill distinguish it from the Wood Ibis which it rather resembles. Often soars. Found in both dry and wet places. Hunts locusts and grasshoppers. In our area a winter visitor and passage migrant from Europe. Reported from many localities, and recorded as frequent in Chad, but on the whole not common.

SADDLEBILL STORK   *Ephippiorhynchus senegalensis*   **Pl. 4**
Identification: 57". Sexes similar. A very large black and white Stork. The massive red bill with its black band and yellow frontal saddle is diagnostic. In flight the pure white primaries identify it. Occurs singly or in pairs. Stalks its prey like a Heron. Given to soaring.
Voice: Silent except for clapping bill noises at the nest.
Distribution and Habitat: Widespread but rather uncommon ranging from Senegal and Gambia east to Chad and the Central African Republic and south to Gaboon and Congo. Breeds in Senegal and Chad. Frequents swamps and large rivers.
Nesting: A solitary nester. In Uganda builds a massive stick nest at the top of a tree and lays two white eggs.

OPENBILL   *Anastomus lamelligerus*   **Pl. 4**
Identification: 36″. The uniformly dark plumage, the large bill and the wide gap between the mandibles when it is closed distinguish it. It occurs in pairs and parties.
Voice: Usually silent, but a weak croak has been recorded.
Distribution and Habitat: From Sierra Leone and Mali east to Chad and the Central African Republic and south to Gaboon and Congo, mainly in savanna localities, occasionally in forest clearings. An aquatic species frequenting rivers, lakes, and marshes.
Nesting: In colonies in tall acacias near water.

MARABOU STORK   *Leptoptilos crumeniferus*   **Pl. 4**
Identification: 50″. Sexes similar. A huge repulsive-looking Stork with a massive bill and a bare dirty pinkish head and neck with sparse woolly short down. Upperparts slate-grey; underparts white; neck pouch pinkish. Stands either erect or hunched-up. In flight black wings contrast with white body. Gregarious; often associates with Vultures; a scavenger, not shy.
Voice: Usually silent. A guttural croak. Bill clacking and a variety of vocal sounds at the nest.
Distribution and Habitat: Widely but irregularly distributed. Locally very common in the open dry savanna areas and infrequent or absent from the forest areas. Frequents swamps, river banks, the vicinity of villages, and the open savanna.
Nesting: Colonial, sometimes together with Pelicans. A platform of sticks built in a tree often located in a village or town. Eggs 2–3, white.

WOOD IBIS   *Ibis ibis*   **Pl. 4**
Identification: 38″. Sexes similar. A medium-sized Stork. At a distance appears black and white; at close range pinkish-mauve and white. Yellow, slightly decurved bill, bare red face, and black tail are characteristic and distinguish it from the White Stork. Immature plumage greyish. Tame. Often gregarious. Feeds in the water and also on dry ground.
Voice: Usually silent. Occasionally a loud nasal sound like a squeaky hinge. Bill clacking at nest.
Distribution and Habitat: Widely distributed in our area from Gambia and Senegal east to Chad and south to Gaboon and Congo, especially in the dry regions north of the forest where it breeds. Rare in the forest zone except for the coastal mud-flats. Frequents the margins of lakes, rivers, and lagoons, and grass-covered flats near water.
Nesting: Breeds in trees in colonies sometimes shared with Marabous, Pelicans, or Herons. A stick nest lined with grass. Eggs 2–3, white with yellowish nest stains.

IBISES AND SPOONBILLS: Threskiornithidae

Medium-sized wading birds with long, strongly or moderately decurved bills except for the Spoonbills in which genus the bill is straight and characteristically flattened and spatulate. Fly with neck extended.

SACRED IBIS *Threskiornis aethiopica* **Pl. 3**

Identification: 35″. Sexes similar. Unmistakable and conspicuous. Pure white, with black head and neck both bare of feathers, a blackish decurved bill, black ornamental plumes over the rump, and (in flight) dark wing tips. In immature plumage the head and neck are feathered and mottled black and white. Usually gregarious. Flies in formation. Flight interspersed with long glides.

Voice: Usually silent. Croaking calls at the nest.

Distribution and Habitat: Widely and commonly dispersed throughout our area from Gambia and Senegal east to Chad and the Central African Republic and south to Gaboon and Congo, especially in the savanna although it also occurs on the lakes and large rivers of the high forest zone and is common in the coastal mangrove creeks. Frequents muddy stagnant waters of marshes and the margins of rivers and also dry open cultivated or grassy ground.

Nesting: Breeds in colonies, on the ground or in trees, either alone or in company with Heron species. Nest of sticks lined with twigs and grass stems. Eggs 2–3, white or white tinged green, spotted, blotched, or pencilled with different shades of brown.

HADADA IBIS *Bostrychia hagedash (Hagedashia hagedash)* **Pl. 3**

Identification: 30″. Sexes similar. A loud unmistakable call. In flight at a distance appears uniformly dark. At close range the metallic bronze, green, and bluish upperparts and wings contrast with the grey-brown head, neck, and underparts. A white stripe on the cheek. A rather thick-set Ibis more stoutly built than the Glossy Ibis. Usually in pairs or small parties and most often heard and seen at dawn and dusk flighting between roosting and feeding grounds.

Voice: Very noisy. A frequent, far-reaching, raucous 'ha ha ha ha ha'.

Distribution and Habitat: Widely but unevenly distributed. Locally common in the savanna and gallery forest zone north of the main body of the forest, and rare in the arid north. Frequents marshes and wooded streams in the savanna and lakes and rivers in the high forest.

Nesting: Solitary. A nest of sticks built in a tree over or near water. Eggs 2–3, pale green blotched and smeared with brown and reddish.

Allied species: The Spotted-breasted Ibis (*Bostrychia rara*), 22″, is a small species distinguished by its crest, its dark upperparts, and spotted neck and breast. It inhabits the main body of the forest and the heavier gallery forests from Liberia to Gaboon and Congo and is uncommon. Generally encountered at dusk when flying between its feeding and roosting grounds. On these flights it utters a repeated loud raucous 'k-hah'. The Olive Ibis (*Bostrychia olivacea*) is even rarer. Similar in size to the common West African Hadada (*Bostrychia hagedash*) it is distinguished from that species by its long crest and by its different cry and from the Spotted-breasted Ibis by its uniform brown underparts and large size. The range is the forest from Sierra Leone and Liberia to Gaboon, but records are few. A very distinct small race (*B. olivacea bocagei*) occurs on the island of Sao Tome.

GLOSSY IBIS *Plegadis falcinellus* **Pl. 3**

Identification: 18″. A slim, slender-legged, Curlew-like Ibis, with a long decurved bill. Smaller than the Hadada Ibis, more buoyant in flight, and more graceful on the ground. At a distance appears black. At close quarters dark brown, the head and neck speckled with whitish, the back and wings with bronzy-green reflections. In nuptial plumage (uncommon in West Africa) neck and underparts chestnut-maroon. Flies in line. Wing beats interspersed with long glides. Wades at the edge of marshes in small flocks.

Voice: Usually silent. Rarely a harsh 'Kaa' when taking flight.

Distribution and Habitat: Resident, but mainly a winter visitor from the Palaearctic Region to Senegal, Mali, Niger, Ghana, northern Nigeria, and Chad. Rare south of the forest. A vagrant to the Cape Verde Islands. Breeds Mali.

Nesting: In colonies with Heron and Cormorant species. A stick nest built in an acacia in a swamp. Eggs dark blue-green.

AFRICAN SPOONBILL *Platalea alba* Pl. 3

Identification: 36″. Sexes similar. White all over, like one of the white Egrets, but with a conspicuous spoon-shaped bill. At close quarters the pinkish forehead, bill, and feet are field marks and distinguish it from the European Spoonbill *Platalea leucorodia*, (which breeds in Mauritania), which has black bill and feet and no pink on the forehead. Immature bird has black wing tips. The neck is extended in flight. Fishes by scything the water from side to side.

Voice: Usually silent. Guttural grunts at the nest.

Distribution and Habitat: Resident. Widespread but local. Recorded from Senegal, Gambia, Mali, Nigeria, Chad, Central African Republic, Portuguese Guinea, Sierra Leone, Ghana, and Gaboon. Frequents shallow running or still water, salt or fresh.

Nesting: A large platform of sticks usually in colonies in trees with Heron and Ibis species. Sometimes on the ground on sandy islands. Eggs 2–3, white, blotched and spotted at the large end with red, brown and violet-grey.

FLAMINGOES: Phoenicopteridae

GREATER FLAMINGO *Phoenicopterus ruber* Pl. 2

Identification: 55″. Sexes similar. A very long-legged, long-necked, pink and white bird with a massive angled bill which can be confused with no other African species except the Lesser Flamingo. In flight red and black wings distinctive. Immature plumage greyish. Gregarious. Flies with neck and legs extended. Usually seen standing or walking slowly in shallow, often brackish, water. Occasionally swims. Immerses head under water to feed.

Voice: A goose-like 'honk'.

Distribution and Habitat: Occurs locally and irregularly in coastal West Africa in Mauritania, Senegal, Gambia, Sierra Leone, Liberia, Gaboon, and Congo, frequenting lagoons, estuaries, and brackish lakes.

Nesting: Breeds in colonies on islets off the Mauritanian coast. Nest a mound of dried mud. Eggs 2, white.

Allied species: The Lesser Flamingo (*Phoenicopterus minor*), **Pl. 2**, 40″, is easily confused at a distance with the Greater Flamingo despite its much smaller size. At close range the darker red bill and the less pronounced angulation of the ridge of the maxilla distinguish it. The habits and habitat resemble those of the Greater Flamingo. An uncommon bird in West Africa recorded from Chad, the Cameroons, Portuguese Guinea, Senegal, and Mauritania.

DUCKS AND GEESE: Anatidae

Essentially water birds. In flight distinguished from most other groups by the extended neck and short tail. Glide rarely or not at all. Flat bill and webbed feet. Often gregarious.

FULVOUS TREE-DUCK *Dendrocygna bicolor (D. fulva)* **Pls. 12, 13**
Identification: 19″. Sexes similar. Fulvous with dark brown back. Rather similar to the White-faced Tree-duck in size, build, habits, and habitat, but on the ground stands a little higher and appears larger and in flight displays white upper and under tail coverts and cream stripes on the flank. In both species in the air the legs extend behind the tail. Call characteristic.
Voice: A very distinctive, soft, hushing 'tsoo-ee tsoo-ee' constantly repeated in flight.
Distribution and Habitat: The lakes, marshes, and inundation zones of the open country north (mainly) of the forest from southern Mauritania (17° N.) and Senegal through Mali, Niger, and northern Nigeria to Chad. A few records from Ghana, Togo, and Gaboon.
Nesting: Nest in reed bed over water. An accumulation of dry reeds fashioned into a shallow cup with living reeds bent down to form an arch over the eggs. Eggs white tinged with yellowish-green and distinctly larger than those of the White-faced Tree-duck. Clutch (in South Africa) 6–12.

WHITE-FACED TREE-DUCK *Dendrocygna viduata* **Pls. 12, 13**
Identification: 19″. Sexes similar. Often on the ground when alert upright stance on long legs is distinctive. White head and throat contrast with black hind crown and nape; upper parts brown and rufous; chest chestnut; lower breast and belly black; flanks barred. In immature plumage face pale grey. In the air a dark-looking duck with a white head, rounded wings, and slow heavy wing beats. Highly gregarious. By day often rest on sandbank or other bare ground near water. Feed and fly at dawn, dusk, and at night. Occasionally perch in trees.
Voice: A very distinctive whistling 'wishi wishi' constantly uttered in flight.
Distribution and Habitat: Widely and commonly distributed north and south of the forest from southern Mauritania, Senegal and Gambia east to Chad and the Central African Republic and south to Gaboon and Congo, frequenting marshes, rice fields, rivers, lakes, and coastal lagoons and swamps. Moves north during the rains.
Nesting: On the ground, sometimes concealed in rank herbage, sometimes quite open in short grass, usually but not always near water. Materials a few wisps of grass; no down. Eggs 10–12, white tinged cream soon becoming nest-stained with yellowish.

EGYPTIAN GOOSE *Alopochen aegyptiaca* **Pls. 12, 13**
Identification: 28″. Sexes similar. A light-brown Goose with a large white patch on the wing and a dark chestnut patch on the chest, both good field marks at rest and also in flight. Size and colour distinguish it from other West African

species. Occurs in pairs or flocks, usually near water, sometimes on dry open ground.
Voice: A loud hoarse honking.
Distribution and Habitat: Widespread and locally common in our area, except in the closed forest, where there are marshes, flooded plains, rice fields, and river sandbanks. Widely distributed, especially in the dry northern territories, from Senegal to Chad and south to Gaboon and Congo.
Nesting: Outside our area very varied nesting sites on the ground and in trees. A nest in Nigeria was a hollow in the sand in a cranny between boulders on a rock in the River Niger. Lined with grass and down it held 9 eggs, white with a bluish tinge.

SPUR-WINGED GOOSE *Plectropterus gambensis* **Pls. 12, 13**
Identification: Male 40″, female much smaller. Great size and long neck distinguish it from other African geese. Upperparts black, the mantle and wings glossed with green; underparts mainly white; bill and feet pinkish. In flight a conspicuous large white wing patch. Gregarious. Sometimes perches in trees. Usually feeds by night on grassland or farmland and rests by day.
Voice: Rather silent. A high-pitched feeble whistle.
Distribution and Habitat: Widespread and abundant in the open country north of the forest from southern Mauritania, Senegal and Gambia to Chad and the Central African Republic, absent from the closed forest and reappearing in more open country south of the forest in Gaboon and Congo. Frequents swamps, rice fields, the flood plains, sandbanks, and margins of the great rivers, lakes, and tidal estuaries.
Nesting: Nest in coarse grass on dry ground near water. A hollow scantily lined with grass; no down. Eggs 9–11, ivory-white.

HARTLAUB'S DUCK *Pteronetta hartlaubii* **Pls. 12, 13**
Identification: 18″. Mainly dark chestnut with a black head and neck and a large light blue shoulder patch formed by the wing coverts which is very conspicuous in flight. Sexes similar. Occurs in pairs or parties. Frequently perches in trees overhanging water. Tame and lethargic.
Voice: Flight-note a grating 'ka-ka-ka-karr'. A duck-like 'quack' and various other calls are described.
Distribution and Habitat: A sedentary species ranging widely in the forest from Sierra Leone to the Central African Republic, Gaboon, and Congo. Partial to secluded shaded streams, ponds, and creeks, and where such habitats are available quite common.
Nesting: Not known.

KNOB-BILLED GOOSE *Sarkidiornis melanota* **Pls. 12, 13**
Identification: 31″, but female smaller. Head and neck white spotted black; upperparts black with a bronze sheen; underparts white. In flight the black wings (there is no white wing patch) contrast with the white under surface of the body. In the male a prominent black comb on the upper mandible. Occurs in flocks. Usually near or on open water but feeds on marshy ground and also on growing crops in dry places.
Voice: Usually silent. Sometimes a short hoarse whistle in flight.
Distribution and Habitat: Widely but locally distributed from southern

Mauritania and Senegal to Chad and south to Gaboon and Congo and especially common in the swamps, inundation zones, and lakes of the semi-arid belt. Absent from the closed forest.

Nesting: Eggs laid in a hole in an acacia tree or on the ground amongst reeds. Eggs 11, pale yellowish.

PIGMY GOOSE   *Nettapus auritus*   **Pls. 12, 13**
Identification: 13″. Smaller and plumper than a Garganey (*Anas querquedula*). Upperparts black with a green sheen; underparts conspicuously white with orange flanks. Male has the face and throat white and the ear coverts pale green bordered with black. These parts in the female are greyish-white. In flight wings black with conspicuous white bar. Seen in pairs or small groups, often amongst water lilies, practically never on the ground. Often feeds by diving. Not shy. Flight low and fast.
Voice: A soft whistling 'choo-choo pee wee'.
Distribution and Habitat: Widely but locally distributed and resident throughout the area even in the forest zone where there is suitable habitat, from Senegal to Chad and south to Gaboon and Congo. Inhabits lakes and backwaters of rivers and coastal lagoons with water lilies or other low surface plants. Prefers deep water.
Nesting: In our area recorded as breeding in a hole in a hollow tree standing in water. In south and east Africa lays 6–9 pale cream eggs.

AFRICAN BLACK DUCK   *Anas sparsa*   **Pls. 12, 13**
Identification: 19″. Sexes similar. A blackish duck with white spots on the upper surface which are however inconspicuous in the field. At rest the light-coloured bill and the white wing bar are field marks and when the bird rises the orange feet catch the eye. Occurs in pairs and flocks. Active at dusk.
Voice: A loud Mallard-like 'quack quack'.
Distribution and Habitat: The crater lakes and the rivers and marshes of the Cameroon highlands. Also a few lowland lake and river localities in the Cameroons and Gaboon forest zone.
Nesting: In southern Africa it nests near water on the ground or on the top of driftwood caught in trees along river banks and lays 5–7 cream-coloured eggs.
Allied species: The Hottentot Teal (*Anas hottentota*), 13″, has been recorded from a few localities in northern Nigeria, and it breeds there. Recorded also from Chad. At rest the very small size, the black cap, and the whitish cheeks distinguish it. In flight the broad white wing bar and the black rump are conspicuous.

PINTAIL   *Anas acuta* (*Dafila acuta*)   **Pls. 12, 13**
Identification: 22″. Slender build, long neck, and pointed tail are field marks. Male in nuptial plumage unmistakable – head chocolate-brown, prominent white stripe on side of neck, white breast, and grey upperparts. Male in eclipse like female but darker above. Female mottled brown and rather resembles the female Wigeon and Gadwall but apart from the slender neck and pointed tail the grey bill distinguishes it from the yellow-billed Gadwall and the brown plumage from the more rufous Wigeon. Also the Wigeon and Gadwall are comparatively rare in West Africa. Often associates with the Garganey. Flight rapid. A surface feeder. Often nocturnal.

Voice: Silent in Africa.

Distribution and Habitat: A non-breeding Palaearctic migrant present from October to March. Widespread in the northern savanna from west to east but absent from the forest and the southern savanna. Locally abundant in Mauritania, Senegal, Mali, northern Nigeria, and Chad, frequenting lakes, lagoons, swamps, and flooded plains.

GARGANEY *Anas querquedula* **Pls. 12, 13**

Identification: 15″. Small size, rapid flight, and ability to perform sudden manoeuvres in the air are characteristic. In the male at rest the broad white stripe extending from eye to nape and the long black and white scapulars are diagnostic. In flight the pale grey-blue front of the wing and the brown breast, sharply demarcated from the white belly, distinguish it. The male in eclipse retains the blue forewing. The female is mottled brown and buff with a thin whitish streak from eye to nape. Occurs in flocks – sometimes of immense size. Feeds at night on rice fields, marshes, and shallow pools with surface vegetation. Rests during the day on open stretches of water.

Voice: Silent in Africa.

Distribution and Habitat: A Palaearctic migrant from October to March occurring abundantly where there is suitable habitat in southern Mauritania, Senegal, Mali, northern Nigeria, and Chad, and also recorded from the Gambia, Portuguese Guinea, Ghana, southern Nigeria, Niger, Cameroons, and Gaboon.

Allied species: The European Teal (*Anas crecca*) is slightly smaller than the Garganey and has the same build and similar rapid erratic flight. The male at a distance appears grey with a dark head and lacks the Garganey's white eyestripe. At close range the chestnut head, large green comma-shaped patch over the eye, white horizontal stripe above wing, and grey speckled back and flanks distinguish it. The female closely resembles the female Garganey but is darker and lacks the whitish streak behind the eye. In the hand the dark green speculum bordered with black distinguish it at once from the female Garganey. A Palaearctic winter migrant to our area occurring regularly in a few localities in Ghana, northern Nigeria and Chad, and recorded from Senegal and the Cape Verde Islands.

SHOVELER *Anas clypeata* (*Spatula clypeata*) **Pls. 12, 13**

Identification: 20″. In flight and at rest the large spatulate bill is clearly visible and distinguishes both sexes. The male in nuptial plumage has the head dark green, back blackish and white, breast white, belly and flanks chestnut, and on the wing a large blue shoulder patch and a green speculum bordered in front with white. Wing characters useful in flight and in eclipse plumage when male body plumage is brown and inconspicuous. Female at all seasons a mixture of browns but blue shoulder patch and green speculum duller. Sits and swims with front well under the water and bill pointing downwards and feeds thus dabbling its bill in the water and sweeping its head from side to side in characteristic fashion. Flight heavy but rapid. Occurs singly, in pairs, or in small parties.

Voice: Silent in Africa.

Distribution and Habitat: Frequents shallow marshes, pools, and lakes with good cover. A Palaearctic migrant widely but usually sparsely spread north of the forest and recorded from Senegal, Gambia, Portuguese Guinea, Mali, Upper Volta, Ghana, Nigeria, and Chad.

Plate 3

DABCHICK, CORMORANTS, IBISES AND SPOONBILL

1. **DABCHICK** *Podiceps ruficollis*   page 15
Whitish spot at gape; chestnut cheeks and neck.

2. **LONG-TAILED SHAG** *Phalacrocorax africanus*   18
Small; relatively long tail; black.

3. **WHITE-BREASTED CORMORANT** *Phalacrocorax carbo*   18
Large; black, but cheeks and throat white.

4. **HADADA IBIS** *Bostrychia hagedash*   26
White stripe on cheek.

5. **AFRICAN DARTER** *Anhinga rufa*   18
Thin pointed bill; white stripe on neck.

6. **GLOSSY IBIS** *Plegadis falcinellus*   26
Small and slim; decurved bill; appears black at a distance.

7. **SACRED IBIS** *Threskiornis aethiopica*   26
Mainly white; head and neck black.

8. **AFRICAN SPOONBILL** *Platalea alba*   27
Spoon-shaped bill; pinkish forehead and feet.

4

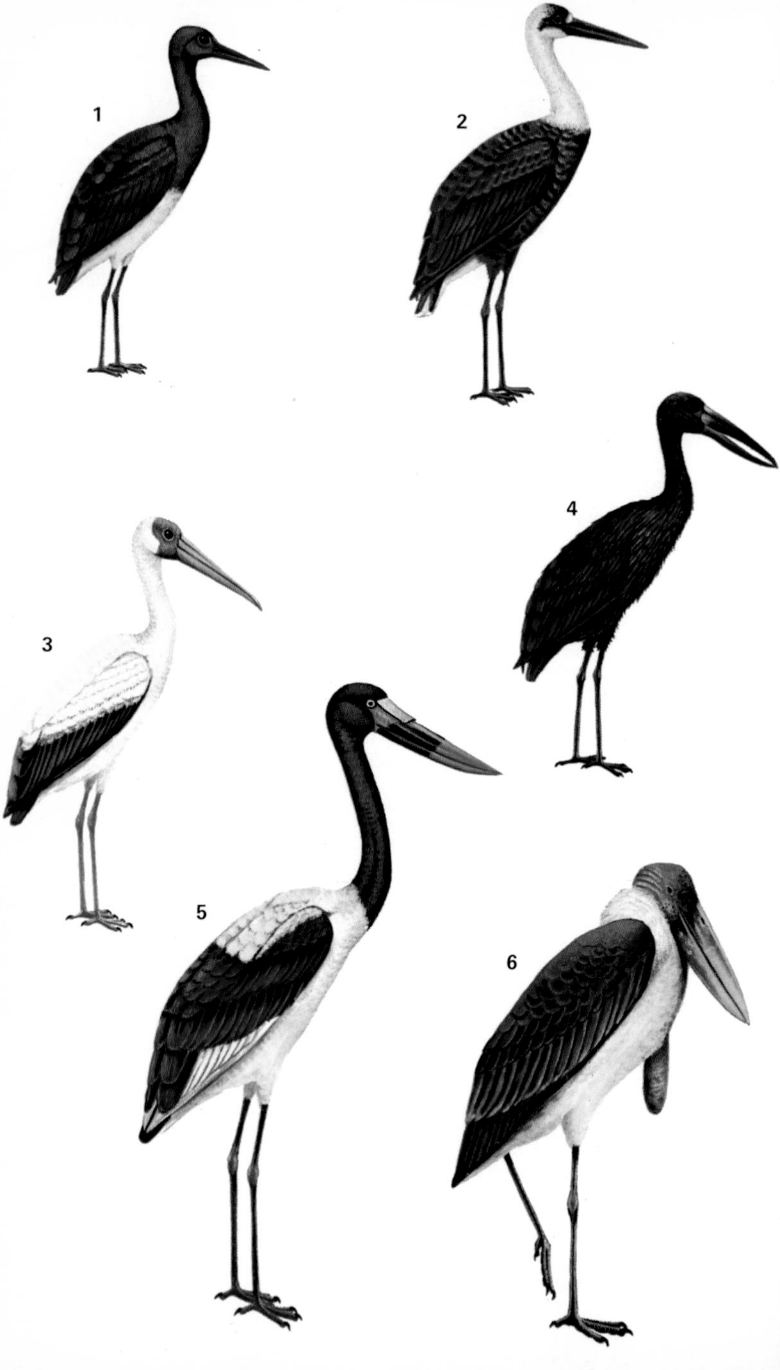

Plate 4

STORKS

FERRUGINOUS DUCK *Aythya nyroca* (*Nyroca nyroca*) **Pls. 12, 13**
Identification: 16″. Male and female distinguished from all other Ducks in our area by rich, dark chestnut head, neck, and breast. Pure white under tail coverts an excellent character, and in flight or at rest when wings are flapped a broad white crescentic bar on the flight feathers. White eye of male conspicuous. Female a little duller, has brown eyes, and at a distance can be confused with a female Tufted Duck (rare in our area) but the conspicuous white under tail coverts distinguish it. A diving duck. Runs along surface before taking off. Flight heavy with abrupt, fast wingbeats.
Voice: Unknown in Africa.
Distribution and Habitat: Habitat marshes and shallow lakes with abundant cover and hidden stretches of open water. North of the forest in our area a rather local Palaearctic migrant. Recorded from the Cape Verde Islands, Senegal, Sierra Leone, Mali, Ghana, Nigeria, and Chad. Not common except on the lakes of northern Nigeria where large flocks congregate some winters.

WHITE-BACKED DUCK *Thalassornis leuconotus* **Pls. 12, 13**
Identification: 17″. Sexes similar. A dark dumpy Grebe-like Duck that sits low on the water. White spot at the base of the mandibles an excellent field mark. At rest mainly dark brown above and fulvous below. In flight pure white back very conspicuous. A diving Duck. Flight low and strong. Take-off laborious. Usually tame. Occurs in pairs or small groups.
Voice: A soft whistle.
Distribution and Habitat: Local and resident in West Africa, being recorded from Senegal, Mali, Nigeria, Cameroons, Chad, and Congo. Absent from the forest area. Frequents swamps and lakes with abundant surface and fringing vegetation.
Nesting: In South Africa the nest is a floating mass of aquatic vegetation among growing reeds in deep water. Eggs 3–7, warm brown and unusually dark for a Duck's egg.

VULTURES, HARRIERS, HARRIER-EAGLES, SPARROWHAWKS AND GOSHAWKS, BUZZARDS, EAGLES, KITES: Accipitridae

Vultures: Characterised by very large size, dull plumage, bare face and (usually) neck, long wings, short tail, and powerful hooked bill. Given to gliding and soaring. In flight the neck is drawn back and the head appears smaller than the head of an eagle of comparable size. Well known for feeding on carrion. Some species difficult to identify, especially in immature plumage.
Harriers: Slender hawks with long wings and tails and buoyant flight. Do not perch. Hunt close to the ground.
Harrier-Eagles or Snake-Eagles: The large size and general appearance of eagles but having the tarsus bare. Large yellow eyes. Feed largely on reptiles.
Sparrowhawks and Goshawks: Much smaller with rather short rounded wings and long tail. When hunting follow their prey tenaciously, unlike the falcons.
Buzzards: Resemble eagles but have broad wings and a bare tarsus. Characteristic sustained gliding in wide circles.

Eagles: Large birds with the tarsus feathered to the toes. Rounded wings. In flight the head seems larger than the vulture's and the shoulders less hunched up round the head.
Kites: Identified by their graceful flight, and, in most species, conspicuously forked tail.

NUBIAN or LAPPET-FACED VULTURE
Aegypius tracheliotus (*Torgos tracheliotus*)   **Pl. 5**
Identification: 40″. The great size, even for a Vulture, distinguishes it. Plumage mainly very dark brown but thick white down of the underparts is conspicuous, being only partly concealed by the long brown breast feathers. Bare skin of head and neck pink. Bill brown. In flight from below the short white streak near the front edge of the wing and white flanks are distinctive. In immature birds the bare head is flecked with white down and the flanks are brown not white.
Voice: Practically silent. A sharp yelp has been recorded.
Distribution and Habitat: The arid northern savanna from Senegal and Gambia through Mali, Niger, and northern Nigeria to Chad. Mainly thinly dispersed but locally common on the fringe of the Sahara. Usually solitary or in pairs. Frequents cliffs in mountainous areas, and slaughter houses.
Nesting: A large nest of sticks in an acacia tree. The single egg is white sparingly spotted and blotched with red-brown.
Allied species: The White-headed Vulture (*Trigonoceps occipitalis*) 32″, is rather thinly dispersed in the savanna, yet it is locally not uncommon. Recorded from Senegal, Gambia, Mali, Chad, Portuguese Guinea, Guinea, Ivory Coast, Ghana, Nigeria, Cameroons, and Gaboon. Adult distinguished by red bill and white head, belly, and secondaries, these white parts contrasting conspicuously in flight with the black breast and forewing. Immature birds mainly brown but belly white.

RUPPELL'S GRIFFON VULTURE *Gyps ruppellii*   **Pl. 5**
Identification: 40″. The light-spotted scapulars and upper wing-coverts are conspicuous and diagnostic. Plumage mainly dark brown. The underparts are light-spotted but less conspicuously so than the wing-coverts. Head and neck mainly bare, greyish. Bill yellowish. White ruff at base of neck. In flight three whitish bands on the under surface of the wing. Immature birds appear pale brown.
Voice: Usually silent. Occasional harsh call.
Distribution and Habitat: Widely distributed and not uncommon in the northern savannas, occurring in southern Mauritania, Senegal, Gambia, Portuguese Guinea, Guinea, Mali, Niger, northern Nigeria, Cameroons, and Chad. Occurs singly, in pairs or in parties. May congregate in large roosts. A Vulture of the open bush avoiding towns.
Nesting: A large nest of sticks in a tree or on a cliff ledge. Singly or in colonies and sometimes with the White-backed Vulture. The single egg is white.

WHITE-BACKED VULTURE *Gyps bengalensis*
(*Pseudogyps africanus*)   **Pl. 5**
Identification: 38″. Medium-sized pale brown Vulture (unspotted) best recognised by its white rump. In flight viewed from above the conspicuous

Plate 5

VULTURES, HARRIER HAWK, BATELEUR AND SECRETARY-BIRD

1. **NUBIAN VULTURE** *Aegypius tracheliotus* page 35
Bare pink head and neck. In flight from below white band near front edge of wing and white flanks.

2. **RUPPELL'S GRIFFON VULTURE** *Gyps ruppellii* 35
Light-spotted scapulars and wing-coverts. In flight from below three light bands on wing.

3. **WHITE-BACKED VULTURE** *Gyps bengalensis* 35
White rump (not visible at rest). In flight from below white front edge of wing.

4. **HOODED VULTURE** *Neophron monachus* 38
Brown; bill slender. In flight relatively short, rounded tail.

5. **HARRIER HAWK** *Polyboroides radiatus* 39
Long legs; barred underparts; white tail band.

6. **PALM-NUT VULTURE** *Gypohierax angolensis* 38
White body plumage; black and white wings. In flight from below black secondaries.

7. **BATELEUR** *Terathopius ecaudatus* 40
Chestnut back. In flight from below very short tail, black body and mainly white underwing; red feet.

8. **SECRETARY-BIRD** *Sagittarius serpentarius* 54
Long tail; long legs; occipital crest.

Plate 6

EAGLES

1. SHORT-TOED EAGLE *Circaetus gallicus*
Unfeathered tarsus; lightly streaked and barred underparts; large yellow eye.

2. BROWN HARRIER EAGLE *Circaetus cinereus*
Unfeathered tarsus; dark brown; large yellow eye.

3. WEST AFRICAN RIVER EAGLE *Haliaetus vocifer*
White head, breast, and tail; chestnut belly.

4. MARTIAL EAGLE *Polemaetus bellicosus*
White lower breast and belly lightly spotted brown; throat and upper breast sepia brown.

5. CROWNED HAWK-EAGLE *Stephanoaetus coronatus*
Heavily barred breast and belly; spotted thighs.

6. LONG-CRESTED HAWK-EAGLE *Lophaetus occipitalis*
Conspicuous untidy crest.

7. TAWNY EAGLE *Aquila rapax*
Brown; short rounded tail.

8. WAHLBERG'S EAGLE *Aquila wahlbergi*
Brown. Smaller than the Tawny Eagle with square relatively longer tail.

Tawny Eagle, *Aquila rapax*

Wahlberg's Eagle, *Aquila wahlbergi*

character is the rump and from below the white fore-edge of the wing. Bill black. Immature bird lacks the white rump and easily confused with immature Ruppell's Griffon Vulture but is generally much darker.

Voice: Usually silent. Harsh cries when fighting over a carcase.

Distribution and Habitat: Locally common and widely distributed in the dry savanna. Absent from the forest and rare in the extreme north. Recorded from Mauritania, Senegal, Gambia, Portuguese Guinea, Guinea, Ivory Coast, Ghana, Togo, Dahomey, Mali, northern Nigeria, Chad, and the Central African Republic. Frequents open country with game and also towns with slaughter houses.

Nesting: Breeds singly or in small scattered colonies, making a small stick nest in a tree. One egg, white, sometimes blotched with reddish.

HOODED VULTURE *Neophron monachus* (*Necrosyrtes monachus*) **Pl. 5**

Identification: 26″. A small dark brown Vulture. In flight appears uniformly dark. Tail short and rounded. Bill slender. Tame, often gregarious, usually scavenging in towns and villages.

Voice: Usually silent. Female utters a weak high-pitched call when mating.

Distribution and Habitat: Widespread and very common in the savanna north of the forest from southern Mauritania and Senegal to the Central African Republic penetrating southwards into the larger forest clearings. Rarer north of 15° N. Affects mainly towns and villages and the surrounding farmland and frequents especially slaughter houses and refuse tips.

Nesting: A bulky stick nest lined with twigs and leaves built in a strong tree fork, often near town or village. Clutch one. Egg white, blotched and smeared with various shades of brown with ashy shell marks.

Allied species: The Egyptian Vulture (*Neophron percnopterus*), 26″, is a small black and white Vulture with a bare yellowish face and a slender bill. In flight the white primaries and the white wedge-shaped tail are distinctive. Immature bird brown resembling the Hooded Vulture but the wedge-shaped tail readily distinguishes it. The Egyptian Vulture is common and resident in the Cape Verde Islands and common (in winter at least) in Chad as far south as 13° N. Elsewhere in West Africa it occurs, on the whole sparingly, in the countries bordering the Sahara, being recorded from Senegal, Gambia, Mali, Ghana, Niger, and Nigeria. Breeding recorded from Senegal, Mali and Chad.

PALM-NUT VULTURE *Gypohierax angolensis* **Pl. 5**

Identification: 23″. Easily recognised by white body plumage, black and white wings, and white tail with broad black band near the tip. Bare skin of face orange. Immature plumage brown, lacking distinctive marks. Occurs singly, in pairs, or small parties. Often perches conspicuously. Given to soaring. Not shy.

Voice: A guttural 'pruk-kurrr'.

Distribution and Habitat: Widely and commonly distributed in the forest clearings and the savannas from Senegal to the Central African Republic and south to Gaboon and Congo, but scarce north of 12° N. (13° N. in Senegal) and absent from the dry zones fringing the desert. From sea-level to 7,000 feet and specially abundant in the mangroves and estuaries of the Niger Delta. Range coincides more or less with that of the oil-palm, whose fruit is its favourite diet.

Nesting: A bulky stick nest lined with twigs and leaves built in a strong fork of a tree usually at a great height. Single egg, white, blotched and smeared with different shades of brown and ashy shell marks.

PALLID HARRIER   *Circus macrourus*   **Pl. 8**
Identification: 18″. The slender build, long wings and tail, and especially the buoyant and ceaseless flight low over the ground identify it as a Harrier. Male very pale grey, almost white at a distance, with black wing tips. Female and young brown above with a conspicuous white rump and buff streaked rufous below. They cannot be distinguished in the field from female and immature Montagu's Harrier. Occurs singly. Occasionally put up from the ground but usually encountered quartering its territory with typical Harrier flight.
Voice: Usually silent in winter quarters.
Distribution and Habitat: A Palaearctic migrant, widely and commonly distributed in winter in the savanna north of the forest, frequenting dry open orchard bush, farmland, grass savanna, marshes, and rice fields, but less partial to wet places than Montagu's Harrier.
Allied species: The male Montagu's Harrier (*Circus pygargus*) 17″, differs from the male Pallid Harrier by having a black wing bar (clearly visible in flight) and rufous streaks on the flank and belly. The brown white-rumped female and immature birds cannot be told in the field from the Pallid Harrier. A Palaearctic winter migrant to the savannas north of the West African forest, occurring abundantly in the rice fields of the Senegal River but rather uncommon in other parts of its range. Recorded from Gambia, Mali, Ivory Coast, Nigeria, Chad, and the Central African Republic.

MARSH HARRIER   *Circus aeruginosus*   **Pl. 8**
Identification: 20″. A larger and heavier bird than the Pallid Harrier, slightly more ponderous in flight, although it shows a similar buoyancy, and, like it, glides with slightly upraised wings. Male brown and rufous with grey tail and secondaries and black primaries. Female brown with a creamy-white crown. Young brown with a tawny crown. The Marsh Harrier never has a white rump. Like the Pallid Harrier in winter quarters, female and immature birds predominate. Wet habitat characteristic.
Voice: Normally silent in winter quarters.
Distribution and Habitat: Abundant in winter in the marshes and rice fields in Senegal and Gambia and recorded from several widely dispersed savanna localities with suitable wet habitat in Mali, Niger, Liberia, Ivory Coast, Ghana, Nigeria, Cameroons, Chad, and the Central African Republic.

HARRIER HAWK   *Polyboroides radiatus* (*Gymnogenys typicus*)   **Pl. 5**
Identification: 25″. A lanky, long-legged grey hawk with broad rounded wings, a long tail, and a rather weak, hesitant flight. Head small and crested. Upperparts grey; underparts below the grey chest closely barred black and white; tail black with a broad whitish band about its mid-length. Bare bright yellow face a good field character. Young bird brown mottled and barred with buff and blackish. The steep diving display flight is characteristic. Often raids the nests of Weavers and other birds.
Voice: A pleasing modulated whistle.
Distribution and Habitat: Widespread and common throughout the area in both forest and savanna and, in the wet season at least, extending its range to

the edge of the desert.

Nesting: A large stick nest lined with fresh green leaves usually built high up in a strong fork of a tree. Eggs 2, buffish heavily smeared and blotched with dark reddish-brown.

BATELEUR   *Terathopius ecaudatus*   Pl. 5

Identification: 24″. In flight unmistakable by reason of its long wings, very short tail, and colour pattern. The black underside of the body contrasts with the white underside of the wings and with the bright orange feet which project beyond the tail. Nearly always seen on the wing. A complete master of the air, gliding at great speed, and named 'Bateleur' because it is given to somersaulting and other acrobatic exercises. Perched it shows its chestnut back. In immature plumage brown and superficially like the Brown Harrier-Eagle and the Tawny Eagle but readily distinguished by its short tail.

Voice: A short, sharp bark.

Distribution and Habitat: Widespread in the open savanna from Senegal east to the ·Central African Republic and south to Congo. North of the forest common between 9° N. and 15° N. Absent from the high forest and from the extreme north.

Nesting: Nest a platform of sticks in a high tree. One creamy-white egg, usually unmarked.

SHORT-TOED EAGLE or SNAKE EAGLE   *Circaetus gallicus*
Pl. 6

Identification: The Harrier Eagles (*Circaetus*), of which the Short-toed Eagle is the European representative, is a small, mainly African group of medium-sized Eagles of rather heavy build, having large, round, rather owl-like heads, un-feathered tarsi, and rather slow clumsy flight. They feed largely on reptiles. The Short-toed Eagle (30″) has these characters. Distinguished when adult from other Harrier-Eagles by its colour. Upperparts brown; underparts white streaked on the throat and lightly barred on the breast and belly with brown. Large yellow eye conspicuous. Immature bird pale brown with blotched and barred underparts. In immature and intermediate dress the different species are sometimes impossible to identify in the field.

Voice: Silent.

Distribution and Habitat: A rather common winter visitor from the Palae-arctic Region to the open thorn savanna of West Africa. Recorded from Mauritania, Senegal, Gambia, Mali, Ivory Coast, northern Ghana, northern Togo, northern Nigeria, and Chad.

Allied species: Beaudouin's Harrier-Eagle (*Circaetus beaudouini*) 32″, some-times regarded as a race of the Short-toed Eagle, is resident in West Africa. In this form the upperparts and chest are brown, and the lower breast and belly white with indistinct narrow chestnut bars. Young birds are very dark brown all over. In West Africa it has much the same range as the Short-toed Eagle but penetrates farther south. Recorded from Senegal, Gambia, Portuguese Guinea, Liberia, Mali, Ghana, Nigeria, Chad, and the Central African Republic.

BROWN HARRIER-EAGLE   *Circaetus cinereus*   Pl. 6

Identification: 29″. Very dark brown all over. In flight from below the dark body and under wing-coverts contrast with the whitish under surface of the flight feathers and the light barred tail. The immature bird is mottled pale and dark brown. The Brown Harrier-Eagle resembles a dark-plumaged Tawny Eagle but can be distinguished by its bare tarsi, large yellow eyes, and light under surface of the wings.

Voice: Usually silent. A deep 'ko-ko-ko'.

Distribution and Habitat. Resident. Widely distributed in the savanna from Senegal east to Chad and the Central African Republic and south to Congo.

Nesting: Builds a large stick nest in a high tree. The single egg is white, sometimes marked with rufous-brown.

Allied species: The Banded Harrier-Eagle (*Circaetus cinerascens*) inhabits the wooded savanna north of the forest and its range extends from Senegal and Portuguese Guinea to the Central African Republic. Size 22″–24″. Distinguished when adult from other Harrier-Eagles by its tail, which is blackish with one broad white band across the middle and a narrow white tip. Immature birds are brown above and dirty white washed with brown below. The Serpent Eagle (*Dryotriorchis spectabilis*) is allied to the Harrier-Eagles. It is smaller than these and possesses relatively shorter wings and a longer tail. Further it is a true forest bird. Dark above, whitish below with a black longitudinal throat stripe and with or without black spots on the breast. Long yellow bare legs. The loud cat-like 'miaow' is distinctive. A snake-eater. In our area it occurs from Sierra Leone to Gaboon.

GREAT SPARROWHAWK   *Accipiter melanoleucus*   **Pl. 7**

Identification: 18″–22″. The size and build of the European Goshawk. In the adult the body is black above and white below with a black patch on the flanks which is a field mark. The immature bird is brown below, heavily streaked. Flight strong and dashing. A notorious chicken thief.

Voice: A shrill 'kek-kek-kek'.

Distribution and Habitat: Widely distributed in the Ethiopian Region. In our area resident and locally common in the forest and the adjoining wooded savanna from Ivory Coast and Ghana south to Gaboon and Congo and east to the Central African Republic. One Senegal record.

Nesting: Builds in a tree making a large stick nest lined with leaves. Eggs 3, bluish-white faintly and sparingly marked with brown.

WEST AFRICAN GOSHAWK   *Accipiter toussenelii*   **Pl. 8**

Identification: Upperparts grey, no white on the rump; underparts vary with locality from uniform rufous to rufous barred with white; tail blackish with three prominent white spots, these latter distinguishing it from the Shikra, which has the tail unspotted. Immature birds are heavily spotted below with dark brown. A typical Sparrowhawk in flight and behaviour, preying on birds, rodents, frogs and lizards.

Voice: A harsh monotonous 'pik-pik-pik . . .' uttered when perched, and also on the wing.

Distribution and Habitat: The forest and the outlying woods in the savanna, and exceptionally the orchard bush from Senegal to Gaboon and Congo. Also Fernando Po. Widespread and locally common. Partial to dense forest second-growth.

Nesting: The closely allied Goshawk of South and East Africa (*Accipiter tachiro*) builds a stick nest in a tree and lays 2–3 white eggs.

Allied species: The Chestnut-flanked Goshawk (*Accipiter castanilius*) is a rather uncommon forest hawk recorded in our area from the Cameroons and Gaboon. Though structurally different and slightly smaller it is virtually indistinguishable in the field from the West African Goshawk; but the race of the latter occurring in the Cameroons and Gaboon has the underparts unbarred or faintly barred whilst *castanilius* has the underparts clearly barred. It inhabits the dense vegetation of the forest.

SHIKRA *Accipiter badius*   **Pl. 8**

Identification: 11″–13″. Female larger than male. Upperparts dove-grey; breast pale rufous finely barred with white; belly and thighs white. No white on the rump. Tail grey, the outer rectrices crossed with six black bands. In immature plumage grey-brown heavily blotched below with reddish-brown. Short wings and long tail apparent in flight. A bold hawk with swift dashing flight. Not at all shy. Often perched quietly concealed in a leafy tree.

Voice: A high-pitched 'ki-ki-ki-ki'.

Distribution and Habitat: Widely and abundantly distributed throughout our area, but absent from closed forest and from the extreme north though there is a movement towards the desert in the wet season.

Nesting: A rather slight platform of sticks usually high up in the fork of a tree. Eggs 2–3, white rather sparsely blotched and spotted with different shades of brown and with grey shell marks.

Allied species: The Ovampo Sparrowhawk (*Accipiter ovampensis*) is a rather rare bird of the open country outside the rain forest, occurring as far west as Senegal. Grey above, finely barred grey and white below. The white spots on the middle tail feathers distinguish it from the Shikra and the absence of clear white on the rump from the Gabar Goshawk.

WEST AFRICAN LITTLE SPARROWHAWK
Accipiter erythropus (*A. minullus*)   **Pl. 8**

Identification: 10″–12″. Known by its small size and colour pattern. Upperparts black with a distinct white patch at the base of the tail. In the race occurring in the Cameroons and Gaboon the breast is rufous and the tail shows one or two white spots. West of the Cameroons the breast is grey faintly barred and the tail is unspotted. The white rump distinguishes this species from the larger West African Goshawk.

Voice: No records. In South Africa the closely related *Accipiter minullus* utters a high-pitched 'kik-kik-kik-kik-kik'.

Distribution and Habitat: Senegal to Gaboon and Congo. It is nowhere common. Its principal habitat is the forest second-growth but it is also found in wooded localities outside the forest.

Nesting: The nest is built in a tree.

CHANTING GOSHAWK *Melierax metabates*   **Pl. 7**

Identification: 20″–22″. Female larger than male. Pale grey upperparts, throat, and breast. Belly and thighs finely barred black and white. Tail edged and tipped white. Cere and legs bright orange. The barred rump appears white in flight. Immature birds mainly brown above and on breast; belly and thighs barred brown and white. Often perched in a tree when the upright carriage is characteristic.

Voice: A prolonged musical fluting cry.

Distribution and Habitat: Common in the savanna north of the forest from Mauritania, Senegal, and Gambia through Portuguese Guinea, Guinea, Mali, Ivory Coast, Ghana, Togo, Niger, northern Nigeria, and Cameroons to Chad and the Central African Republic. Most plentiful in the dry northern thorn scrub provided there are a few tall trees.

Nesting: Builds in the fork of a tree standing alone or on the edge of a wood. Made of sticks with various materials incorporated in the lining. Eggs 2, occasionally 1. Pure white or white tinged blue.

GABAR GOSHAWK *Melierax gabar* (*Micronisus gabar*) Pl. 8

Identification: 12″–14″. Female larger than male. Same size as the Shikra. Broad white rump an excellent field character. Upperparts excluding rump, throat, and breast grey; belly narrowly barred grey and white. Tail barred dark and light, and tipped white. Legs red. Melanistic phase fairly common. Immature plumage resembles the Shikra, but the rump is white. Rapid dashing direct flight. Often perched concealed in thick cover inside a tree.

Voice: A weak high-pitched chittering.

Distribution and Habitat: A common hawk of the thorn scrub zone from southern Mauritania, Senegal and Gambia east through Mali, Ivory Coast, Niger, northern Nigeria, and northern Cameroons to Chad. Recorded from Gaboon.

Nesting: Located, usually high up, in the fork of a tree. A platform of sticks lined with leaves. Eggs 1–3, dull white with yellowish nest stains.

LONG-TAILED HAWK *Urotriorchis macrourus* Pl. 7

Identification: Readily distinguished from all other forest hawks in our area by its disproportionately long graduated tail. Grey above; mainly chestnut below; rump white; tail spotted and tipped with white.

Voice: A shrill cry.

Distribution and Habitat: A rather uncommon rain forest species that occurs in Liberia east to the Central African Republic and south to Gaboon. Its habitat is the forest both in the thick undergrowth and in the tree tops.

Nesting: Habits unknown.

LIZARD BUZZARD *Kaupifalco monogrammicus* Pl. 8

Identification: 14″. A thick-set, medium-sized grey hawk. The black line down the white throat is distinctive, as is, especially in flight, the broad white bar across the black tail. Mantle grey, rump black, breast grey, belly and thighs barred black and white. *Melierax metabates* (p. 42) is larger and lacks the throat streak and tail bar. *Melierax gabar* (above) is smaller and has a white rump. Call distinctive. When hunting perches for a time on a tree watching the ground intently and then flies on to another tree with characteristic very direct flight.

Voice: A very distinctive musical far-carrying series of whistles in descending pitch.

Distribution and Habitat: Widespread and common in the wooded savanna and in the forest clearings from Gambia and Senegal east to the Central African Republic and south to Gaboon and Congo. Uncommon in the arid north and rare in Mali and Chad.

Nesting: Nest of sticks built in the fork of a tree. Eggs 3, white tinged blue.

Plate 7

HAWKS, BUZZARD, OSPREY AND KITE

BIRDS OF PREY

GRASSHOPPER BUZZARD   *Butastur rufipennis*   **Pl. 8**
Identification: 16″–18″. Female larger than male. A long-winged, long-tailed hawk, immediately recognised in flight by its rufous-chestnut wings. Upperparts ashy-brown; underparts light rufous. Immature dress mainly rufous. Flight Harrier-like. Often seen in numbers near grass fires catching insects. Frequently perches high in a tree.
Voice: Silent.
Distribution and Habitat: Widely distributed in the savanna north of the forest. Mainly in the orchard bush zone but extending its range seasonally north to the desert and south nearly to the savanna-forest edge. Recorded from Mauritania, Senegal, Gambia, Ivory Coast, Mali, Ghana, Nigeria, Cameroons, Chad, and the Central African Republic.
Nesting: A platform of sticks lined with leaves and built high up in a tree. Eggs 3, white sparingly marked with brown and lilac.

RED-TAILED BUZZARD   *Buteo auguralis*   **Pl. 7**
Identification: 18″–20″. A typical broad-winged Buzzard easily recognised in flight and when perched by its rufous tail. Given to soaring. Upperparts, throat, and chest mainly brown. Remainder underparts and under surface of wing white, the breast and flanks spotted with brown. The immature bird has the underparts whitish, spotted with brown, and the tail is rufous-brown barred darker.
Voice: A Buzzard-like 'mew'.
Distribution and Habitat: Resident and common in West Africa from Senegal east to Chad and Gaboon frequenting large clearings in the lowland forest zone and wooded areas in the savanna and also the grassy highlands of the Cameroons and the Bauchi Plateau of Nigeria. Subject to migration.
Nesting: Nests in a tree or on the ledge of a crag making a stick nest and laying 2–3 eggs, which are whitish and very sparingly marked.

LONG-CRESTED HAWK-EAGLE   *Lophaetus occipitalis*   **Pl. 6**
Identification: 22″. Perched appears as a small completely dark brown (at a distance black) Eagle with a long untidy crest which blows about in the wind. In flight, from above, a large white patch on the wing; from below most of the wing white, and tail mainly white tipped black. Often perches for long periods on high exposed branch in stiff erect pose. Also soars and glides. Not shy.
Voice: A series of high-pitched shrill whistles.
Distribution and Habitat: Widespread and rather common throughout the area in the savanna and forest clearings but absent from closed forest and from the desert and its borders.
Nesting: A nest of sticks lined with green leaves built in the upper branches of a tree. Eggs 1–2, white sparingly blotched and smeared with red-brown, with lilac shell marks.

CROWNED HAWK-EAGLE   *Stephanoaetus coronatus*   **Pl. 6**
Identification: 32″. A very large powerfully-built Eagle. Head crested. In the adult black above, barred black and buff below. In flight from below the wings are conspicuously barred. The immature bird has the head and under-parts white but the thighs are spotted, as can be observed in the field. Soars to great heights above the forest. Preys especially on monkeys and also on goats and sheep and other smaller animals. Wary of human beings.

Voice: Call a rapid 'hu-hu-hu- . . .' rising in pitch and a slow 'ouhu-ouhu . . .' also rising in pitch.

Distribution and Habitat: The forest from Portuguese Guinea east to the Central African Republic and south to Gaboon and Congo, occasionally penetrating the wooded savanna outside the forest.

Nesting: For the greater part of the year the life of these eagles is centred upon their nest. The fledgling period is very extended. The huge stick nest which is used year after year is built in a forest tree. The clutch is one.

Allied species: Cassin's Hawk-Eagle (*Hieraaetus africanus*), 22″, is a rather rare forest species recorded in our area from Liberia, Ivory Coast, Togo, Cameroons, and Gaboon. The adult is dark above, and white below with a dark patch on either side of the chest and dark axillaries. Ayres' Hawk-Eagle (*Hieraaetus dubius*) is a rare, mainly forest eagle recorded from Liberia, Ivory Coast, Togo, Cameroons, Chad, and Spanish Guinea. 18″–22″. When adult dark above, and below white blotched with black. The African Hawk-Eagle (*Hieraaetus spilogaster*), 26″, is a savanna species, local in our area and recorded from Senegal, Gambia, Portuguese Guinea, Ghana, Togo, and Nigeria. Like Ayres' Hawk-Eagle the adult is dark brown above and white blotched black below, but the blotches are less heavy and more linear so that at a distance the underparts appear white. It is larger than Ayres' Hawk-Eagle and has a noticeably longer tail.

MARTIAL EAGLE   *Polemaetus bellicosus*   Pl. 6

Identification: 31″–33″. The largest and most powerful Eagle of the open savanna. Upperparts, throat, and upper breast brown; lower breast and belly white spotted brown. Eye yellow. Tarsus feathered. In immature plumage upperparts pale brown and underparts including the tarsus unspotted white. Distinguished from Beaudouin's Harrier-Eagle by its larger size, spotted not barred underparts, and feathered tarsus. Often seen perched erect on a tree top watching for its prey. Hunts Guinea-fowl.

Voice: Usually silent. A short bark and a loud ringing cry have been described.

Distribution and Habitat: Widely but sparingly distributed in the savanna north of the forest being recorded from Senegal, Gambia, Portuguese Guinea, Sierra Leone, Mali, Ivory Coast, Ghana, Nigeria, Cameroons, Chad, and the Central African Republic.

Nesting: A massive stick nest at the top of a tree. The single egg is white sparingly marked with brown at the large end.

TAWNY EAGLE   *Aquila rapax*   Pl. 6

Identification: 26″–30″. Female much larger than male. A brown Eagle, usually uniformly dark when adult but the shade varies with abrasion and according to race. Immature bird pale brown. Seen from below in flight the light tips contrast with the rest of the wing, which is dark. The tail appears rounded. Flight slow but powerful. Sometimes soars. A sluggish sedentary Eagle. Not shy. Takes carrion and also kills its own prey.

Voice: A harsh barking cry. Usually rather silent.

Distribution and Habitat: Widely distributed in the open savanna north of the forest and locally common. Rarer in the extreme north. Numbers perhaps augmented by Palaearctic migrants in winter. Recorded from Mauritania, Senegal, Gambia, Ivory Coast, Upper Volta, Ghana, Niger, Nigeria, Cameroons, Chad, Central African Republic and Congo.

Plate 9

FALCONS

10

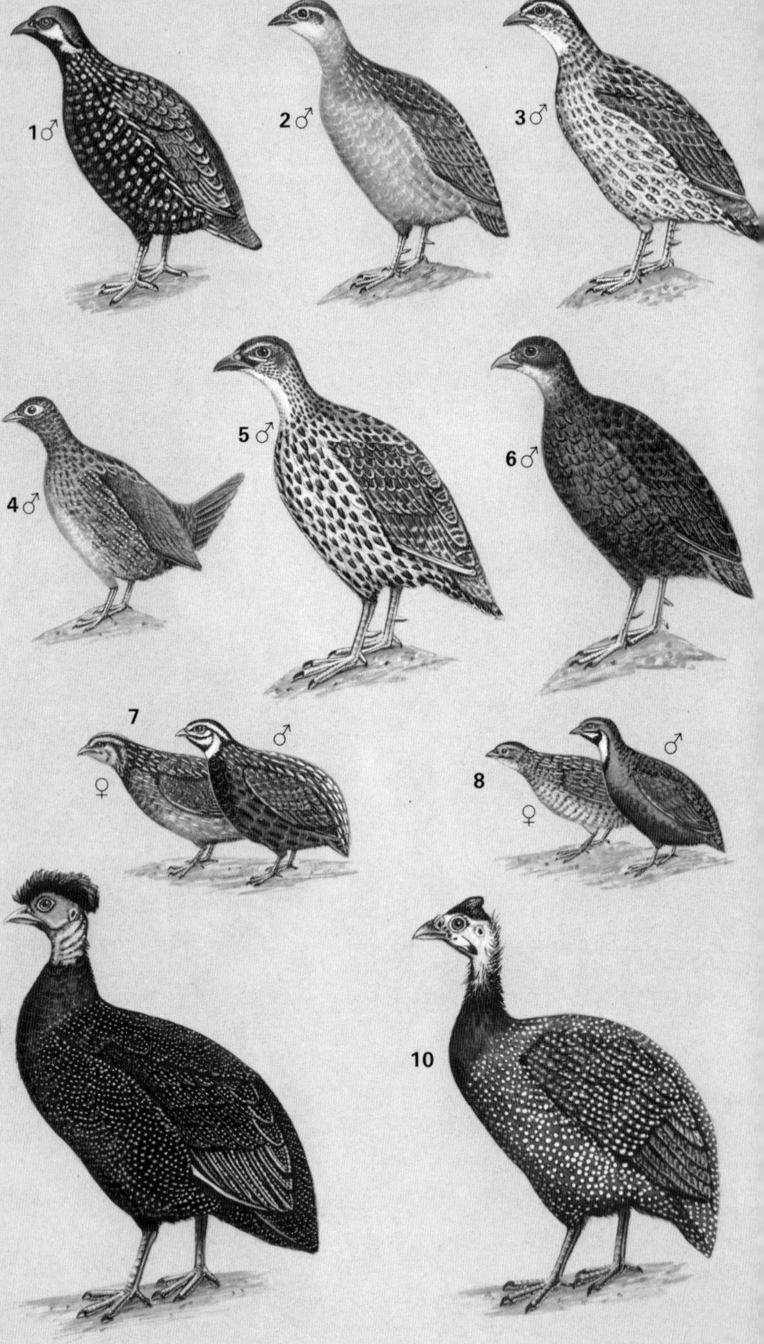

Plate 10

FRANCOLINS, QUAILS, STONE-PARTRIDGE, AND GUINEA-FOWLS

1. **LATHAM'S FRANCOLIN** *Francolinus lathami* page 55
Dark underparts boldly spotted white.

2. **WHITE-THROATED FRANCOLIN** 55
Francolinus albogularis
Eye-stripe; rufous-yellow neck; mainly pale buff underparts.

3. **DOUBLE-SPURRED FRANCOLIN** 56
Francolinus bicalcaratus
Long white stripe above eye; heavily spotted underparts.

4. **STONE-PARTRIDGE** *Ptilopachus petrosus* 58
Cocked tail.

5. **CLAPPERTON'S FRANCOLIN** *Francolinus clappertoni* 56
Creamy-white underparts boldly marked with black.

6. **SCALY FRANCOLIN** *Francolinus squamatus* 56
Orange-red legs.

7. **HARLEQUIN QUAIL** *Coturnix delegorguei* 57
Male: black and white patterned throat; black breast; mainly chestnut flanks.
Female: white throat bordered by black dots.

8. **AFRICAN BLUE QUAIL** *Coturnix chinensis* 57
Male: mainly dark body plumage; white throat; chestnut wings.
Female: dark barred underparts.

9. **CRESTED GUINEA-FOWL** *Guttera edouardi* 58
Curly black crest.

10. **GREY-BREASTED HELMET GUINEA-FOWL** 58
Numida meleagris
Helmet crest; bare head and neck; red wattle.

Nesting: A large stick nest lined with leaves built high up in a tree. Eggs 1–2, white irregularly washed with pale grey.

WAHLBERG'S EAGLE   *Aquila wahlbergi*   **Pl. 6**

Identification: 23″–25″. A rather small Eagle uniformly dark brown in colour. The smaller size, the short crest on the nape, and, in flight, the relatively much longer and almost square tail distinguish it from the Tawny Eagle. In flight the blackish under wing-coverts contrast with the brown wings.

Voice: A clear two-note whistle.

Distribution and Habitat: Locally distributed in our area from Senegal, Gambia, and Mali to Nigeria, in the savanna north of the forest. Subject to migration.

Nesting: A stick nest is built in a fork of a tree. The egg is chalky-white sparingly to heavily marked with brown and lilac. The clutch is one, occasionally two.

WEST AFRICAN RIVER EAGLE   *Haliaetus vocifer*
(*Cuncuma vocifer*)   **Pl. 6**

Identification: 28″–30″. Female larger than male. Easily recognised by colour pattern. Head, mantle, breast and tail white, belly chestnut, wings black with chestnut shoulder patches. White head and bib conspicuous. Far-carrying arresting cry. The Palm-nut Vulture is superficially similar but has the entire underparts white and the white tail is crossed by a broad black band. The immature River Eagle is brown above and streaked buff and brown below, but the plumage is variable and birds in intermediate dress can be puzzling. Feeds on both live and dead fish and robs other fish-eating birds.

Voice: High-pitched and ringing. A 'kiou——Kiou-kiou-kiou-kiou'.

Distribution and Habitat: Always near water. Estuaries, mangrove creeks, rivers, and lakes attract it. Where such habitat available common. From Mauritania, Senegal, and Gambia east to the Central African Republic and south to Gaboon and Congo. Particularly common in Senegal and Gambia.

Nesting: A large stick nest built in a tree near water and often at no great height. Eggs 2, white.

BLACK KITE   *Milvus migrans*   **Pl. 7**

Identification: 22″. Uniformly dull rufous-brown. Recognised by its forked tail. In the resident African race (*parasitus*) the bill is yellow. It is black in the migratory European race (*migrans*) and the latter also has a lighter-coloured head. But immature *parasitus* has a black bill and cannot be distinguished from *migrans*. Often in the air. Flight light and graceful. A scavenger; often in great numbers about towns and villages. Bold and familiar though migrants from Europe by comparison rather shy.

Voice: Frequent shrill mewing cries.

Distribution and Habitat: Very abundant and widespread throughout the area, especially near human habitation. Absent from closed forest. Resident race subject to local migration. Population increased in winter by Palaearctic immigrants.

Nesting: A stick nest lined with rags and other trash. Built in a tree at a height of twenty to eighty feet. Eggs 2–3, white blotched and spotted with different shades of brown. Usually poorly marked.

Allied species: The Honey Buzzard (*Pernis apivorus*) 22″–24″, is recognised by its small slender head and long tail, the latter tipped with black and showing two dark bands near its base. Upperparts brown; underparts variable being brown, or white heavily or lightly marked with brown. Inner lining of wings whitish with dark bars. A visitor from the Palaearctic Region wintering in the forest clearings and the moist savanna from Liberia to the Cameroons and Fernando Po and occurring on passage in Mali and Chad. On the whole rather uncommon.

WEST AFRICAN CUCKOO FALCON   *Aviceda cuculoides*   **Pl. 8**
Identification: 15″. Upperparts dark and uniform. Underparts below the grey breast heavily barred white and chestnut. In flight the long pointed wing and long tail, both barred, are field marks. Sometimes soars but usually seen flying with heavy slow flapping flight. Rather shy. Largely insectivorous.
Distribution and Habitat: The forest and the wooded savanna north of the forest from Gambia and Senegal to the Cameroons and Gaboon and the Central African Republic. Frequents primary and secondary forest and is nowhere common.
Nesting: In South Africa the nest is a platform of sticks built in a large tree. Eggs 2–3, white spotted and scrolled with brown.

BLACK-SHOULDERED KITE   *Elanus caeruleus*   **Pl. 8**
Identification: 12″. A small thick-set, long-winged, short-tailed hawk. Upperparts light grey with a conspicuous black patch on the shoulders. Underparts white. In immature plumage upperside brownish with light edges to the scapulars and wing-coverts; underside streaked with yellowish-brown. Flight characteristically buoyant and graceful. Hovers like a Kestrel. Feeds largely on rodents. Often seen perched, scanning the ground for prey.
Voice: Generally silent. Occasionally a piping whistle.
Distribution and Habitat: Common and widespread in the savanna from Senegal and Gambia east to the Central African Republic and south to Gaboon and Congo. Absent from the closed forest and rare in the arid north. Prefers open cultivated country where field mice and other rodents abound.
Nesting: A shallow platform of sticks and twigs built in the branches of a tree. Eggs 3–4, white or pale brown, blotched and smeared with different shades of reddish-brown.

SWALLOW-TAILED KITE   *Elanus riocourii (Chelictinia riocourii)*   **Pl. 8**
Identification: 15″. Unmistakable. A slight, slender hawk with the build and grace of a Tern. Long pointed wings; deeply forked tail. Upperparts light grey; underparts white. In flight usually displays a black patch on the under surface of the wing near the elbow. Often gregarious. Buoyant in flight; quarters the ground like a Kestrel; sometimes hovers. Feeds mainly on insects.
Voice: Usually silent. A mewing cry recorded.
Distribution and Habitat: Widespread and locally common in the drier northern savanna, especially between 13° N. and 17° N. from Gambia and Senegal in the west to Chad in the east. Subject to irregular movements dictated by the supply of its insect prey.
Nesting: A small nest of twigs in a thorn tree at no great height. Eggs 3–4, whitish, closely and finely speckled with umber-brown.

BAT HAWK   *Macheirhamphus alcinus*   **Pl. 7**
Identification: 18″. Its very rapid falcon-like flight, its silhouette, particularly the pointed wings, the dark plumage (in our area at least), and its habit of appearing at dusk, all help to identify it. Wary. Predominantly a bat-eater, which explains its crepuscular habits; occasionally hunts during the day. Shows a preference for large clearings in the forest.
Voice: Described as a shrill falcon-like 'kwik-kwik-kwik . . .'.
Distribution and Habitat: The forest and the wooded savanna from Gambia and Senegal to the Cameroons and the Central African Republic and south to Congo. Widely but thinly distributed.
Nesting: In South Africa nests in tall trees making a stick nest lined with green leaves. Eggs 1–2. Pale bluish-green, immaculate or marked with brown and purple.

OSPREY   *Pandion haliaetus*   **Pl. 7**
Identification: 22″–25″. The best field mark is the white crown and the dark line through the eye. Upperparts, wings, and tail brown. Underparts white with a patch of brown on the breast. In the air the buoyant flight and long narrow slightly flexed wings are characteristic. Hovers over water and plunges in with a splash to retrieve a fish. Often perches on a high dead limb over water.
Voice: A succession of short shrill musical whistles.
Distribution and Habitat: A fairly widespread Palaearctic migrant to our area where there are fish-stocked rivers, lakes, reservoirs, lagoons, estuaries, and coastal waters. Occurs from Senegal and Gambia east to the Central African Republic and south to Gaboon and Congo. Breeds on the Cape Verde Islands and suspected of doing so on the West African coast.
Nesting: A massive stick nest on a rock or cliff edge. Eggs 2–3, cream, handsomely blotched with rich shades of brown.

FALCONS: Falconidae

Thick-set birds with long pointed wings and swift, usually direct flight. Some capable of spectacular aerial manoeuvres. Usually catch their prey on the wing, the true falcons in the course of a stoop at great speed. Usually lay on a rock ledge or in the nest of another bird. Do not build nests of sticks. Moustachial streak is a character of many species.

LANNER FALCON   *Falco biarmicus*   **Pl. 9**
Identification: 16″–18″. Female larger than male. A large Falcon with the build, size, and direct flight of a Peregrine but not so fierce or dashing. The rufous crown and nape is diagnostic but not always useful as a field character for the Lanner flies high and perches high. Upperparts dark grey. Underparts pinkish-buff spotted with brown on the breast and flanks. Stoops like a Peregrine.
Voice: A high-pitched 'kii kii kii'.
Distribution and Habitat: Widely and fairly commonly distributed in the savanna north of the forest from Mauritania and Senegal to Chad and the Central African Republic. Likes mountainous country or open savanna with granite outcrops or tall solitary trees.
Nesting: Eggs laid on a cliff ledge or in a high tree in the appropriated nest of some other bird, a few fresh green leaves being added. Eggs 3–4, yellowish or

pinkish-buff washed, blotched, and smeared with different shades of red and brown.

Allied species: The Peregrine Falcon (*Falco peregrinus*), 13″–15″, resembles the Lanner but has a blackish not rufous crown, the black moustachial patch is bolder and broader, and the underparts are barred not spotted. A Palaearctic migrant and a resident in West Africa, rather rare and reported from Gambia, Liberia, Ivory Coast, Ghana, Niger, Chad, Nigeria, Cameroons, and Fernando Po. Breeds on the Cape Verde Islands and presumably also on the African mainland.

AFRICAN HOBBY *Falco cuvieri* Pl. 9

Identification: 12″. In appearance and habits recalls the European Hobby. Slate above, rufous below heavily streaked with black on the breast. Black moustachial streak. Flight rapid and dashing. The European Hobby (*Falco subbuteo*), a rare winter visitor to West Africa, is similar but has much paler underparts.

Voice: A shrill 'ke-ke-ke . . .'.

Distribution and Habitat: The savanna except the more arid parts from Senegal and Gambia east to the Central African Republic and south to Congo. Occasionally in extensive clearings in the forest zone. Widely but thinly distributed.

Nesting: In South Africa nests in high trees laying three cream eggs heavily marked with red-brown.

RED-NECKED KESTREL *Falco chicquera* Pl. 9

Identification: 12″–14″. Female larger than male. The bright chestnut head and nape, pinkish-buff breast, and narrowly barred upperparts and underparts distinguish it. A typical, dashing Falcon which preys on birds and bats. Active at twilight. Usually in the vicinity of palm trees, especially the Borassus palm.

Voice: A shrill 'kii kii kii'.

Distribution and Habitat: Widely distributed but nowhere abundant in the savanna north of the forest from Senegal and Gambia to Chad and the Central African Republic. Absent from the forest. Palm trees an essential component of the habitat.

Nesting: In the crown of a Borassus palm laying its eggs on the upper hollow surface of a leaf stem. Eggs in east Africa are creamy-white, unmarked.

GREY KESTREL *Falco ardosiaceus* Pl. 9

Identification: 14″. Grey all over. Cere and bare skin round eye chrome-yellow and conspicuous at close range. Bill blackish. In the air the dark tips of the wings catch the eye. Of heavier build than the Kestrel and slower in flight. Sometimes hovers. Given to perching and often chooses a bare dead limb, telegraph pole, or other exposed site.

Voice: Usually silent. A harsh whistling at the nest.

Distribution and Habitat: Widely distributed in the savanna north and south of the forest but nowhere common, occurring from Senegal and Gambia east to Chad and south to Gaboon and Congo. Lightly wooded savanna and plains dotted with trees attract it and it avoids closed rain forest and also the thorn scrub bordering the desert.

Nesting: Eggs laid inside a Hammerkop's nest or in the hollow of a tree. No nesting materials. Eggs 4–5, resemble the eggs of a Kestrel (*Falco tinnunculus*) but tend to be paler.

KESTREL *Falco tinnunculus* **Pl. 9**

Identification: 13"–14". Adult male has grey head, rump, and tail, the last with a black band near the tip; dark-spotted rufous upperparts; buff underparts streaked blackish. Female and immature bird have upperparts rufous barred blackish; underparts pale buff streaked blackish; tail barred. Flight rapid. When hunting characteristically hovers scanning the ground below. Not shy. Hunts in the open and prefers exposed perches such as cliff ledges, ant-hills, trees, overhead cables, and telegraph poles. Attracted by the insects and other animals raised by bush fires.

Voice: A shrill 'kik kik kik kik' most often heard at the nest.

Distribution and Habitat: A winter visitor from the Palaearctic Region. Widespread and common in the savanna, rare or absent from the forest. Also a resident population mainly in mountainous areas such as the Cameroons highlands and the Jos Plateau, and in the savanna where there are granite outcrops or cliffs. Resident in the Cape Verde Islands.

Nesting: Breeds on cliff ledges or in a hollow tree making little or no nest. Eggs 2–3 (in the Cape Verde Islands 5), buff or cream usually heavily marked with red and brown.

Allied species: The Lesser Kestrel (*Falco naumanni*), 12", is slightly smaller than the Kestrel, which it closely resembles. Adult male distinguished from the latter by the absence of dark spots on the mantle and female and immature birds distinguishable at close range when perched by their whitish not black claws. Highly gregarious. Less given to hovering than the Kestrel and more given to catching insects in the air. A Palaearctic migrant and winter visitor. Common locally in winter in Chad and northern Nigeria, common some years on passage in Senegal, and recorded also from a few widespread localities in Mauritania, Gambia, Mali, Ivory Coast, Ghana, and Congo.

FOX KESTREL *Falco alopex* **Pl. 9**

Identification: 16"–17". Obviously a Kestrel. Very accomplished on the wing. Entire plumage in male and female foxy-red, the body above and below streaked with black and the long tail narrowly barred with black. Often attracted to grass fires.

Voice: The call is described as like that of other Kestrels.

Distribution and Habitat: The open parts of West Africa north of the forest from Ivory Coast and Mali to Chad and the Central African Republic. Local, being virtually restricted to crags, rocky hills, and inselbergs. Subject to local movements and absent from the southern moister parts of its West African range during the rains.

Nesting: Nests on the ledge of a cliff.

SECRETARY-BIRD: Sagittariidae

SECRETARY-BIRD *Sagittarius serpentarius* **Pl. 5**

Identification: The long legs and tail, the raptor bill, the occipital crest, and the black and pale grey plumage, are, collectively, quite diagnostic. Largely terrestrial. A stalking gait. A snake-eater pounding its victim to death with its powerful feet.

Voice: Described as a frog-like croak.

Distribution and Habitat: Widely but rather thinly distributed in our area but absent from the forest zone. Its range includes the grassy highlands of the Cameroons and the Bauchi Plateau and the arid areas bordering the Sahara.
Nesting: In South Africa the massive stick nest is built in a tree, often at no great height. Eggs 2–3, white.

FRANCOLINS, QUAILS AND GUINEA-FOWLS: Phasianidae

Terrestrial birds with heavy bodies, generally rotund form, and drooping hindquarters. Bill strong, short and arched. Wings short and rounded. Tail short. Plumage usually finely and intricately patterned. Sexes usually alike. Young precocious, nidifugous, and developing flight feathers at a very early age.

LATHAM'S FRANCOLIN *Francolinus lathami* **Pl. 10**
Identification: A true forest Francolin. The bold white spots on the dark ground colour of the underparts serve to identify both male and female, and the male also shows white marks on the mantle. In high forest with scanty undergrowth it may be seen singly or in small parties walking over the leaf-strewn ground and searching for termites of which it is fond.
Voice: A clucking call.
Distribution and Habitat: Strictly confined to the forest from Sierra Leone to southern Cameroons, Gaboon, and Congo. It does not enter the grassy clearings nor the farm patches.
Nesting: Nest a depression on the forest floor scantily lined with leaves. The clutch is two. The eggs have a remarkably hard and thick shell. Elongate-ovate in shape, buff to coffee-brown in colour, the shade sometimes varying in different parts of the shell.

WHITE-THROATED FRANCOLIN *Francolinus albogularis* **Pl. 10**
Identification: 9″. Plumage varies individually and with locality. In the male, crown rufous, eye-stripe white or buff, neck rufous-yellow, back chestnut-brown or greyish-brown streaked and barred whitish and dusky, wings and wing-coverts mainly chestnut, chin and throat white, rest of underparts mainly pale buff. Female differs by being barred blackish below, especially on the chest and flanks. The call, the small size, and, in flight, the chestnut wings, are the best field marks. Occurs in pairs or coveys; usually lies close; flight low, rapid and direct.
Voice: A loud strident distinctive 'kili kili kili', especially at dawn and dusk.
Distribution and Habitat: Locally distributed in the savanna in Senegal, Gambia, Guinea, Ivory Coast, Ghana, Nigeria, and Cameroons. Frequents fallow fields with regenerating bushy growth and also open rolling country with a light covering of scrub.
Nesting: Nest in the open; a slight depression in the ground scantily lined with grass and leaves. Eggs 6, buff, slightly glossy, and minutely pitted.
Allied species: The Coqui Francolin (*Francolinus coqui*) is about the same size as the White-throated Francolin but has a slightly longer tail. The general colour of the upperparts is rufous, barred and vermiculated with greyish-black. The underparts are whitish or pale buff except for the breast, which is heavily barred black and white. This last is a field mark. Sparingly distributed in the

arid belt bordering the desert and recorded from Mauritania, Mali, Upper Volta, northern Nigeria, and northern Cameroons. It reappears in the short-grassed savanna of Congo.

DOUBLE-SPURRED FRANCOLIN *Francolinus bicalcaratus* **Pl. 10**
Identification: 14″. Sexes similar except that female is smaller. Plumage variable. Upperparts at a distance dark brown, at close range streaked, mottled, and barred blackish, dark brown, rufous, buff, and cream; crown earth-brown separated from the conspicuous long white supercilium by a black band extending from the forehead to the nape; underparts buffish boldly marked with tear-shaped chestnut and blackish spots. A plump Francolin which runs with upright carriage; often seen in the open; not shy; occurs in coveys or pairs; flight strong and noisy; cry distinctive.
Voice: A loud harsh 'kor-ker kor-ker' usually at dawn and dusk and often delivered from the top of an ant-hill or other prominent perch.
Distribution and Habitat: The most abundant and widespread of the Francolins in our area ranging south of 17° N. from Senegal and Gambia east to Chad and the Cameroons. Habitat very varied, from arid plain to bleak grassy upland, but absent from closed forest. Fond of cultivated or recently abandoned farmland.
Nesting: Nest on the ground in herbage or crops. A shallow circular depression scantily lined with grass, twigs and feathers. Eggs 5–6, buff, shell very strong, and surface minutely pitted.

CLAPPERTON'S FRANCOLIN *Francolinus clappertoni* **Pl. 10**
Identification: 12″–13″. About the same size and build as the Common Bush-fowl (*Francolinus bicalcaratus*) of West Africa. The upperparts are pale brown; the underparts are creamy-white with prominent black pear-shaped marks. At sunrise and sunset the male crows from some vantage point such as a termite-hill.
Voice: Loud and harsh and rather similar to that of the Common Bush-fowl.
Distribution and Habitat: The range is the semi-arid belt near the desert and it is recorded from Mali, Niger, Nigeria north of 12° N., Chad, and the Central African Republic. It is locally common in these areas.
Nesting: Undescribed in West Africa.

SCALY FRANCOLIN *Francolinus squamatus* **Pl. 10**
Identification: 12″–13″. The loud crowing call often heard about sunrise or sunset is the surest means of identification. There is nothing distinctive about its plumage of various shades of brown and buff. The orange-red legs, which can be glimpsed when it is flushed, are an excellent field mark. A mainly terrestrial species difficult to see in the thick undergrowth it affects.
Voice: Well described as 'a blend of a whistle and grating call, a far-carrying "hu-hu-hu-hurrrr" '.
Distribution and Habitat: The forest belt from eastern Nigeria through the Cameroons to Gaboon and Congo. Also the derived savanna of eastern Nigeria north of the forest. Widespread and common. Absent from true forest. Partial to the thick herbage of plantations, to native farm patches, and especially to the impenetrable tangle of abandoned clearings.

Nesting: The nest is a shallow scrape sparingly lined with grass and plant stems. The six unspotted buff eggs are stout-shelled.

Allied species: The Ahanta Francolin (*Francolinus ahantensis*) takes the place of the Scaly Francolin from the vicinity of Benin in southern Nigeria west to the Gambia. It has rather similar habits and habitat, a similar loud call, and the same conspicuous red legs. In the hand readily distinguished from the Scaly Francolin by the feathers of the underparts which have white margins; but this is not a good field character.

HARLEQUIN QUAIL *Coturnix delegorguei* Pl. 10

Identification: 7″. About the same size as the Common Quail (*Coturnix coturnix*). Male distinguished by the black anchor-shaped mark on the white chin and throat; breast black, belly chestnut. The female lacks distinctive characters, being sandy-brown above marked with black, and cream and rufous-buff below except for the throat, which is white bordered by a ring of black dots. Swift whirring flight.

Voice: In South Africa described as a loud ringing 'whit-whit-it'.

Distribution and Habitat: Of local occurrence in West Africa, being recorded from Senegal, the Ivory Coast, from several localities in Nigeria but not in closed forest, from Chad and Cameroons, and from the grasslands of Gaboon. Occurs also on Fernando Po and Sao Tome. Subject to migratory movements. A savanna species.

Nesting: Undescribed in West Africa.

Allied species: The Common Quail (*Coturnix coturnix*), 6″, occurs widely but locally in West Africa as a migrant and winter visitor in the open country north of the forest in Mauritania, Senegal, Gambia, Sierra Leone, Mali, Ivory Coast, Ghana, Nigeria, Cameroons and Chad. Particularly common in the dry zone bordering the Sahara. In the Cape Verde Islands both resident and migratory. Upperparts mainly light brown streaked cream, crown blackish with pale buff medial stripe, supercilium white, middle of chin and throat black, breast rufous, belly dull white. Female differs by having throat entirely white and the breast spotted with black. Frequents grassland and farmland. Sits close, takes off noisily, and drops again after a short, rapid, skimming flight.

AFRICAN BLUE QUAIL *Coturnix chinensis* (*Excalfactoria adansoni*)
Pl. 10

Identification: 5½″. The tiny size and the short swift low flight accompanied by a faint whirr of wings are field characters. In the male in flight the chestnut on the wing and the white on the breast contrast with the dark body plumage. In the brown female the dark barring on the under surface is a useful diagnostic character. Encountered in pairs and, immediately after breeding, in family parties. Difficult to flush a second time.

Voice: Silent, but a whistling cry has been recorded.

Distribution and Habitat: A savanna species, found also in the forest zone where there are extensive grassy clearings such as airfields. Ranges from Sierra Leone and Mali to the Central African Republic and south to Gaboon. Widespread and locally common. Migratory.

Nesting: Nest a slight hollow in the ground lined with grass stems. The 6–8 eggs are yellowish-clay in colour and unmarked.

STONE-PARTRIDGE   *Ptilopachus petrosus*   **Pl. 10**
Identification: 10″. With its cocked tail and alert appearance resembles a
dark brown bantam fowl. Characteristically in parties creeping or running
nimbly amongst boulders or stony ground; difficult to see; reluctant to take
wing. Upperparts brown delicately marked with whitish and buff. Throat
streaked, breast buff, belly mainly brown.
Voice: A pleasing characteristic 'ouit ouit ouit' rising slightly in pitch. Vocal
mainly at dawn and dusk.
Distribution and Habitat: Widely distributed where there is suitable terrain
from Senegal, Gambia and Portuguese Guinea through Sierra Leone, Mali, Ivory
Coast, Ghana and Nigeria to Chad, Cameroons and the Central African Republic.
Mainly restricted to granite kopjes and lateritic outcrops but also found on
sandy scrub-covered plains.
Nesting: A small depression in the soil in the lee of a grass tuft, scantily lined
with grass. Eggs 4, immaculate pale buff.

GREY-BREASTED HELMET GUINEA-FOWL
Numida meleagris   **Pl. 10**
Identification: 22″. Sexes similar. Easily recognised as a Guinea-fowl with
its large plump body, rounded back, and drooping tail. Plumage dark grey
profusely spotted white above and below except for the chest and upper mantle,
which are unspotted. Head and neck bare, casque brown, cheeks and sides of
neck mainly bluish-white, wattle red. Occurs in flocks, runs strongly, mainly
terrestrial but usually roosts in trees, call characteristic.
Voice: An unmistakable loud cackling call heard especially at the roost.
Distribution and Habitat: Abundant and widespread except in the rain
forest from Senegal east to Chad and the Central African Republic and south
to Gaboon and Congo. Also in the Cape Verde Islands. Habitat varied.
Nesting: Nest a slight depression in the ground scantily lined with grass.
Eggs 6–12, creamy-yellow or buff, marked with pores.

CRESTED GUINEA-FOWL   *Guttera edouardi*   **Pl. 10**
Identification: About the same size as the common Grey-breasted Helmet
Guinea-fowl (*Numida meleagris*). In the field it appears darker than that species.
The best characters are the crest of curly black feathers, the bare red throat
and the bare blue neck. Easily heard and located but difficult to see clearly in
the undergrowth.
Voice: The members of the flock make clucking sounds as they feed on the
forest floor.
Distribution and Habitat: Widely distributed in the Ethiopian Region. In
West Africa found in the forests and gallery forests from Portuguese Guinea
to the Central African Republic and Congo. Shows a preference for rather
dense woody second growth and occurs in large scattered parties.
Nesting: In East Africa nests on the ground in a shallow scrape scantily lined
with grass. Eggs 8–10, white or buff, pitted and finely spotted all over with
brown.
Allied species: Three other forest Guinea-fowl, all much rarer than the
Crested Guinea-fowl, occur in our area. The Plumed Guinea-fowl (*Guttera
plumifera*) is about the same size as the Crested Guinea-fowl. Its plumage is
black finely spotted with white. It is distinguished by its crest feathers being

stiff and erect, not curly, and by the bare grey skin of the head and neck. Found in the Cameroons, Gaboon, and Congo, in primary forest and in old overgrown clearings. Gregarious. The White-breasted Guinea-fowl (*Agelastes meleagrides*) is local and rare and so far recorded only from the lowland forests of Liberia, Ivory Coast and Ghana. Easily recognised by its colour pattern – black except for the white breast and mantle and the bare red head. The Black Guinea-fowl (*Agelastes niger*) occurs in the lowland forests of the Cameroons, Gaboon and Congo, in the true forest and occasionally in the cultivated patches on its border. A black unspotted Guinea-fowl distinguished by its head and neck, which are mainly naked and coloured yellowish-pink.

RAILS, CRAKES, GALLINULES AND COOTS: Rallidae

Many species difficult to observe, being secretive and fond of thick vegetation, often in marshy places. Long legs and toes adapted to their usual habitat of marsh or lake. Wings short and rounded and flight usually brief and seemingly weak; yet some species strongly migratory. The Rails and Crakes have narrowed, compressed bodies suited to progress in tough, close vegetation. The Gallinules and Coots are the least secretive members of the family. They often frequent open water, are strong paddlers, and jerk their heads as they swim.

GREY-THROATED RAIL   *Canirallus oculeus*   Pl. 14
Identification: 12″. A shy forest Rail. Upperparts mainly brown, wings spotted and barred with white, tail chestnut, chin and upper throat grey, breast chestnut, belly brown barred buff.
Voice: Captive birds make snoring and cooing noises.
Distribution and Habitat: The rain forest from Liberia east to the Central African Republic and south to Gaboon but not many records. Restricted to shaded forest streams and swamps.
Nesting: Nest of broad blades of grass placed on a low stump at the swampy margin of a forest stream. Eggs 3, cream boldly marked with chestnut-brown and ashy blotches.
Allied species: The Nkulengu Rail (*Himantornis haematopus*) has a similar habitat and is most difficult to observe but its voice is distinctive. A large Rail (17″), its plumage forms an inconspicuous pattern of brown, grey and blackish. The red eye and red legs are field marks. The native name 'nkulengu' is a representation of its low gruff sonorous call. The call is audible at a great distance and is heard especially at dawn and dusk. The range is the forest from Liberia to Gaboon and Congo.

AFRICAN CRAKE   *Crex egregia* (*Crecopsis egregia*)   Pl. 14
Identification: 9″. Upperparts brown blotched with black, breast grey, flanks and belly conspicuously barred black and white. At short range the red eye is noticeable. Elusive and skulking.
Voice: A rapid series of eight or nine whistling notes in a monotone.
Distribution and Habitat: Widely distributed in the savanna and in the forest clearings from the Gambia and Senegal east to Chad and south to Gaboon; also Sao Tome. The habitat is rank herbage in either dry or wet terrain. Resident and locally migratory.

Nesting: Nest in rank herbage near marshy ground; a shallow scrape sparingly lined with grasses and leaves. Eggs 7–8, white or pinkish-white, blotched with chestnut-brown and ashy-purple mainly about the large end.

Allied species: The European Corn Crake (*Crex crex*), 11″, occurs locally as a migrant and winter visitor and is recorded from Mali, Chad, Ghana, Nigeria, Cameroons, and Congo. The bright chestnut wing-coverts are conspicuous in flight and distinguish it from other West African Crakes. Plumage mainly pale brown, the upperparts with dark streaks, and the flanks barred. Typical sluggish flight of a Rail, legs dangling, seldom sustained. Frequents dry or wet herbage. Silent in winter quarters. The Striped Crake (*Porzana marginalis*), 7″, is a little-known species recorded from our area from Ghana, Nigeria (where it breeds), the Cameroons, and Gaboon. Upperparts mainly brown, the mantle and wing-coverts faintly streaked light brown, and the underparts are mainly grey. Its dull plumage, lack of distinctive fieldmarks, and addiction to dense herbaceous cover make its identification in the field virtually impossible.

BLACK CRAKE   *Limnocorax flavirostra*   **Pl. 14**
Identification: 9″. Sexes similar. Readily identified by sooty-black plumage, yellowish-green bill, and bright red legs. Absence of white under tail-coverts distinguishes it from Waterhen species. In unfrequented places shy; in frequented places often confiding. Frequents vegetation at the water's edge and where there are water lilies ventures into the open running nimbly over the lilies fluttering its wings at times to maintain its balance, or taking short flights across open stretches of water.
Voice: Noisy. A variety of loud clucking and churring calls, one of them resembling the 'pruk' of a Moorhen.
Distribution and Habitat: Widely distributed throughout the area south of 17° N. where there are lakes, pools, or sluggish streams fringed with reedy or other sheltering aquatic vegetation.
Nesting: A shallow cup of dry rush blades resting on a platform of bent-over reeds and grasses and usually built in reeds near the water's edge. Eggs 3–5, cream, usually fairly evenly spotted and flecked with chestnut-brown and pale purple.

WHITE-SPOTTED PIGMY RAIL   *Sarothrura pulchra*   **Pl. 14**
Identification: 6″. At all seasons the distinctive far-carrying call identifies it. Best field mark in the male the jet-black back and wing-coverts boldly spotted with white. Chestnut head, mantle, and tail inconspicuous in the forest shade and underparts usually hidden. In the female the chestnut-red is duller in tone and the parts that are white-spotted in the male are marked with close wavy bars of buff on a blackish ground. Restless, strictly terrestrial, and usually shy, although the male at least can be brought to one's feet by imitating its call.
Voice: A clear, whistling, resonant, low-pitched 'hoo-hoo-hoo-hoo-hoo-hoo' delivered in measured time and unmistakable.
Distribution and Habitat: The habitat is forest or shrubby growth, or occasionally thick herbage, and always near water, either stream, lake, marsh, or tidal creek. A sedentary species. The range is the forest and its gallery extensions from Gambia east to the Central African Republic and south to Gaboon. Particularly common in the swamp forest of the Niger delta.

Nesting: Nest a domed structure of leaves and plant stems placed on the leaf-strewn forest floor, and practically invisible so well does it match its surroundings. Eggs 2, white.

Allied species: The Red-chested Pigmy Rail (*Sarothrura rufa*), 5″, is another elusive and skulking member of the same group. It frequents dense herbage, often in marshy places, in clearings in forest country, and in our area is recorded from Sierra Leone, Nigeria, the Cameroons, the Central African Republic, Gaboon and Congo. In South Africa the call is described as a strong 'dúeh-dúeh-dúeh' continued for ten to fifteen seconds. The male has a rufous head, nape and breast and a blackish back, wings, tail and belly, the dark upperparts being streaked and spotted with white. The call of the Buff-spotted Pigmy Rail (*Sarothrura elegans*), 6″, identifies it. The prolonged, mournful, musical, far-carrying whistle is one of the characteristic nocturnal sounds of the forest. The colour pattern of the male resembles the Red-chested Pigmy Rail but the markings on the upperparts take the form of spots (not streaks) and they are buff (not white). This Rail inhabits mainly the low dense second-growth of forest clearings. It is recorded from the forest of Guinea, Sierra Leone, Liberia, Nigeria, the Cameroons and Fernando Po.

MOORHEN *Gallinula chloropus* Pl. 14

Identification: 13″. Sexes similar. Plumage dull black but thin white streak along flanks and white under tail-coverts conspicuous when tail is flirted. Frontal shield and bill (except for yellow tip) red and conspicuous. Swims, dives, walks and runs. Nods head characteristically when swimming and flirts tail when walking or swimming. Flight laboured with long greenish legs dangling. Rather shy and secretive.

Voice: A loud explosive high-pitched 'krrrk'.

Distribution and Habitat: Locally distributed from Senegal and Gambia to Chad and the Cameroons and in a few places common. Breeds Cape Verde Islands and recorded Sao Tome and Annobon. The Palaearctic race, a migrant, is mainly found north of 14° N., whilst the Ethiopian race ranges south of this limit. Frequents lakes, swamps and backwaters with fringing or covering vegetation.

Nesting: A bulky deep cup of aquatic grasses usually over water amongst reeds or sedges. Eggs 4–7, buff or greyish with reddish-brown spots and ashy shell marks and with typical suffusions around the markings.

Allied species: The Lesser Moorhen (*Gallinula angulata*), 10″, resembles the Moorhen (*Gallinula chloropus*) and like it has a red frontal shield, a white flank streak, and white under tail-coverts. The yellow beak of the Lesser Moorhen and its much smaller size distinguish it. Also the sexes are dissimilar, the female Lesser Moorhen being duller and browner than the male. Its habitat is the dense aquatic vegetation of marshes and the borders of lakes and it is widely if locally distributed in West Africa being recorded from Senegal, Mali, Ivory Coast, Ghana, Nigeria, the Cameroons, Chad, and Sao Tome.

KING REED-HEN *Porphyrio porphyrio* (*P. madagascariensis*) Pl. 14

Identification: 17″. Sexes similar. Unmistakable. At a distance appears mainly blue with a turquoise sheen. Under tail-coverts white. Frontal shield, massive bill, and long sturdy legs red. Walks and runs amongst the reeds and over floating vegetation but does not swim. Flirts its tail as it walks. In short flights legs dangle, in longer flights they are extended. In breeding season aggressively territorial.

Voice: A loud trumpeting call.

Distribution and Habitat: Occurs locally in Senegal, Mali, Ghana, Togo, Nigeria, Chad and the Central African Republic, frequenting reed or sedge fringed or covered lakes and marshes.

Nesting: A bulky mass of aquatic grasses slightly hollowed on top. Amongst sedges or reeds. In tall reed beds sometimes attached to the reed stems and quite clear of the surface of the water. Eggs 3–5. Variable. Pale green to deep buff fairly thickly and evenly blotched and spotted with purplish-brown, reddish-brown, and chocolate-brown and with ashy-violet shell marks.

ALLEN'S REED-HEN *Porphyrio alleni* (*Porphyrula alleni*) **Pl. 14**
Identification: 10″. Sexes similar. Resembles the King Reed-hen but much smaller and the frontal shield is greenish-blue not red. Bill and feet red. Immature bird is olive-brown above, pale buff below, and has the bill and legs brown. Walks and runs and clambers nimbly and swims well. Sometimes shy, sometimes bold.

Voice: At the nest a series of harsh 'chucks' increasing in volume and rate and rising in pitch and continuing for several seconds.

Distribution and Habitat: Where the terrain is suitable fairly widely distributed from Senegal and Gambia east to Chad and the Cameroons and south to Gaboon and Congo. Also Fernando Po and Sao Tome. Inhabits rice fields, lakes, and backwaters where there are reeds, water lilies, or other floating vegetation.

Nesting: Over water amongst sedges or rice. A shallow cup of dry sedges sometimes with the surrounding vegetation arched over and screening it above. Eggs 3–5, pinkish-cream evenly marked with reddish-brown and pale lilac spots and speckles which are clearly defined from the ground colour.

Allied species: The European Coot (*Fulica atra*), 15″, is an uncommon winter visitor to Senegal, Nigeria, Chad and the Central African Republic. The slate-black plumage and conspicuous white bill and frontal shield distinguish it. No white under the tail. In flight a narrow white wing bar. Aquatic; fond of open stretches of water; given to diving; gregarious.

FINFOOT: Heliornithidae

FINFOOT *Podica senegalensis* **Pl. 14**
Identification: 25″. Plumage varies individually and with age, sex and locality. Head and nape black separated by a white stripe from the slate-grey throat. Upperparts mainly blackish or dark brown washed with iridescent green and spotted with white. Underparts mainly whitish, sometimes blotched or barred with black. Bill red and conspicuous. Feet bright orange-red but seldom in view. A long-necked aquatic bird superficially similar to a Cormorant or a Grebe. Shy. Usually skulks at the edge of lake, river, or mangrove creek in the shadow of overhanging foliage. Swims, dives, and (rarely) flies. Swims low in the water, sometimes with the whole body submerged and only head visible. Sometimes clambers and creeps about the undergrowth at the water's edge.

Voice: Shrill and guttural calls described. Usually silent.

Distribution and Habitat: Widely but locally distributed in suitable localities from Gambia and Senegal east to Chad and the Central African Republic and south to Gaboon and Congo. Restricted to lakes and water courses with wooded banks. Common in mangrove creeks.

Nesting: In southern Africa nest is built amongst debris on a branch overhanging water, the clutch is two, and the eggs pale buffy-green streaked and blotched with different shades of brown.

CRANES: Gruidae

CROWNED CRANE *Balearica pavonina* **Pl. 11**

Identification: 40″. Sexes similar. At a distance appears as a long-legged blackish Crane with much white on the wings. At close range the conspicuous straw-coloured bristly crest, black crown, and bare pink and white cheeks readily identify it. In flight the neck and legs are held at an angle to the body and the white wing-coverts are conspicuous. Loud cry and nuptial dance also identify it. Usually in flocks except when nesting.

Voice: A powerful trumpeting cry usually uttered in flight.

Distribution and Habitat: South of 17° N. widely distributed in the open country north of the forest from Senegal to Chad and the Central African Republic, frequenting wet plains, rice fields, grassy marshland, and also dry terrain including growing crops.

Nesting: Nests solitarily in a marsh. A pile of grass or other vegetation fashioned into a large circular platform. Eggs 2–3, white tinged blue, very sparingly marked with brown and chocolate.

BUSTARDS: Otididae

Large terrestrial birds that inhabit dry open savanna or desert country. Long necks and rather long legs. Upperparts dull and often cryptically coloured. Powerful, sustained flight with neck and legs extended. On the whole rather silent but the call usually loud and distinctive.

SUDAN BUSTARD *Otis arabs* (*Ardeotis arabs*) **Pl. 11**

Identification: 30″–38″. Female much smaller than male. A very large Bustard. Crested crown buff broadly bordered with black; upperparts mainly tawny; hind and foreneck and breast finely barred black and white appearing grey at a distance, the lax feathers of the neck making it seem thick; rest of underparts whitish. Large area of white on the wing visible in flight at a great distance. Occurs in pairs or small parties. Shy.

Voice: Usually silent. Sometimes utters a powerful barking cry.

Distribution and Habitat: The arid region south of 18° N. in southern Mauritania, Senegal, Gambia, Mali, Niger, northern Ivory Coast, northern Ghana, northern Nigeria, Chad, and the Central African Republic, but absent from the southern part of this range in the wet season.

Nesting: Eggs 2, laid on the bare ground, yellowish or olive blotched with dark brown and grey.

Plate II

CROWNED CRANE AND BUSTARDS

Plate 12

DUCKS AND GEESE IN FLIGHT

1. WHITE-FACED TREE DUCK *Dendrocygna viduata*   page 28
White head.

2. AFRICAN BLACK DUCK *Anas sparsa*   30
White wing bar; orange feet.

3. SHOVELER *Anas clypeata*   31
Heavy spatulate bill; large blue shoulder-patch.

4. FULVOUS TREE-DUCK *Dendrocygna bicolor*   28
White upper and under tail-coverts.

5. HARTLAUB'S DUCK *Pteronetta hartlaubii*   29
Large light blue shoulder-patch.

6. FERRUGINOUS DUCK *Aythya nyroca*   34
White wing-bar; white under tail-coverts.

7. PINTAIL *Anas acuta*   30
Long pointed tail; white neck stripe.

8. GARGANEY *Anas querquedula*   31
Grey-blue shoulder-patch; brown breast sharply demarcated from
white belly; conspicuous white eye stripe.

9. WHITE-BACKED DUCK *Thalassornis leuconotus*   34
White back.

10. PIGMY GOOSE *Nettapus auritus*   30
Female: white wing-bar; white underparts.
Male: white wing-bar; white underparts.

11. KNOB-BILLED GOOSE *Sarkidiornis melanota*   29
All-black wings; white underparts.

12. SPUR-WINGED GOOSE *Plectropterus gambensis*   29
Large white wing-patch.

13. EGYPTIAN GOOSE *Alopochen aegyptiaca*   28
Large pure white shoulder-patch.

DENHAM'S BUSTARD *Neotis denhami* **Pl. 11**

Identification: 32″–40″. Female much smaller than male. The other very large Bustard in our area. Distinguished from the Sudan Bustard by the less conspicuous crest, rufous hindneck, dark brown upperparts, darker grey foreneck, and, particularly in flight, by the contrasting black and white wings. Occurs singly or in small parties. Usually wary.

Voice: Usually silent. A guttural barking cry described.

Distribution and Habitat: Widely distributed and locally common with much the same range as the Sudan Bustard but penetrates farther south in the dry season. Recorded from Mauritania, Senegal, Gambia, Mali, Guinea, Sierra Leone, Ivory Coast, Upper Volta, Ghana, Niger, Nigeria, northern Cameroons, Chad, Central African Republic and Congo. Not uncommon locally.

Nesting: A single egg laid on the bare ground, olive-brown washed with reddish-brown.

Allied species: The Nubian Bustard (*Neotis nuba*) occurs sparingly in Niger and Chad in the arid scrub country bordering the desert. A massive bird (30″), though considerably smaller than the well-known Denham's Bustard (*Neotis denhami*). The large white wing patch and the white under surface of the wing are conspicuous in flight, and the broad black band bordering the crown, and the black throat, are diagnostic.

SENEGAL BUSTARD *Eupodotis senegalensis* **Pl. 11**

Identification: 24″. A small Bustard with a conspicuous blue-grey neck and crop. In the male the crown, a line bordering the nape, and a patch on the throat black. Upperparts warm sandy-rufous with dark vermiculations; breast tawny; belly white. Female has only a touch of grey on the neck and the crown is brown with fine vermiculations and is otherwise the same colour as the male, except for a cream belly. For a Bustard the flight is quite buoyant and light. Solitary or in small flocks.

Voice: A powerful far-reaching 'korwaak' uttered especially at dawn and dusk.

Distribution and Habitat: Widely distributed and locally common from southern Mauritania, Senegal and Gambia east to Chad and the Central African Republic and south to the Congo savanna frequenting open places in the thorn scrub and orchard bush and grassland bordering cultivation.

Nesting: Eggs 2, laid on the bare ground, greenish-buff blotched and spotted with lightish-brown and stone markings.

Allied species: Savile's Pigmy Bustard (*Eupodotis ruficrista*), 16″, is even smaller than the Senegal Bustard. The neck is noticeably short. Distinguished by its black underparts. (Very much smaller than *Eupodotis melanogaster*, the other West African Bustard with black underparts.) Tuft of pinkish feathers on nape specially conspicuous in male. Upperparts sandy-rufous with black lanceolate markings. Arresting, far-carrying, ventriloquial, piping call, uttered day and night in the breeding season. Local, ranging in the dry scrub savanna from Senegal to Chad and the Central African Republic.

BLACK-BELLIED BUSTARD *Eupodotis melanogaster*
(*Lissotis melanogaster*) **Pl. 11**

Identification: 24″. A medium-sized long-necked, long-legged Bustard. Male distinguished from other Bustards by large area of white on the wing. Upperparts including rump and tail vermiculated dark brown and buff, and blotched with black. Male has entire underparts including a thin line up the throat black; female has breast buff, throat and belly white. Usually in pairs in the open short grassy savanna.

Voice: A harsh strident cry.

Distribution and Habitat: Widespread and common in the savanna and thorn scrub from Senegal and Gambia east to Chad and the Central African Republic, and south to Congo.

Nesting: Clutch 2. Eggs laid on the bare ground in open scrub country; brownish-buff mottled and clouded with brownish and underlying markings of grey.

LILY-TROTTERS: Jacanidae

Rail-like water birds with long legs and very long toes suited to running over water vegetation, which is their usual habitat.

LILY-TROTTER *Actophilornis africana* **Pl. 14**

Identification: 9″–11″. Female larger than male. A bright chestnut long-legged water bird usually encountered running nimbly over water lilies or other floating water vegetation. Field marks at close range are the frontal shield bluish at the breeding season and greyish at other times, black crown and hindneck, and golden collar separating the white throat from the chestnut breast. Immature birds are brown above and white below. Not shy. Where numerous gregarious when not breeding.

Voice: Rather noisy. A series of short staccato notes.

Distribution and Habitat: Widely and commonly distributed south of 17° N. where there are lakes, backwaters, and other still waters with plenty of floating vegetation.

Nesting: An accumulation of floating weeds which scarcely shows above the surface of the water. Eggs 4, pyriform, highly glossed, yellow-brown boldly, thickly and evenly scrolled with blackish-brown.

Allied species: The Lesser Lily-trotter (*Microparra capensis*), 6″, is distinguished by its much smaller size from the adult Common Lily-trotter (*Actophilornis africana*) but is easily confused with the young of the latter species. The best field character is the chestnut crown of the Lesser Lily-trotter and the absence of a frontal shield. Recorded from a few localities in Mali, Niger, the north of Nigeria, and Chad.

THICK-KNEES OR STONE CURLEWS: Burhinidae

Medium-sized, dull-coloured, long-legged birds with a preference for sandy river banks or dry open country. Large head and the large eyes of nocturnal species. When surprised run away with head down and neck extended, taking off after a few metres. Rather noisy at night. Do not perch.

Plate 13

DUCKS AND GEESE

1. **WHITE-FACED TREE-DUCK** *Dendrocygna viduata* page 28
   White head and throat; chestnut chest.

2. **FULVOUS TREE-DUCK** *Dendrocygna bicolor* 28
   Dark brown back; cream flank stripes.

3. **HARTLAUB'S DUCK** *Pteronetta hartlaubii* 29
   Mainly chestnut; black head; light blue wing-patch.

4. **SHOVELER** *Anas clypeata* 31
   Heavy spatulate bill; chestnut flanks.

5. **FERRUGINOUS DUCK** *Aythya nyroca* 34
   Chestnut head and breast; white under tail-coverts.

6. **AFRICAN BLACK DUCK** *Anas sparsa* 30
   Mainly light-coloured bill; white wing-bar.

7. **PINTAIL** *Anas acuta* 30
   Long neck; long pointed tail; white neck stripe.

8. **GARGANEY** *Anas querquedula* 31
   White head stripe; long black and white scapulars.

9. **PIGMY GOOSE** *Nettapus auritus* 30
   Female: smaller and plumper than a Garganey.
   Male: green, black, and white head colours.

10. **WHITE-BACKED DUCK** *Thalassornis leuconotus* 34
    White spot at base of bill.

11. **KNOB-BILLED GOOSE** *Sarkidiornis melanota* 29
    Black comb on upper mandible.

12. **SPUR-WINGED GOOSE** *Plectropterus gambensis* 29
    Large size; long neck; white wing-patch.

13. **EGYPTIAN GOOSE** *Alopochen aegyptiaca* 28
    Chestnut circumorbital patch and chestnut breast patch.

13

14

Plate 14

RAILS, FINFOOT, THICK-KNEES AND LILY-TROTTER

1. **BLACK CRAKE** *Limnocorax flavirostra* page 60
   Black; yellow bill; red legs.

2. **AFRICAN CRAKE** *Crex egregia* 59
   Dark blotched upperparts; barred belly and flanks.

3. **WHITE-SPOTTED PIGMY RAIL** *Sarothrura pulchra* 60
   Female: black and buff barred back.
   Male: black back boldly spotted white.

4. **FINFOOT** *Podica senegalensis* 62
   Red bill and feet; white head stripe.

5. **GREY-THROATED RAIL** *Canirallus oculeus* 59
   Grey throat; chestnut breast.

6. **KING REED-HEN** *Porphyrio porphyrio* 61
   Red bill and frontal shield; red legs; white under tail-coverts.

7. **ALLEN'S REED-HEN** *Porphyrio alleni* 62
   Red bill; greenish-blue frontal shield; red legs; white under tail-coverts.

8. **MOORHEN** *Gallinula chloropus* 61
   Red bill tipped yellow; red frontal shield; white streak on flanks; white under tail-coverts.

9. **SENEGAL THICK-KNEE** *Burhinus senegalensis* 70
   Broad pale wing band.

10. **SPOTTED THICK-KNEE** *Burhinus capensis* 70
    Underparts boldly spotted black.

11. **LILY-TROTTER** *Actophilornis africana* 67
    Mainly bright chestnut; black and white head and neck.

SENEGAL THICK-KNEE   *Burhinus senegalensis*
(*Oedicnemus senegalensis*)   **Pl. 14**

Identification: 14″. A typical, large-eyed, round-headed Thick-knee. Upperparts sandy with blackish streaks; underparts buffish-white, the throat streaked with black. Closed wings show pale band bordered by two dark bands. In flight prominent white wing bar. When disturbed usually runs before taking flight. Active by night, calling. Sometimes frequents dirt roads. For distinctions from the rather similar Spotted Thick-knee (*Burhinus capensis*) and Water Thick-knee (*Burhinus vermiculatus*) see those species.

Voice: A resonant, plaintive, descending 'tui tui tui tui'. Cry usually nocturnal and often taken up by other birds of the species.

Distribution and Habitat: Widespread and common in suitable localities from Gambia and Senegal east to Chad and the Central African Republic and south to Congo. Likes bare sandy country usually near water and is specially common on the sandbanks of the larger rivers.

Nesting: Two eggs laid in a depression on the bare ground not far from water. Stone-coloured handsomely blotched with sepia-brown and with inconspicuous spots and streaks of the same shade and sparse ashy shell marks.

Allied species: The Water Thick-knee (*Burhinus vermiculatus*) occurs on certain of the large rivers and estuaries of Liberia, Ivory Coast, Ghana, Nigeria, Gaboon and Congo, usually in localities near the sea. It resembles rather closely the commoner and widespread Senegal Thick-knee (*Burhinus senegalensis*). At close quarters the markings on the closed wing distinguish the two species, the Water Thick-knee having a narrow white band near the bend of the wing and the Senegal Thick-knee a broad white band (on the greater coverts) about the middle of the wing. The colour of the tarsus is not a reliable diagnostic.

SPOTTED THICK-KNEE   *Burhinus capensis* (*Oedicnemus capensis*)
Pl. 14

Identification: 14″. Resembles the Senegal Thick-knee but upperparts rufous with conspicuous large black spots. Tail barred. White wing spots visible in flight but no wing-bar. Legs chrome-yellow. Squats and runs. Mainly nocturnal. Habitat distinctive.

Voice: Similar to cry of Senegal Thick-knee, usually uttered at night.

Distribution and Habitat: A dry-country species that usually avoids water. Affects bare sandy or stony places in the savanna or the open orchard bush where the grass has been fired. Much scarcer than the Senegal Thick-knee but widely though locally distributed in the dry northern regions from Mauritania and Senegal east to the Central African Republic and Chad, in which last territory it is common, and south to Gaboon.

Nesting: The two eggs are laid on the bare ground and are dark buff blotched and spotted with chocolate-brown.

PLOVERS, SANDPIPERS AND SNIPE: Charadriidae

A large, heterogeneous group of small to medium-sized wading birds that frequent shores and marshes except for certain Plovers with a dry open habitat. Many of these Waders are non-breeding visitors from the Palaearctic. Often highly gregarious.

SPUR-WINGED PLOVER *Vanellus spinosus (Hoplopterus spinosus)*

Pl. 17

Identification: 11″. Sexes similar. Readily identified by black crown, greyish-brown upperparts, pure white cheeks and side of neck, and black throat and breast. Wings and tail patterned black and white. Legs black. A noisy aggressive Plover on its nesting territory, flying and crying above the intruder.

Voice: Loud plaintive cries and a metallic 'tic tic tic'.

Distribution and Habitat: A common and widely distributed Plover of the drier northern savannas from Mauritania, Senegal, and Gambia east to Chad and the Central African Republic. Absent from the coast and the moister savannas. Never far from water and usually found on rivers, and the borders of lakes, swamps, and rice fields.

Nesting: Sometimes no nest, the eggs being laid on the bare rock or soil; sometimes a substantial structure of dead grasses and reed stems. Eggs 3–4, typically limicoline, clay or buffish-stone evenly marked with blotches and spots of black, dark brown and ash.

Allied species: The White-faced Lapwing (*Vanellus crassirostris*) is similar in size and build to the Spur-winged Plover (*Vanellus spinosus*). It is readily distinguished by its white forecrown, face, throat, and chest, which contrast with the black hindcrown, nape and breast. It occurs in Nigeria and Chad in the vicinity of Lake Chad.

BLACK-HEADED PLOVER *Vanellus tectus (Sarciophorus tectus)*

Pl. 17

Identification: 11″. Sexes similar. Crown, crest, and side of neck black; line encircling crown white; eye wattle red; upperparts greyish-brown; underparts white with a broad black streak down the middle of the breast; wings and tail patterned black and white; legs dark red. Found in pairs or small parties. Usually tame.

Voice: A rasping cry like that of the Spur-winged Plover but less harsh.

Distribution and Habitat: Widely distributed in the northern savannas between 11° N. and 17° N. from Mauritania, Senegal and Gambia to Chad and the Central African Republic. Frequents bare, dry, open terrain usually remote from water.

Nesting: In an open place. A circular scrape in the ground sometimes lined with flakes of dried mud. Eggs 3, clay or buff thickly and evenly blotched and spotted with black, dark brown, and ash.

WHITE-HEADED PLOVER *Vanellus albiceps*
(*Xiphidiopterus albiceps*)

Pl. 17

Identification: 12″. Sexes similar. A common Plover of the river sandbanks. The grey head and neck, white crown, and long yellow eye wattles distinguish it. Mantle pale brown; underparts white; tail white with a black tip; wing closed mainly black, wing open mainly white, showing more white than any other of the genus.

Voice: A loud repeated piping call. Often silent at a nest with eggs.

Distribution and Habitat: Widely distributed along the great rivers where there are sandbanks following them down even into the coastal forest zone. Ranges from Senegal and Liberia east to Chad and south to Gaboon and Congo. Also Fernando Po.

Nesting: A scrape in a sand or shingle bank usually close to the water's edge. Bare or lined with small sticks or pebbles. Eggs 2–4, clay, buff, or stone tinged with green, blotched, spotted, and lined with different shades of brown and with ashy shell marks.

SENEGAL PLOVER *Vanellus lugubris (Stephanibyx lugubris)* **Pl. 17**
Identification: 9″. A rather slight long-winged Plover with brown upperparts and chest, a conspicuous white patch on the forehead and a white lower breast and belly. Tail white tipped with black. The patterned black and white upper and undersurfaces of the wing are evident in flight.
Voice: A clear plaintive trisyllabic whistling cry frequently heard at the breeding season.
Distribution and Habitat: A broken distribution, in the savanna, from Sierra Leone and Liberia to Gaboon and Congo. In the two last territories it is rather common. Short grassy plains, recently burnt areas, and ground cleared for cultivation attract it.
Nesting: A nest in Sierra Leone was a circular depression on the bare ground scantily lined with grass stems. It held two pyriform eggs, buff-coloured, heavily blotched and spotted with dark brown and yellow-brown.

SENEGAL WATTLED PLOVER *Vanellus senegallus*
(Afribyx senegallus) **Pl. 17**
Identification: 13″. Sexes similar. Wattled, and somewhat resembles the White-headed Plover but the white crown is bordered with black, the throat is black, the side of the neck is streaked, and the closed wing is mainly pale brown, not black Occurs in pairs or small parties. Mobs intruders into its territory. Not shy.
Voice: On breeding ground shrill high-pitched cries. Often calls at night.
Distribution and Habitat: Widely but locally distributed in the savanna from Senegal and Gambia east to the Central African Republic and south to Congo. Frequents rivers and marshes and also dry open places and cleared farmland at a distance from water.
Nesting: Nest a depression in the ground lined with pebbles and small bits of grass. Eggs 2–4, buff blotched and spotted with black and dark brown.

BROWN-CHESTED WATTLED PLOVER *Vanellus superciliosus*
(Anomalophrys superciliosus) **Pl. 17**
Identification: 9″. The black crown, pale rufous forehead, and bright yellow wattle are field marks and so also in good light is the large chestnut patch on the breast. Mantle brown, belly white, wings and tail patterned black and white.
Voice: A characteristic shrill call heard especially at the breeding ground.
Distribution and Habitat: A migrant species, breeding in the West African savanna, arriving there in December and departing in July to spend the off-season in the savanna south of the equator. It occurs locally from Ghana east to the Central African Republic showing preference for dry open orchard bush or farmland clearings in the savanna. Records from forested Cameroons and Congo are probably of passage migrants.
Nesting: Nest of small pebbles lining a depression on the ground. Eggs variable; some closely resemble the eggs of the Lapwing (*Vanellus vanellus*) but most clutches show marked erythrism and match the red soil on which they are laid.

GREY PLOVER   *Pluvialis squatarola (Squatarola squatarola)*   **Pl. 17**
Identification: 12″. Sexes similar. A plump, round-headed Plover with relatively short bill and long legs. The black axillaries, conspicuous in flight, are diagnostic. In winter upperparts grey but rump white; underparts whitish. Bill black, feet grey. In nuptial (summer) plumage underparts mainly black and mantle spotted black and white. Powerful, agile, and fast flight. Runs in starts, bending forward to pick at the ground between runs.
Voice: A melodious piping 'tlui tlui'.
Distribution and Habitat: A fairly common winter visitor to West African coasts from Cape Verde Islands and Senegal to Congo frequenting sandy shores, mudflats and estuaries. A few inland records, mainly on the Niger and at Lake Chad at the migration periods.

RINGED PLOVER   *Charadrius hiaticula*   **Pl. 17**
Identification: 7½″. Sexes similar. A small, active, alert shore-bird usually seen running rapidly over the sand with head drawn back between the shoulders. Forehead white separated by a black line from the brown crown. Black mark through eye. Remainder upperparts brown except for white collar separating head from mantle. Underparts white with broad black band across chest. Bill orange tipped black; legs orange. White wing bar conspicuous in flight. Immature has brown not black incomplete chest band.
Voice: A melodious 'poo-eep', but not often heard in Africa.
Distribution and Habitat: A common winter visitor and passage migrant to West African coasts from Senegal to Gaboon. Also occurs Cape Verde Islands and recorded from a few inland localities mainly at the spring and autumn migration. Frequents sandy shores and estuaries.

LITTLE RINGED PLOVER   *Charadrius dubius*   **Pl. 17**
Identification: 6″. Sexes similar. Resembles Ringed Plover but smaller and lacks the white wing bar. The flesh-coloured not orange legs and a white line behind the black forecrown (not well shown in plate) are further differences. Immature bird has brown, usually incomplete chest band.
Voice: Melodious, rather like that of the Ringed Plover but shriller. Seldom heard in Africa.
Distribution and Habitat: A widely distributed winter visitor occurring on the coasts and on inland lakes and rivers from Senegal east to Chad (where it is common) and south to Gaboon. Also recorded Cape Verde Islands and Fernando Po.

KITTLITZ'S SAND PLOVER   *Charadrius pecuarius*
(*Leucopolius pecuarius*)   **Pl. 17**
Identification: 6½″. Rather similar to the White-fronted Sand Plover (*Charadrius marginatus*) (p. 74) but has darker upperparts and distinctive head markings. A narrow black line (brown in female) borders the white forehead. Another black line, bounded above by a white line, extends from behind the eye down the side of the neck and then across the nape forming a collar below the white line. Mantle brown. Underparts white, the breast washed with rufous. Not shy. Runs at great speed with occasional sudden stops to pick at the sand. In small companies when not breeding.
Voice: A plaintive whistling 'tu-wit'.
Distribution and Habitat: Widely distributed on the sandbanks and sandy

margins of the great rivers, lakes, and coastal lagoons, and sometimes visiting bare cultivated or fallow land quite far from water. From Senegal east to Chad and the Central African Republic and south to Gaboon and Congo.

Nesting: Nest a scrape in the sand or mud-dust. Eggs 2, yellowish-white or stone thickly and evenly pencilled with black and grey. Before leaving the eggs, the incubating bird covers them with material from the nest.

FORBES'S BANDED PLOVER   *Charadrius forbesi*
(*Afroxyechus forbesi*)   **Pl. 17**

Identification: $7\frac{1}{2}''$. The two dark bands across the chest distinguish it from the Ringed Plover (*Charadrius hiaticula*) (p. 73), which it rather resembles in habits and appearance. Forehead brown; a prominent white streak from the eye to the nape. On the ground the swift runs alternating with long pauses and in the air the jerky zig-zag flight are characteristic.

Voice: A plaintive piping call.

Distribution and Habitat: Widely and commonly distributed in the savanna and in open places in the forest belt from Senegal and Portuguese Guinea east to the Central African Republic and south to Gaboon and Congo. Partial to sandy or recently burnt ground and to airfields, parade grounds, golf courses, and similar bare open places, occurring in open flocks. Subject to local movements.

Nesting: Pairs nest singly, choosing an open situation on the top of a granite kopje or on the plain. Eggs laid in a scrape in the shingle. Clutch 2–3, cream-coloured with brown primary blotches and spots and thickly distributed ashy secondary suffusions and blotches.

WHITE-FRONTED SAND PLOVER   *Charadrius marginatus*
(*Leucopolius marginatus*)   **Pl. 17**

Identification: $7''$. Upperparts rusty-grey, the forehead white with, in the adult, a black band separating forehead from crown. Underparts white with a rusty patch on either side of the breast. Much paler upperparts and lack of black streak on side of face are best distinctions from Kittlitz's Plover (*Charadrius pecuarius*).

Voice: A soft liquid 'woo-eet'. Alarm note a low drawn-out 'pirr'.

Distribution and Habitat: The sandbanks of the larger rivers, the seashore, and the coastal lagoons from Mali and Liberia east to the Central African Republic and south to Gaboon.

Nesting: Nest an unlined depression in the sand bordering river or lagoon. Eggs 2, clay-coloured lined and spotted with brown and ash-grey.

Allied species: The Kentish Plover (*Charadrius alexandrinus*), $6\frac{1}{2}''$, is distinguished from the White-fronted Sand Plover by the absence of a rust-coloured wash on the ash-brown upperparts, by its blackish not greenish legs, and by the black (brownish in female) not rust-coloured patches on either side of the neck. Distinguished from the Ringed and Little Ringed Plover by its blackish bill and legs and absence of black breast band. The Kentish Plover breeds in the Cape Verde Islands and is a rather scarce winter visitor and passage migrant to the West African coast as far east as Nigeria, with a few inland records from Senegal and Lake Chad. Recently reported breeding in Senegal.

WHIMBREL   *Numenius phaeopus*   **Pl. 18**
Identification: 16″. A large white-rumped greyish-brown wader with a long decurved bill which can be confused with no other species except the Curlew. Distinguished from the Curlew by smaller size, boldly striped crown, and call. Usually in small parties.
Voice: A very distinctive far-carrying tittering 'ti ti ti ti ti ti ti' in a monotone. Sometimes imitates the 'cour-li' call of the Curlew.
Distribution and Habitat: Widely distributed in winter along the whole West African coast line, particularly where there are estuaries, from Senegal to Congo. Some birds over-summer. A few inland records on passage from Mali and Lake Chad. Also the Cape Verde Islands and islands of the Gulf of Guinea.

CURLEW   *Numenius arquata*   **Pl. 18**
Identification: 22″. Larger than the Whimbrel with a very long curved bill. Similar in plumage but lacks the boldly striped crown. Call distinctive.
Voice: A resonant pure whistling 'courli'.
Distribution and Habitat: A Palaearctic winter visitor recorded from many coastal localities from Senegal to Congo but far outnumbered by the Whimbrel. Several inland passage records from Mali, Niger, Ghana, Lake Chad and Chad. Frequents coastal mud-flats, mangrove swamps, and sandy shores, and inland rivers, lakes, and swamp edges.

BLACK-TAILED GODWIT   *Limosa limosa*   **Pl. 18**
Identification: 16″. A rather large wader with a very long straight bill and long legs which in flight extend far beyond the tail. In winter grey-brown above, whitish below, and showing in flight a broad white wing-bar and a pure white tail with a terminal black band. In summer plumage (seldom seen in West Africa) the chest is rufous. Flight fast and straight. Gregarious; sometimes in large flocks.
Voice: A harsh 'gritto-gritto-gritto' frequently uttered when in flocks.
Distribution and Habitat: A common winter migrant to the swamps, rice fields, and inundated areas bordering the great inland rivers from Senegal through Mali, Niger and northern Nigeria to Chad. Many summer records. Also occurs but less commonly and chiefly on passage on the coast from Cape Verde Islands, Senegal and Gambia to the Cameroons.
Allied species: The Bar-tailed Godwit (*Limosa lapponica*), 15″, resembles the Black-tailed Godwit but is smaller, has an upturned bill, and lacks the white wing-bar. The tail is barred (not white with a terminal dark band) and in flight the legs scarcely project beyond it. In summer the chest is rich rufous. Recorded in winter, sometimes in flocks, from coastal Senegal, Gambia, Sierra Leone, Ivory Coast, Ghana and Nigeria, and inland from Chad and Nigeria, but on the whole uncommon.

GREENSHANK   *Tringa nebularia* (*Glottis nebularius*)   **Pl. 18**
Identification: 13″. Considerably larger than a Redshank and with long green legs. Large area of white on back and rump conspicuous in flight. Upperparts pale grey; underparts whitish. No white wing-bar. Usually occurs singly.
Voice: A ringing distinctive 'tew tew tew'.
Distribution and Habitat: Widely distributed and fairly common winter

Plate 15

PIGEONS AND DOVES

PARROTS AND PLANTAIN-EATERS

visitor and passage migrant to the inland marshes, rivers and lakes, and the
coastal sand-bars, tidal estuaries and mangrove swamps. From Senegal and
Gambia east to Chad and the Central African Republic and south to Congo.
Also Cape Verde Islands.

MARSH SANDPIPER   *Tringa stagnatilis (Glottis stagnatilis)*   **Pl. 18**
Identification: 9″. Resembles a Greenshank but distinguished by its much
smaller size, slimmer figure, proportionately longer, finer legs, and very slender
straight bill. Like the Greenshank conspicuous white back and rump in flight;
no white wing-bar.
Voice: A single whistled 'tew'. Not very arresting.
Distribution and Habitat: Occurs as a winter visitor and passage migrant
along the whole West African coastline from Senegal to Congo, and locally
common. Also recorded from several inland localities. Occasional Cape Verde
Islands. Frequents lagoons and coastal mudflats and inland rivers, lakes, and
inundated areas.

WOOD SANDPIPER   *Tringa glareola*   **Pl. 18**
Identification: 8″. In winter upperparts brown faintly speckled white; underparts white washed with grey on the breast. In flight white rump, barred tail,
light underwing, and absence of wing-bar aid identification. Most likely to be
confused with the Green Sandpiper (*Tringa ochropus*) but the latter has a much
darker almost black mantle and shows more white on the rump and tail. Frequently bobs head and tail. In winter quarters often gregarious. Fairly tame.
Voice: A shrill 'gui gui gui' when put up.
Distribution and Habitat: A common Palaearctic migrant and winter visitor
to West Africa occurring on the coast and on inland waterways and marshes
from Senegal and Gambia, east to Chad and the Central African Republic and
south to Gaboon. Occurs Cape Verde Islands and Sao Tome. Frequents
lagoons, estuaries, mangrove swamps, marshes and inundated areas alongside
the great rivers.

GREEN SANDPIPER   *Tringa ochropus*   **Pl. 18**
Identification: 9″. In winter in the field the upperparts appear black and in
flight contrast strongly with the pure white rump and basal half of the tail.
Underwing blackish (light in the Wood Sandpiper) and tip of tail strongly
barred black and white. Underparts white but breast greyish-brown. No wing-
bar. Shy, solitary, and easily alarmed, rising with a cry and making off with
rapid zig-zag flight.
Voice: A loud clear 'tui tui' on rising.
Distribution and Habitat: Much less out in the open than the Wood Sandpiper or the Common Sandpiper, affecting drainage ditches and channels,
isolated pools, swamps, and rice fields. A common Palaearctic passage migrant
and winter visitor to inland localities, but rare on the coast. Widespread and
recorded from Senegal and Gambia east to Chad and the Central African Republic and south to Gaboon.

COMMON SANDPIPER   *Tringa hypoleucos (Actitis hypoleucos)*   **Pl. 18**
Identification: 7½″. Sexes similar. A small Sandpiper, dark olive-brown above
and white below, faintly streaked on the breast. In flight white wing-bar and

dark rump and tail, the latter edged white. Flight characteristic, low over the water, with light, fluttering, shallow wing beats and interspersed with short glides. On the ground constantly bobs head and tail. Not shy.

Voice: A rather thin 'tee wee wee' call.

Distribution and Habitat: A passage migrant and winter visitor from the Palaearctic very widely and commonly distributed throughout our area wherever there is open water. Frequents rivers, lakes, estuaries and the seashore.

REDSHANK *Tringa totanus* Pl. 18

Identification: 11″. Sexes similar. In flight recognised by white edges at the back of the dark wing, and white rump and back; on the ground by long orange-red legs. Upperparts grey-brown; underparts white but breast grey. Call characteristic. Rather shy. Bobs head, especially when alarmed.

Voice: The melodious, piping, far-reaching, whistled 'too-hoo' or 'too-hoo-hoo', the last notes pitched lower, is an excellent and reliable field character.

Distribution and Habitat: A Palaearctic migrant occurring on passage and in winter, mainly on the coasts and estuaries from Senegal to the Cameroons, and also inland in Mali, Chad and Nigeria. Not uncommon, yet local.

Allied species: The Spotted Redshank (*Tringa erythropus*), 12″, in winter plumage rather resembles the Redshank, but is larger and lacks the pure white wing-bar. The white-spotted grey mantle, longer legs and call help to identify it. Orange legs and darker tail distinguish it from the Greenshank. In summer plumage, acquired at the end of March, very dark, with spotted upperparts and dark red legs. The call is a loud typical 'tiruit'. A passage migrant and winter visitor on the coast and also inland, recorded from Senegal, Gambia, Mali, Ivory Coast, Ghana, Nigeria, Chad and Congo. Locally common coastal Ghana.

TURNSTONE *Arenaria interpres* Pl. 18

Identification: 9″. A shore-bird easily distinguished from other waders by general appearance and colour. Short but conspicuous orange legs, short, strong, pointed dark bill In winter upperparts variegated brown and black, rump and tail white crossed by black bands; underparts white but breast brown. In flight conspicuous white wing-bar. Summer plumage with distinctively patterned black and white head and neck and variegated black and rufous upperparts sometimes seen in West Africa. Gregarious. Forages vigorously on the sea shore among pebbles and piles of seaweed, turning over the shells and small stones.

Voice: Call a sharp 'ki-ti-tit'.

Distribution and Habitat: A maritime species showing a strong preference for rocky shores. A common visitor from the Palaearctic to the Cape Verde Islands and on the mainland occurring, though less commonly, from Senegal to Gaboon where there is suitable habitat. A few inland records on migration.

COMMON SNIPE *Gallinago gallinago (Capella gallinago)* Pl. 18

Identification: 10½″. A brownish wader which sits tight and is not usually seen till it is flushed and takes off with fast zig-zag flight and typical harsh cry. Long straight bill. Upperparts streaked black, brown and buff, the crown with a light buff central stripe; tail mainly rufous-brown with only a little white on the outer edges. Does not forage in the open. Solitary.

Plate 17

PLOVERS

Plate 18

SANDPIPERS AND ALLIES (IN WINTER PLUMAGE)

1. **WOOD SANDPIPER** *Tringa glareola* page 78
Brown upperparts indistinctly speckled white; underwing whitish.

2. **COMMON SANDPIPER** *Tringa hypoleucos* 78
Olive-brown above; white below; brown patch either side of chest.

3. **GREEN SANDPIPER** *Tringa ochropus* 78
Blackish mantle contrasting with pure white rump; underwing blackish.

4. **MARSH SANDPIPER** *Tringa stagnatilis* 78
Like Greenshank but smaller, slimmer, with very slender bill and legs.

5. **GREENSHANK** *Tringa nebularia* 75
Long green legs; in flight white lower back and rump.

6. **REDSHANK** *Tringa totanus* 79
Orange-red legs; in flight dark wing with conspicuous broad white hind edge.

7. **TURNSTONE** *Arenaria interpres* 79
Short dark bill; short orange legs; variegated brown, black, and white plumage.

8. **RUFF** *Philomachus pugnax* 83
Size, proportions, and carriage of Redshank, but distinguished by scaly upperparts, absence of white wing-bar, and greenish or orange-yellow (not bright orange-red) legs.

9. **BLACK-TAILED GODWIT** *Limosa limosa* 75
Long straight bill; long legs; pure white tail tipped black.

10. **COMMON SNIPE** *Gallinago gallinago* 79
Long bill; buff-striped head and mantle.

11. **WHIMBREL** *Numenius phaeopus* 75
Long decurved bill; boldly striped crown.

12. **CURLEW** *Numenius arquata* 75
Like Whimbrel but larger and lacks boldly striped crown.

Voice: A harsh rasping 'krrek' or 'retsch' uttered as the bird takes off.

Distribution and Habitat: Shows a preference for swamps and pools with muddy edges and grass clumps. Widely but unevenly distributed in winter and locally common where there is suitable terrain from Senegal and Gambia east to Chad, the Cameroons and Fernando Po.

Allied species: The Great Snipe (*Gallinago media*), 11″, and the Jack Snipe (*Gallinago minima*), 7½″, resemble the Common Snipe in colour and markings. The Great Snipe can be distinguished in flight by its slower, heavier, direct flight without zig-zagging and by its silent take-off. In the hand the white outer tail feathers distinguish it and this is also a field character in flight if a good view is obtained. The Jack Snipe is best recognised by its much smaller size, usually silent take-off, and quick return to earth after a short (not zig-zag) flight. In the hand the lack of any white on the tail and the lack of a pale central crown stripe distinguish it. The Great Snipe is locally common in winter in Mali, Ivory Coast and Nigeria and is recorded as a winter visitor or passage migrant from Senegal, Sierra Leone, Ghana, Chad, Gaboon and Congo. The Jack Snipe is reported to be rather common in Chad in winter and there are a few scattered records from Senegal, Gambia, Ivory Coast and Nigeria, and a sight record from Ghana.

CURLEW SANDPIPER   *Calidris ferruginea* (*Erolia testacea*)   **Pl. 19**

Identification: 7½″. Sexes similar. In winter streaked pale brownish-grey upperparts; white underparts; white rump and wing-bar; slender slightly decurved bill. In summer chestnut and black upper parts and chestnut underparts. Mainly a shore bird, occurring in flocks and small parties.

Voice: Call a liquid 'tchirrip' uttered on the wing.

Distribution and Habitat: A Palaearctic winter visitor and passage migrant well distributed along the coast from Senegal to Gaboon and also recorded on passage from several inland localities in Mali, Ghana, Nigeria and Chad. Visits Cape Verde Islands. Frequents the sea-shore, estuaries, brackish lagoons, and inland lakes and rivers.

Allied species: The Dunlin (*Calidris alpina*), 7″, in winter resembles the Curlew Sandpiper but the bill is straight or only very slightly decurved, the legs are shorter, and only the sides of the rump are white. In summer easily distinguished by the large black patch on the breast and belly. The Dunlin is an uncommon winter visitor and passage migrant to West Africa recorded from the Cape Verde Islands, Senegal, Gambia and Lake Chad. The winter plumage of the Knot (*Calidris canutus*), 10″, somewhat resembles that of the Curlew Sandpiper but the Knot is a much larger, more stoutly built bird with relatively short bill and legs and in flight a light rump and tail and a rather indistinct pale wing-bar. A shore bird, usually in flocks. Recorded from the Cape Verde Islands and on the mainland on the coast from Senegal east to Nigeria. Apparently it is uncommon.

LITTLE STINT   *Calidris minuta* (*Erolia minuta*)   **Pl. 19**

Identification: 5¼″. A very small Wader, in winter plumage resembling a Dunlin (*Calidris alpina*) but much smaller and with a relatively shorter bill. In flight the V pattern on the back, the indistinct pale wing-bar, the white sides of the rump, and the grey sides of the tail are field marks. Usually in flocks. Not shy.

Voice: A sharp 'ti-ti-tit'.

Distribution and Habitat: A common and widespread passage migrant and winter visitor from Gambia and Senegal east to Chad and the Central African Republic and south to Gaboon and Congo, occurring on the estuaries and shores of the sea coast and also on inland rivers, lakes and marshes. Occasional visitor Cape Verde Islands.

Allied species: Temminck's Stint (*Calidris temminckii*), 5¾", resembles the Little Stint but is greyer and less brown and in flight exhibits no V pattern on the back, and the sides of the tail are white not grey. The greenish or brownish not black legs also a field character. Cry a ringing 'tirrr'. Much rarer than the Little Stint and shows a preference for inland waters. Regular on migration in Chad and at Lake Chad, sometimes in large numbers, and sparingly recorded from Senegal, Mali, Ivory Coast, Ghana and Nigeria in localities besides Lake Chad.

SANDERLING *Calidris alba* (*Crocethia alba*) **Pl. 19**

Identification: 8". Sexes similar. A sea-shore Wader characteristically seen running at great speed over the sand just out of reach of the waves. In flight white sides to rump and a very distinct white wing-bar. Bill and legs black. In winter appears very white; upperparts palest grey with black shoulder patch; underparts white. In summer head, back and breast rusty spotted with blackish; belly white.

Voice: A short soft 'quit' at take-off and in flight.

Distribution and Habitat: A fairly common winter visitor and passage migrant to sandy beaches on the coast from Senegal to Gaboon and Congo. Also the Cape Verde Islands. A few inland records on passage from Ghana, Nigeria and Chad.

RUFF *Philomachus pugnax* **Pl. 18**

Identification: Male 12". Female smaller. The size, proportions and carriage of a Redshank (*Tringa totanus*) (p. 79). In winter scaly grey-brown upperparts, pale grey breast, whitish belly. Short dark bill. Legs orange-yellow or greenish (seldom the bright orange-red of a Redshank). In flight the absence of a conspicuous white wing-bar and the presence of an oval white patch on each side at the base of the dark tail distinguish it. Males in spring or autumn sometimes show traces of nuptial ruff. In winter characteristically in large flocks, from a distance looking like clouds. Forage on flooded or dry plains, sometimes on roads.

Voice: Silent in winter.

Distribution and Habitat: Very common in winter on the flooded plains, marshes and rice fields in Senegal, Mali, Niger, northern Nigeria and Chad, and recorded on passage from many inland and coastal localities from Gambia to Gaboon and Congo. Occasionally winters Cape Verde Islands.

BLACK-WINGED STILT *Himantopus himantopus* **Pl. 19**

Identification: 15". Easily identified on the ground and in flight by contrasting black and white plumage and very long pink legs. Lower mantle and wings (both upper and underside) black in male, dark brown in female. Male in summer has black nape. Immature birds have brown head, neck and mantle. Long, thin, straight black bill. Stands motionless or walks sedately in the water. Not shy.

Voice: Frequent harsh 'kik-rik' cries in flight.

Distribution and Habitat: Widely distributed, especially in winter, where there is suitable terrain, both inland and on the coast, from Senegal and Gambia east to Chad and south to Gaboon and Congo. Breeds in coastal Ghana and in the Cape Verde Islands. Frequents lagoons, estuaries, larger rivers with sand-banks, lakes and marshes.

Nesting: Near water. A depression in the mud, very scantily lined and some-times well concealed by surrounding herbage. Eggs 4, clay or buff, blotched and spotted with black and ashy-grey.

Allied species: The Oyster-catcher (*Haematopus ostralegus*) (Family: *Haematopodidae*), 17″, is a rather uncommon winter visitor and passage migrant to the West African coast from Senegal and Gambia as far east as the Niger Delta. Occasional Cape Verde Islands. The black and white plumage, orange-red bill and pink legs distinguish it. At rest head, chest and upperparts black; under-parts white. In flight black above, with broad wing-bar, rump, and base of tail white. In winter a white band across the black throat.

PAINTED SNIPE   *Rostratula benghalensis*   **Pl. 19**

Identification: 10″. Female larger than male and more brightly coloured. Superficially resembles a Snipe and has similar habitat. Male: crown blackish with buff coronal stripe; upperparts grey with dark vermiculations; upper surface of wing-coverts and flight feathers heavily spangled with golden-buff; throat grey; under surface white. Female: in flight V-shaped buff mark on back and gold markings on flight feathers conspicuous. Nape, throat and chest chestnut separated from white under surface by black chest band. Pure white ring round eye. Lacks golden-buff spots on wing-coverts. The Painted Snipe sits close and when flushed flies off slowly and clumsily and soon drops again. Unobtrusive and crepuscular.

Voice: Female has deep croaking note. Male has a mellow note likened to the sound made by blowing into a bottle.

Distribution and Habitat: Widely but locally distributed from Gambia and Senegal east to Chad and the Central African Republic and south to Gaboon and Congo frequenting the muddy edges of swamps, reed beds and rice fields.

Nesting: A slight depression in the ground lined with sticks and leaves. Eggs buff heavily blotched, suffused, scrawled, and spotted with black and sepia.

CROCODILE BIRD, COURSERS AND PRATINCOLES:
Glareolidae

Small or medium-sized Plover-like birds. The Coursers are terrestrial, have long, slender legs, and are great runners. They frequent dry open country. The Pratincoles are short-legged. In the air they are Tern-like with buoyant flight, long, pointed wings and forked tails. They mainly frequent rivers.

CROCODILE BIRD   *Pluvianus aegyptius*   **Pl. 19**

Identification: 9″. Sexes similar. A small thick-set Plover-like species. Unmistakable colour pattern. Crown, face and mantle black; long white super-ciliary stripe; closed wing and tail mainly grey; underparts pale buff but chest band black. Feet light blue-grey. In flight the wings and tail are conspicuously patterned black, white and grey. Frequents river sandbanks. Tame. Runs swiftly and has characteristic jerky flight low over the water or sand. In pairs and in the non-breeding season sometimes also in flocks.

Voice: A rapid shrill 'krrr krrr krrr'.

Distribution and Habitat: Rather common on the larger rivers with sandbanks or sandy shores, from Senegal and Gambia east to Chad and the Central African Republic and south to Gaboon and Congo, reaching to the river mouths provided there are sandbanks but avoiding salt water. Occasional on lake margins.

Nesting: Breeds on sandbanks. No nest. Incubating eggs normally partially buried in the sand and before the brooding bird leaves them they are completely buried and so difficult to locate. Small chicks are also buried by the parents. Eggs 2–3, buff, spotted, streaked, and lined with various shades of brown with slate undermarkings.

CREAM-COLOURED COURSER   *Cursorius cursor*   Pl. 19

Identification: 9″. Sexes similar. Plover-like with a slim, graceful build; a swift runner and swift in the air when the black under-surface of the wing is a field mark. Mainly sandy-buff but primaries black. A conspicuous white band bordered below by black extends from the eye to the nape.

Voice: Usually silent. A short whistle and also a harsh 'hark hark' recorded.

Distribution and Habitat: Resident in the Cape Verde Islands. On the mainland of West Africa in the semi-arid belt bordering the desert in Senegal, Mauritania, Mali and Niger, where it is possibly a winter visitor only from the Sahara, most records falling between October and February.

Nesting: In the Canary Islands the two eggs are laid on the bare sandy or stony ground. Cream or buff uniformly and profusely speckled and pencilled with various shades of brown and underlying ash-grey shell marks.

TEMMINCK'S COURSER   *Cursorius temminckii*   Pl. 19

Identification: 8″. Sexes similar. A small, slim Courser with earth-brown upperparts and chest, chestnut breast, and white belly with black central patch. The bright chestnut crown bordered by a white band and below that by a black band are the main features of the conspicuous head markings. In flight the short tail, black wing tips, and black under surface of the wing aid identification. Legs whitish. Runs swiftly and occurs in pairs or parties in open places.

Voice: A piping call uttered in flight. Silent when settled.

Distribution and Habitat: Partial to burnt bare ground in the savanna, short grassy or arid plains, and open places such as airfields, polo fields, and parade grounds. Widely and commonly distributed from Senegal and Gambia east to Chad and the Central African Republic and south to Gaboon and Congo but absent from the forest and from north of 16° N.

Nesting: No nest. The 2 eggs are laid on the bare ground, sometimes amongst animal droppings. Whitish, densely and evenly speckled and lined with black and sepia.

Allied species: The Bronze-wing Courser (*Cursorius chalcopterus*), 10″, is locally distributed in the savanna from Senegal and Gambia east to Chad and the Central African Republic and also south of the forest in the Congo savanna. Absent from the forest and in the north near the desert a wet season visitor only. A large long-legged Courser with earth-brown upperparts and chest, black breast-band and white belly. At close range the white forehead, superciliary streak, and side of face and the blackish ear-coverts are field marks. In flight the black primaries (tipped metallic violet) and white upper tail-coverts catch the eye. Penetrates the bushy or wooded savanna provided there are bare earthy or recently burnt patches. Mainly nocturnal and sometimes seen on the earth roads in the beam of the car headlights.

PRATINCOLE   *Glareola pratincola*   **Pl. 19**
Identification: 10½″. Wing span 22″. Sexes similar. Long-winged and fork-tailed with buoyant Tern-like flight. Runs swiftly. Very demonstrative at nest. Gregarious. White base of tail, chestnut under wing-coverts, and pale throat with narrow black border are field marks. Upperparts mainly olive-brown.
Voice: On its breeding ground a variety of harsh Tern-like calls, the most frequent a strident 'tit-ir-it'. Also a guttural 'purk'.
Distribution and Habitat: Widely but locally distributed in the dry northern areas in Senegal, Gambia and Portuguese Guinea through Mali to Niger, northern Nigeria, Central African Republic and Chad. Also locally in coastal Ghana and Nigeria. Resident and subject to local movements. Resident population almost certainly augmented in winter by Palaearctic migrants. Recorded from Cape Verde Islands. Frequents mud-flats, rice fields, coastal lagoons, deltas, and the vicinity of lakes and great rivers.
Nesting: Colonial. Nest a slight depression in the bare ground. Eggs 2, greyish-white or buff boldly blotched and spotted with blackish and dark brown and with ashy-grey secondary markings.

COLLARED PRATINCOLE   *Glareola nuchalis*   **Pl. 19**
Identification: 7½″. Somewhat Tern-like; long pointed wings, forked tail and short legs. Plumage sooty-brown with a broad white band at the base of the tail conspicuous in flight and a white or rufous collar at the base of the neck. At close range the red basal half of the bill and the red legs are visible. Habitat, erratic buoyant flight, and display and call at the nest are aids to identification.
Voice: At the breeding season a musical trilling song. Also a faint trisyllabic piping call.
Distribution and Habitat: Locally common on the great rivers of West Africa, occurring at the breeding season in scattered colonies in places where the surface is broken by rocks, and in the non-breeding season visiting inland lakes, coastal beaches and lagoons. Ranges in the savanna and forest from Sierra Leone, Liberia, Ivory Coast and Mali through Ghana, Togo, Niger, Nigeria and Cameroons to the Central African Republic, Gaboon and Congo.
Nesting: Nest usually on an islet, the two eggs lying, often precariously, in a little niche or fissure in the bare uneven rock surface. Eggs greenish-white or greyish-white well covered with blotches, spots and twisted irregular hair lines in different shades of brown and grey.

GREY PRATINCOLE   *Glareola cinerea*   **Pl. 19**
Identification: 7½″. Long narrow wings, slightly forked tail, build, and posture mark it as a Pratincole. At rest very inconspicuous against its usual background of white sand. In flight the pattern of the black and white wings and tail identify it. Rump white. Base of bill and feet orange-red.
Voice: On its breeding ground a trilling song. Soft liquid call-note.

D istribution and Habitat: Ranges in the savanna and forest from· Mali and Ghana east to Chad and the Central African Republic and south to Gaboon and Congo, inhabiting the sandbanks of the rivers and in the non-breeding season at least visiting also the estuaries and coastal lagoons. Its local movements coincide with the rise and fall of the river.

Nesting: Ordinarily in colonies. Nest an unlined scrape in the sand or shingle. Clutch 1–2. Eggs buff or cream, marbled and blotched in various shades of brown with underlying markings of greyish-purple and usually a few dark hair lines.

GULLS AND TERNS: Laridae

Aquatic, mainly coastal birds though some species frequent rivers and lakes. Long wings and easy, graceful flight. Grey and white the predominant colours of the adult plumage. Often gregarious. Gulls have webbed feet and swim well. Usually have square tails and strong, hooked bills. Terns have straight and more slender bills and, usually, forked tails. Flight buoyant. Feed mainly on fish captured by diving from a height.

GREY-HEADED GULL *Larus cirrhocephalus* Pl. 20
Identification: 17″. Sexes similar. Grey head clearly demarcated from white neck and underparts. Back and wing coverts grey. Bill and feet red. In flight the primaries are almost entirely black with just a little white. In winter plumage the head is very pale grey. The Black-headed Gull (*Larus ridibundus*) is distinguished by its mainly white not black primaries.

Voice: Usually rather silent. Call a ringing laugh.

Distribution and Habitat: Widespread but local from Mauritania, Senegal and Gambia eastward inland on the great rivers and lakes to Chad and along the coast to Ghana.

Nesting: In colonies on off-shore islands and on the edges of lakes. Nest on the ground; built of sticks and rootlets. Eggs 2–3, olive-brown blotched and spotted with blackish-brown and purplish shell marks.

Allied species: The Black-headed Gull (*Larus ridibundus*) of Europe is a fairly common winter visitor (mainly November–April) to the coasts and estuaries of Senegal and Gambia and there are coastal records from as far east as Nigeria and inland records from the Niger in Mali and Nigeria and also from Lake Chad. Occasional in the Cape Verde Islands. In adult plumage grey and white with black-tipped wings. The small size (16″), slender short carmine bill, carmine feet, and broad white margin on the front edge of the wing are field marks. Head in winter white except for a dark patch behind the eye and a smaller black patch in front of the eye. In breeding dress head dark brown. The Slender-billed Gull (*Larus genei*) resembles the Black-headed Gull (*Larus ridibundus*) but has a white head at all seasons and the underparts have a rosy tinge at the breeding season. Bill and legs dark red. Local and a breeding resident on the coasts of Mauritania and Senegal. Has occurred in the Cape Verde Islands.

LESSER BLACK-BACKED GULL *Larus fuscus* Pl. 20
Identification: 21″. Sexes similar. A large white Gull with slaty-black (*Larus*

f. fuscus) or slaty-grey (*Larus f. graellsii*) upperparts, easily distinguished from the other Gulls of our area except perhaps from *Larus argentatus atlantis*, which form, however, has dark pearl-grey upperparts. In winter plumage head and neck streaked brown. Feet and bill yellow. Immature plumage mottled brown.

Distribution and Habitat: A non-breeding migrant from Europe to the West African seaboard from Mauritania and Senegal east to the Cameroons River delta, occurring commonly from November to May and occasionally in other months. A maritime species frequenting the lagoons, estuaries, harbours and sea-shore. A few inland records from the Niger in Mali and Nigeria and occurs regularly at Lake Chad (October–April). Rare in the Cape Verde Islands.

Allied species: The Herring Gull (*Larus argentatus*), 22", is a winter visitor (November–April) in small numbers to the seaboard of Senegal and Gambia and has occurred as far east as Lagos, and also visits the Cape Verde Islands. The only race known certainly to occur in our area is the yellow-legged *L. a. atlantis*, the Atlantic Islands Gull. In this race the mantle is grey, darker in shade than that of the familiar Herring Gull of Western Europe (*L. a. argentatus*) but appreciably lighter in shade than *L. fuscus graellsii*, the paler of the two forms of the Lesser Black-backed Gull occurring in West Africa.

AFRICAN SKIMMER   *Rynchops flavirostris*   **Pl. 20**
Identification: 15". A conspicuous Tern-like bird with long narrow black wings, blackish upperparts, white underparts, and a conspicuous orange-red bill. The mode of feeding when, with wings raised in a V shape, it skims over the water with the lower mandible grazing the surface, is unique. Usually gregarious. Spends much time settled on sandbanks.
Voice: A harsh 'kree'.
Distribution and Habitat: The great rivers and lakes of the savanna belt from Gambia and Senegal east to Chad and south to Gaboon and Congo. Sandbanks and large stretches of open water characterise its habitat. Locally common especially in Nigeria and Mali. Occasionally visits coastal lagoons. Subject to local movements determined by the rise and fall of the rivers.
Nesting: Breeds in scattered colonies on sandbanks. Nest a large deep unlined scrape in the sand. Eggs 2–3, buff or pale grey with bold brown blotches and sometimes also speckles and fine linear markings and with ashy secondary blotches and spots.

GULL-BILLED TERN   *Sterna nilotica* (*Gelochelidon nilotica*)   **Pl. 20**
Identification: 15". Sexes similar. Upperparts pearl-grey, underparts white. Head in breeding dress black, in non-breeding dress white streaked with black. Tail slightly forked. Distinguished from other large Terns by its massive all-black bill. Buoyant and graceful in flight and an expert diver.
Voice: On its breeding ground rasping and laughing calls.
Distribution and Habitat: A Tern of cosmopolitan range. Breeds on the fringe of our area on islands off the Mauritanian coast. Elsewhere in West Africa a non-breeding visitor (mainly September–May) occurring on the coast east to Ghana and inland on the Senegal, Niger and Chari Rivers and at Lake Chad. Frequents rivers, lakes, rice fields, lagoons and estuaries.
Nesting: Colonial, sometimes in vast numbers. Nest a simple depression in the bare ground or sand. Eggs 1–2, greenish or yellowish rather sparingly spotted with brown and ashy-grey.

CASPIAN TERN *Sterna caspia (Hydroprogne caspia)*   **Pl. 20**
Identification: 20″. Sexes similar. A very large Tern with a conspicuous stout
red bill. Tail forked. In flight the dark-tipped primaries are a field mark.
Upperparts pearl-grey, underparts white. Crown and nape black, but streaked
with white at the non-breeding season. An expert diver. Flight less buoyant
than in smaller Terns.
Voice: Call-note loud and harsh.
Distribution and Habitat: A breeding resident on the coasts of Mauritania,
Gambia, Senegal and Portuguese Guinea, and a non-breeding visitor to the
whole West African seaboard as far east as Gaboon. Occurs inland on the
Senegal and Gambia Rivers, the Niger in Mali and Nigeria, and at Lake Chad
and Lake Fittri. Rivers, estuaries, lagoons and the sea-shore are its habitat.
Nesting: Colonial; sometimes in great numbers. Nest a rather deep depression
in the ground or in drifted vegetation. Eggs 2, yellowish-green or greyish
spotted with dark brown or black.

COMMON TERN *Sterna hirundo*   **Pl. 20**
Identification: 14″. Sexes similar. Flies buoyantly, dives expertly. A small
slender Tern with long wings and a deeply forked grey tail. Upperparts pearl-
grey, underparts white. Crown black, streaked with white at the non-breeding
season. Bill red tipped black at the breeding season and blackish with a red base
at the non-breeding season. The rather similar Arctic Tern (*Sterna paradisea*)
has in breeding dress an entirely red bill and in non-breeding dress an entirely
blackish bill.
Voice: Loud strident and chattering cries on breeding ground.
Distribution and Habitat: A common Palaearctic passage migrant and
winter visitor to West African coasts and a local breeding resident in Mauritania,
Senegal, Portuguese Guinea and Nigeria. Recorded from the Cape Verde
Islands. Absent from inland waters except as a vagrant.
Nesting: In colonies; sometimes alongside other Tern species. Nest a shallow
circular depression in the ground. Eggs 2–3, greenish, blotched and spotted
with dark brown and ashy-grey.
Allied species: The Royal Tern (*Sterna maxima*), 19″, nests locally on the
coasts of Mauritania, Senegal and Gambia in May and June, and is a common
migrant and non-breeding visitor to the West African seaboard as far east as
the Cameroons and Gaboon, frequenting the sea-shore and the lagoons. A
large Tern with a black crown (streaked white in non-breeding dress), pale grey
mantle and white underparts and a conspicuous heavy orange bill. Rather
similar to the Caspian Tern (*Sterna caspia*) but smaller and having a more
slender bill and a longer more deeply forked tail. The Sandwich Tern (*Sterna
sandvicensis*), 17″, sexes similar, is another large Tern with a black crown
(heavily streaked white in non-breeding dress), pale grey mantle, and white
underparts. Distinguished from other large West African Terns by its long
slender yellow-tipped black bill (the stout bill of *Sterna nilotica* is also black
but has no yellow tip). Tail slightly forked. The Sandwich Tern is a common
passage migrant and winter visitor to the West African sea coasts in their whole
length and some non-breeding birds remain through the summer. The Arctic
Tern (*Sterna paradisea*), 15″, sexes similar, is a spring and autumn passage
migrant and winter visitor to the West African sea coasts from Senegal to the
Cameroons. Difficult to distinguish in the field from the Common Tern (*Sterna
hirundo*). At close quarters the colour of the bill (see above) distinguishes it.

WHITE-WINGED BLACK TERN *Sterna leucoptera*
(*Chlidonias leucoptera*) **Pl. 20**

Identification: 9″. Sexes similar. A rather short almost square tail. Easily distinguished in summer dress by black head, neck, mantle and underparts, dark grey wings, white shoulders, and white upper tail-coverts and tail (the tail of the Black Tern is grey). In winter and immature dress the head and neck are mottled black and white and the underparts are entirely white, there being no dark patch on the side of the breast. Bill reddish-black in summer, black in winter. Picks its food from the surface of the water and rarely dives.

Distribution and Habitat: A passage migrant and non-breeding winter visitor to West Africa. In late spring before its departure often encountered in summer dress. Occurs on lagoons and estuaries from Senegal to Gaboon and frequently on inland lakes and rivers. Common in the Niger Inundation Zone in Mali and on Lake Chad.

Allied species: The Whiskered Tern (*Sterna hybrida*), 9½″, sexes similar, is in summer dress distinguished from the rather similar White-winged Black Tern and Black Tern by its conspicuous white face sharply demarcated from the black crown and by its crimson bill. In winter dress it is virtually indistinguishable from the White-winged Black Tern. A winter visitor and passage migrant from the Palaearctic Region occurring in West Africa mainly on inland waters such as Lake Chad and less frequently on the sea coast. Fairly common in Senegal. The Black Tern (*Sterna nigra*), 9″, sexes similar, is usually encountered in non-breeding (winter) dress. It resembles the White-winged Black Tern (*Sterna leucoptera*) except that in breeding dress the shoulders and tail are grey not white and the under wing-coverts are whitish not black, and in non-breeding dress the white underparts show a dark patch on each side of the breast just in front of the wing. In behaviour resembles the White-winged Black Tern. A passage migrant and winter visitor, and some non-breeding birds summer. In West Africa mainly a marine species frequenting the coasts, estuaries and lagoons from Senegal to Gaboon and Congo. A few inland records.

LITTLE TERN *Sterna albifrons* **Pl. 20**

Identification: 8″. Sexes similar. The small size, black crown and nape, white forehead, and dusky-tipped yellow bill are field marks. The crown is speckled greyish and white in non-breeding dress. Tail slightly forked. Flight buoyant with rapid wing beats.

Voice: Various rasping and chattering calls on breeding ground.

Distribution and Habitat: Widely but locally distributed on the coast and on inland lakes and rivers ranging from Mauritania and Senegal to Gaboon, Chad, and the Central African Republic. Numbers in winter augmented by Palaearctic migrants as far east at least as the Ivory Coast.

Nesting: Breeds singly or in small colonies on the sandbanks of the great rivers or lagoons. Nest a small shallow circular unlined scrape in the sand or shingle. Eggs 2–3. Variable. Clay, ochraceous, greenish-grey or buff, evenly blotched and spotted with different shades of brown and with ashy or pale violet shell marks.

SANDGROUSE: Pteroclididae

Birds of arid regions. Thickset, about the size of a Turtle Dove, with short legs feathered to the toes. The cryptically patterned plumage mainly chestnut and sandy. Do not perch but fly fast and direct in flocks, like Pigeons. Drink at regular intervals.

CHESTNUT-BELLIED SAND-GROUSE *Pterocles exustus* **Pl. 20**
Identification: 11″. The only Sand-grouse in our area with a long sharp tail except for the Spotted Sand-grouse (*Pterocles senegallus*) (see Checklist, p. 271), a desert species which just reaches the northern edge of our area. In the male the head, mantle, throat, and chest are sandy-buff, the lower breast and belly are chestnut, and the breast is crossed by a narrow black band. The female is yellowish-buff and has the upperparts spotted with yellow and streaked and barred with black, the throat and chest spotted with black, the breast unspotted, and the belly heavily barred with black. In flight both sexes show some white on the wing. Usually observed in small parties and sometimes in large flocks at or flighting to or from their drinking places by pond, lake, or river margin.
Voice: Loud, harsh, yet musical chuckling calls uttered in flight. Also a soft, twittering call.
Distribution and Habitat: The arid belt bordering the desert from southern Mauritania, Senegal and Gambia east through Mali, where it is common to Niger, northern Nigeria and Chad.
Nesting: Eggs 2–3, regular ovals, the creamy ground spotted and speckled with brown and mauve. Laid in a slight hollow on the bare ground.

FOUR-BANDED SAND-GROUSE *Pterocles quadricinctus* **Pl. 20**
Identification: 10″. On the ground at a distance can be confused with the Chestnut-bellied Sand-Grouse, but in flight the rounded not pointed tail distinguishes it. Seen at close range the male has a black and white forehead, heavily barred upperparts, and a buffish chest separated from the dark barred lower breast and belly by three contiguous bands of chestnut, white, and black. Female rather similar but lacks the distinctive head marks and breast bands and the chest is uniform deep rufous buff. In flight the black wing tips show up.
Voice: A shrill piping note uttered at dusk when flighting to watering place.
Distribution and Habitat: Less of a desert species than the other Sand-Grouse in our area. Strongly migratory. In the dry season penetrates as far south as 9° N. and in the wet season as far north as 17° N. From Mauritania, Senegal, Gambia, and Portuguese Guinea east through Ivory Coast, Ghana and Nigeria to Chad and the Central African Republic. Frequents bare, stony or sandy ground, cultivation clearings, short grassy plains, scrubland and lightly wooded savanna.
Nesting: A slight depression in the ground sometimes sheltered by a shrub. Eggs 2–3, blunt ovate, salmon-buff sparsely and evenly spotted and flecked with orange-brown and with a few mauve blotches.

BUTTON-QUAILS: Turnicidae

Birds superficially like tiny Quails. Usually hidden on the ground in a grassy place. Characteristic short skimming flight when flushed and difficult to put up a second time.

AFRICAN BUTTON-QUAIL *Turnix sylvatica* **Pl. 20**
Identification: Male 5½″. Female 6½″. A tiny Quail-like bird which in flight can be mistaken for a Quail, but the curved expanse of the wing together with the virtually invisible tail produce a characteristic crescent-shaped outline, and on landing the body is held quite straight and seems to be suspended from the two wings. When flushed flies only a few yards, then settles and runs swiftly through the herbage to one side and hides. No distinctive plumage characters. Underparts creamy with the centre of the breast rust-coloured and the sides spotted with black. Female larger and more brightly coloured than the male.
Voice: A fluty whistle heard at night.
Distribution and Habitat: Frequents dry or wet open grass country and crop-bearing or fallow farmland. Widely distributed but local ranging from southern Mauritania, Senegal and Gambia east to Chad and the Central African Republic and south to Gaboon and Congo. Absent from the forest.
Nesting: A little hollow in the soil scantily lined with grasses and twigs. Eggs 3, ovate-pyriform, pale brown evenly and thickly spotted and blotched with brown, yellow-brown and slate.
Allied species: The Black-rumped Button-quail (*Turnix hottentotta nana*) resembles the African Button-quail in size and colour except that it has rufous cheeks and a conspicuous blackish rump. Recorded only from savanna localities in Sierra Leone, Ivory Coast, Ghana, Nigeria, the Cameroons and Congo. The Quail-Plover (*Ortyxelos meiffrenii*), 6″, has the upperparts rufous finely streaked with cream and the underparts mainly white. On the ground a small Button-Quail-like secretive bird. In the air recognised by its buoyant lark-like jerky flight, white shoulder-patches and white-bordered black wings. Local and restricted to arid areas between 13° N. and 17° N. from Senegal through Mali, Niger, Ghana and northern Nigeria to Chad and the Central African Republic.

PIGEONS AND DOVES: Columbidae

Medium-sized, strong-winged, fast-flying birds with small heads, slender bills, short, strong legs, and soft, usually delicately coloured plumage. The Pigeons are larger and stoutly built with rounded or square tails. The Doves are slender in form with long graduated tails. Call generally cooing in character, varies from species to species, and useful in identification.

GREY WOOD PIGEON *Columba unicincta* **Pl. 15**
Identification: 16″. A large grey pigeon of the true forest best identified by its far-carrying call. The white tail band is noticeable in flight. Usually hidden in the crown of a tall forest tree.
Voice: Call a deep vibrant 'coooor'.

Distribution and Habitat: The rain forest from Liberia to Gaboon and Congo but there are few records of it from west of the Cameroons. Usually a pair together in the highest tree tops but occasionally attracted to some fruiting tree in a forest clearing.

Nesting: A nest in Zaire was lodged in a small fork near the top of a tall forest tree. The egg is white.

Allied species: The Olive Pigeon (*Columba arquatrix*), 16″, is easily distinguished from other pigeons by its coloration. Mantle, breast and belly purplish-maroon heavily spotted with white; head and rump grey. In our area it is a mountain species found only in the highland forests of Fernando Po, the Cameroons and the Obudu Plateau of Nigeria. In this restricted range fairly common. A very distinct race (*C. a. thomensis*) which differs in being practically unspotted occurs on the island of Sao Tome. The Bronze-naped Pigeon (*Columba malherbii*) is a small (11″) rather local arboreal forest species ranging from Guinea and Sierra Leone to Gaboon and Congo in the main body of the forest and its gallery extensions. Also on Principe, Sao Tome and Annobon. The call is a characteristically phrased mournful cooing. In the male the head and upperparts are grey, the mantle being copper glossed with green or violet; underparts mainly vinous. In the female the crown is rufous and the underparts grey-brown washed with chestnut. In both sexes a broad buff band at the tip of the tail. In the well marked race (*C. m. malherbii*) of the Gulf of Guinea islands the male is grey below and the female has a grey not a rufous crown.

SPECKLED PIGEON   *Columba guinea*   Pl. 15

Identification: 15″. Sexes similar. A large robust pale grey Pigeon with vinous-chestnut mantle and wing-coverts, the latter conspicuously spotted with white. At close range the collar of stiff chestnut and grey feathers and the bare red skin round the eye are field marks. In flight the light grey rump contrasts with the dark mantle and wings. Gregarious when not breeding.

Voice: A series of deep sonorous well-separated 'coos'.

Distribution and Habitat: A savanna species that penetrates as far as 15° N. in the semi-arid belt but is absent from the forest and the adjoining moist savanna and from the savanna south of the forest in Gaboon and Congo. Widespread and locally common ranging from Senegal and Gambia to Chad and the Central African Republic. Fond of farmland with Borassus palms and scattered thickly foliaged trees. Often near or in towns and villages.

Nesting: A platform of twigs and rootlets built in a tree or in buildings. Eggs 2, white.

RED-EYED DOVE   *Streptopelia semitorquata*   Pl. 15

Identification: 13″. Sexes similar. A large dark Dove with grey head, greyish-brown upperparts, and vinous underparts. A black half-collar at the base of the neck. Bare skin round eye dark red and conspicuous. Tail brown, crossed in the middle by a broad blackish band. For differences between the Red-eyed Dove and the rather similar Mourning Dove see the latter species (p. 94). Towering display flight. Often gregarious.

Voice: Characteristic 'coo-coo' followed after a short pause by a slow descending 'coo-coo-coo'. On landing a sort of nasal 'hui'. The voice is the best distinguishing character from the Mourning Dove.

Distribution and Habitat: Abundant and widespread in savanna and forest

but rare in the thorn scrub and uncommon in Nigeria and Chad north of 10° N.
Fond of cultivated ground with scattered shady trees, and also fringing mangrove, swamp and montane forest.

Nesting: A platform mainly of twigs usually in a thick leafy tree and often
near water. Eggs 2, white.

Allied species: The European Turtle-Dove (*Streptopelia turtur*), 10½″, occurs
numerously in winter (September–May) in Senegal, especially on the rice fields
of the Senegal River and is recorded on migration from Gambia and off the
Portuguese Guinea coast. Farther east there are winter and passage records from
Mali, northern Nigeria and northern Cameroons, and many records from Chad.
In the vicinity of Lake Chad it is a regular spring and autumn migrant, sometimes abundant in March–April. The resident Saharan race (*S. turtur hoggara*)
occurs in our area in the Air Massif. Head grey, mantle brown, breast vinous,
shading into white on the belly. The black-and-white half collar on the side of
the neck, rufous wing-coverts with conspicuous black centres to the feathers,
and the long dark white-tipped tail are good field characters. The Adamawan
Turtle-Dove (*Streptopelia lugens hypopyrrhus*), 12″, is the West African race of
a dove widely but locally distributed in the highlands of tropical Africa. Found
in the Jos Plateau of Nigeria, the uplands of north Cameroons and Fianga
(Chad) along wooded or scrub-covered banks of streams. A black half-collar on
either side of the hind neck, crown grey, mantle brown, chest grey, breast and
belly pinkish-cinnamon, tail feathers black tipped with grey except for the
central pair which are entirely dark brown.

MOURNING DOVE: *Streptopelia decipiens*   **Pl. 15**

Identification: 12″. Sexes similar. Resembles the Red-eyed Dove but is
slightly smaller, lower breast and belly are pale grey not vinous, and the tail is
grey tipped white and lacks the dark band of the Red-eyed Dove's. The quavering throaty chuckling call uttered by both sexes is a sure guide to identification.

Voice: 'coo——roo-oo-oo' or 'coo-roo-roo', the first note pitched higher than
the last two. Also the characteristic chuckling call already mentioned.

Distribution and Habitat: A dry-country species with a more northerly
range than the Red-eyed Dove though the two overlap. Found from southern
Mauritania (17° N.) and Senegal east through Mali, Niger, Togo, northern
Nigeria and northern Cameroons to Chad. Fond of riverine fringing vegetation.

Nesting: A flimsy platform mainly of twigs built at a height of 5 to 40 feet in a
variety of trees. Eggs 2, white.

VINACEOUS DOVE *Streptopelia vinacea*   **Pl. 15**

Identification: 10″. Sexes similar. A rather small Dove with a broad black
collar on the hind neck, grey-brown upperparts, and vinous-pink underparts.
Outer tail feathers broadly tipped white. In flight dark brown remiges a field
mark. Tame. Occurs in pairs and seasonally in flocks. Frequents both cultivated
ground and the open bush.

Voice: A characteristic high-pitched rapid far-carrying 'coor-coo-coo——coor-
coo-coo . . .' with the first note emphasised. On landing utters a nasal cry.
Sometimes calls at night.

Distribution and Habitat: Common and widespread in the savanna north
to 17° N. Absent from the forest and its clearings and from Gaboon and Congo
and in the moist savanna bordering the forest a dry season visitor only.

Nesting: 5 to 25 feet from the ground in the smaller branches of a tree. A flimsy circular saucer of twigs and rootlets. Eggs 2, pure white.

Allied species: The Rose-grey Dove (*Streptopelia roseogrisea*) is black-collared and resembles the Vinaceous Dove but is a little larger, the plumage is paler, and in flight the under surface of the wing is white not slate. The call is softer and more Dove-like than that of the Vinaceous Dove and resembles that of the domestic Collared Dove of Europe. A Dove of the sub-desert areas very common between 15° N. and 17° N. Ranges from Mauritania and Senegal through Mali, Niger, and northern Nigeria to Chad.

LAUGHING DOVE *Streptopelia senegalensis*
(*Stigmatopelia senegalensis*)   **Pl. 15**

Identification: 11″. Sexes similar. A small Dove without any black collar on the hind neck and distinguished from all other Doves by a black-spotted reddish foreneck. Head vinous, mantle brown, rump dark grey. Underparts vinous becoming white on the belly. Grey-blue wing-coverts and secondaries conspicuous at rest and in flight. Tame. Numerous in villages and towns. Spends much time on the ground feeding on fallen seeds.

Voice: A cooing 'ro-too-too-too-too', hurried in the middle and not very loud.

Distribution and Habitat: Widespread and very common throughout our area south of 18° N. but absent from the closed forest. Mainly, but not entirely, restricted to villages and surrounding farmland. Occurs on Sao Tome and Principe.

Nesting: A very flimsy platform of twigs, rootlets and tendrils, built in a small tree at a height of from 4 to 18 feet. Eggs 2, white.

LONG-TAILED DOVE *Oena capensis*   **Pl. 15**

Identification: 10″. A tiny slenderly built Dove with a very long graduated tail which can be well seen in flight and is diagnostic. Black mask and chest, grey crown and tail, brown upperparts, white breast and belly. At close range two blackish bands on the rump and metallic blue patches on the wing. In flight a large cinnamon patch on the wing. In the female the mask and chest are greyish-brown. Immature plumage varies with age, usually showing rufous, black and white spots above and dark bars below. Usually feeds on the ground. Perches low. Flight swift.

Voice: Rather silent. A low subdued 'hoo-hoo'.

Distribution and Habitat: The northern arid belt between 9° N. and 20° N. from Mauritania and Senegal through Mali, northern Ghana, northern Nigeria, Niger, and northern Cameroons to Chad and the Central African Republic, and reappearing south of the forest in the coastal savannas of Gaboon.

Nesting: Nest usually within 2 feet of the ground in dwarf shrub or on a heap of dead twigs in open arid country. A slender platform of rootlets, tendrils and small twigs. Eggs 2, elliptical, cream-coloured.

TAMBOURINE DOVE *Turtur tympanistria*
(*Tympanistria tympanistria*)   **Pl. 15**

Identification: 8½″. The male readily distinguished by its white forehead, eyestripe and underparts. Upperparts brown with a blackish band across the rump. In the female the white parts are washed with grey. Occasionally perches on trees but essentially a ground Dove. Shy. Flight rapid, low and direct.

Plate 19

PRATINCOLES, COURSERS, PAINTED SNIPE, STILT AND SANDPIPERS

1. **SANDERLING** *Calidris alba*   page 83
Palest grey above; white below; black shoulder patch; in flight white wing-bar.

2. **LITTLE STINT** *Calidris minuta*   82
Very small; short bill, short legs; in flight V-shaped pattern on back; white sides of rump.

3. **CURLEW SANDPIPER** *Calidris ferruginea*   82
Slightly decurved bill; in flight white rump and wing-bar.

4. **BLACK-WINGED STILT** *Himantopus himantopus*   83
Black and white plumage; long pink legs; straight black bill.

5. **PAINTED SNIPE** *Rostratula benghalensis*   84
Female: white round eye; chestnut sides of head and neck.
Male: light buffish round eye; pale coronal streak.

6. **PRATINCOLE** *Glareola pratincola*   86
Forked tail; white base of tail; pale throat narrowly bordered black.

7. **COLLARED PRATINCOLE** *Glareola nuchalis*   86
Forked tail; long pointed wings; red legs and base of bill; white or rufous collar.

8. **GREY PRATINCOLE** *Glareola cinerea*   86
At rest mainly pale grey and inconspicuous; in flight patterned black and white wings and tail.

9. **CREAM-COLOURED COURSER** *Cursorius cursor*   85
Slim; Plover-like; sandy-buff. In flight black under-surface of wing.

10. **TEMMINCK'S COURSER** *Cursorius temminckii*   85
Small; chestnut breast; black patch on belly; chestnut crown.

11. **CROCODILE BIRD** *Pluvianus aegyptius*   84
Distinctive black, white, and grey colour pattern.

Plate 20

SAND-GROUSE, BUTTON-QUAIL, TERNS AND GULLS

1. **CHESTNUT-BELLIED SAND-GROUSE**   page 91
   Pterocles exustus
   Male: long sharp tail; narrow black chest-band; white wing-bar.
   Female: long sharp tail; white wing-bar.

2. **FOUR-BANDED SAND-GROUSE**   *Pterocles quadricinctus*   91
   Rounded tail; barred mantle, breast, and belly.

3. **AFRICAN BUTTON-QUAIL**   *Turnix sylvatica*   92
   Rust-coloured patch on breast.

4. **COMMON TERN**   *Sterna hirundo*   89
   Bill red tipped black (breeding); bill blackish with red base (non-breeding).

5. **GULL-BILLED TERN**   *Sterna nilotica*   88
   Massive black bill.

6. **WHITE-WINGED BLACK TERN**   *Sterna leucoptera*   90
   Short square tail; entirely white underparts.

7. **CASPIAN TERN**   *Sterna caspia*   89
   Massive red bill.

8. **LITTLE TERN**   *Sterna albifrons*   90
   Small; black-tipped yellow bill; white forehead.

9. **AFRICAN SKIMMER**   *Rynchops flavirostris*   88
   Conspicuous orange-red bill; blackish upperparts; white underparts.

10. **LESSER BLACK-BACKED GULL**   *Larus fuscus*   87
    Large; slaty-black or slaty-grey upperparts.

11. **GREY-HEADED GULL**   *Larus cirrhocephalus*   87
    Grey head; red bill and feet.

Voice: A protracted series of mournful coos.
Distribution and Habitat: Sedentary and well-distributed in the forest and its gallery extensions from Sierra Leone to Gaboon and Congo and Fernando Po. In the mountain forests of Cameroons up to 7,000 feet. Usually in thick places in the primary or second-growth; also in forest clearings planted with rubber, kola or cocoa.
Nesting: Nest a slight platform of twigs, plant stems and rootlets, built in a forest tree or shrub. Two dark cream coloured eggs are laid.

RED-BILLED WOOD-DOVE   *Turtur afer*   Pl. 15
Identification: 8½″. The yellow-tipped red bill distinguishes it from the closely similar Black-billed Wood-Dove. Upperparts brown with two dark bands on the rump; underparts vinous. In flight the rufous on the wing is conspicuous. Usually first seen rising with characteristic suddenness from the ground or a low perch and flying off through the foliage to alight again at no great distance. Often flushed from farm plots or footpaths.
Voice: A series of plaintive coos, monotonous and protracted.
Distribution and Habitat: Sedentary and common in the savanna and the forest clearings from Senegal and Gambia to the Central African Republic, Gaboon and Congo. Favours especially native farmland.
Nesting: A slight platform usually built low down in a farmland tree or shrub. The two eggs are dark cream coloured.
Allied species: The Black-billed Wood-Dove (*Turtur abyssinicus*) closely resembles the Red-billed Wood-Dove and is distinguished by its black not red bill and at close range by its greyish not brown mantle. The call is rather similar. A bird of the arid north common between 12° N. and 16° N. and extending south to 8° N. and in Ghana to 5° N. In the south its range widely overlaps that of the Red-billed Dove. Found from Senegal and Mauritania, east to Chad and the Central African Republic.

BLUE-HEADED DOVE   *Turtur brehmeri* (*Calopelia puella*)   Pl. 15
Identification: 10″. Distinguished from other doves by its colour pattern. Cinnamon-rufous except for the blue-grey head. Metallic green or golden-copper spots on the wing. A shy secretive forest species usually discovered on or near the ground in places where there is thick cover.
Voice: A plaintive cooing, louder and more abrupt than the cooing of the Tambourine Dove or the Wood-Dove.
Distribution and Habitat: In the rain forest interior from Sierra Leone to Gaboon. Widely distributed but nowhere common.
Nesting: Nest a platform of twigs and rootlets built low down in a forest tree. Eggs 1–2, buff.
Allied species: The Lemon Dove (*Aplopelia larvata*) has a wide but discontinuous and mainly mountain range in Africa. In our area it is recorded from the forested mountains of the Cameroons and from a few lowland forest localities in Liberia, Cameroons, Gaboon and Congo. It occurs also on the islands of Fernando Po, Principe, Sao Tome and Annobon. The plumage varies greatly individually, sexually, with age, and with locality. The upperparts are usually brown with metallic reflections. The underparts in the male are usually grey and in the female brownish-grey or cinnamon. In the islands of the Gulf of Guinea and in the Cameroon highlands locality is a good guide to recognition of the species.

GREEN FRUIT-PIGEON *Treron australis (Vinago australis)* **Pl. 15**
Identification: 11″. The only green Pigeon in our area except for the Yellow-bellied Fruit-Pigeon, which latter has a yellow not a green breast. An arboreal species of the savanna and the forest where there are edible fruit-bearing trees. Usually encountered in parties. After feeding they sit quietly for hours in the higher branches.
Voice: A curious chuckling call.
Distribution and Habitat: Senegal and Gambia east to Southern Chad and the Central African Republic and south to Gaboon and Congo and all the islands of the Gulf of Guinea. Common and widespread in the forest and wooded savanna but rare or absent from the northern thorn-scrub zone. Subject to local migrations.
Nesting: The nest is a circular platform of dry twigs built in a tree. The single white egg is an elongated oval with both ends distinctly pointed.

YELLOW-BELLIED FRUIT-PIGEON *Treron waalia*
(*Vinago waalia*) **Pl. 15**
Identification: 12½″. Sexes similar. The only other green Pigeon on the mainland is the Green Fruit-Pigeon (*Treron australis*), from which it is distinguished by its lemon-yellow breast and belly. Head and throat ashy-olive; upperparts olive-green. Mauve shoulder patch. Bill lilac tipped white. In *T. australis* the bill is red tipped bluish-white. Occurs in flocks. Arboreal. Despite its bright colouring difficult to see in the foliage because of its immobility. Noisy flight when moving from branch to branch is typical. Climbs rather like a Parrot. Addicted to fig trees.
Voice: Does not coo. Various calls, one a chuckling yapping cry, another a trill.
Distribution and Habitat: A Pigeon of the thorn-scrub savanna penetrating north to 15° N., which is about the limit for fig trees. From Senegal, Gambia and Portuguese Guinea through Mali, Ivory Coast, northern Ghana, Togo, Dahomey, Niger, northern Nigeria and Cameroons to southern Chad and the Central African Republic. Also on the dry coastal plain of Ghana.
Nesting: A flimsy platform of twigs and rootlets in a tree, often at the end of a bough. Eggs 1–2, white.

PARROTS: Psittacidae

Arboreal, usually vividly coloured birds with large heads and strong, curved, sharp-edged bills useful for cracking nuts and gripping the branches of trees whilst climbing. Strong, direct, rapid flight. Loud squawking, screeching or twittering calls.

BROWN-NECKED PARROT *Poicephalus robustus* **Pl. 16**
Identification: 12″. Characteristic top-heavy appearance due to very large horn-grey bill. General colour green but head, neck and throat mainly brown, bend of the wing and thighs orange-red (visible when settles), and wing and tail feathers dark brown. Female resembles male but has a red forecrown. Flight fast and powerful with regular wing beats. Usually in pairs or parties clambering about the trees or flying high overhead.

Plate 21

CUCKOOS

1. **EMERALD CUCKOO** *Chrysococcyx cupreus* page 110
Green upperparts and breast; yellow belly.

2. **DIDRIC CUCKOO** *Chrysococcyx caprius* 110
Outer tail feathers dark with white spots. Female duller, more extensively barred below.

3. **KLAAS' CUCKOO** *Chrysococcyx klaas* 110
Outer tail feathers almost entirely white.

4. **GREAT SPOTTED CUCKOO** *Clamator glandarius* 106
Spotted upperparts; long white-tipped graduated tail.

5. **BLACK CUCKOO** *Cuculus clamosus* 107
Forest race (*C. clamosus gabonensis*): black upperparts; barred underparts; rufous chin, throat, and breast.

6. **PIED CRESTED CUCKOO** *Clamator jacobinus* 106
Black upperparts; white underparts; white patch on wing.

7. **LEVAILLANT'S CUCKOO** *Clamator levaillantii* 106
Resembles Pied Crested Cuckoo, but larger and throat is heavily streaked black.

8. **RED-CHESTED CUCKOO** *Cuculus solitarius* 107
Slate-grey upperparts and chin; reddish chest.

9. **COMMON CUCKOO** *Cuculus canorus* 107
Long white-tipped tail; pointed wings; grey upperparts; bill (African race) mainly yellow tipped black.

21

Plate 22

MOUSEBIRDS, TROGONS AND COUCALS

1. **BLUE-NAPED MOUSEBIRD** *Colius macrourus*   page 123
   Blue nape patch; red bill and face.

2. **BAR-BREASTED MOUSEBIRD** *Colius striatus*   123
   Black face; bright coral-red feet.

3. **NARINA TROGON** *Apaloderma narina*   123
   Outer tail feathers white.

4. **BAR-TAILED TROGON** *Apaloderma vittatum*   124
   Outer tail feathers closely barred black and white.

5. **YELLOWBILL COUCAL** *Ceuthmochares aereus*   111
   Long graduated tail; yellow bill.

6. **BLACK COUCAL** *Centropus grillii*   111
   Entire underparts black.

7. **SENEGAL COUCAL** *Centropus senegalensis*   114
   Upperparts black glossed green; underparts whitish.

8. **BLACK-THROATED COUCAL** *Centropus leucogaster*   111
   Throat and chest black; lower breast and belly whitish.

Voice: Various harsh grating cries.
Distribution and Habitat: Gambia, southern Senegal, Portuguese Guinea, Ivory Coast, Ghana, Togo, Nigeria, Gaboon and Congo. Local and usually uncommon except in Gambia, where it is frequent in the mangrove forest. Frequents mangove forest, gallery forest and savanna woodlands.
Nesting: In southern Africa 3–4 rounded white eggs laid in a hole in a tree.
Allied species: The Red-crowned Parrot (*Poicephalus gulielmi*) occurs in small flocks in the forest. It ranges from Liberia to Gaboon and Congo but is nowhere common. A rather small (12″) green Parrot with a scarlet or orange forehead and a scarlet or orange patch at the bend of the wing. The call is a high-pitched screech. The flight is fast and direct.

SENEGAL PARROT   *Poicephalus senegalus*   Pl. 16

Identification: 10″. Sexes similar. In flight easily recognised by short tail and orange or red belly and under tail-coverts, the shade varying geographically. Head dull grey, breast and upperparts bright green. Well known as a cage bird. Wary. Hard to see when perched, the plumage blending with the foliage. Feeds on fruits and ripening millet, maize and groundnuts.
Voice: Loud chattering calls often uttered in flight.
Distribution and Habitat: A fairly common savanna species showing a preference for open woodland with large trees such as oil and Borassus palms. Ranges from Senegal, Gambia and Portuguese Guinea through Mali, Ivory Coast, Upper Volta, Ghana and Nigeria to southern Chad.
Nesting: Eggs 2, white, rounded. Laid in a hole high up in a large tree.

GREY PARROT   *Psittacus erithacus*   Pl. 16

Identification: Unmistakable. A grey parrot with a scarlet tail. Draws attention to itself, especially at dawn and dusk when flocks pass high overhead, with swift direct flight between their roosting and feeding grounds, screeching and whistling. The evening roost may number several hundred birds. By day they feed on fruiting trees in the forest and are particularly partial to the oil palm.
Voice: A variety of loud whistles and screeches.
Distribution and Habitat: The lowland forest from Sierra Leone to Gaboon and Congo and the islands of Fernando Po and Principe. Locally abundant, especially in swamp and mangrove forest.
Nesting: The usual clutch is three and the eggs are laid high up in a forest tree in a knot-hole or other cavity. Eggs white, ovate, and slightly glossy.

SENEGAL LONG-TAILED PARRAKEET   *Psittacula krameri*
Pl. 16

Identification: 16″. A slim, red-billed, green Parrot with a very long graduated bluish-green tail. The adult male is further distinguished by its black throat, bluish nape, and narrow pink collar. Cry distinctive. Usually in flocks. Flight high, rapid and graceful.
Voice: An incessant, noisy, shrill 'kio kio kio'.
Distribution and Habitat: A common, widespread Parrot of the drier savanna ranging from southern Mauritania, Senegal, Gambia and Portuguese Guinea through Guinea, Mali, Ivory Coast, Ghana, Togo and Nigeria to Chad and the Central African Republic.
Nesting: Nesting holes high up in a tree top. Eggs 4, white.

RED-HEADED LOVEBIRD   *Agapornis pullaria*   **Pl. 16**

Identification: A tiny green Parrot, the male with a red crown, face and throat, and the female with these parts yellowish. In flight the blue rump and (in the male only) the black underside of the wing are conspicuous. Feeds principally on grass seeds.

Voice: A squeaky chirruping uttered in flight.

Distribution and Habitat: The savanna from Guinea and Sierra Leone east to southern Chad and the Central African Republic and south to Gaboon and Congo. Also Fernando Po and Sao Tome. Occasionally penetrates the forest zone in places where there are extensive grassy clearings. Rather local, occurring in pairs or parties.

Nesting: The nest is a round chamber approached by a tunnel excavated by the parrots in a termites' or ants' nest attached to the bole or branch of a tree. The eggs are white and the clutch 4–5.

Allied species: The Black-collared Lovebird (*Agapornis swinderniana*) is about the same size as the Red-headed Lovebird. It is distinguished by having the entire head green and a black collar on the hind neck. It is a rare species of the forest and its gallery extensions recorded in our area from a few localities in Liberia, the Cameroons, Gaboon and Congo. It feeds principally on figs.

TOURACOS OR PLANTAIN-EATERS: Musophagidae

An exclusively African family. Large, conspicuous, arboreal, fruit-eating birds of the forest and savanna. Often brightly coloured. Agile, swift, hopping and running progression along the branches characteristic. Call usually loud and resonant.

GREEN-CRESTED TOURACO   *Tauraco persa* (*Turacus persa*)   **Pl. 16**

Identification: 17″. The loud cry, in flight the conspicuous crimson wings, and, as it moves about the branches, the strange hopping progression, are all arresting field characters, but they are shared with certain other Touraco species in our area. The head, mantle and breast are green, the entirely green head crest being the most reliable distinguishing character of this Touraco. Back, wing-coverts and tail glossy violet. Wing feathers crimson. It moves rapidly about the branches with long springing hops; it also runs. Flight mainly gliding.

Voice: A series of resonant far-carrying cries, 'kaw-kaw-kaw . . .', at first slow, then increasing in volume and speed, then gradually fading away. Often when one bird calls, others in the area take up the call so that in a few moments all the Touracos within earshot are swelling the chorus.

Distribution and Habitat: Widespread and common in the forest and its gallery extensions from Senegal and Gambia east to the Central African Republic and south to Gaboon and Congo. An arboreal species mainly in the tree tops of the primary and old second-growth.

Nesting: Nest a flimsy platform of twigs built in a forest tree. Eggs two, white, almost spherical.

Allied species: Bannerman's Touraco (*Tauraco bannermani*) is restricted in range and found only in the montane forests of the Bamenda highlands above 6,000 feet. Similar in size and build to the Green-crested Touraco but easily distinguished by its red head and crest. The call, too, is similar but is higher-pitched and less resonant.

VERREAUX'S TOURACO   *Turaco macrorhynchus*
(*Turacus macrorhynchus*)   **Pl. 16**

Identification: 17″. In habits, appearance and habitat resembles the Green-crested Touraco but the crest on the head is differently coloured. In the race occurring from Sierra Leone to Ghana (*T. m. macrorhynchus*) the crest is green tipped with black with a subterminal white bar. In the race occurring from Nigeria to Congo (*T. m. verreauxi*) the crest is green tipped with red with a subterminal black bar. In the Green-crested Touraco the crest is entirely green.

Voice: Similar to the call of the Green-crested Touraco but louder and harsher. As in that species birds scattered over a wide area sometimes call in unison.

Distribution and Habitat: The forest from Sierra Leone to Gaboon and Congo and the island of Fernando Po. Widespread and locally common in the lowland forest. In the Cameroons it is also abundant in the mountain forests at least up to 6,000 feet.

Nesting: Nest a flat slight platform of twigs and sticks concealed in the foliage of a tree top. Eggs two, creamy white, regular ovals.

WHITE-CRESTED TOURACO   *Turaco leucolophus*
(*Turacus leucolophus*)   **Pl. 16**

Identification: 16″. The conspicuous all-white crest and the white cheeks and nape readily distinguish it from other Touracos. Upperparts mainly glossy-violet, breast green, quills crimson. Active and agile darting along the branches with the curious half-running, half-hopping progression characteristic of the genus.

Voice: A deep guttural 'kuroo' repeated a varying number of times.

Distribution and Habitat: In our area a rather limited zonal range extending in the wooded savanna north of the forest from Benue Province of Nigeria through the Cameroons to southern Chad and the Central African Republic.

Nesting: Nest a slight structure of twigs built in the fork of a savanna tree. The two eggs are rounded ellipses, white tinted with palest grey.

VIOLET PLANTAIN-EATER   *Musophaga violacea*   **Pl. 16**

Identification: Sexes similar. A large slimly-built Touraco. In flight at a distance blackish with crimson wings and yellow bill. At close range crown crimson, bare area of face scarlet, and line below and behind face white; upperparts violet-blue; underparts blackish, glossed with green on the breast. At rest the edge of the crimson wing is just visible. Bill yellow tipped scarlet. Hard to see when perched but often betrayed by its call. Runs and leaps about the branches in the way characteristic of the group.

Voice: A rapid 'courou-courou-courou...' which carries a long way and is often repeated by several birds at once. Also utters a harsh cry.

Distribution and Habitat: The gallery forests and outliers of the savanna south of 13° N. and north of the closed forest from Gambia and Senegal east to northern Cameroons, Chad and western Central African Republic.

Nesting: A frail platform of sticks, of open construction like the nest of a Dove, in a leafy tree at a height of 20–25 feet. Eggs 2, rounded ovals, glossless white tinged with creamy-grey.

Allied species: Lady Ross's Violet Plantain-eater (*Musophaga rossae*) resembles the Violet Plantain-eater but can be distinguished by its prominent erect crimson crest and by the bare skin round the eye being orange-yellow not scarlet. It is uncommon in our area being recorded from a few localities in eastern Cameroons and the Central African Republic where there are outlying woods or gallery strips in the savanna.

GREY PLANTAIN-EATER   *Crinifer piscator*   **Pl. 16**
Identification: 20″. Sexes similar. A long-tailed grey Touraco with a conspicuous lemon-yellow bill. In flight the large white patch on the rounded wing identifies it. At close range upperparts dark grey streaked with black, chest brown, breast and belly white conspicuously streaked with blackish. A noisy bird, easy to observe, and not at all shy. In pairs at the breeding season; in small parties at other times.
Voice: A series of loud screeching 'coo-coo' calls rising and then falling in pitch. Also various cackling and chuckling sounds.
Distribution and Habitat: A common widespread savanna species extending north to 16° 30′ N. in localities with trees but absent from the closed forest. Fond of leafy trees in open woodland, gardens and farmland. Ranges north of the forest from Senegal and Gambia to western Chad and the Central African Republic and reappears south of the forest in the Congo savanna.
Nesting: A fairly substantial platform of sticks and twigs in the fork of a tree. Eggs 2–3, rounded ovate, greyish-white and slightly glossy.
Allied species: The Abyssinian Grey Plantain-eater (*Crinifer zonurus*) resembles the Grey Plantain-eater in habits and appearance but the lower breast and belly are unstriped and, except for the central pair, the dark tail feathers show a broad white band across their middle third. In our area it occurs in southern Chad and eastern Central African Republic.

BLUE PLANTAIN-EATER   *Corythaeola cristata*   **Pl. 16**
Identification: 30″. Unmistakable. By far the largest Plantain-eater. Plumage mainly blue; belly and thighs chestnut; long tail tipped with black; head with conspicuous black crest. Hops and runs along the branches in the tree tops.
Voice: A variety of loud calls, the most frequent a deep guttural 'koorook koorook . . .' and an explosive clamorous 'ko ko ko ko . . .'.
Distribution and Habitat: The forest and its gallery extensions from Senegal and Portuguese Guinea east to the Central African Republic and south to Gaboon and Congo; also Fernando Po. In the Cameroons it ascends the mountain forests at least to 7,000 feet. Widespread and locally abundant occurring in small parties in the primary forest and also in the old second-growth, where it may often be seen eating the fruit of the umbrella tree (*Musanga*).
Nesting: Nest a platform of twigs built in the top of a forest or farmland tree. Eggs 2; very pale greenish-blue rounded ellipses.

CUCKOOS AND COUCALS: Cuculidae

A family well represented in Africa. Includes the true Cuckoos, which are parasitic in their nesting habits, and the Coucals, which construct their own nests and rear their young. Stoutly built with long graduated tails. Small species brilliantly coloured. Calls loud and usually distinguish the species.

GREAT SPOTTED CUCKOO *Clamator glandarius* Pl. 21

Identification: 15″. Sexes similar. Recognised by crest, brown upperparts boldly spotted with white, long graduated tail conspicuously tipped with white, and creamy-white underparts. Juveniles lack the crest and have rufous primaries. Not shy. Perches conspicuously. Very noisy in the breeding season.

Voice: A loud repeated 'krit-chit-chik' and a 'kook' alarm call. Silent outside the breeding season.

Distribution and Habitat: Local but widespread in the savanna, especially in the arid north, and numbers augmented in dry season by wintering European birds. Widely recorded except in the wet forest from Senegal east to Chad and the Central African Republic and south to the Congo savanna.

Nesting: In West Africa commonly parasitises the Pied Crow (*Corvus albus*), as many as ten Cuckoo's eggs being laid in one nest with those of the fostering Crow. Eggs pale bluish-green spotted and blotched with brown and lilac and closely matching the eggs of the Crow but smaller, heavier and more elliptical.

PIED CRESTED CUCKOO *Clamator jacobinus* Pl. 21

Identification: 13″. A long-tailed crested Cuckoo, black above, white below. Occasionally black or grey breasted examples (migrant *C. j. serratus* from southern Africa). White patch on the wing a field mark. Distinguished from the rather similar Levaillant's Cuckoo (*Clamator levaillantii*) by its smaller size, slimmer build, and the absence of bold black streaks on the throat. Flight straight and swift.

Voice: In the breeding season a variety of loud calls, harsh, guttural, or piping.

Distribution and Habitat: Senegal through Mali, Upper Volta, Ghana, Niger, and Nigeria to Chad. Especially common in the semi-arid parts of Mali and Niger bordering the Sahara. Records from the forest are probably of birds on passage. Resident and migrant.

Nesting: Brood-parasitic. In Ethiopia it victimises the Babbler (*Turdoides fulvus*) and in southern Africa it victimises mainly Bulbul and Shrike species. An oviduct egg collected near Timbuctoo was white but the usual colour in tropical Africa is immaculate bluish-green.

LEVAILLANT'S CUCKOO *Clamator levaillantii* Pl. 21

Identification: 16″. Sexes similar. In flight large white wing patch and long graduated white-tipped tail catch the eye. Settled, upperparts glossy black except for small white wing patch, underparts white with heavy black streaks on the throat. Head crested. Immature plumage brown above, buff below, and lacks white tail tips. The larger size and streaked breast distinguish it from the rather similar Pied Cuckoo (*Clamator jacobinus*). Feeds largely on caterpillars.

Voice: Loud, raucous, far-carrying and characteristic, consisting of several well-spaced 'kiou' calls followed by a rapid series of up to twenty 'kiou' notes.

Distribution and Habitat: Common and widely distributed throughout the area in all zones south of 16° N. but absent from closed forest. Frequents mainly trees and thickets in the savanna. Migratory with a general movement north in the rains and south in the dry season.

Nesting: In West Africa parasitises the Brown Babbler (*Turdoides plebeja*). Eggs pale greenish-blue, pink or white, sometimes closely matching the fosterer's in shade.

RED-CHESTED CUCKOO   *Cuculus solitarius*   **Pl. 21**
Identification: 12". Reddish chest a good field mark. Upperparts and chin
slate-grey, lower breast and belly creamy-buff heavily barred with black. See
Black Cuckoo for plumage differences from that species. Usually perched
motionless in the foliage of a tree top and easily overlooked were it not for its
loud distinctive call.
Voice: A loud resonant descending 'mak-bak-bo'. Calls persistently through
the day and often into the night.
Distribution and Habitat: Widespread in Africa. In our area from Senegal
and Gambia to Nigeria, the Cameroons, Chad, Central African Republic,
Gaboon and Fernando Po. A common resident forest species, found also in the
moister wooded savanna. Ascends the mountain forests to 6,000 feet.
Nesting: Breeds in West Africa but its breeding habits are unknown. In
southern Africa it parasitises mainly Thrush species and lays a glossy uniform
chocolate-brown egg.

BLACK CUCKOO   *Cuculus clamosus*   **Pl. 21**
Identification: 12". The voice is most distinctive and the best guide to
recognition. The savanna race (*C. c. clamosus*) appears blackish all over in the
field except that in immature birds the underparts are barred rufous and
blackish. The forest race (*C. c. gabonensis*) is black above but has a rufous
throat and breast and the remainder of the underparts are banded blackish
and buff. In the field it is very like the Red-chested Cuckoo but its upperparts
are darker and glossier and its chin is reddish not grey.
Voice: Three plaintive notes rising in pitch with occasionally a pause followed
by a repetition of the third note of the phrase. Less commonly a bubbling trill
that ascends and then descends the scale. Call heard at all times of the day,
quite commonly in the late evening when other birds are silent, and occasionally
through the night.
Distribution and Habitat: The rufous-chested forest race (*C. c. gabonensis*)
is resident and common in the lowland and montane forest belt of Liberia,
Ivory Coast, Ghana, Nigeria, the Cameroons and Gaboon. It affects primary
and second-growth and the trees of clearings. The black-breasted race (*C. c.
clamosus*) occurs in the savanna as far west as the Gambia and also occasionally
in the forest. Its status is uncertain. It may be a migrant only in our area.
Nesting: Egg cream profusely marked especially about the large end with
brown and grey blotches and spots. The Black Cuckoo is parasitic. In southern
Africa it victimises mainly Shrike species.

COMMON CUCKOO   *Cuculus canorus*   **Pl. 21**
Identification: 15". Sexes rather similar. The rather hawk-like appearance in
flight, the long pointed wings, long graduated white-tipped tail, and, especially,
the call distinguish it. Upperparts and chest grey; breast and belly white with
dark bars. The migrant (European) race has the bill mainly blackish. The
resident (African) race has the bill mainly yellow with a black tip.
Voice: At the breeding season the resident race utters a far-carrying 'coo-coo',
the second syllable of the call being stressed.
Distribution and Habitat: The Cuckoo is represented in West Africa by a
resident race (*C. canorus gularis*). It also occurs as a spring and autumn migrant
from Europe (*C. c. canorus*) recorded from the Cape Verde Islands, Senegal,

Plate 23

KINGFISHERS AND ROLLERS

23

24

Plate 24

BEE-EATERS, HOOPOE AND WOOD-HOOPOES

Gambia, Portuguese Guinea, Liberia, Nigeria, Cameroons and Chad. The resident race is widely distributed in the savanna ranging from Senegal and Gambia east to the Cameroon highlands and Chad and south to Congo.

Nesting: In breeding condition and calling January–April. In southern Africa the eggs of *C. c. gularis* are variable in colour: some resemble the eggs of the Drongo (*Dicrurus adsimilis*), an authenticated host.

KLAAS'S CUCKOO *Chrysococcyx klaas (Lampromorpha klaasi)* **Pl. 21**
Identification: 7″. Call unmistakable. In both sexes practically white three outermost tail feathers distinguish it from the Didric Cuckoo. Male has metallic green and bronze upperparts, white underparts, and green patch on each side of the throat. Female has mainly bronzy upperparts and white underparts finely barred brown on the flanks. Juvenile closely barred upper and underparts and hardly separable in the field from juvenile Emerald Cuckoo (*Chrysococcyx cupreus*) but the latter has white-tipped crown feathers.
Voice: A quite diagnostic 'phay-it-it phay-it-it' rather plaintive in quality.
Distribution and Habitat: Widely and in the main commonly distributed throughout the area in a wide variety of habitat in both savanna and forest but absent from the desert edges north of 16° 30′ N. A local migrant.
Nesting: In West Africa parasitises Flycatcher and Warbler species and the White-eye (*Zosterops senegalensis*). Eggs in southern Africa variable, white or blue, spotted or unmarked.

DIDRIC CUCKOO *Chrysococcyx caprius (Lampromorpha caprius)* **Pl. 21**
Identification: 7½″. Call unmistakable. In both sexes outer tail feathers dark with white spots. Male has metallic green and bronze upperparts, white eyebrow, and conspicuous white spots on wing; white underparts but flanks barred greenish. Female duller and also more extensively barred below; white eyebrow indistinct. Juvenile resembles female. Its coral red bill distinguishes it from juvenile Klaas and Emerald Cuckoos.
Voice: A diagnostic 'deea-deea-deedaric', far-carrying and at the breeding season at least frequently repeated.
Distribution and Habitat: Very widely and commonly distributed throughout the area south of 17° N. in a wide variety of habitat in forest (except closed forest) and savanna. A local migrant, absent from the arid north in the dry season.
Nesting: Parasitic, particularly on Weaver species. In southern Africa eggs are pale blue or white, immaculate or variously marked.

EMERALD CUCKOO *Chrysococcyx cupreus*   **Pl. 21**
Identification: 9″. Call-note is unmistakable. Usually perched motionless, hidden high up in the foliage. When seen the male easily distinguished by iridescent green upperparts and breast and vivid yellow belly. The female and the juvenile are copper and green above and finely barred green and white below.
Voice: A characteristic clear vehement far-carrying whistle of three syllables. The male is a persistent caller.
Distribution and Habitat: Common and resident in the high rain forest from Sierra Leone to Gaboon and Congo. Its range extends into the gallery forests of the savanna from Gambia and Senegal to the Central African Republic

and it is resident on the islands of Fernando Po, Principe and Sao Tome. Usually in the high forest tree-tops; occasionally low down in the second-growth, or in the trees of forest clearings.

Nesting: Breeding habits in our area unknown. In southern Africa it parasitises Warbler and Weaver species and its egg is white or white speckled with brown or purple.

YELLOWBILL COUCAL *Ceuthmochares aereus*   Pl. 22

Identification: 13″. A slimly built long-tailed species with a conspicuous yellow bill. Upperparts except the head dark glossy blue with purplish or greenish reflections. Head and underparts grey. Active and agile and usually concealed in thick leafy growth. Often in pairs and occasionally joins the mixed bird parties of the forest.

Voice: A curious harsh low-pitched 'chaaa' repeated two or three times a minute. A prolonged clicking chatter is also described.

Distribution and Habitat: In forest or savanna where there is good cover. Thickets in outlying savanna woods and dense second-growth in the main body of the forest attract it. Usually near the ground yet found at all heights provided the foliage is dense. Ranges from Senegal and Gambia east to the Central African Republic and south to Gaboon and Congo. Also Fernando Po.

Nesting: Eggs 2–3, white ellipses, unglossed. A nest in Ghana was built of twigs and leaves and placed in the fork of a sapling about 8 feet from the ground.

BLACK COUCAL *Centropus grillii*   Pl. 22

Identification: 14″. Sexes similar. Entirely black underparts distinguish it in breeding plumage from all other Coucals. Head, neck and tail black, mantle brown, wings mainly rufous. In non-breeding and immature plumage upperparts streaked rufous and black and underparts buff with blackish spots on the breast. Characteristic clumsy, heavy Coucal flight. Shy and seldom emerges from thick herbaceous cover.

Voice: A bubbling call resembling that of the Senegal Coucal but softer and mellower.

Distribution and Habitat: Characteristically inhabits open plains of rank grass or reeds near or in water. Widespread but local and mainly in savanna localities. Not north of 14° 30′ N. Recorded from Senegal, Gambia, Portuguese Guinea, Ivory Coast, Mali, Ghana, Togo, Nigeria, Cameroons, Chad, Central African Republic, Gaboon and Congo.

Nesting: A large spherical grass nest well-concealed low down in rank herbage. Eggs 4, white.

BLACK-THROATED COUCAL *Centropus leucogaster*   Pl. 22

Identification: 20″. A large ungainly forest Coucal with a long and broad tail, a slow laboured flight, and a deep sonorous call. Shy and skulking; usually near the ground. Head, throat, chest and upperparts black except for the back and wings which are chestnut. Lower breast and belly white.

Voice: A typical Coucal call, lower pitched and louder than that of the familiar Senegal Coucal, with a hollow plaintive quality; a succession of about twenty 'hoos' which at first increase in rate and volume and at the end die away.

Distribution and Habitat: The range is the forest zone from Guinea and Sierra Leone to the Cameroons and Gaboon. It frequents thick cover in partially

Plate 25

OWLS

1♂

2♂

3♀

4♂

♀

5

Plate 26

NIGHTJARS

1. **PLAIN NIGHTJAR** *Caprimulgus inornatus* page 118
White-tipped outer rectrices; in flight white wing-patch.

2. **WEST AFRICAN FRECKLED NIGHTJAR**
Caprimulgus tristigma 118
Blackish upperparts; white-tipped outer rectrices.

3. **LONG-TAILED NIGHTJAR** *Caprimulgus climacurus* 119
Long graduated tail; in flight white wing-patch.

4. **PENNANT-WINGED NIGHTJAR** *Macrodipteryx vexillarius* 120
Mainly white lower breast and belly.

5. **STANDARD-WING NIGHTJAR** *Macrodipteryx longipennis* 119
Female: resembles male but lacks standards.
Male: conspicuous standards; square tail; no white tail spots or wing patches.

cut-out primary forest, old second-growth, and young oil-palm plantations in forest clearings.

Nesting: Eggs usually 2, white, elliptical. Nest domed, a large ball of leaves and grass built in a shrub or young tree.

Allied species: The Blue-headed Coucal (*Centropus monachus*) ranges from Ghana east to Lake Chad and the Central African Republic and south to Gaboon and Congo. It is locally common in the thick herbage of forest clearings, especially in damp places, and also occurs sparingly in the savanna zone adjoining the forest. Its range overlaps that of the Senegal Coucal, the common savanna species. The two birds have the same general appearance and colour pattern but the Blue-headed Coucal can be distinguished by its larger size and the bluish not greenish sheen on the nape and mantle.

SENEGAL COUCAL   *Centropus senegalensis*   **Pl. 22**

Identification: 15″. Sexes similar. Crown, nape and tail black glossed with green, mantle and wings chestnut, underparts whitish. Can be confused with the Blue-headed Coucal but the latter is larger and the sheen on the nape and mantle is bluish not greenish. In immature dress upperparts barred black and breast buff. A rufous phase with rich chestnut underparts (formerly known as *C. epomidis*) occurs and is particularly common in south-western Nigeria. Flies low with weak uncertain wing beats and pitches awkwardly into its perch in bush or thicket. Often on the ground, where it walks slowly and hunts small vertebrates and grasshoppers.

Voice: A prolonged 'hu-hu-hu-hu-hu-hu-hu' in descending pitch aptly likened to water bubbling from a bottle. Also sharp clucking calls.

Distribution and Habitat: Widespread and abundant south of 17° N. except in closed forest. Frequents thickets, dense grass patches, reed-beds and gardens with shrubs.

Nesting: A large, loosely built, domed, spherical nest of coarse grasses lined with leaves and placed low down in a shrub. Eggs 2–4, white.

OWLS: Strigidae

Large or medium-sized birds of prey that usually hunt by night and roost during the day. Plumage soft and flight silent. Large head and eyes and strong, hooked bill. Facial discs and, in many species, 'ear tufts' are characteristic. Upright posture when perched. Call often distinctive.

BARN OWL   *Tyto alba*   **Pl. 25**

Identification: 12″. Sexes similar. A pale Owl. Upperparts pale golden-buff vermiculated with grey-brown and white; underparts white lightly spotted. White facial discs. Black eyes. No ear-tufts. Upright stance on long legs. Nocturnal.

Voice: Call a shrill screech. Also various hissing and snoring noises. Snaps bill loudly when disturbed at nest.

Distribution and Habitat: Widespread and common from Mauritania, Gambia and Senegal east to Chad and the Central African Republic and south to Gaboon and Congo, in plain, mountain, desert, savanna and forest. Also

Cape Verde Islands, Fernando Po and Sao Tome. Varied habitat but partial to built-up areas where the rodents associated with man are available.
Nesting: Eggs laid in hollows in rocks or trees, in buildings, chimneys or roofs, or in the old nests of the Hammerkop. Clutch 4–6 and up to 12 recorded. Eggs white.

SCOPS OWL *Otus scops* (*O. senegalensis, O. leucopsis*) Pl. 25

Identification: 7″–8″. Sexes similar. A very small nocturnal Owl. Ear-tufts usually erect and prominent when the bird is perched. At a distance brown. At close range grey or rufous-grey finely streaked and vermiculated with brown and black.
Voice: Call a single far-carrying piping, quavering 'kloo' frequently repeated.
Distribution and Habitat: Widespread but local in the savanna. The West African mainland race is recorded from Senegal, Gambia, Portuguese Guinea, Mali, Ivory Coast, Ghana, Nigeria, Chad, Central African Republic and Congo. Island races occur on Sao Tome and Annobon, and the larger migratory Palaearctic race, which is indistinguishable in the field, is recorded (September–March) from Senegal, Liberia, Ivory Coast, Mali, Ghana, Nigeria and Chad.
Nesting: Eggs 3, white, laid in a hole in a tree.

WHITE-FACED OWL *Otus leucotis* (*Ptilopsis leucotis*) Pl. 25

Identification: 10″. Sexes similar. Appreciably larger than the Scops Owl. The white face encircled with a thin black line and the long black ear-tufts are distinctive. At close range bill whitish, crown dark brown, mantle grey-brown with dark streaks, underparts whitish with black streaks. Mainly nocturnal, perching by day in a savanna tree.
Call: A rather soft 'kuh-cooo'.
Distribution and Habitat: Widely distributed and locally common except in closed rain forest, ranging from Senegal and Gambia east to Chad and south to Gaboon and Congo. Penetrates at least to 17° N. and in the Cameroons highlands ascends to 5,000 feet.
Nesting: Eggs laid in a tree in a natural hole or on top of the nest of a hawk, dove, or other species. Eggs 2–4, white.
Allied species: The Maned Owl (*Lophostrix letti*) is a rare species recorded in our area from Liberia, Ghana, the Cameroons, and Rio Muni from localities in the main body of the forest and its gallery extensions. Length 12″. Colour predominantly rufous. The facial disc is rufous rimmed with black; the prominent ear-tufts are rufous and white tipped with black; the crown and wing-coverts are white-spotted, and the underparts are dark-streaked.

SPOTTED EAGLE-OWL *Bubo africanus* Pl. 25

Identification: 17″. Finely and profusely vermiculated and obscurely barred, spotted, and blotched in brown, grey, sepia, white and buff. The general appearance is of a large greyish Owl without any outstanding plumage characters. The tail is barred but not prominently. The ear-tufts are apparent in the field. Facial disc ill-defined. Known by its call, nocturnal activity, tameness, addiction to open places near towns and villages, and its habit of settling on the earth roads at night or perching conspicuously on a roadside tree or rock.
Voice: A soft 'hoo-hoo' or 'hoo-hoo-hoo' not nearly so loud or resonant as the call of the European Tawny Owl.

Distribution and Habitat: Widely and commonly distributed in the savanna from Senegal and Portuguese Guinea east to Chad and the Central African Republic and south to Gaboon and Congo. Found in the vicinity of towns and villages, in orchard-bush, thorn-scrub and remote rocky hills. Absent from the true forest.

Nesting: Eggs white rounded ovals, two in number, laid in a hole in a tree or on the ground under a rock on a hillside, or on a cliff ledge. No nest made.

FRASER'S EAGLE-OWL *Bubo poensis*   **Pl. 25**
Identification: 17″. Nocturnal, roosting by day in thick foliage where it is sometimes mobbed by small birds. Dark rufous above, pale rufous below, narrowly barred all over in a darker shade, conspicuous ear-tufts and black-rimmed facial disc.

Voice: A captured bird uttered high-pitched dismal moaning sounds during the night and also made snapping noises with its bill.

Distribution and habitat: A lowland forest Owl found from Liberia to Gaboon and on the island of Fernando Po.

Nesting: Habits unknown.

Allied species: The Akun Eagle-Owl (*Bubo leucostictus*), 18″, is another little-known species that ranges in the forest from Sierra Leone to Gaboon. Upper-parts very dark brown indistinctly barred with pale brown; upper breast dark brown; lower breast and belly white, blotched and lightly barred with brown. Prominent long ear-tufts, dark with a white inner margin.

MILKY EAGLE-OWL *Bubo lacteus*   **Pl. 25**
Identification: 23″. Sexes similar. A massive grey-brown Owl with very pale underparts and long ear-tufts. At close range the large brown eyes, pink eyelids, long thick rictal bristles and greyish facial discs fringed with black distinguish it. Plumage finely vermiculated. Tail barred. By day sits immobile in the foliage of a tall tree.

Voice: A very low, muted 'hoo-hoo-hoo', the notes rising in pitch. Sometimes calls in broad daylight.

Distribution and Habitat: Widely but rather thinly distributed in the dry open belt of West Africa north of the forest from southern Mauritania, Senegal and Gambia east to Chad and the Central African Republic. Tall trees on a river bank attract it.

Nesting: In southern Africa lays 2 white eggs in a hollow tree or on top of an old nest of a Hawk or a Hammerkop.

PEL'S FISHING OWL *Scotopelia peli*   **Pl. 25**
Identification: 24″. A nocturnal, riverine Owl, stockily built with a massive round head. No ear-tufts. Known by its tawny plumage, rich in shade above with dark barring, and paler in shade below with dark spotting. It feeds on fish and the powerful feet are spiculate on the under surface like an Osprey's.

Voice: A loud resonant snoring note. Also a loud screech.

Distribution and Habitat: Inhabits forested river banks in the main body of the forest and its gallery extensions in the savanna, ranging from Senegal and Gambia east to the Central African Republic and south to Gaboon and Congo, but nowhere common.

Nesting: In south Africa the site of the nest is a hole in a tree.

PEARL-SPOTTED OWLET *Glaucidium perlatum* **Pl. 25**
Identification: 7″. Sexes similar. A small, compact Owl without ear-tufts, having the upperparts including the wings and tail brown spotted with white and the underparts white blotched and streaked with rufous-brown. Nocturnal but sometimes discovered by day in flight or being mobbed at its perch by small birds.
Voice: Far-carrying and often heard by day and constantly at night. A series of shrill piping notes ascending and then descending the scale and ending softly. Also a 'hui-oo' cry.
Distribution and Habitat: Well distributed in the wooded and bushy savanna north of the forest from Senegal (to 16° N.) and Gambia east to Chad and the Central African Republic.
Nesting: Eggs 3, white, laid in a hole in a tree.
Allied species: The Yellow-legged Owlet (*Glaucidium tephronotum*), 8″, is about the same size as the Pearl-spotted Owlet. It is a rare forest bird known in our area only from Liberia, Ghana and the Cameroons. Upperparts slate-grey or chocolate-brown, the mantle spotted with white; underparts, except for the rufous breast, mainly white with blackish spots and streaks; white spots on the inner webs of the tail feathers. Sjöstedt's Barred Owlet (*Glaucidium sjöstedti*) is another little-known forest Owl recorded from the Cameroons and Congo. It is larger than the Pearl-spotted Owlet. Mainly chestnut above, narrowly barred with white on the mantle and tail; buff below barred with chestnut on the breast and flanks.

WEST AFRICAN WOOD-OWL *Ciccaba woodfordi*
(*Strix woodfordi*)   **Pl. 25**
Identification: 13″. A nocturnal forest Owl with a distinctive call. Distinguished by its dark chocolate upperparts spotted on the scapulars with white and its barred chocolate and white underparts. No ear-tufts. Roosts by day in a thickly foliaged forest tree and often mobbed by small birds.
Voice: A characteristic 'hoo-hu hoo-hu hu-hu' of constant rhythm.
Distribution and Habitat: Widely distributed in Africa. In our area resident in the forest and its gallery extensions from Senegal and Sierra Leone to the Central African Republic and south to Gaboon and Congo, being recorded from many localities. It ascends the forested mountains to over 7,000 feet.
Nesting: The site is a hole in a forest tree. One white egg is laid.

AFRICAN MARSH-OWL *Asio capensis* **Pl. 25**
Identification: 14″. Diurnal and nocturnal. When it is flushed it often circles round tamely and inquisitively. It is then easy to see the black circles round the eye which are very conspicuous and contrast sharply with the rest of the facial disc, which is whitish. Plumage mainly brown but thighs and belly pale rufous-buff.
Voice: A croaking 'kaaa' uttered in flight and also on the ground.
Distribution and Habitat: Locally common in the Niger Inundation Zone in Mali, on the Jos Plateau of Nigeria and the grasslands of the Cameroon highlands and recorded from a number of other localities in Chad and Nigeria. The habitat is thick marshy herbage or swamp in open country. Resident.
Nesting: The nest is on the ground well concealed in rank herbage in a swamp. The eggs, three to six in number, are white rounded ovals.

Allied species: The Short-eared Owl (*Asio flammeus*), 15″, is an uncommon winter visitor (November–April) from the Palaearctic region recorded from Senegal, Gambia, Lake Chad and the Jos Plateau of Nigeria. It frequents open damp grasslands. The habitat, slow deliberate flight usually near the ground, long wings, virtually invisible ear-tufts and well-marked facial disc are the best field characters.

NIGHTJARS: Caprimulgidae

Nocturnal, insectivorous birds that capture their prey in flight. Rest by day on the ground where their immobility and cryptic coloration make them hard to see. Large eyes and gapes. Soft plumage and silent flight. Some species have conspicuous nuptial plumes projecting from the wing or tail.

PLAIN NIGHTJAR   *Caprimulgus inornatus*   **Pl. 26**
Identification: 9″. Some examples are grey, some rufous, and some inter-mediate in shade. The male has a white wing patch and the two outermost tail feathers are broadly tipped with white. In the female the wing patches and tail tips are rufous. No white throat patch and only a few dark angular markings on the upper surface. Active in the late evening when it can be seen flying up from the ground in pursuit of insects or flitting noiselessly over the thorn scrub.
Voice: Described as a sewing machine-like 'tchur-rr'.
Distribution and Habitat: In the wet season common along the southern edge of the Sahara in Mauritania, Senegal, Mali, Niger and Chad. In the dry season a movement south. In Liberia, Ivory Coast, Ghana, Nigeria, the Cameroons, and the Central African Republic population probably a mixed one of sedentary residents and (in the dry season) immigrants from the north.
Nesting: No local records. In the Somali Republic it nests on the bare ground and lays two eggs. These are highly polished, ivory coloured, marbled with light red-brown shading into lilac.
Allied species: The Golden Nightjar (*Caprimulgus eximius*) is a species of the southern edge of the Sahara. It is distinguished by its upperparts, which are golden-buff barred and speckled with black and white. The underparts are mainly palest buff. The white throat patch and wing patch and the white-tipped outer rectrices of the male are all field marks but they are shared with several other Nightjars. The call is a low-pitched 'churr'. The Golden Nightjar so far as is known is sedentary and inhabits the dry grassy scrub country of Senegal, Mali, Niger, northern Nigeria and Chad.

WEST AFRICAN FRECKLED NIGHTJAR   *Caprimulgus tristigma*
Pl. 26
Identification: 10½″. A heavy squat, noticeably dark-coloured Nightjar. The upperparts are blackish, finely freckled with grey. Both sexes have a broad white throat patch and a white wing patch and the male has also white-tipped outer rectrices. Associated with bare rocky hills in the savanna. By day they rest on the bare rock when their immobility and protective coloration make them almost impossible to see. More easily located at night for then they frequent the laterite roads and can be picked out and identified in the headlights of a car.
Voice: Call described as a weird 'whow-whow' repeated over and over again.

Distribution and Habitat: Recorded from scattered savanna localities in Guinea, Ivory Coast, Mali, Ghana, Nigeria, Cameroons and the Central African Republic, always apparently where there are rocky hills.

Nesting: The two eggs are laid on the bare rock of a granite inselberg and are described as white spotted with brown and grey.

Allied species: The Black-shouldered Nightjar (*Caprimulgus pectoralis*), 9″, is richly coloured, the upperparts warm brown heavily blotched and streaked with black and rufous. Both sexes have the white patches on the throat, wings and outer tail feathers found in many species of Nightjar. The tail is square. This is a somewhat local bird recorded from Portuguese Guinea, Sierra Leone, Nigeria, the Cameroons, Gaboon and the Central African Republic from places where the forest and savanna meet. By day it rests quietly on the ground in primary or secondary forest near its edge. The call, which is heard at night, is a melancholy, tremulous, 'twip-turr-r-r-r-r-r'. The White-tailed Nightjar (*Caprimulgus natalensis*) is distinguished by the large amount of white on the two outer tail feathers; on the outer web the white extends nearly to the base of the feather. The upperparts are greyish-brown with bold triangular black markings. Recorded from a few localities in Mali, Liberia, Ghana, Nigeria, the Cameroons, Chad, Gaboon and Congo. Addicted to marshy patches in open savanna country and sometimes flushed at night from roads and tracks near such places.

LONG-TAILED NIGHTJAR   *Caprimulgus climacurus*
(*Scotornis climacurus*)   **Pl. 26**

Identification: 11″. A small Nightjar with a very long graduated tail. Often seen on the road at night when its red shining eyes show up in the lights of the car. Plumage varies geographically. Upperparts greyish-brown or rufous-brown or blackish-brown, streaked, freckled and barred with gold and blackish, and with a small white shoulder patch visible at rest and a large white wing patch visible in flight. Underparts mainly buff. Female has a much shorter tail and the wing patches are washed with rufous. By day lies closely in the lee of some shrub or tuft of grass. Active at night frequenting bush paths and motor roads.

Voice: Noisy. Song a sustained purr. Call a frequent 'chong'.

Distribution and Habitat: Very common and widespread throughout the area south of 17° N. in the thorn scrub, moist savanna, and forest clearings, but not in the closed forest. Part of the population migratory, shifting south in the dry season.

Nesting: Eggs 2, laid on the bare ground. Buff or cream suffused, marbled, and blotched with pale grey, brown and tawny.

STANDARD-WING NIGHTJAR   *Macrodipteryx longipennis*   **Pl. 26**

Identification: 9″. Sexes similar but female lacks breeding plumes. Male readily recognised in breeding season by greatly elongated ninth primary consisting of 9″ of bare shaft terminating in 7″ of broad web. At dusk or in moonlight the shafts are invisible and the plumes 'follow' the Nightjar like two black butterflies. A small square-tailed Nightjar mainly dark brown above with, at close range, a faint rufous collar, black and buff shoulder markings, and barred rufous and black flight feathers. No white patches on wing shoulder. Underparts mainly buff with narrow dark bars. By day rests on the ground and seldom seen till kicked up.

Voice: A shrill churring.

Distribution and Habitat: Widespread and common north of the forest from Gambia and Senegal to Chad and the Central African Republic penetrating in the wet season at least as far as 17° N. Shows a preference for bare stony ground with scattered shrubs.

Nesting: Eggs 2, laid on the bare ground. Pale salmon blotched, smeared, and spotted with chestnut and brown and with ashy shellmarks.

PENNANT-WINGED NIGHTJAR *Macrodipteryx vexillarius*
(*Cosmetornis vexillarius*) **Pl. 26**

Identification: 12″. A large stoutly built Nightjar having the belly mainly white. Males in breeding plumage easily identified by the very long streamer-like ninth primary; but these streamers are usually shed before the birds arrive in West Africa from their southern breeding places and are usually only partly developed at the time they depart.

Voice: Silent in West Africa.

Distribution and Habitat: The Pennant-winged Nightjar breeds south of the equator and migrates to pass the non-breeding season in the savannas of West Africa north of the forest, where it is found from February until July. Also recorded on migration from a few localities in Cameroons and Fernando Po.

Nesting: Does not breed within our limits.

SWIFTS: Apodidae

Insectivorous aerial birds with long, curved, pointed wings and powerful, swift and often erratic flight. The plain colours, rapid flight, and the difficulty of observing them at rest hinders their specific identification. Flight, silhouette, habitat and locality are useful aids to identification.

MOTTLED SWIFT *Apus aequatorialis* **Pl. 27**

Identification: 8¼″. A very large Swift with unusually powerful and rapid flight. Normally seen on the wing. Dark brown with a white throat. In the race occurring in Sierra Leone the middle of the breast and belly are barred dark brown and white, but in the Bamenda race these parts appear uniformly dark in the field.

Voice: A shrill cry, often uttered in chorus by a compact flock of birds displaying spectacularly over the crags where they live.

Distribution and Habitat: Widely but discontinuously distributed in Africa, usually in mountainous localities with crags and escarpments. In West Africa it occurs in Sierra Leone, the Bamenda highlands of the Cameroons, and the Ennedi mountains of Chad. A sight record from Ghana.

Nesting: Unrecorded.

EUROPEAN SWIFT *Apus apus* (*Micropus apus*) **Pl. 27**

Identification: 6½″. Sexes similar. Uniformly dark brown plumage, very long and narrow wings, short, slightly forked tail, and strong, rapid, wheeling, erratic flight are all distinctive. Usually gregarious, and, except when roosting, aerial. In the field difficult to distinguish from the paler Mouse-coloured Swift (*Apus pallidus*) (see Checklist, p. 274), which occurs sparingly in the dry northern zone, and from the darker Black Swift (*Apus barbatus*) (see Checklist, p. 274), which is, however, mainly restricted to Fernando Po.

Distribution and Habitat: A spring and autumn passage migrant from the Palaearctic Region widely recorded in West Africa in all vegetation zones from Mali and Senegal to the Cameroons and Chad. Winter records comparatively few but from February to May numbers progressively increase.

Allied species: The Alpine Swift (*Apus melba*), 8½", is known from West Africa by a very few scattered sight records. The pale brown upperparts and breast band and the white belly distinguish it.

BATES'S BLACK SWIFT   *Apus batesi* (*Micropus batesi*)   **Pl. 27**
Identification: A small slender glossy black Swift without any white in the plumage; tail forked when open, pointed when shut; flight rapid and sustained. Usually in small flocks hawking for insects.

Voice: Not known.

Distribution and Habitat: A rare species known from two or three localities in the Cameroons and Gaboon forest and the adjoining savanna. Sight record from Liberia.

Nesting: They occupy the retort-shaped mud nests of a forest Swallow, probably *Hirundo fuliginosa*, the whole interior of the nest being relined with vegetable down, feathers, and inspissated saliva. Two white eggs are laid.

WHITE-RUMPED SWIFT   *Apus caffer* (*Micropus caffer*)   **Pl. 27**
Identification: 6". A dark Swift with a white rump. Distinguished from the commoner Little African Swift (*Apus affinis*), which also has a white rump, by the form of the tail, which is forked when the rectrices are spread and pointed when they are closed. *Apus affinis* has a square tail. Differs from the Horus Swift (*Apus horus*) (see Checklist, p. 274), which occurs in Cabinda and Chad by being slimmer and in having the tail more deeply forked.

Voice: A low twittering chatter.

Distribution and Habitat: In West Africa recorded from several localities, mainly in the savanna, in Senegal, Gambia, Ivory Coast, Ghana, Nigeria, Chad, Central African Republic, Gaboon and Congo.

Nesting: They breed in the retort-shaped mud nests built in road and rail culverts and under house eaves by *Hirundo abyssinica* and *Hirundo semirufa*, dispossessing the Swallows and relining the interior of the nest with grass, vegetable down, feathers and inspissated saliva. The eggs are pure white and two in number.

LITTLE AFRICAN SWIFT   *Apus affinis* (*Colletoptera affinis*)   **Pl. 27**
Identification: 5". Sexes similar. A blackish Swift with a very conspicuous white rump, a white throat and a pale forehead. Flight strong and swift with occasional glides. Ussher's Spine-tailed Swift (*Chaetura ussheri*) at a distance is rather similar but has the characteristic 'loose-jointed' Spinetail flight. The White-rumped Swift (*Apus caffer*) is also rather similar but has a strongly forked tail. Tame. Gregarious. Town-lover. Life centred on the breeding colony throughout the year.

Voice: A short, sharp squeal.

Distribution and Habitat: Widely and abundantly distributed throughout the area including the islands of Fernando Po, Sao Tome and Principe. In the dry season numbers swelled by immigrant Palaearctic *A. affinis galilejensis*. Seldom seen at any distance from towns and villages.

Nesting: Usually in colonies in such sites as the eaves and thatched roofs of buildings and the masonry of bridges. An untidy nest of grass and feathers stuck together with saliva. Occasionally utilises spouted Swallows' nests in the manner of *Apus caffer*. Eggs 2–3, white.

PALM SWIFT *Cypsiurus parvus*   **Pl. 27**
Identification: 7″. A very slender grey-brown Swift nearly always found near palm trees. Long and narrow wings; long tail strongly forked when spread, pointed when closed.
Voice: A shrill, thin scream.
Distribution and Habitat: Common and widespread throughout the area south of 16° N., usually associated with the Borassus Palm or the Dum Palm in the savanna and with the Oil Palm or Coconut Palm in the forest. Sedentary. Usually in small colonies.
Nesting: Nest on the underside of a drooping palm frond. A pad of feathers cemented together and to the palm with saliva. Two white eggs laid on a little hollowed-out shelf at lower end of pad and stuck to the nest with saliva.

USSHER'S SPINE-TAILED SWIFT *Chaetura ussheri*   **Pl. 27**
Identification: 5½″. A dark Swift with a white rump and a white patch on the belly. Could be mistaken for the Little African Swift (*Apus affinis*) but the loose-jointed flight characteristic of the Spine-tails, the call, and the white on the belly distinguish it. Tail noticeably longer than in Cassin's Spine-tail. Occurs in pairs.
Voice: A distinctive, rasping, twittering call, frequently uttered.
Distribution and Habitat: Widely but locally distributed in both forest and savanna from Senegal and Gambia to the Cameroons. Common in parts of the Cameroons forest where most large village clearings boast a pair or two. Often in the vicinity of dwellings or tall hollow forest trees.
Nesting: A small saucer-shaped nest inside a hollow tree. The eggs are pure white. Clutch 2.
Allied species: Sabine's Spine-tail (*Chaetura sabini*), 4½″, is a glossy black Swift distinguished by its small size and its conspicuous white belly, rump, upper and under tail-coverts. The call is a rather feeble high-pitched note not unlike that of the Palm Swift. Partial to lakes, large rivers, and open waterways in the mangroves and the swamp forest. Usually in small parties, but as many as fifty seen on occasions. Often keeps company with Cassin's Spine-tail and other Swift species. It ranges in the forest from Sierra Leone to the Cameroons and Gaboon and the island of Fernando Po.

CASSIN'S SPINE-TAILED SWIFT *Chaetura cassini*   **Pl. 27**
Identification: 6″. Easily identified as a Spine-tail by its silhouette and peculiar loose-jointed flight. The large size, the long notched wings and the very short tail identify it as Cassin's Spine-tail. The white rump and belly are useful field marks only at close range; high in the sky it appears black. Usually encountered hawking for insects over lakes or clearings in forest country and often in the company of Swallows and other Swifts.
Distribution and Habitat: The forest belt of Liberia, Ivory Coast, Ghana, Nigeria, the Cameroons, Gaboon and Fernando Po. In the Cameroons it is rather common in the high forest where there are lakes. Usually in small flocks but sometimes up to forty together.
Nesting: Nest inside a hollow forest tree. Eggs white.

COLIES OR MOUSEBIRDS: Coliidae

BAR-BREASTED MOUSEBIRD *Colius striatus* **Pl. 22**
Identification: 12″. Unmistakable. A slim, crested, short-winged bird with a very long tail; brownish in colour with a black face and bright coral-red feet, which are conspicuous when it is perched with legs straddled. In parties of five to ten or even twenty individuals. They clamber actively about the twigs and branches, often hanging upside down, and fly from shrub to shrub in straggling formation.
Voice: Little sharp cries uttered at rest and in flight.
Distribution and Habitat: The moister savanna and the edges and clearings of the forest from Nigeria east to the Central African Republic and south to Gaboon and Congo. In the Cameroons where it is abundant on the borders of the mountain forests it ascends to 7,500 feet. Widespread and locally common. Fond of gardens, hedges and thick leafy shrubbery. A fruit eater.
Nesting: Nest in a tree or shrub, usually substantially built with a rather shallow cup for the eggs which are white and number 2–3.

BLUE-NAPED MOUSEBIRD *Colius macrourus* **Pl. 22**
Identification: 14″. Sexes similar. In flight appears grey with a very long stiff tail. Settled often clings vertically. At close range crest, pale blue patch on the nape, and red face and bill are field marks. Flight fast and direct. Usually in parties. Fruit-eating.
Voice: A soft, piping, two-toned 'pi-hu', the second note slightly lower than the first. Cries constantly in flight and when perched.
Distribution and Habitat: Restricted to the semi-arid region from southern Mauritania, Senegal and Portuguese Guinea east through Guinea, Mali, Upper Volta, Niger and northern Nigeria to Chad. Partial to open thorn scrub.
Nesting: A shallow cup of twigs scantily lined with grass, built in a shrub at no great height. The tail of the brooding bird hangs over the edge of the nest. Eggs 3–4, white spotted and scrawled with brown and rufous.

TROGONS: Trogonidae

NARINA TROGON *Apaloderma narina* **Pl. 22**
Identification: 12″. Vividly coloured. The male is mainly iridescent green, with the lower breast and belly scarlet and the three outer pairs of tail feathers white. In the female the throat and upper breast are brown not green, and the scarlet on the under surface is paler and less extensive. Best located by the dove-like call of the male. Shy and difficult to approach; often perched motionless on a bough, where it is inconspicuous despite its bright colours. Very closely similar in appearance to the Yellow-cheeked Trogon (*Apaloderma aequatoriale*) (see Checklist, p. 275), which inhabits the high forest of Cameroon and Gaboon, but the call of the latter, a plaintive, resonant 'ho-ho-ho-ho-' has a different quality.
Voice: A repeated dove-like 'coo-coo'.

Distribution and Habitat: The high forest from Sierra Leone to the Cameroons and Gaboon, and, rarely, the wooded savanna north of the forest. Rather uncommon, occurring singly or in pairs, and occasionally as a member of the insect-hunting bird armies.

Nesting: Not recorded in our area. In South Africa it nests in holes in tree trunks and lays 3–4 glossy white round eggs.

Allied species: The Bar-tailed Trogon (*Apaloderma vittatum*), **Pl. 22**, 10″, is rather similarly coloured but may be distinguished by its black and white barred tail, a good character when the bird is perched and viewed from below. Its call – a prolonged, mournful, far-reaching 'wheeee-oh' – is distinctive. This is a montane forest species whose range in our area is restricted to Fernando Po, the west Cameroon highlands, and the Obudu Plateau of Nigeria. Where it occurs it is common.

KINGFISHERS: Alcedinidae

A well-characterised family ranging in size from that of a small Sparrow to that of a Pigeon. Most have straight, strong, pointed bills, short legs, rather short tails, and generally a thick-set appearance. Many are brilliantly coloured. Divisible into an aquatic diving group mainly subsisting on fish and a terrestrial group mainly subsisting on ground insects and other invertebrates and small vertebrates on which they swoop down from a perch.

GIANT KINGFISHER   *Ceryle maxima* (*Megaceryle maxima*)   **Pl. 23**
Identification: 18″. The largest African Kingfisher. Massive black bill. Upperparts slate-grey speckled with white, the speckling sometimes very sparse in forest birds. Throat white, breast rufous, belly barred black and white. The female differs by having the breast blackish and belly chestnut. Often solitary. Perches quietly over water. Fish-eating. In flight at a distance can be confused with the Green-backed Heron (*Butorides striatus*) (see p. 21), and the loud calls of the two species are somewhat similar.
Voice: A loud carrying 'kek-kek-kek-kek'.
Distribution and Habitat: Widely distributed south of 16° N. yet local, ranging from Gambia and Senegal east to Chad and the Central African Republic and south to Gaboon and Congo. Frequents mainly the lakes and larger wooded streams of the savanna and forest and also the sandy seashore and mangrove waterways.
Nesting: Eggs 3–5, white, laid at the end of a long tunnel dug by the birds in a river bank or aqueduct.

PIED KINGFISHER   *Ceryle rudis*   **Pl. 23**
Identification: 10″. The only black and white Kingfisher. Upperparts mixed black and white. Underparts white except for two black chest bands in the male and a single incomplete band in the female. Crested black crown and massive black bill. Tame and usually conspicuous. Eats fish, diving for its prey from a perch. Often hovers over water.
Voice: Noisy. Call a sharp 'kik-kik'.
Distribution and Habitat: Widely and commonly distributed south of 17° N.

wherever rivers, lakes, ponds, marshes, rice fields, lagoons or mangrove creeks offer suitable habitat with fish.

Nesting: A rounded chamber without nesting materials at the end of a long tunnel in a river bank or canal. Sometimes in colonies. Eggs 4–6, white.

SHINING-BLUE KINGFISHER *Alcedo quadribrachys* Pl. 23

Identification: 7½″. Blue above, chestnut below, with a large black bill. The Malachite Kingfisher is smaller and has a red bill. A true Kingfisher and an expert diver. Encountered singly, usually perched quietly on a branch overhanging the water or flying near the surface along the course of a stream.

Voice: Call a high-pitched rapid 'cheep-cheep-cheep-cheep' uttered in flight. Ordinarily silent.

Distribution and Habitat: The main body of the forest and the fringing forests of the savanna from Senegal, Gambia and Portuguese Guinea east to the Central African Republic and south to Gaboon and Congo. Well distributed and locally common on the lakes, rivers and creeks of the forest and the mangrove swamps.

Nesting: Nests are tunnels in the bank of a stream, gravel pit or saw pit in the forest. In Uganda the clutch is 5–6 and the eggs are described as white, glossy and rounded.

MALACHITE KINGFISHER *Alcedo cristata (Corythornis cristata)*
Pl. 23

Identification: 5¼″. Sexes similar. A tiny, mainly aquatic Kingfisher with blue upperparts and chestnut underparts. Face chestnut, throat white, bill red. At close range the barred blue and black erect crest and the white streak on the side of the neck are diagnostic and distinguish it from the mainly non-aquatic Pigmy Kingfisher (*Ceyx picta*). Immature bird has black bill. Usually seen perched over water, or diving for fish or insects, or streaking along the surface.

Voice: A little sharp 'peep-peep' uttered in flight.

Distribution and Habitat: Widely and commonly distributed south of 17° N. on the rivers, streams, lakes and pools of the savanna and in the coastal lagoons and mangrove creeks. More sparingly distributed on the rivers and lakes of the high forest. Ranges from Gambia and Senegal east to Chad and the Central African Republic and south to Gaboon and Congo.

Nesting: A small unlined chamber at the end of a burrow in the bank of a river or dam. Eggs 4–6, glossy white, almost spherical.

WHITE-BELLIED KINGFISHER *Alcedo leucogaster*
(*Corythornis leucogaster*) **Pl. 23**

Identification: 5¼″. The White-bellied Kingfisher is about the same size as the familiar Malachite Kingfisher. It may be distinguished in most of its range by its mainly white underparts, only the flanks and a patch on each side of the breast being rufous; back blue; bill red.

Voice: Not recorded.

Distribution and Habitat: Ranges from Portuguese Guinea to Gaboon and Congo and Fernando Po. On the islands of Principe and Sao Tome there occur very distinct races with the underside more rufous than white.

Nesting: The nest is a tunnel in a bank. Eggs undescribed.

PIGMY KINGFISHER *Ceyx picta (Ispidina picta)* **Pl. 23**
Identification: 5″. Sexes similar. A tiny Kingfisher with violet-blue upper-parts and pale rufous underparts. Resembles the Malachite Kingfisher (*Alcedo cristata*), but has no crest, the ear-coverts are violet not chestnut, and there is no white streak on the side of the neck. Further distinguished by habits and habitat. Very seldom dives though frequently picks insects off surface of water. Often in dry terrain far from water. Hunts for terrestrial insects from a perch.
Voice: A small sharp piping cry. During display a reedy sustained 'cheeeeeeeer' uttered on the wing.
Distribution and Habitat: Commonly and widely distributed in the area in varied habitats in the savanna and the forest clearings. Less common in the semi-arid belt of the savanna but penetrates to 16° N.
Nesting: An unlined chamber at the end of a tunnel in a ditch, borrow pit, road cutting or anthill. Eggs 3–4, glossy white spheres.
Allied species: The Red-headed Dwarf Kingfisher (*Ceyx lecontei*) is a rare species recorded in our area from a few localities from Guinea and Sierra Leone in the west to Gaboon in the east. It is an insect-eater and the driver ant columns attract it. It perches near the ground in shaded tangled second-growth or in the primary forest. It is even smaller (4″) than the Pigmy Kingfisher and it may be distinguished from the latter and from other small Kingfishers by its orange-rufous head and the black frontal band at the base of the bill.

SENEGAL KINGFISHER *Halcyon senegalensis* **Pl. 23**
Identification: 9″. Sexes similar. Entire upper surface brilliant light blue but head and neck pale grey and wing-coverts and wing tips black. Underparts white, the breast tinged grey. Upper mandible black, lower mandible red. For differences from the Blue-breasted Kingfisher see that species. Usually perched on a bough watching the ground beneath for insects and small vertebrates. Very occasionally fishes. Cry characteristic.
Voice: A piercing trill starting with a high detached note followed by a cascade of descending notes.
Distribution and Habitat: A savanna species also common in clearings in the forest belt but absent from closed forest. Frequents parkland, clearings with trees, gardens and mangrove swamps. Abundant and widely distributed throughout, penetrating to 17° N. in the rains.
Nesting: Nesting hole in a tree, house-roof, tree-termite nest, anthill, road cutting or river bank. Eggs 3–4, glossy white, subspherical.

BLUE-BREASTED KINGFISHER *Halcyon malimbica* **Pl. 23**
Identification: 11″. Sexes similar. Resembles the Senegal Kingfisher but is larger, has the scapulars as well as the wing-coverts black, and the breast blue. Upper mandible black, lower mandible red. Prefers well-wooded country. Mainly insectivorous. Occasional member of forest bird parties. Seldom fishes.
Voice: A far-carrying whistling 'piou-piou-piou . . .' descending in pitch and decreasing in volume.
Distribution and Habitat: Well distributed and locally common throughout south of 13° N. frequenting fringing forest and leafy woodland in the savanna and old second-growth and (especially) mangroves in the forest belt. Common on Principe.

Nesting: Eggs 2–4, glossy white and round, laid inside a hollow termite's nest in a tree. ·

Allied species: The Chocolate-backed Kingfisher (*Halcyon badia*), 8″, is easily recognised by its colour pattern. It is dark chestnut above with a blue wing-patch, rump and tail; underparts white; the massive bill red. A rather local forest species. It ranges from Liberia and Sierra Leone to the Central African Republic, Gaboon and the island of Fernando Po. An insect-eating Kingfisher that keeps out of sight in the forest interior. The characteristic call is a succession of hollow whistles which gradually diminish in volume and fall in pitch.

STRIPED KINGFISHER   *Halcyon chelicuti*   Pl. 23

Identification: 7″. Sexes similar. The least brightly coloured of the King-fishers. Head grey streaked blackish, hind neck white, mantle grey-brown, rump and tail blue, underparts dull white obscurely streaked. Bill blackish above, salmon-red below. Perches quietly and unobtrusively on a branch looking out for insects on the ground beneath.

Voice: A whistling 'hoo-ee'. Also a detached note followed by a rapid trill somewhat resembling the voice of the Senegal Kingfisher but more subdued and less of a monotone. Beats its wings when calling.

Distribution and Habitat: Well distributed and locally common in the savanna south of 17° N. Rare in the forest and there only in the larger clearings in the dry season. Reappears south of the forest in the Congo savanna. Prefers dry country with scattered trees.

Nesting: Eggs 3, white rounded ellipses, laid in a hole in a tree.

GREY-HEADED KINGFISHER   *Halcyon leucocephala*   Pl. 23

Identification: 8″. Sexes similar. Field marks are the black mantle and wing-coverts contrasting with the cobalt-blue wings, rump and tail, and the bright chestnut belly. Head grey, throat and breast white. Bill and feet red. Insectivorous.

Voice: A rapid rather weak 'dji-dji-dji-dji-dji' usually uttered in flight.

Distribution and Habitat: A common, widespread savanna species. Strongly migratory. In the wet season penetrates to 17° N. and in the dry season south to the forest clearings. Rare south of the forest in Gaboon and Congo. There is a resident pale-headed race *H. l. acteon* in the Cape Verde Islands.

Nesting: Nest an unlined chamber at the end of a burrow tunnelled into a river bank, ditch or borrow pit. Eggs 3–5, glossy white, spherical.

BEE-EATERS: Meropidae

Conspicuous, brilliantly coloured birds with long, decurved, pointed bills, short legs and long tails, the latter sometimes forked and sometimes with the central pair of feathers greatly elongated. Many species gregarious, especially when breeding. Feed on bees and other flying insects. These are caught during a circular flight from a perch or in the course of an extended cruising flight.

Plate 27

SWIFTS

1. **EUROPEAN SWIFT** *Apus apus*   page 120
   Uniformly dark brown; slightly forked tail.

2. **MOTTLED SWIFT** *Apus aequatorialis*   120
   Large; white throat.

3. **LITTLE AFRICAN SWIFT** *Apus affinis*   121
   Square tail; white rump.

4. **WHITE-RUMPED SWIFT** *Apus caffer*   121
   Forked tail; white rump.

5. **PALM SWIFT** *Cypsiurus parvus*   122
   Long narrow wings; long strongly-forked tail.

6. **BATES' BLACK SWIFT** *Apus batesi*   121
   Entirely black; forked tail.

7. **CASSIN'S SPINE-TAILED SWIFT** *Chaetura cassini*   122
   Long notched wings; short tail; white rump and belly.

8. **USSHER'S SPINE-TAILED SWIFT** *Chaetura ussheri*   122
   Long notched wings; tail short but longer than Cassin's Swift;
   white rump.

28

Plate 28

HORNBILLS

1. **BLACK-CASQUED HORNBILL** *Ceratogymna atrata* page 138
Male: large; black cylindrical casque; plumage black except for white tail tips.
Female: rufous head and neck.

2. **BLACK-AND-WHITE-CASQUED HORNBILL** 139
Bycanistes subcylindricus
Resembles the Brown-cheeked Hornbill but central pair of rectrices entirely black.

3. **BROWN-CHEEKED HORNBILL** 138
Bycanistes cylindricus cylindricus
White tail; all the rectrices with a broad black band across the middle.

4. **RED-BILLED DWARF HORNBILL** *Tockus camurus* 137
Brown; red bill; double white wing-bar.

5. **WHITE-CRESTED HORNBILL** 137
Tropicranus albocristatus cassini
Very long tail; white crown and crest.

6. **RED-BEAKED HORNBILL** *Tockus erythrorhynchus* 136
Red bill; white supercilium; white central stripe on mantle.

7. **GREY HORNBILL** *Tockus nasutus* 136
Grey-brown; broad white supercilium.

8. **PIPING HORNBILL** *Bycanistes fistulator* 138
Black and white wings; more stoutly built than the Black-and-white-tailed Hornbill.

9. **BLACK-AND-WHITE-TAILED HORNBILL** 137
Tockus fasciatus semifasciatus
Black wings; second and third outermost rectrices white or white-tipped.

10. **GROUND HORNBILL** *Bucorvus abyssinicus* 139
Massive; black except for white primaries.

EUROPEAN BEE-EATER *Merops apiaster*   **Pl. 24**
Identification: 11″. Sexes similar. Chestnut crown and back and in the adult the projecting middle tail feathers are excellent field marks in flight and at rest. The white forehead, black line through the eye, and narrow black pectoral band separating the bright yellow throat from the bluish underparts are also good characters at close range. Flight graceful, undulant, gliding and far-ranging. Gregarious.
Voice: A liquid resonant 'toorook toorook', often uttered in West Africa.
Distribution and Habitat: A spring (February–April) and autumn (September–October) passage migrant in West Africa and a rather scarce winter visitor. Without being common widely recorded from the savannas and forest clearings from Gambia and Senegal to the Cameroons, Chad, Gaboon and Congo.

BLUE-CHEEKED BEE-EATER *Merops superciliosus*
(*M. persicus*)   **Pl. 24**
Identification: 12″. Sexes similar. Plumage mainly green. A broad black line through the eye, bordered above and below by pale blue. Forehead pale blue, chin yellow, throat chestnut, no black pectoral band. The central tail feathers are greatly elongated. Graceful but strong Swallow-like flight. Gregarious.
Voice: A musical resonant clear note rather like that of the European Bee-eater.
Distribution and Habitat: Migratory. The West African population includes resident birds and, in the dry season, migrants also from North Africa. Widely but locally distributed in the open savanna north of the forest from Mauritania and Senegal to the Cameroons and Chad with breeding colonies in southern Mauritania, Senegal, Mali and northern Nigeria. Also encountered on migration in Gaboon, Congo and Sao Tome.
Nesting: Colonial. A burrow in a sandy river bank or in the mud wall of a building. Nesting chamber unlined. Clutch 5. Eggs glossy immaculate white rounded ovals.

LITTLE GREEN BEE-EATER *Merops orientalis*   **Pl. 24**
Identification: 10″. Sexes similar. Small and green all over with no other noticeable colour. Tail square but with two conspicuous long narrow projecting central rectrices. At close range a black streak through the eye and a narrow dark band across the chest. In flight wings golden-brown tipped black. Young lacks elongated central tail feathers. Gregarious or solitary when breeding. Often in pairs at other times. Hunts insects, usually from low perch.
Voice: A pleasing high-pitched 'cree-cree-cree-cree' usually uttered on the wing.
Distribution and Habitat: Where there are trees or shrubs for perching widespread and sedentary in the dry northern savanna from Mauritania, Senegal and Gambia through Mali, Niger, northern Nigeria and northern Cameroons to Chad.
Nesting: Nests in tunnels excavated in the hard clayey banks of river beds, and in road cuttings and sandbanks.

CARMINE BEE-EATER *Merops nubicus*   **Pl. 24**
Identification: 13″. Sexes similar. A large distinctively coloured Bee-eater with long projecting central tail feathers. Carmine all over but head greenish-blue and rump and vent pale blue. Gregarious. Gliding, graceful flight and hunts

in flight or from a perch. Attracted by bush fires and cattle herds and sometimes perches on the backs of cattle and other animals. Partial to locusts and winged ants.

Voice: A distinctive, soft, liquid, disyllabic call uttered in flight.

Distribution and Habitat: Widely distributed and common in the semi-arid belt of the savanna extending its range southward in the dry season almost to the edge of the forest. Ranges from Senegal, Gambia and Portuguese Guinea east to Chad and the Central African Republic.

Nesting: Usually in very large colonies (up to several thousands of burrows) in steep river banks. Long tunnel with terminal unlined egg chamber. Eggs 3–5, glossy white, sub-globular.

Allied species: The Rosy Bee-eater (*Merops malimbicus*) is usually found in the vicinity of wide rivers or lagoons. It is somewhat locally distributed from Ivory Coast to Gaboon and Congo, occupying mainly the moister savanna country and the forest edge. It is absent from the main body of the forest. Gregarious. The colour pattern is distinctive. The upperparts are grey, the underparts rose-pink, and there is a long and broad white streak below the eye.

WHITE-THROATED BEE-EATER *Merops albicollis*
(*Aerops albicollis*) **Pl. 24**

Identification: 12″, including long central tail feathers. Distinguished by white forehead, supercilium, and throat which contrast with the black crown, stripe below eye, and chest band. Rest of body plumage mainly pale green. Belly white. Spread flight feathers cinnamon. Highly gregarious. Usually hunts from low perch.

Voice: A pleasing, liquid, low-pitched 'trooee trooee' frequently uttered.

Distribution and Habitat: Abundant and widely dispersed throughout the area, nesting in the rains in the countries bordering the Sahara from Mauritania to Chad and migrating south in the dry season to the moister savanna, the forest clearings, and the savanna south of the forest in Congo and Gaboon.

Nesting: Breeds colonially or singly, burrowing into the flat ground or into a bank. Eggs 6–7, white, sub-globular.

LITTLE BEE-EATER *Merops pusillus* (*Melittophagus pusillus*) **Pl. 24**

Identification: 7″. A square-tailed Bee-eater with a bright yellow throat sharply defined from a blackish chest band. Upperparts green, stripe through eye black, upper breast chestnut, rest underparts yellowish. In flight wing and tail feathers fawn tipped black. Young birds lack the dark chest band. Can be confused with the Blue-breasted Bee-eater (*Merops variegatus*) (see Checklist, p. 275), but the latter has a white patch on the side of the neck and a blue not black chest band, and in West Africa is confined to savanna country in the Cameroons and Gaboon. Non-gregarious. Usually in pairs, hunting in circular flycatcher fashion from a perch near the ground.

Voice: An occasional short 'tsip'.

Distribution and Habitat: Widely and commonly yet irregularly distributed from Mauritania and Senegal east to Chad and the Central African Republic and south to Congo, in the savanna and in the larger forest clearings. Fond of swamp edges.

Nesting: Nests solitarily in sandy roadside banks or borrow pits, the tunnel ending in an oval egg chamber. Eggs 4–6, glossy white, subglobular.

RED-THROATED BEE-EATER   *Merops bulocki*
(*Melittophagus bullocki*)   **Pl. 24**

Identification: 8½". Sexes similar. A square-tailed Bee-eater of the savanna distinguished by the bright red throat, mainly green upperparts, thick black stripe through and below the eye, cinnamon breast, and blue under tail-coverts. Usually in parties hawking for insects above the tree tops of open woodland.

Voice: A soft liquid disyllabic note. Calls frequently.

Distribution and Habitat: Widespread and locally abundant in the mid-zone of the savanna from Senegal and Gambia to southern Chad and the Central African Republic. Absent from the driest parts of the thorn scrub bordering the desert and from the wettest zone of the grass savanna bordering the forest. Frequents the edges of woods, fringing forest, and savanna and farmland with trees.

Nesting: Breeds colonially, sometimes alongside the Carmine Bee-eater, in burrows excavated in river banks, road cuttings or borrow pits. Eggs 2–5, glossy white and rounded ovate.

BLACK BEE-EATER   *Merops gularis*   **Pl. 24**

Identification: A small square-tailed forest Bee-eater. The upperparts, except for the blue rump, are black; the throat is scarlet; the breast black streaked with blue, and the rest of the underparts mainly blue; chestnut on the wings in flight. Conspicuously coloured birds, usually seen in pairs or small parties hawking for insects from the branches of a tree, sometimes at a considerable height.

Voice: Usually silent. The song is described as quavering and pleasant.

Distribution and Habitat: The forest and its outliers in the savanna from Sierra Leone and Liberia to Gaboon and Congo. It inhabits trees on the edge of the true forest, in old clearings, and in second-growth. Well distributed but nowhere really abundant.

Nesting: The nesting holes are dug in banks, cuttings or drainage ditches. Eggs white; clutch 2–4. Usually a solitary nester, but sometimes colonial.

Allied species: The Blue-headed Bee-eater (*Merops muelleri*) is another small, brilliantly coloured and rather rarer forest species that ranges from Sierra Leone to Gaboon and Fernando Po. The rich chestnut back and wings serve to identify it. It has a black throat with a scarlet patch, and blue head, tail and underparts.

SWALLOW-TAILED BEE-EATER   *Merops hirundineus*
(*Dicrocercus hirundineus*)   **Pl. 24**

Identification: 9". Sexes similar. The strongly forked tail is diagnostic and distinguishes adult and immature birds from all other Bee-eaters. Upperparts mainly green. Broad, black infraorbital stripe. Tail blue-green. Throat yellow, narrow chest band blue, breast green, belly and under tail-coverts blue. Occurs singly or in pairs or small parties. Hawks for insects from tree perch. Unobtrusive.

Voice: A cry of two shrill notes.

Distribution and Habitat: Widely but locally distributed in the savanna. Recorded from Senegal (to 15° N.), Gambia, Portuguese Guinea, Sierra Leone, Ivory Coast, Ghana, Togo, Nigeria, southern Chad and the Central African Republic.

Nesting: Nests singly. In southern Africa lays 3 glossy white eggs in a burrow in a sandbank.

ROLLERS: Coraciidae

Sturdy birds about the size of a Pigeon. Strong, slightly hooked bills. Brightly coloured plumage, always with some blue. Seldom walk but perch for long periods on a bush, telegraph wire or other look-out post from which they swoop down on their prey on the ground. The two *Eurystomus* species are, however, aerial hunters. Not very wild.

ABYSSINIAN ROLLER *Coracias abyssinica* **Pl. 23**
Identification: 18″. Sexes similar. Vivid colouring and very long narrow outer tail feathers distinguish it. Bright blue all over but back brown and shoulders and flight feathers purple. In immature plumage lacks elongated tail and very closely resembles European Roller (*Coracias garrulus*) but the white on the forehead is more extensive and the flight feathers are purple not black. Descends on its prey on the ground from a conspicuous perch on telegraph wire, tree or shrub. Pugnacious. Noisy. Attracted by grass fires.
Voice: An unpleasant harsh croaking 'kraa'.
Distribution and Habitat: Widely and commonly distributed in the savanna especially in the dry northern parts (up to 18° N.) from Senegal and Gambia east to Chad and the Central African Republic. Absent from the forest. Frequents orchard bush, thorn scrub and open grass or farmland provided there are tree perches.
Nesting: Lays in a hole in a tree or building. Eggs 4–5, white, glossy, rounded ovate.
Allied species: The European Roller (*Coracias garrulus*), 12″, sexes similar, resembles the Abyssinian Roller but is square-tailed, lacking the long streamers of the African species. It is virtually indistinguishable in the field from immature examples of the latter (see above). Occurs in West Africa on spring or autumn passage and less frequently in winter, being recorded from Gambia, Senegal, Ivory Coast, Nigeria, the Cameroons, Chad, Congo and the islands of Principe and Sao Tome in the Gulf of Guinea.

RUFOUS-CROWNED ROLLER *Coracias naevia* **Pl. 23**
Identification: 15″. Sexes similar. A stockily built square-tailed Roller. Settled rather dull-coloured with mainly brown upperparts and vinous-rufous underparts streaked narrowly with white. At close range a white streak over the eye and a white patch on the nape. In flight the blue on the wings and tail is conspicuous. Occurs singly. Pugnacious. Drops from its perch to the ground to retrieve its prey.
Voice: Less noisy than the Abyssinian Roller. Call harsh and grating.
Distribution and Habitat: Less common than the Abyssinian Roller and occupying the same terrain though showing a preference for the better-wooded savanna. Ranges from southern Mauritania, Senegal and Gambia east to Chad and the Central African Republic.
Nesting: In southern Africa breeds in tree holes laying 2–3 white eggs.

BLUE-BELLIED ROLLER *Coracias cyanogaster* **Pl. 23**
Identification: 14″. Sexes similar. Colour pattern distinctive. Head, nape and breast pale pinkish-fawn; back blackish; underparts below breast deep blue.

In flight wings ultramarine with a broad bar of light cobalt; tail greenish-blue and forked. Occurs singly or more characteristically in small parties. Perches on trees or other conspicuous vantage points.

Voice: An explosive 'ah' and in the breeding season a loud 'ah-ah-ah-ah'.

Distribution and Habitat: Widely distributed in the savanna but local. Absent from the arid far north and from the grass savannas bordering the forest. Partial to clearings in the wooded savanna. Recorded from Senegal, Gambia, Portuguese Guinea, Guinea, Sierra Leone, Ivory Coast, Mali, Ghana, Togo, Nigeria and the Central African Republic.

Nesting: Site a hole in a tree. Eggs white.

BROAD-BILLED ROLLER *Eurystomus glaucurus* **Pl. 23**

Identification: 10″. Sexes similar. Less conspicuous than the *Coracias* group by reason of its smaller size, duller colouring and virtual restriction to the tops of large trees. Large bright yellow bill. Upperparts dark rufous; underparts lilac. In flight wings and tail mainly blue. Tail square. The closely similar Blue-throated Roller is distinguished by its blue throat patch. Often gregarious. Very active at dusk wheeling over the tree tops with erratic buoyant flight. Pugnacious. Noisy. Catches insects in the air.

Voice: A variety of loud discordant cries.

Distribution and Habitat: Provided there are tall trees, widely and abundantly distributed in savanna and forest clearing. Penetrates to 12° 30′ N. in Nigeria and to 15° N. in Senegal. In south of range numbers increase greatly in dry season.

Nesting: Site a hole high up in a tall tree. Eggs 3, white, glossy.

Allied species: The Blue-throated Roller (*Eurystomus gularis*) closely resembles the Broad-billed Roller in appearance and habits but may be distinguished by its shriller call and by the patch of blue on the throat. Further, it is a sedentary forest species whilst the Broad-billed Roller is predominantly a savanna species especially in the wet season. The range is the forest from Guinea and Sierra Leone to Gaboon and Congo and the island of Fernando Po.

HOOPOES AND WOOD-HOOPOES: Upupidae

The Hoopoe with its crest, pinkish body plumage and patterned black and white wings and tail is unmistakable. The Wood-Hoopoes are slender birds with long decurved bills and long graduated tails. Mainly dark glossy plumage with some white. Arboreal, searching the bark for insects.

HOOPOE *Upupa epops (U. senegalensis)* **Pl. 24**

Identification: 11″. Sexes rather similar. The cinnamon body plumage, boldly barred black and white wings and tail (conspicuous at rest and in flight), prominent black-tipped erectile crest, and curved bill are, taken together, quite distinctive. The resident West African races (*U. epops senegalensis* and *U. e. africana*) cannot certainly (in immature dress at least) be distinguished in the field from the migratory European race (*U. epops epops*). The flight is leisurely, undulating, and butterfly-like. Mainly terrestrial. Solitary or in pairs.

Voice: A low-pitched resonant hollow-sounding 'hoo-hoo'.

Distribution and Habitat: The European race is a winter visitor and passage migrant to the savanna, especially to the northern drier areas, occurring from August to April. The resident race (*U. e. senegalensis*), which is a partial migrant, is widely distributed and locally common in the savanna from Senegal to Chad and the Central African Republic, and another race (*U. e. africana*) occurs south of the forest in the Gaboon and Congo savannas. Usually in open country in orchard bush or thorn scrub.

Nesting: Eggs laid in a hole in a tree or dry-stone wall or in the base of an ant hill. No nesting materials. Egg white tinged with bluish-green.

SENEGAL WOOD-HOOPOE *Phoeniculus purpureus*
(*P. erythrorhynchus*, *P. senegalensis*)   **Pl. 24**

Identification: 18". Sexes similar. Slimly built and glossy black with a very long graduated tail and a conspicuous curved red or red-tipped bill. In flight conspicuous white patches on the wing and white bands on the tail. In immature dress bill black. Gregarious. Arboreal, climbing about the branches in character-istic jerky fashion exploring the cracks and holes. Fly in single file.

Voice: A frequent, hard, metallic 'ak-ak-ak' usually uttered in chorus.

Distribution and Habitat: Widely but locally distributed in the savanna provided there are trees of some sort, from 16° N. south to the forest edge. Ranges from Senegal, Gambia and Portuguese Guinea east to Chad and the Central African Republic.

Nesting: Eggs laid on a pile of wood chips in a natural hole in a tree. Clutch 2–3. Immaculate blue tinged grey with a lustreless, somewhat roughened surface.

LESSER WOOD-HOOPOE *Phoeniculus aterrimus*
(*Scoptelus aterrimus*)   **Pl. 24**

Identification: 9". Characteristic build, proportions and actions of a Wood-Hoopoe, but much smaller. Glossy black with, in flight, a conspicuous white wing bar. In female and immature dress the breast is dark brown and unglossed. Bill blackish. Occurs singly and in pairs climbing about the trunks and branches of the savanna trees, and at times when perched swaying its whole body back-wards and forwards in the same curious manner as the Senegal Wood-Hoopoe.

Voice: A dry metallic 'ha-ha'.

Distribution and Habitat: Widely distributed in the savanna, especially in the arid zone, penetrating northwards right up to the edge of the desert. In the dry season the range extends as far south as 6° 30′ N. in Nigeria. From southern Mauritania, Senegal and Gambia through Portuguese Guinea, Guinea, Ivory Coast, Mali, Ghana, Togo, Niger, Nigeria and northern Cameroons to Chad and the Central African Republic.

Nesting: Eggs 3, laid in a natural hole in a tree.

Allied species: The Buff-headed Wood-Hoopoe (*Phoeniculus bollei*), 13", has the head and neck white tinged with buff; rest of the plumage black with metallic reflections; conspicuous red bill and feet. It is found along the northern edge of the West African lowland forest from the Ivory Coast and Guinea through Nigeria and the Cameroons to Congo and the Central African Republic. An isolated race (*P. bollei okuensis*) characterised by the greatly reduced amount of white on the head is found at 7,000 feet in the montane forest of Lake Oku in the Bamenda highlands. The Forest Wood-Hoopoe (*Phoeniculus castaneiceps*) is a rather rare and local species of the high forest. In our area it ranges from

Liberia and the Ivory Coast to the Cameroons. Black with a rufous head; but in part of its range males have the head either black or whitish. These last are distinguished from *Phoeniculus bollei* by their smaller size (11″ against 13″) and by their blackish not red bills.

HORNBILLS: Bucerotidae

Large or medium-sized generally conspicuous birds of the forest or wooded savanna, with slow, laboured and often undulating flight with long glides. Most species have loud, characteristic, raucous voices. Bill large, curved and strong, and in many species surmounted by a prominent casque whose shape is often a useful diagnostic. Most forms are arboreal and fruit-eating. Highly specialised nesting habits.

GREY HORNBILL   *Tockus nasutus (Lophoceros nasutus)*   **Pl. 28**
Identification: 18″. In flight at a distance appears as a lanky grey-brown bird with a long, curved bill, rounded wings and long tail, with an undulating flight characterised by several wing beats followed by a long downward glide with wings closed. At close range upperparts grey, the wings spotted and the outer tail feathers tipped with white. A broad white supercilium. Underparts creamy-white. Bill in the male black with a patch of cream at the base; in the female the upper mandible yellow and lower mandible blackish, both tipped red. Occurs in pairs or parties. Call characteristic. Sometimes spectacular large flocks on migration.
Voice: A loud plaintive 'pee-yoo' repeated several times and heard throughout the year. Calls with bill in vertical position and wings flapping.
Distribution and Habitat: Common and widespread in the savanna in the northern arid parts as far north as the desert edge provided there are trees. Less common in the humid savanna immediately north of the forest and there only in the dry season. Ranges from southern Mauritania, Senegal and Gambia east to northern Cameroons, Chad and the Central African Republic.
Nesting: In a hollow in a tree which is walled up after the female starts to incubate. Eggs 2–4, dull white.

RED-BEAKED HORNBILL   *Tockus erythrorhynchus*
(*Lophoceros erythrorhynchus*)   **Pl. 28**
Identification: 17″. A slender, lanky, black and white Hornbill with a long curved red bill and no casque. Upperparts blackish with a broad white stripe above the eye and a long white stripe down the middle of the back. Underparts white. Wings black and white. Tail black with an increasing amount of white on the outer rectrices. Dipping flight like the Grey Hornbill.
Voice: A monotonous, melancholy, high-pitched tooting. Also a long drawn-out whistle. Call delivered with bill raised and wings flapping.
Distribution and Habitat: Ranges from Mauritania and Senegal east through northern Ivory Coast, Mali, Niger, Ghana, Nigeria and Cameroons to Chad and northern Central African Republic. More restricted to the arid belt than the Grey Hornbill it reaches the edge of the desert at 18° N. and is absent from the moist savanna zones.
Nesting: Nests in holes in trees at varying heights from the ground. Female walled in. Eggs 3–6, dull white.

RED-BILLED DWARF HORNBILL   *Tockus camurus*
(*Lophoceros camurus*) **Pl. 28**

Identification: 15". A small forest Hornbill with a conspicuous red bill and two white bars on the wing formed by the tips of the coverts. Plumage mainly brown, but whitish on the lower breast and belly. A far-carrying distinctive call. An insect hunter sometimes associated with mixed bird parties.

Voice: Loud and plaintive, a series of notes in a descending scale and diminishing volume 'hoo-oo-hoo-oo-hoo-oo . . .'. Also a high-pitched musical 'choork-choork-choork . . .' with a distinct pause between 'choorks'.

Distribution and Habitat: The lowland forest from Liberia to Gaboon and Congo. Locally fairly common in old second-growth and primary forest occurring in pairs or small parties.

Nesting: Habits unknown.

Allied species: The Black Dwarf Hornbill (*Tockus hartlaubi*), an equally small Hornbill, is rather rare and mainly restricted to unspoilt primary forest. It ranges from Sierra Leone to Gaboon and Congo. The head and upperparts are blackish, the underparts grey and white, the bill black, tipped red in the male. The best field mark is the long broad white superciliary streak.

BLACK-AND-WHITE-TAILED HORNBILL   *Tockus fasciatus*
(*Lophoceros fasciatus, L. semifasciatus*) **Pl. 28**

Identification: 21". A scraggy, loose-jointed, black-and-white Hornbill, gregarious, tame and vocal; often seen in straggling formation passing from one tree to another with slow, weak, undulating flight. The underparts from lower breast to under tail-coverts are white, as are the second and third outermost tail feathers; rest of the plumage black. The bill is cream tipped and streaked dark red. In the race that occurs from Nigeria westwards (*Tockus f. semifasciatus*) the tips only of the second and third outermost tail feathers are white and the bill is cream tipped and streaked black.

Voice: A shrill querulous laughing cry.

Distribution and Habitat: Senegal and Gambia east to the Central African Republic and south to Gaboon and Congo in the forest and its gallery extensions and the savanna woods. Abundant and widespread affecting mainly old second-growth, forest borders, overgrown clearings and oil palm and rubber plantations.

Nesting: The eggs are laid in a plastered-up hole in a tree. They are white and slightly rough in texture.

WHITE-CRESTED HORNBILL   *Tropicranus albocristatus* **Pl. 28**

Identification: 30". A forest Hornbill easily recognised by its very long strongly graduated tail. Black in colour with a white crown and crest, white-tipped tail feathers and, in the eastern half of its range (*T. a. cassini*), white-tipped wing feathers. A rather silent, furtive species that keeps to the forest interior, seen singly or in pairs, and often in the company of monkeys.

Voice: Usually silent. The call has been likened to the clucking of a hen. Another call is a clear plaintive wail.

Distribution and Habitat: From Guinea and Sierra Leone to Gaboon, in the main body of the forest and its gallery extensions. It frequents primary and old second-growth.

Nesting: The nest site is a hollow in the trunk of a forest tree. As in other Hornbill species the female is imprisoned in the nest throughout the incubation and fledgling period and is fed by her mate. Two eggs are laid.

BLACK-CASQUED HORNBILL   *Ceratogymna atrata*   **Pl. 28**
Identification: 36″. The great size, large casque, and the loud swishing noise made by the wings in flight distinguish it from all other forest birds except the Yellow-casqued Hornbill. Male plumage black except that all but the central pair of tail feathers have the terminal third white. Gular pouch and naked skin round the eye light blue. The large blackish casque is cylindrical in shape. The female is similar except that the head and neck are rufous and the casque is much smaller. Flight slow, laborious and noisy. Usually a pair or a pair and a young one keep company.
Voice: A loud clamorous resonant call with a nasal quality, audible at a distance of half a mile.
Distribution and Habitat: The lowland forest and its outliers from Liberia to the Central African Republic, Gaboon and Congo. Also Fernando Po. In the Cameroons forest where it is common it ascends to 4,500 feet.
Nesting: The nest is a hollow high up in a large forest tree and the opening is plastered up in Hornbill fashion leaving a small aperture through which the brooding female is fed by the male.
Allied species: The Yellow-casqued Hornbill (*Ceratogymna elata*) ranges in the forest and its outliers from Portuguese Guinea to Western Cameroons. Its appearance, loud voice, noisy flight and habits generally recall the black-casqued species. It differs in the pattern of the tail which is entirely white except for the middle pair of feathers, which are black. Further, the casque is whitish not black, and in the male its shape differs, being truncated.

PIPING HORNBILL   *Bycanistes fistulator (B. sharpii)*   **Pl. 28**
Identification: 20″. Head, neck, breast and upperparts except for the rump black; underparts below the breast and rump white. Wings and tail black and white, the proportion of each colour varying with locality. The only other black and white Hornbill of comparable size in our area is the Black-and-white-tailed Hornbill (*Tockus fasciatus*) from which the present species is readily distinguished by the heavier bill, the stouter build, the much more powerful and swifter flight, and the different call. A noisy, conspicuous bird, encountered in pairs and parties of up to a dozen individuals.
Voice: A variety of loud shrill raucous cries.
Distribution and Habitat: Senegal and Portuguese Guinea east to the Central African Republic and south to Gaboon and Congo. A widespread locally common forest Hornbill which penetrates far into the savanna in the gallery forests and kurimis.
Breeding: The nest is in a hollow in a forest tree; the clutch is two; the eggs are white.

BROWN-CHEEKED HORNBILL   *Bycanistes cylindricus*
(*B. albotibialis*)   **Pl. 28**
Identification: 30″. A large black and white forest Hornbill recognised by its tail, which is white crossed near the middle by a broad black band. Casque whitish. Two distinct races in our area, from Dahomey westwards *B. cylindricus cylindricus* with brown cheeks and chin and (in the male) a high abruptly truncated casque, and from Nigeria eastwards *B. cylindricus albotibialis* with black cheeks and chin and a strongly curved pointed casque. Often hidden in the heavily foliaged tops of tall forest trees. Flight undulating with noisy wing beats.

Voice: A variety of loud clamorous and whistling calls.

Distribution and Habitat: The lowland forest with its gallery extensions from Sierra Leone to Gaboon and Congo. Locally common, occurring in pairs and small parties.

Nesting: In Zaire the nest is located high up in a hollow forest tree trunk and one egg is laid.

BLACK-AND-WHITE-CASQUED HORNBILL
Bycanistes subcylindricus   **Pl. 28**

Identification: 30". Closely resembles the Brown-cheeked Hornbill (*Bycanistes cylindricus*) but the tail pattern differs, the central pair of rectrices being entirely black. Tail characters in many Hornbill species are useful in the field for these birds often spread the tail momentarily on alighting, and when launching into flight they may fly for some considerable distance with the tail spread. The casque is white at the base and black distally.

Voice: Described as 'a loud mournful note, slowly repeated'. Also a 'shorter, hoarser, reiterated call'.

Distribution and Habitat: A rather local species recorded from a few localities along the northern edge of the West African forest from Ivory Coast to the Cameroons and the Central African Republic.

Nesting: Nesting hole high up in a forest tree, the entrance being plastered up in the usual Hornbill fashion. The clutch is one.

GROUND HORNBILL   *Bucorvus abyssinicus*   **Pl. 28**

Identification: 43". Unmistakable. A dark terrestrial Hornbill as large as a Turkey with a massive black bill surmounted by a black truncated casque. Plumage entirely black except for white primaries which show up in flight. Bare patch on the throat red in the male, blue in the female. Usually encountered in pairs feeding on the ground where it walks sedately.

Voice: A prolonged deep booming call.

Distribution and Habitat: The wooded savanna from Senegal, Gambia and Portuguese Guinea east to Chad and the Central African Republic but absent from the arid belt next to the desert and from the moist belt next to the rain forest. Fond of burnt ground, the edges of cultivation clearings, and other open spaces in the wooded savanna.

Nesting: A large natural hole in a tree (often a baobab) scantily lined with leaves. The female is not walled in. Eggs 2, white, with a rough, pitted surface.

BARBETS: Capitonidae

Medium-sized or small thick-set arboreal fruit-eating birds of the forest and the wooded savanna. Variable but usually conspicuously coloured plumage. Call usually loud and often of one note repeated again and again.

BEARDED BARBET   *Lybius dubius* (*Pogonornis dubius*)   **Pl. 33**

Identification: 10". Sexes almost alike. Conspicuously coloured. Upperparts black with white rump; underparts red with a broad, black breast band and a white patch on the flanks. Massive bill and bare skin round eye yellow. At close range a tuft of bristles at base of bill. In flight white rump and flanks show up.

The black breast band distinguishes it from the rather similar Tooth-billed Barbet (*Lybius bidentatus*).

Voice: Various harsh guttural cries.

Distribution and Habitat: In the savanna in places where there are trees and particularly between 10° N. and 14° N. A fruit-eating arboreal species especially addicted to wild figs. Absent from the extreme north and also from the southern belt adjoining the rain forest. From Senegal, Gambia and Portuguese Guinea east through the Ivory Coast, Mali and Ghana to northern Nigeria and Chad.

Nesting: Breeds in a hole excavated in a rotten tree. Eggs 2.

TOOTH-BILLED BARBET   *Lybius bidentatus*
(*Pogornis bidentatus*)   **Pl. 33**

Identification: A large thickset Barbet with a conspicuous whitish bill. Mainly black above and red below, the rump and a patch on each side of the breast white, and a red wing bar. Rather like the Bearded Barbet (*Lybius dubius*) but lacks that species' black breast band. Sexes alike. Often in pairs in fruiting trees.

Voice: Described by Jackson as a loud, long-drawn-out, rattling 'chur-r'.

Distribution and Habitat: Portuguese Guinea, east to the Central African Republic, south to Gaboon. It occurs in the gallery forests, woodlands and scattered trees of the savanna adjoining the forest, and less commonly in the second-growth trees of the fringe of the forest and of its larger clearings. Absent from the rain forest interior.

Nesting: The nesting hole is excavated in the trunk or branch of a dead tree. Eggs 3–4, white.

Allied species: The White-headed Barbet (*Lybius leucocephalus*) is distinguishable from other Barbets in our area, being white with dark back, wings, tail and belly. It is locally common in the savannas from northern Nigeria to the Central African Republic.

VIEILLOT'S BARBET   *Lybius vieilloti*   **Pl. 33**

Identification: 6″. Sexes similar. Call and colour pattern diagnostic. Head, throat and breast mainly scarlet; rest of underparts including wings and tail brown, but lower back, rump and margins of wing feathers yellow; belly mainly yellowish-white. Bill black. Red head and yellow rump clearly seen in flight. Tame and easily observed. Often in wild fruit trees, especially figs. Usually singly or in pairs.

Voice: A 'kree-kree' (resembling the call of the Double-spurred Francolin) followed by a rhythmic series of flute-like 'poop-poops' uttered by a duetting pair of birds.

Distribution and Habitat: Widely and commonly distributed in the thorn-scrub and wooded savanna in a wide belt extending northwards to the edge of the desert and southwards almost to the forest edge and from Mauritania, Senegal and Gambia in the west to Chad and the Central African Republic in the east.

Nesting: A hole excavated in a rotten branch at a height of 4 to 25 feet. Eggs 2–3, white.

HAIRY-BREASTED TOOTHBILL *Lybius hirsutus*
(*Tricholaema hirsutum, T. flavipunctatum*) **Pl. 33**

Identification: A medium-sized forest Barbet, occurring usually alone or two together and sometimes as a member of the mixed forest bird parties. Sluggish in habit and easily overlooked. A fruit eater. Apart from two whitish stripes on the side of the head the plumage appears rather featureless in the forest shade. At short range the yellow-flecked dark upperparts and dark-streaked-and-spotted yellowish underparts are visible. A well-marked race (*Lybius hirsutus flavipunctatus*, formerly regarded as a species), which lacks the white stripes on the side of the head, occurs in the Cameroon and Gaboon forest.

Voice: Described by Chapin as a series of 12–14 'coos', beginning rather rapidly and later slowing down.

Distribution and Habitat: Sierra Leone to the Central African Republic, Gaboon and Congo, inhabiting the primary and second-growth forest.

Nesting: Habits unknown.

NAKED-FACED BARBET *Gymnobucco calvus* **Pl. 33**

Identification: A dumpy dull-coloured Barbet, brown all over with a naked blackish head. At close range tufts of short bristles on the chin, at the gape, and at each nostril, are visible. Noisy, restless, sociable and quarrelsome. Often encountered in colonies at their nests in great dead forest trees whose trunks are sometimes riddled with Barbet holes. Arboreal, feeding on figs and the fruit of Musanga and other trees, restlessly jumping and flying from branch to branch and balancing tit-like in every conceivable position as they eat the fruit.

Voice: A shrill monosyllabic rasping 'shreep', frequently repeated.

Distribution and Habitat: Widespread in the forest belt from Sierra Leone to Gaboon and Congo. In the Cameroons it ascends in the mountain forests to over 5,000 feet.

Nesting: In a colony in holes excavated in dead trees. Eggs 3–5, white.

Allied species: The Bristle-nosed Barbet (*Gymnobucco peli*) and the Grey-throated Barbet (*Gymnobucco bonapartei*), two closely-related Barbets with similar plumage, habits and habitat, can be distinguished from the Naked-faced Barbet by their prominent, erect nasal tufts, much longer than in that species. Further, in the Grey-throated Barbet the head is feathered, not naked. The Bristle-nosed Barbet ranges from Ghana to Gaboon and the Grey-throated Barbet occurs in the Cameroons, Gaboon and Congo.

DUCHAILLU'S YELLOW-SPOTTED BARBET
Buccanodon duchaillui **Pl. 33**

Identification: Apart from the characteristic purring call, identified by black plumage spotted and barred with yellow, crimson crown, and conspicuous yellow stripe on the side of the head and neck. Often solitary and hidden in the thick foliage of a tall tree, but as many as twelve together may be seen in fruiting trees in forest clearings, and this Barbet occasionally joins the mixed forest bird parties. A fruit-eater that occasionally takes insects.

Voice: A soft musical 'p-r-r-r-r-r' lasting a second or two.

Distribution and Habitat: Sierra Leone to Gaboon and Congo in the lowland forest. It also occurs in the savanna woods and montane forests of the Cameroon highlands ascending to 7,000 feet.

Nesting: Breeds in a hole in a tree. Eggs 4.

SPECKLED TINKER-BIRD   *Pogoniulus scolopaceus*   **Pl. 33**
Identification: A small Barbet, dark above speckled with yellow, washed-out
yellowish below with dark mottlings. Usually found singly or in pairs, searching
in the second-growth trees for fruit and insects, progressing spasmodically in
short jumps or flights.
Voice: A series of 'toks' in a monotone, the tempo increasing towards the end
of the series. It also taps like a Woodpecker.
Distribution and Habitat: Sierra Leone to Gaboon and Congo, and including Fernando Po, in the forest and its clearings and in outlying woods of
the savanna.
Nesting: Nest usually excavated in a decaying stump in second-growth. Eggs
3–4, white.
Allied species: The Mountain Barbet (*Pogoniulus coryphaeus*) is locally common
in the montane forest and the tree-dotted mountain grasslands of west Cameroons. A tiny, usually solitary Barbet, its call a rattling 'tik-tik-tik-tik . . .', but
often silent. Blackish above with a broad central yellow streak from the crown
to the rump, a yellow wing bar, and a white moustachial stripe. Dull olive
underparts.

YELLOW-FRONTED BARBET   *Pogoniulus chrysoconus*   **Pl. 33**
Identification: 4½". Sexes similar. A very small Barbet with a conspicuous
golden-yellow forecrown and a boldly streaked black and white face. More
often heard than seen for it is often hidden in the foliage of tree tops. Upperparts
streaked black and white but rump yellow; underparts sulphur-yellow. Bill
black. Searches the branches and twigs for insects in Warbler fashion.
Voice: A characteristic fluty rhythmic 'poop-poop' repeated monotonously for
prolonged periods with short pauses.
Distribution and Habitat: A common savanna species, especially in the semi-
arid belt ranging from Gambia, Senegal and Portuguese Guinea through Mali,
Ivory Coast, Ghana, Togo, Niger, Nigeria and northern Cameroons to Chad
and the Central African Republic. Absent from the moist savanna belt next to
the forest.
Nesting: A small hole excavated in a dead branch 6 to 12 feet from the ground.
Eggs 2, white.

LEMON-RUMPED TINKER-BIRD   *Pogoniulus bilineatus*
(*P. leucolaima*)   **Pl. 33**
Identification: Glossy black above with a yellow rump; two prominent white
stripes on the side of the head; mainly yellow below, but the throat white. Best
known by its 'touking' call, which persists throughout the day, even in the hot
hours when most birds are silent.
Voice: A far-carrying monotonous 'touk-touk-touk . . .' with brief pauses
between series of 'touks' and sometimes lasting for several minutes.
Distribution and Habitat: A wide-ranging common African species. The
West African races differ from those of South and East Africa by their lemon,
not yellow, rump, and are sometimes considered specifically distinct. In West
Africa from the Gambia to Congo, and including Fernando Po. Occurs in the
main body of the forest (but not in virgin growth) and in the gallery extensions
and orchard bush of the savanna. It penetrates the highland forests to 6,500 feet
at least. Frequents gardens.

Nesting: Breeds in a small shallow excavation in a decaying tree or stump in a forest clearing, laying 2–3 white eggs.

Allied species: The Yellow-throated Tinker-bird (*Pogoniulus subsulphureus*), another common species which ranges from Guinea to Gaboon and Congo, living in the clearing trees and the second-growth of the forest, is remarkably like the Lemon-rumped Tinker-bird. At close range the yellow, not white, throat can be seen, and in some of its races the stripes on the side of the head are also yellow. The call is like that of the Lemon-rumped Tinker-bird but the rhythm is different.

RED-RUMPED TINKER-BIRD *Pogoniulus atroflavus*
(*P. erythronotos*)   **Pl. 33**

Identification: Somewhat resembling the Lemon-rumped Tinker-bird but recognisably larger in the field and having a scarlet not a yellow rump. The stripes on the side of the head are less conspicuous, and are yellow.

Voice: A long-continued loud 'ho-ho-ho-ho . . .', slower and pitched lower than the call of the Lemon-rumped Tinker-bird.

Distribution and Habitat: One of the less common Barbets of the forest frequenting trees on the forest edge and in the clearings and second-growth. Its range extends from Senegal to Gaboon.

Nesting: Nesting hole excavated in a tree or stump. Eggs two, white.

YELLOW-BILLED BARBET *Trachyphonus purpuratus*
(*Trachylaemus purpuratus*)   **Pl. 33**

Identification: The call is unmistakable. A large strikingly coloured Barbet; glossy blue-black above; below, a narrow red band separating the white-streaked black breast from the blotched black and yellow belly. A conspicuous yellow bill and circumorbital patch. A white wing patch, conspicuous in flight. The well-marked race *T. purpuratus goffini* found from Ghana westwards differs in having the throat and breast streaked pinkish and grey and the belly yellow without any black. Occurs singly or in pairs.

Voice: A low-pitched slowly-repeated regular 'poop-poop-poop . . .'.

Distribution and Habitat: Sierra Leone to Gaboon and Congo, in the forest, mainly in its second-growth trees and the fruit-bearing trees of cultivated clearings.

Nesting: The nest is a hole excavated in a dead tree. Eggs 3–4, white.

Allied species: The Yellow-breasted Barbet (*Trachyphonus margaritatus*) inhabits the semi-arid belt from Mali and Niger through northern Nigeria to Chad. A large conspicuous noisy Barbet, boldly spotted with white on the upper parts and tail; yellow below with a black throat patch (male only) and red under tail-coverts.

HONEY-GUIDES: Indicatoridae

Plain-coloured woodland birds without distinctive markings except for the white pattern on the tail which is conspicuous in flight. Partial to beeswax, honey and bee larvae. Parasitic in breeding habits.

144

Plate 29

HONEY-GUIDES

1. **BLACK-THROATED HONEY-GUIDE**
   Indicator indicator
   Mainly white outer tail feathers. Male has black throat and pale cheek patch.

2. **LYRE-TAILED HONEY-GUIDE** *Melichneutes robustus*
   Lyre-shaped tail.

3. **CASSIN'S SHARP-BILLED HONEY-GUIDE**
   Prodotiscus insignis
   Fine-pointed bill; white outer rectrices not tipped with brown.

4. **LEAST HONEY-GUIDE** *Indicator exilis*
   Closely resembles Lesser Honey-Guide but shows black malar stripe.

5. **LESSER HONEY-GUIDE** *Indicator minor*
   No distinct black malar stripe; white outer rectrices tipped brown.

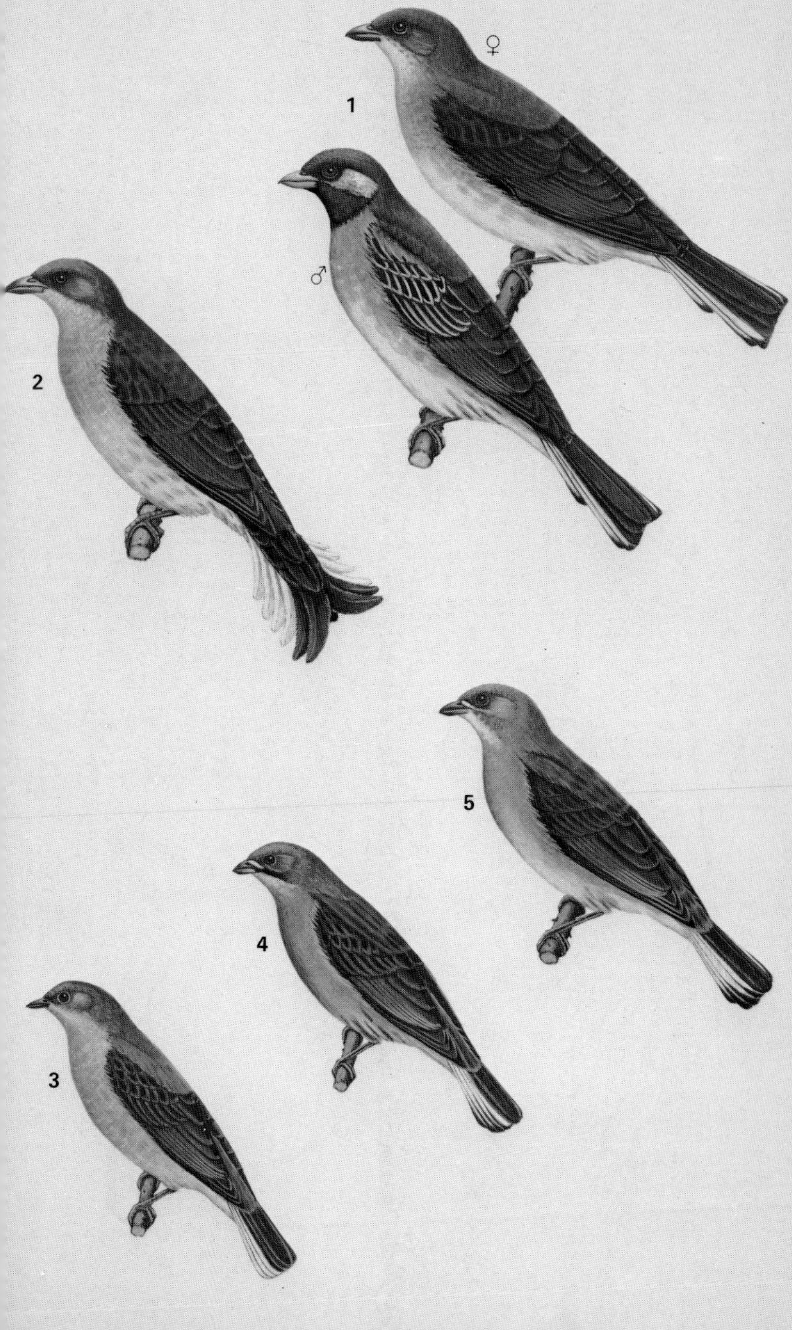
1
♀
♂
2
5
4
3

Plate 30

LARKS, PIPIT, WAGTAILS AND LONG-CLAW

1. **RUFOUS-NAPED LARK** *Mirafra africana* page 153
Black-spotted breast; mainly rufous wing.

2. **SINGING BUSH-LARK** *Mirafra javanica* 153
No crest; mainly sandy-brown with darker streaks; white-edged tail.

3. **CHESTNUT-BACKED FINCH-LARK** *Eremopterix leucotis* 154
Black crown; white ear-coverts and collar across nape.

4. **FLAPPET LARK** *Mirafra rufocinnamomea* 153
Upperparts mainly cinnamon-brown or rufous-brown.

5. **RUFOUS-RUMPED BUSH-LARK** *Mirafra nigricans* 154
White-striped head; boldly blotched breast; cinnamon-rufous rump.

6. **CRESTED LARK** *Galerida cristata* 154
Crested.

7. **YELLOW WAGTAIL** *Motacilla flava* 159
Yellow underparts.

8. **WHITE WAGTAIL** *Motacilla alba* 159
Grey mantle (winter).

9. **AFRICAN PIED WAGTAIL** *Motacilla aguimp* 162
Black mantle.

10. **YELLOW-THROATED LONG-CLAW** *Macronyx croceus* 163
Vivid yellow underparts; black gorget.

11. **PLAIN-BACKED PIPIT** *Anthus leucophrys* 162
Plain unstreaked upperparts.

BLACK-THROATED HONEY-GUIDE   *Indicator indicator*   **Pl. 29**
Identification: 8″. The adult male has brown upperparts, whitish underparts, a black throat, a pale cheek patch, and mainly white outer tail feathers, which are conspicuous in flight. The female lacks the black throat, as does the immature bird, which is further distinguished by its yellowish underparts. Feeds largely on beeswax and is one of the 'guiding' Honey-Guides. Often inconspicuous.
Voice: A dry, repeated 'ker ker' used to lead humans to bees' nests. After calling they approach the person and then move off slowly towards the bees' nest.
Distribution and Habitat: Widely distributed throughout the area except in the desert and the rain forest. Shows a preference for open woodland and orchard bush.
Nesting: Parasitic. In West Africa known to parasitise at least five species of Bee-eater, Gordon's Swallow, and almost certainly the Senegal Wood-Hoopoe and the Abyssinian Roller. Many other host species, especially Barbets and Woodpeckers, are recorded in other parts of Africa. The egg is pure white.

LESSER HONEY-GUIDE   *Indicator minor* (*I. conirostris*)   **Pl. 29**
Identification: The shade of the rather drab body plumage varies locally, the forest forms being darker than the savanna forms. Upper parts olive, the mantle mottled darker; underparts grey; a short stumpy bill. No distinct blackish malar stripe. In flight, which normally is direct, rapid, non-undulating and cuckoo-like, the mainly white outer tail feathers are very conspicuous. Feeds on beeswax and insects; not certainly known to guide to honey.
Voice: In South Africa described as a monotonous 'lew-lew-lew . . .' uttered 10–30 times with intervals of $\frac{1}{2}$ a minute to 3 minutes between series and delivered from a song post in a tree.
Distribution and Habitat: Widespread in Africa and catholic in its choice of habitat. In our area it occurs from Senegal in the west to Chad and the Central African Republic in the east, and south to Gaboon. Found both in forest and savanna but nowhere abundant.
Nesting: Parasitic, mainly on Barbet species, laying a pure white, glossy, ovate egg.
Allied species: The Spotted Honey-Guide (*Indicator maculatus*) is a rather rare forest species which ranges from Gambia to Gaboon. Olive-green above, olive-brown below, the underparts profusely spotted with yellowish or cream. In flight and also at rest when seen from below the tail is mainly white, only the two central pairs of tail feathers and the tips of the others being brown.

LEAST HONEY-GUIDE   *Indicator exilis*   **Pl. 29**
Identification: In proportions and colour rather like the Lesser Honey-Guide (*Indicator minor*) but smaller. It has a similar short stumpy bill and a similar tail pattern. Upperparts rather bright olive streaked with black; underparts pale olive-grey. Adults show a narrow white line between the eye and the nostril, and a blackish malar stripe. Field notes in the literature on voice, feeding habits, breeding habits, etc., are difficult to assign with certainty to the Least Honey-Guide since till recently it was confused with the very similar Willcocks's Honey-Guide.
Distribution and Habitat: Sierra Leone to Gaboon, including Fernando Po; in the forest and the savanna bordering the forest.
Allied species: Willcocks's Honey-Guide (*Indicator willcocksi*) occurs in the

forest and in the gallery extensions north of the forest, ranging from Portuguese Guinea to the Cameroons and the Central African Republic. On plumage characters virtually indistinguishable in the field from the Least Honey-Guide. The adult lacks the white loral streak and the dark malar stripe of the latter species.

LYRE-TAILED HONEY-GUIDE *Melichneutes robustus* **Pl. 29**
Identification: Unmistakable during its remarkable aerial display. It undulates and spirals high over the forest and in the course of rapid descents during its display produces a loud nasal tooting sound, a 'hein-hein' repeated from 10–30 times, first increasing in intensity and rising in pitch and then falling away. The sound is produced mechanically by the vibrating tail feathers. At rest the graduated lyre-shaped tail is diagnostic. The long curved inner rectrices which give the tail its lyrate shape are black; the narrow, short outer rectrices are white. Otherwise a dull-coloured bird.
Distribution and Habitat: A rather rare Honey-Guide of the high forest of Liberia, Ivory Coast, southern Nigeria, the Cameroons and Gaboon.

CASSIN'S SHARP-BILLED HONEY-GUIDE
Prodotiscus insignis   **Pl. 29**
Identification: Recognised by its small size, by its very fine (for a Honey-Guide) pointed bill, by the olive-washed back, and the white outer rectrices untipped with brown, all these characters being observable with field glasses under favourable conditions. This Honey-Guide is not known to guide to bees' nests nor does it take beeswax. It feeds principally on insects which it finds on the leaves and small branches of the forest trees and also catches in the air like a Flycatcher.
Voice: Usually silent. In West Africa it has been heard to utter a weak 'whi-hihi'.
Distribution and Habitat: Sierra Leone to Gaboon in the forest, especially in the trees of its clearings and edges. Widely distributed in Africa but nowhere abundant.
Nesting: No local records. In other parts of Africa it is known to parasitise Flycatchers, Warblers and White-eyes.

WOODPECKERS: Picidae

Arboreal birds with strong, straight, pointed bills with which they tap and drill into the bark for insects. Stiff tails, strong feet, and sharp claws are adaptations for climbing and the pointed bill and long sticky tongue for extracting insects and larvae from holes and cracks in the bark. Often with red in the plumage. Undulating flight. Many have resonant, shrill voices.

EUROPEAN WRYNECK *Jynx torquilla*   **Pl. 33**
Identification: 6½". Sexes similar. Mainly arboreal, perching in the usual passerine way and also clinging to the trunk like a Woodpecker. Sometimes on the ground, where it hops. Unobtrusive in behaviour and inconspicuously coloured. A mixture of brown, grey and rufous streaks, vermiculations, and

spots on a whitish or grey-brown ground. At close range the narrow dark bars on the whitish throat and breast are visible.

Distribution and Habitat: A winter visitor to West Africa from August to April encountered most frequently on spring or autumn passage. Nowhere common yet widely distributed in the savanna from Senegal and Gambia through Portuguese Guinea, Sierra Leone, Liberia, Ivory Coast, Ghana, Togo and Nigeria to the Cameroons, Chad and the Central African Republic.

PIGMY WOODPECKER   *Verreauxia africana*   Pl. 34

Identification: 3″. By its actions a Woodpecker and distinguished from all other African Woodpeckers by its diminutive size. A patch of bare red skin round the eye is a field mark. The upperparts are golden-olive, the underparts grey. The male has a rufous forehead. It finds its insect and larval food on and inside the small branches of the trees and undershrubs, often within a few feet of the ground. Its tapping is loud for so tiny a bird.

Voice: A rather weak high-pitched trill in a monotone.

Distribution and Habitat: Cameroons and Gaboon in the forest second-growth.

Nesting: The two white eggs are laid in a hole excavated in a small tree stump.

FINE-SPOTTED WOODPECKER   *Campethera punctuligera*   Pl. 34

Identification: 8″. Male has forehead, crown, crest and moustachial stripe crimson. Female has only the hind crown and crest crimson, the forehead being black striped with yellow. Both sexes have upperparts yellowish-olive spotted pale yellow and underparts pale yellow with black spots heaviest on the chest. Flight undulating. Feeds on the trunks and branches of trees and also on the ground on ants and termites. Occurs singly, in pairs, and as members of mixed bird parties.

Voice: A loud, laughing 'piu-piu-piu-piu-piu'.

Distribution and Habitat: Common and widespread ranging north to the edge of the desert and south to the forest edge. From Mauritania, Senegal and Gambia east to western Chad and the Central African Republic.

Nesting: Nest in a hole excavated in a tree or an ant-hill. Eggs 4.

GREEN-BACKED WOODPECKER   *Campethera cailliautii*
(*C. permista*)   Pl. 34

Identification: A medium-sized Woodpecker, green above and olive-yellow heavily barred with black below. The head markings are conspicuous. In the adult male the forehead, crown and nape are red; in the female and the juvenile of either sex, the nape only is red, the forehead and crown being black finely spotted with buff. Note the absence of any red or black moustache. Generally discovered searching the trunks and branches for ants and termites, on which it feeds almost exclusively. Usually solitary. An occasional member of the mixed bird parties. Flight undulating.

Voice: A shrill, high-pitched whistle, not often heard.

Distribution and Habitat: A rather common, sedentary, forest species, ranging from Ghana to Gaboon and Congo affecting the primary and especially the second growth. Found also in the gallery forests of the forest-savanna edge.

Nesting: Nest excavated in a hole in a tree. Eggs three, white.

Allied species: The Golden-backed Woodpecker (*Campethera maculosa*), whose range is the lowland forest from Portuguese Guinea to Ghana, has rather similar appearance and habits. The female differs in having no red on the head, but the males of the two forms differ only slightly in shade and markings and are virtually indistinguishable in the field. Fortunately the area of geographical overlap is small.

BUFF-SPOTTED WOODPECKER *Campethera nivosa* Pl. 34

Identification: A small forest Woodpecker, the upperparts varying in shade from brownish-olive to golden-olive according to locality; the head dark brown with, in the male, a splash of crimson on the nape; ear-coverts streaked brown and whitish; throat whitish with dark streaks; rest of the underparts olive-brown profusely spotted with greenish-buff or buff. Usually searching the branches for ants and termites which constitute its principal food and whose nests it appropriates for breeding. Seldom heard tapping. A frequent member of mixed bird parties.

Voice: Normally silent. A sharp rattling call is recorded.

Distribution and Habitat: Resident and common in the primary and second-growth forest and its gallery extensions and outliers from Gambia and Portuguese Guinea to Gaboon and Congo. Occurs in Fernando Po and in the Cameroon highlands ascends to 5,000 feet.

Nesting: Nest a hole excavated by the Woodpecker in an ant's or termite's nest. Eggs 2, white and glossy.

Allied species: The Brown-eared Woodpecker (*Campethera caroli*) resembles *Campethera nivosa* but is slightly larger, the spots on the underside are bolder and extend on to the throat, and the ear-coverts are solid maroon-brown. Its range is the forest from Sierra Leone east to the Central African Republic and south to Gaboon and Congo. It nests in holes in trees. Tullberg's Woodpecker (*Campethera tullbergi*) is a highland species locally common in the montane forests of Cameroon, the Obudu Plateau of eastern Nigeria and the island of Fernando Po. It may be recognised by its conspicuous plumage. Green above; below yellow speckled and spotted with black; the male with a scarlet head, the female with the forehead and crown black spotted with yellow and only the hind crown scarlet. The Golden-tailed Woodpecker (*Campethera abingoni*) widely distributed but nowhere common, inhabits the dry savanna belt from southern Senegal and Gambia in the west to Chad and the Central African Republic in the east. It also occurs in the Gaboon grasslands. Identified by the heavy dark streaking on the breast and by the head markings. In the male the forehead, crown, nape and malar stripe are crimson; in the female the nape only is crimson.

CARDINAL WOODPECKER *Dendropicos fuscescens* Pl. 34

Identification: Probably the commonest small Woodpecker in West Africa. Olive above faintly barred; whitish below finely streaked with black. The intensity of the barring and streaking and the shade of the ground colour vary with locality. Forehead brown; crown and nape scarlet in male, dark brown in female. It explores the branches for insects and larvae; it sometimes climbs downwards and backwards; it both taps and calls. Often in pairs. An occasional member of insect-foraging bird parties in forest or savanna.

Voice: A loud 'bwee-bwee-bwee . . .'; also a sharp rattling trill, rather tinny in tone.

Distribution and Habitat: An adaptable species widely and commonly distributed in the savanna and the forest clearings provided there are trees. Absent from virgin forest. Its range extends from Senegal and Gambia east to Chad and the Central African Republic and south to Gaboon and Congo.

Nesting: In South Africa 2–3 glossy white eggs are laid in a hole excavated in a dead trunk or branch.

Allied species: The Least Grey Woodpecker (*Dendropicos elachus*), 4½″, occurs in the arid savanna south of the desert in Senegal, Gambia, Mali, Niger, northern Nigeria and Chad. Both sexes have a red rump. Upperparts barred grey-brown and white. Underparts whitish indistinctly spotted with brown. The male has a scarlet crest.

GABOON WOODPECKER   *Dendropicos gabonensis*   Pl. 34

Identification: It is fairly easy to distinguish in the field the three races of this West African Woodpecker. The race occurring in Congo, Gaboon and southern Cameroons (*D. g. gabonensis*) has bright green upperparts and yellowish-green underparts streaked with black. The crown and nape are scarlet in the male and dark brown in the female. The race occurring from Ghana west to Guinea (*D. g. lugubris*) has the upperparts olive-green tinged with golden, the underparts are altogether darker than those of *gabonensis* due to the heavy olive-brown streaking, and only the hind crown and nape of the male are scarlet. An intermediate race (*D. g. reichenowi*) with head markings like *gabonensis* and underparts like *lugubris* inhabits west Cameroons and south-eastern Nigeria. It feeds mainly on the larvae of wood-boring insects, which it finds in the decaying trees or soft wood of the forest clearings and second-growth. It taps loudly. It is not an ant or termite eater.

Voice: A shrill piercing cry.

Distribution and Habitat: Guinea to Congo as outlined above. Restricted to the forest zone where it frequents the trees in cultivated clearings and the second-growth. Absent from virgin forest.

Nesting: The nesting hole is excavated in a dead tree.

LESSER WHITE-SPOTTED WOODPECKER
Dendrocopos obsoletus (*Dendropicos obsoletus*)   Pl. 34

Identification: A dry-country Woodpecker occurring singly or in pairs. Brown above; whitish faintly streaked below. The conspicuous white spots on the wing and tail distinguish it from most other small Woodpeckers of the West African semi-arid zone. The male has a scarlet patch on the nape. There is no red on the rump. Found singly, in pairs, or in small parties quietly searching the savanna trees for insects and larvae.

Voice: A feeble high-pitched trill.

Distribution and Habitat: The savanna belt north of the forest from Senegal and Gambia east to Chad and the Central African Republic.

Nesting: Nests in a hole in a dead branch. Eggs 2, white and glossy.

GREY WOODPECKER   *Mesopicos goertae*   Pl. 34

Identification: 8″. A mainly grey Woodpecker without conspicuous spots or barring. Back and wings olive-gold. Male has crown, rump and upper tail-coverts red, and patch on belly yellow or orange-red. Female and immature bird similar but with grey crown. Partial to high trees such as Oil-palms.

Voice: A loud shrill 'peet-peet-peet-peet' or 'peeuh-peeuh . . .'
Distribution and Habitat: Widely and commonly distributed throughout the area wherever there are trees, extending as far as the desert edge, and, where there are clearings, into the rain forest. Also occurs south of the forest in the Gaboon and Congo savanna.
Nesting: Nest in a hole excavated in a tree trunk or stump or in an ants' nest. Eggs 2–4, glossy white.

FIRE-BELLIED WOODPECKER *Mesopicos pyrrhogaster*   **Pl. 34**
Identification: The large size, striking plumage, and loud drumming serve to identify it. Golden-olive mantle; crown, rump and middle line of the breast and belly crimson; the sides of the body spotted and barred black and white; two prominent black streaks on the side of the head. The female lacks the crimson crown. Usually in pairs in the high dead and dying trees left in forest patches cleared for crops, and found also in primary and second-growth and in swamp forest. The larvae of wood-boring beetles and other insects form its main diet.
Voice: A shrill cry.
Distribution and Habitat: Resident in the forest zone from Guinea and Sierra Leone to Nigeria.
Nesting: Nothing recorded. The related Golden-crowned Woodpecker excavates its nesting hole in a dead tree.
Allied species: The Golden-crowned Woodpecker (*Mesopicos xantholophus*) has rather similar habits and occupies the same ecological niche. Its range is the forest of Cameroons, Gaboon, Congo and the Central African Republic. Easily distinguished from *M. pyrrhogaster* by the absence of crimson markings. Its field characters are the black-and-white striped head, the yellow-tipped crown feathers (in the male), and the white-spotted olive underparts.

ELLIOT'S WOODPECKER *Mesopicos ellioti*   **Pl. 34**
Identification: Green above; pale yellow underparts heavily streaked with black; the male with the forecrown black and the hindcrown scarlet, the female with the whole crown black. The montane races *M. ellioti johnstoni* and *M. ellioti kupeensis* can be distinguished in the field by the finer and sparser streaking of the underparts. It occurs in pairs and often joins the mixed forest bird parties. Seen at all heights from the lowest undershrubs to the high forest canopy exploring the branches for insects and larvae.
Voice: A shrill cry. It also drums loudly on the branches.
Distribution and Habitat: The lowland forest of the Cameroons, Gaboon and Congo, and also the montane forests of Fernando Po, the Cameroons and the Obudu Plateau of eastern Nigeria. It is quite common in the montane forest.
Nesting: The nest and eggs are unknown.

BROADBILLS: Eurylaemidae

BLACK-CAPPED BROADBILL *Smithornis capensis*   **Pl. 35**
Identification: 5″. The very broad heavy bill, which is a family character, the black crown, the heavily-streaked breast and flanks, and in flight the white patch on the middle of the back, make identification easy. Females have the

crown grey. A small squat bird usually seen quietly perched on a low spray in the forest second-growth, and from and back to its perch making characteristic very short circular flights.

Voice: A curious loud vibrant 'prrrrr . . .', usually uttered during its circuit flight.

Distribution and Habitat: Locally distributed in the forest from Sierra Leone to Gaboon, in the thick second-growth; absent from the primary forest.

Nesting: Nest suspended from a low branch. An elongated pouch with a side opening. Rather roughly made, mainly of strips of fibre, with a 'beard' like that of a Sunbird's nest trailing from the lower end. Eggs 2–3, glossy white.

Allied species: The Rufous-sided Broadbill (*Smithornis rufolateralis*) differs from the Black-capped Broadbill in having an orange patch on either side of the chest and a double white wing bar. Its circular display flight, call and other habits are rather similar, but it differs in its habitat preference, usually frequenting the shady interior of primary rain forest. Its range is the forest from Liberia to Gaboon.

PITTAS: Pittidae

ANGOLA PITTA   *Pitta angolensis*   **Pl. 35**
Identification: 7″. Seldom seen, being mainly terrestrial, shy and addicted to thick cover in the forest. A long-legged, plump, thrush-like bird, easily identified, if seen, by its brilliant plumage, a pattern of green, cobalt-blue, red, black and fawn.

Voice: In East Africa a loud call heard at the breeding season has been described as a deep, liquid, short trill, 'p-r-r-r-p'.

Distribution and Habitat: The forest from Sierra Leone to Gaboon and Congo, in primary and second-growth, especially the latter. It breeds in West Africa and as yet there is no clear evidence that it is migratory in this part of its range.

Nesting: Takes place during the rainy season. The large domed globular nest composed mainly of leaves and leaf skeletons is set among the branches and twigs of a forest tree or undershrub. Eggs 3, glossy rounded ellipses, cream with a few bold purplish-black blotches and spots and ashy shell-marks, mainly about the large end.

Allied species: The Green-breasted Pitta (*Pitta reichenowi*) is rather similar to the Angola Pitta but the breast is green instead of fawn. Its range is more restricted; in our area it has been recorded from a few forest localities in south-eastern Cameroon and Gaboon.

LARKS: Alaudidae

A group of ground-loving birds (though some forms perch at times) living mostly in sparsely wooded or arid regions. Progress by walking or running. Colouring usually dull, sandy or earth-brown. Rather heavily built. Claw of hind toe often elongated and straight. Song and call often distinctive.

SINGING BUSH-LARK *Mirafra javanica (M. cantillans)*   **Pl. 30**
Identification: 5″. Sexes similar. A small, uncrested, sandy-coloured Lark
with a white-edged tail which is conspicuous in flight but with no other distinctive markings. Sandy-brown above with dark streaks, the wings edged with
rufous. Dirty white below, the chest lightly streaked with brown. At the breeding
season the call and display flight attract notice. At other times shy and inconspicuous, creeping about the grass or stubble.
Voice: At the breeding season male sings a great deal either from a perch on
the ground or a shrub or as he flutters round in circles over his territory. A
high-pitched piping trill with a squeaky quality that recalls the song of the
Corn Bunting.
Distribution and Habitat: Open wooded or shrubby grassland in the arid
zone bordering the desert in southern Mauritania, Senegal, Guinea, Mali,
northern Nigeria, Niger, northern Cameroons and Chad. Local over most of
its range.
Nesting: On the ground in or near a tuft of grass. A fragile bowl of fine grass
with a rather sketchy dome. Eggs 4, whitish, thickly and evenly spotted and
mottled with dark brown and grey.

RUFOUS-NAPED LARK *Mirafra africana*   **Pl. 30**
Identification: A rather large, sturdy, relatively short-tailed Lark. The
plumage varies with locality, the upperparts from pinkish-brown to dark
rufous, streaked and mottled with black; the underparts from cream to deep
cinnamon, with black spots on the breast. In flight the rufous wings are a field
mark. Locality is a good guide to identification.
Voice: A characteristic sweet musical whistle of two to four syllables, usually
delivered from a small shrub or other low perch.
Distribution and Habitat: A widespread African Lark which in West Africa
is local, occurring in certain areas of montane grassland or open upland savanna
in Guinea, Liberia, Ivory Coast, Nigeria (Jos Plateau), the Cameroons and
eastern Chad, and reappearing in the grass savannas of southern Gaboon and
Congo.
Nesting: In East Africa it builds its nest on the ground in an open grassy place
laying two to three profusely spotted eggs.

FLAPPET LARK *Mirafra rufocinnamomea (M. buckleyi)*   **Pl. 30**
Identification: A small inconspicuously marked lark, cinnamon-brown or
cinnamon-rufous above and mainly buff below, the shades varying with locality.
The rhythmic, loud whirring clap of wings as the bird soars round high overhead
with dipping flight is the best character for field recognition. It often squats on
earth roads. It does not perch on trees.
Voice: Usually silent. A soft two-note whistle has been recorded.
Distribution and Habitat: A savanna Lark from Gambia in the west to
Chad and the Central African Republic in the east, reappearing south of the
rain forest in the savannas of Gaboon and Congo. Frequents the lightly wooded
or open grass savanna, including the derived savanna of the forest belt, but not
the forest itself. Rarer in the northern arid areas. Locally common. More than
half a dozen displaying males may be within earshot simultaneously.
Nesting: Eggs 2, closely streaked and spotted with brown and grey. A domed
nest in a hollow on the ground.

RUFOUS-RUMPED BUSH-LARK *Mirafra nigricans*
(*Pinarocorys erythropygia*) **Pl. 30**

Identification: A large Lark, upright stance, noticeably dark upperparts, whitish below boldly blotched with black on the throat and breast. The most distinctive features are the white stripes on the side of the head and the cinnamon-rufous rump, the latter being a character of the West African race only, which is sometimes recognised as a full species (*Mirafra erythropygia*). Seeks out bare recently burned ground; not infrequently perches in the savanna trees.

Voice: A fine full-throated song uttered as the Lark, with undulating flight, circles widely round high over its territory.

Distribution and Habitat: The savanna north of the forest from Gambia and Mali to Chad and the Central African Republic, migrating northwards in the wet (the non-breeding) season to the semi-arid belt. Locally fairly common.

Nesting: Eggs 2, thickly spotted and speckled with olive-brown and grey. Nest a hole in the ground scantily lined with fibres and grass stems.

CHESTNUT-BACKED FINCH-LARK *Eremopterix leucotis* **Pl. 30**

Identification: 4½″. A little Sparrow-like Lark. Adult male distinctively coloured. Head and neck black with contrasting white ear-coverts and collar across nape. Rest of upperparts mainly chestnut and white. Underparts black. Female plumage duller and variable, with the mantle brownish, no conspicuous white head markings, and underparts mainly buff with a black patch on the breast and belly. Usually on the ground. Fond of dusty roads, bare, charred and open fallow ground, and the vicinity of water. Sometimes perches. Often in small flocks.

Voice: Call a repeated sharp 'twit-twit', not very distinctive. Also sings during display flight.

Distribution and Habitat: Widely distributed and locally abundant in the semi-arid belt between 10° N. and 18° N. with a general shift northwards in the rains. From southern Mauritania, Senegal and Gambia through Mali, northern Ghana, Niger, northern Nigeria and northern Cameroons to Chad.

Nesting: A slight depression in the ground scantily lined with fine grass and usually up against and in the shade of a tuft of grass, stone or heap of dried dung. Eggs 1–3, usually 1, greyish-white thickly freckled with olive-brown with a dark ring at the larger end.

Allied species: The White-fronted Finch-Lark (*Eremopterix nigriceps*) is more of a desert bird and inhabits the Cape Verde Islands and the southern edge of the Sahara in Mauritania, Mali, Niger and Chad. The male is similar in build and size to the Chestnut-backed Finch-Lark and has the same black underparts, but the white forehead and grey-brown back distinguish it. The female is sandy-brown all over, paler in shade underneath.

CRESTED LARK *Galerida cristata* **Pl. 30**

Identification: 7″. Sexes similar. A fairly large sturdy Lark with a fair-sized crest, which is often erect and is the best field character. Upperparts sandy-brown, the crest streaked with black and the mantle with dark brown. Underparts mainly cream, the breast having heavy dark streaks. Outer tail feathers sandy-rufous. The shade of plumage varies geographically and with wear. A terrestrial Lark. Seldom perches.

Voice: Regardless of the season often utters a pleasant, fluty, liquid 'dee-lee-oo'.

Distribution and Habitat: A common and widespread savanna Lark found in varied terrain but showing a preference for clearings with crops or pasture. Ranges in the northern savanna from Mauritania, Senegal, Gambia and Portuguese Guinea east to Nigeria, Chad and Central African Republic.

Nesting: On the ground amongst low crops or tufted grass. Eggs 2–4, yellowish-white densely spotted with yellowish-brown and purplish-grey with a cap at the large end.

Allied species: The Sun-Lark (*Galerida modesta*), 5½″, is smaller than the Crested Lark with a less conspicuous crest and a darker appearance especially above due to the heavy dark streaks and the darker ground colour of the mantle and back. The ranges overlap but the Sun-Lark is absent from the arid north and penetrates farther south. From southern Senegal, Guinea and Sierra Leone through southern Mali, Ivory Coast, Upper Volta, Ghana, Nigeria and northern Cameroons to the Central African Republic. The Red-capped Lark (*Calandrella cinerea*), 6″, is rare in West Africa, being recorded only from the Jos Plateau of Nigeria, where it breeds, and from Brazzaville in Congo. A small, slimly-built, mainly terrestrial Lark easily recognised at close range by its rufous cap and rusty patch on either side of the breast.

SWALLOWS AND MARTINS: Hirundinidae

A well-defined family of rather small, slimly-built birds with long pointed wings and often forked tail. Short flattened bill with a wide gape. Short legs and feet but strong claws that aid perching and clinging. Strong, agile, graceful fliers spending much time in pursuit of aerial insects, their only food.

AFRICAN SAND MARTIN *Riparia paludicola* **Pl. 35**

Identification: 5″. Entire upperparts brown, throat and breast grey, belly white. Sexes similar. Resembles Common Sand Martin (*Riparia riparia*) in mode of flight and general behaviour. Gregarious.

Voice: A variety of weak twittering cries usually uttered in flight.

Distribution and Habitat: Resident. Locally distributed in the savanna from Senegal and Mali east through Nigeria to Chad and south to the Bamenda highlands in which latter locality it is common. Partial to rivers and streams with steep sandy or clay banks.

Nesting: Usually in colonies, sometimes singly. Burrows excavated by the birds in river banks or cuttings near water. In the terminal nesting chamber a bulky nest of grass and rootlets lined with feathers. Eggs 2–3, white.

Allied species: The European Sand Martin (*Riparia riparia*), 5″, sexes similar, resembles the African Sand Martin but has white underparts with a well-demarcated brown chest band. It can be confused with the Banded Martin (*Riparia cincta*), an African species, but the latter is larger and more heavily built and shows a white streak on the side of the forehead. A passage migrant and winter visitor from the Palaearctic region showing a preference for inland lakes and large rivers. Common in winter in Senegal, abundant on spring and autumn passage at Lake Chad, where it also winters, and recorded from several widely separated localities, mainly as a migrant, in Cape Verde Islands, Gambia, Sierra Leone, Liberia, Ivory Coast, Mali, Ghana, Nigeria and Chad.

EUROPEAN SWALLOW   *Hirundo rustica (H. lucida)*   **Pl. 35**
Identification: 7″. Sexes similar. The deeply-forked white-mirrored tail, dark blue-black upperparts, dark blue pectoral band and white breast and belly are distinguishing marks. (The resident African race (*H. rustica lucida*) is distinguished when mature from the more widespread migrant Palaearctic race (*H. rustica rustica*) by the shorter streamers and narrower pectoral band.) Given to perching on telegraph wires and bare tree branches. By day hawks for insects in larger or smaller flocks. At night gathers at large communal roosts in rank herbage.
Voice: Song a pleasing twittering warble. Twittering call notes.
Distribution and Habitat: The Palaearctic race is a common spring and autumn migrant throughout West Africa and an abundant winter visitor in the forest belt clearings and the moister savanna in Ghana, Nigeria, the Cameroons, Gaboon and Congo. The resident West African race inhabits the drier savanna and semi-arid belt from Senegal, Gambia and Portuguese Guinea east through Mali, Upper Volta and northern Ghana to Niger and northern Nigeria.
Nesting: An open mud nest lined with feathers usually lodged on a ledge or beam in a building. Eggs 3–4, white profusely spotted with brown.

WHITE-THROATED BLUE SWALLOW   *Hirundo nigrita*   **Pl. 35**
Identification: Dark shining blue with a white chin spot visible at rest and in flight. In the air the white marks on the rectrices catch the eye when the bird momentarily spreads its tail. Tail square. Sexes similar. Riverine habitat typical. Frequently rests on rocks in mid-stream or on projecting snags. Easy graceful flight, usually close to the water.
Voice: A twittering song.
Distribution and Habitat: Rivers and lakes with forested banks in the rain forest zone from Sierra Leone to Gaboon and Congo. Fairly common in this restricted habitat occurring mainly as isolated pairs. Occasionally in flocks when the water level is high.
Nesting: Nest an open mud cup lined with fine grasses and feathers. Usually built against a rock or fallen tree trunk or framework of a pier overhanging the water. Eggs 2–3. White evenly blotched and spotted with chestnut and tawny-brown and underlying ashy-purple marks.

WIRE-TAILED SWALLOW   *Hirundo smithii*   **Pl. 35**
Identification: 5½″. Long outermost rectrices, pure white underparts, chestnut-red crown and dark glossy blue upperparts distinguish it.
Voice: Usually silent. Call note a sharp 'twit'. Occasionally a twittering song.
Distribution and Habitat: Widely but unevenly dispersed in the savanna north of the forest from Senegal, Gambia and Portuguese Guinea through Niger and Ghana to the Cameroons and Chad, occurring in pairs or flocks. Partial to rivers but ranges widely over a variety of terrain.
Nesting: Nests are solitary and are open cups of mud lined with grass and feathers. Usually stuck on to rock overhanging the river. Eggs three, white blotched, spotted, and speckled especially about the large end with red-brown.
Allied species: The Ethiopian Swallow (*Hirundo aethiopica*), 5½″, is a common resident in Ivory Coast, Niger, Ghana, Nigeria, the Cameroons, Chad and the Central African Republic in the open country north of the forest. In south-

western Nigeria it penetrates the forest zone where there are large clearings. Specially common about towns and villages where it breeds in the roofs of the thatched houses. The upperparts, except for a chestnut patch on the forehead, are black glossed with purplish-blue. The underparts are whitish with a black patch on the upper breast on either side.

PIED-WINGED SWALLOW *Hirundo leucosoma* **Pl. 35**

Identification: 5″. A large white wing patch, very conspicuous in flight, distinguishes it from all other West African Swallows. Upperparts dark glossy blue, underparts white. Tail slightly forked. Sexes similar. Given to perching on telegraph wires and trees. When hawking for insects often associates with other Swallow species by which it is usually outnumbered.

Voice: Not described.

Distribution and Habitat: Somewhat local. Usually only a pair at a place. Resident. It ranges in the savanna, mainly in the zone bordering the forest, from Senegal and Gambia to Nigeria.

Nesting: The nest is an open cup lined with fibres, built on a support of the roof of a house or hut. Clutch 4.

MOSQUE SWALLOW *Hirundo senegalensis* **Pl. 35**

Identification: 9″. Sexes similar. The large size, long wings, deeply-forked tail and colour pattern distinguish it. Upperparts blue-black except for rufous collar and rump. Chin and throat cream, breast and belly rufous. The shade of the rufous parts varies geographically. The rather slow ponderous flight is characteristic. Distinguished from Gordon's Swallow by its larger size and pale rufous not black cheeks, and from the Red-rumped Swallow by its much larger size.

Voice: A piping call when on the wing. Also a short musical song, and at the nest a guttural croak.

Distribution and Habitat: Widely but unevenly distributed and locally common in the savanna and the larger clearings in the forest but absent from the most arid savanna and from closed forest. From Senegal, Gambia and Portuguese Guinea east to Chad and the Central African Republic and south to Gaboon and Congo.

Nesting: A large saucer-shaped mud nest lined with feathers, inside a hollow baobab or other large tree or under the eaves of a building. In East Africa lays 3–4 pure white eggs.

Allied species: The Red-rumped Swallow (*Hirundo daurica*), 7″, sexes similar, has the upperparts glossy blue except for a rufous collar and rump, and the underparts white or pale rufous. Widely but locally distributed in the savanna in Senegal, Gambia, Portuguese Guinea, Sierra Leone, Ivory Coast, Ghana, Nigeria, Cameroons and Chad. The Palaearctic race in which the forehead is crossed by a thin band of chestnut is common in winter in Senegal and is also recorded from Chad.

LESSER STRIPED SWALLOW *Hirundo abyssinica* **Pl. 35**

Identification: 5½″ to tip of folded wings, 7½″ to tip of tail. A slight, slim Swallow with a deeply forked tail. Head and rump rufous-chestnut; mantle dark glossy blue; underparts whitish streaked with black, the streaking being particularly heavy and conspicuous in the race occurring in the Cameroon highlands. Graceful, buoyant flight. In pairs or parties and often hawks for insects with other species of Swallow.

Voice: A sweet twittering song. Call note a rather soft wheezy 'wheet'.

Distribution and Habitat: Widespread and common in the savanna and locally distributed in the forest clearings from Senegal and Mali to the Cameroons, Chad, Gaboon and Congo. Rocky hills attract it and especially at the breeding season bridges and modern dwellings. Subject to local migrations.

Nesting: Corrugated iron verandahs and roofs and concrete or iron railway and road culverts and bridges are the usual nest sites; less often natural sites such as caves and rock faces in the hills. The mud retort-shaped nests are lined with grasses and feathers. Eggs 2–4, white, either immaculate or marked, usually faintly and sparingly, with spots and blotches of orange-brown and chestnut.

Allied species: The Rufous-breasted Swallow (*Hirundo semirufa*) is slightly larger than the Lesser Striped Swallow, is similarly proportioned, often shares the same terrain, and chooses similar nesting sites. It is distinguished by its colour pattern. The upperparts except for the chestnut rump are dark glossy blue and the underparts are rufous-chestnut. The white markings on the deeply forked tail are conspicuous in flight. It ranges in the savanna and the forest clearings from Senegal and Mali to Gaboon, and is common.

EUROPEAN HOUSE MARTIN   *Delichon urbica*   Pl. 35

Identification: 5″. Sexes similar. Field marks are the forked tail, dark glossy blue upperparts except for a conspicuous clear-cut white rump, and pure white underparts. The only Swallow with which confusion is likely in West Africa is the resident rather local Preuss's Cliff Swallow (*Hirundo spilodera preussi*) (see Checklist, p. 279), but the latter has a creamy or buffish rump and dirty white or pale brown underparts and is further distinguished at close quarters by a chestnut patch behind the eye.

Distribution and Habitat: A widespread but local, erratic and on the whole uncommon passage migrant and winter visitor in West Africa. Most records come from the savannas of Nigeria and the Cameroons where in places it occurs in good numbers. Rare visitor Cape Verde Islands.

FANTI ROUGH-WINGED SWALLOW   *Psalidoprocne obscura*
                                                        Pl. 35

Identification: 7″. A unicoloured dark Swallow with an oily green or bluish gloss. The long deeply-forked tail, slender build and swift buoyant flight are field marks. Usually in pairs or small parties hawking for insects in a clearing in the woodland savanna or on the border of a gallery forest. Given to resting on a high slender bare branch on the edge of a clearing.

Voice: Call a soft 'seep'.

Distribution and Habitat: Senegal and Portuguese Guinea to western Cameroons, in the savanna in the zone adjoining the forest. Also in the forest itself where there are extensive clearings.

Nesting: Burrows excavated by the birds themselves in road cuttings, pits or river banks. These penetrate horizontally for about two feet and terminate in a rounded egg chamber. Eggs 2, white, laid on a pad of fibre and moss.

Allied species: The Square-tailed Rough-winged Swallow (*Psalidoprocne nitens*), 4½″, is a true forest species which ranges from Sierra Leone to Gaboon and Congo. Village clearings and areas recently felled and cleared for farming attract it. Its square tail and uniformly dark somewhat glossy plumage serve to identify it over most of its range, but in the Cameroons and Gaboon forest it can easily be confused with the Forest Cliff Swallow (*Hirundo fuliginosa*). At close range the rusty-brown throat of the latter is distinctive. On the forested slopes of the Cameroon Mountain the Mountain Rough-winged Swallow (*Psalidoprocne fuliginosa*) is yet another species with which it may be confused. The larger size and at close range the unglossed sooty-brown plumage of *P. fuliginosa* are diagnostic.

WAGTAILS AND PIPITS: Motacillidae

A predominantly terrestrial group of small slimly-built birds with strong feet and usually long tails. Walk and run on the ground, and, especially the Wagtails, wag their tails up and down. Mainly found in open savanna or cultivated terrain or near water. Pipits usually brown with streaks, and difficult to identify in the field. Wagtails usually patterned grey, black and white, and sometimes yellow.

YELLOW WAGTAIL   *Motacilla flava* (*Budytes flavus*)   **Pl. 30**
Identification: 6½″. In our area distinguished by its yellow underparts from all other Wagtail species except the Grey Wagtail (*Motacilla cinerea*) (see Checklist, p. 279). The latter occurs sparingly in winter in Senegal and Gambia and is distinguished from the Yellow Wagtail by its very long tail, grey mantle, yellowish rump, and vivid sulphur-yellow under tail-coverts. Several races of the Yellow Wagtail, differentiated mainly on head markings, occur in West Africa, and after the spring moult males can often be racially identified in the field. In appearance and actions a typical Wagtail. By day usually in small flocks in any open place where there are insects on or near the ground. Grazing herds, the outskirts of villages, rice fields, damp meadows, lakesides and seashores attract it. By night gathers in great roosts, often in tall grass.
Distribution and Habitat: A widespread and abundant passage migrant and winter visitor (September–April) from the Palaearctic Region recorded from all the territories in our area and from all vegetation zones except closed forest. There is an isolated breeding population just north of our area on the islands of the Banc d'Arguin in Mauritania.

WHITE WAGTAIL   *Motacilla alba*   **Pl. 30**
Identification: 7″. Sexes rather similar. Readily recognised as a Wagtail by its pose, actions and build. In winter dress crown black, mantle grey, tail black and white, forehead, face and underparts white with a black pectoral band. The African Pied Wagtail (*Motacilla aguimp*), sometimes regarded as a race of the White Wagtail, is similar but has the entire upper surface black.
Distribution and Habitat: A winter (September–April) visitor from the Palaearctic Region recorded from Gambia, Senegal, Sierra Leone, Liberia, Mali, northern Nigeria, the Central African Republic and Chad. Mainly in the arid north bordering the desert. In Senegal where it is common it affects especially the African villages, irrigated fields and rice fields, as well as the earth roads, dispersing during the day and gathering into large roosts at night.

Plate 31

BABBLERS, DRONGO, MAGPIE, ROCK-FOWL AND CROW

Gilbert's Babbler, *Kupeornis gilberti*, page 201

31

Plate 32

WARBLERS

1. EUROPEAN WHITETHROAT *Sylvia communis* page 205
White throat; chestnut wing-patch; white outer tail feathers.

2. BLACKCAP *Sylvia atricapilla* 205
Sharply demarcated black cap.

3. GARDEN WARBLER *Sylvia borin* 205
Brown above; buffish-white below. No arresting plumage characters.

4. SINGING CISTICOLA *Cisticola cantans* 207
Plain dark grey upperparts; rust-brown wing-patch.

5. STRIPED CISTICOLA *Cisticola natalensis* 210
a. Winter dress: heavily-striped upperparts; long tail.
b. Summer dress: mottled upperparts; russet-edged flight feathers;
stout bill.

6. REDPATE CISTICOLA *Cisticola ruficeps* 211
Summer dress: rust-brown head and nape; conspicuous black and
white tipped tail.

7. RUFOUS GRASS-WARBLER *Cisticola galactotes* 210
Summer dress: brown head; boldly mottled back.

8. RED-WINGED WARBLER *Prinia erythroptera* 212
Summer dress: plain grey upperparts; bright chestnut on wing;
tawny-buff underparts.

9. SHORTWING CISTICOLA *Cisticola brachyptera* 211
Male, summer dress: plain back; patterned tail.

10. DESERT FANTAIL WARBLER *Cisticola aridula* 212
Male, summer dress: mottled head and mantle.

11. COMMON FANTAIL WARBLER *Cisticola juncidis* 211
a. Male, summer dress: heavily mottled head and mantle.
b. Male, winter dress: head and mantle more streaked than mottled.

12. WEST AFRICAN PRINIA *Prinia subflava* 212
a. Male, summer dress: plain mantle; white stripe over eye.
b. Male, winter dress: long tail; rusty-tinged upperparts.

AFRICAN PIED WAGTAIL *Motacilla aguimp* **Pl. 30**

Identification: A typical Wagtail in appearance and habits. Head and back black; underparts white with black breast band; wings and tail patterned black and white. The closely related White Wagtail of Europe which occurs in West Africa in winter is distinguished by having a grey (not a black) back.

Voice: Note a sharp 'chizzit'. Song a pleasing warble.

Distribution and Habitat: Widely distributed in West Africa in forest and savanna from Senegal and Portuguese Guinea east to Chad and the Central African Republic and south to Gaboon and Congo. Partial to large rivers and river beds and the vicinity of human habitation. Resident, occurring in pairs or small parties.

Nesting: Nests in holes in buildings and river banks, laying three eggs so profusely marked with pale yellowish-brown as to appear almost unicoloured.

Allied species: The Mountain Wagtail (*Motacilla clara*) is locally distributed from Portuguese Guinea to Gaboon and Congo and Fernando Po. It affects the smaller streams especially in hilly country such as the Cameroon highlands. It is distinguished from the White Wagtail and the African Pied Wagtail by having both crown and back grey.

PLAIN-BACKED PIPIT *Anthus leucophrys* **Pl. 30**

Identification: 7½". Sexes similar. The plain unstreaked upperparts are distinctive. Upperparts earth-brown, throat white, moustachial streak blackish. Underparts pale buff, the breast streaked indistinctly with brown. Tail dark brown except for mainly buff outer rectrices. The Tawny Pipit (*Anthus campestris*) is paler and is unstreaked below. Outside breeding season usually in small flocks. Typical Pipit action, running actively, pecking at the ground, or pausing with head uplifted and tail jerking up and down. Occasionally perches on trees.

Voice: A soft 'sissit' frequently uttered on the wing and a monosyllabic note usually uttered on the ground.

Distribution and Habitat: Widely and commonly distributed in the savanna from Mauritania, Senegal and Gambia east to Chad and the Central African Republic and south to Congo. In the Cameroon highlands to 6,000 feet. Absent from the closed forest. Fond of fallow farmland, recently burnt savanna, short grass and other open places.

Nesting: On the ground among crops or pasture. A little hollow scantily lined with grass and fibre. Eggs 3, greyish-white thickly mottled, spotted and streaked with brown and purplish-grey.

Allied species: The Tawny Pipit (*Anthus campestris*), 6½", sexes similar, is a passage migrant and winter visitor (October–May) to West Africa from the Palaearctic region. Widely but locally distributed in the territory bordering the desert being recorded from Gambia, Senegal, Mali, northern Ghana, northern Nigeria, Niger and Chad, and it favours open arid stony or sandy wastes. A slimly built, pale-coloured Pipit almost unstreaked in adult plumage. Upperparts pale sandy-brown; throat and belly whitish; breast buff; a conspicuous light eye-stripe. Usually single or in pairs. The wide-ranging Richard's Pipit (*Anthus novaeseelandiae*) occurs in West Africa as a breeding resident on the upper open grassy slopes of the mountains of the Cameroon highlands. Occurs throughout the year in the Ennedi Mountains. Also recorded from a few lowland localities in northern Nigeria, northern Cameroons and Chad, where its status is probably that of a non-breeding visitor. A large (7″) long-legged streak-breasted Pipit. The general colour is dark brown or rufous, the shade varying with locality and wear. Unfortunately usually indistinguishable in the field from Nicholson's Pipit (*Anthus similis*) which in the Cameroon highlands often occupies the same ground. The Tree-Pipit (*Anthus trivialis*), 6″, sexes similar, is a common and widespread visitor (September–April) to West Africa from the Palaearctic Region. In the northern arid zones mainly a passage migrant but in the moister savanna and the forest clearings resident, frequenting mainly orchard bush and cultivated clearings. Occurs singly or in small parties, feeding on the ground, and often flying up to perch in trees. Upperparts olive-brown, breast yellow-buff, belly white. Mantle streaked, rump plain, breast boldly streaked. The Red-throated Pipit (*Anthus cervinus*), 6″, sexes similar, is a rather uncommon or overlooked winter visitor to West Africa recorded from a few widely separated localities in Senegal, Gambia, Ivory Coast, Ghana, Chad and Nigeria, in which last territory it is fairly common on the Jos Plateau. Partial to short grass meadows, marshes, and the borders of rivers and lakes. Often associates with Yellow Wagtails. The pink throat and breast are distinctive but in most individuals appear only a few weeks before their spring departure for their Palaearctic breeding grounds. In general appearance resembles the Tree-Pipit but the rump is streaked not plain.

YELLOW-THROATED LONG-CLAW *Macronyx croceus* Pl. 30
Identification: A large stoutly built Pipit readily recognised by its call, its slow flight during which glides alternate with fluttering wing beats and by its vivid yellow underparts and black gorget. White tail marks are conspicuous in flight.
Voice: The call is a characteristic frequently repeated short melodious whistle often uttered on the wing. Also a sweet unpretentious song.
Distribution and Habitat: A common resident species widely distributed in the West African savanna. Absent from the country bordering the desert and from the rain forest interior. Partial to damp meadows and low herbaceous growth in cultivation clearings.
Nesting: The cup-shaped nest is built on the ground. The 2–3 whitish eggs are well spotted and speckled with ashy-violet and different shades of brown.

SHRIKES: Laniidae

A large family of medium-sized or small birds that are widespread in the forest and savanna. Strong, hooked bill and rather short rounded wings are characters. Feed mainly on insects captured in the foliage or on the ground. Some are conspicuously coloured. Calls often resonant, harsh or musical, and, especially in those species which skulk in thick foliage, a useful means of identification.

LONG-CRESTED HELMET-SHRIKE *Prionops plumata* Pl. 36
Identification: 8″. Sexes similar. Easily recognised by long crest, distinctive black and white plumage, noisy chattering, fearlessness and social habit. Head, neck and underparts white but hind crown and sides of face grey. Upperparts blackish, the wing conspicuously barred with white and the tail edged and tipped white. A fleshy yellow wattle round the eye. Shape and length of crest

Plate 33

BARBETS

1. **BEARDED BARBET**   *Lybius dubius*   page 139
   Massive yellow bill; black breast band; white patch on flanks.

2. **TOOTH-BILLED BARBET**   *Lybius bidentatus*   140
   Whitish bill; red wing-bar; no black breast band.

3. **VIEILLOT'S BARBET**   *Lybius vieilloti*   140
   Red head; yellow rump.

4. **HAIRY-BREASTED BARBET**   *Lybius hirsutus*   141
   Two whitish stripes on side of head.

5. **YELLOW-BILLED BARBET**   *Trachyphonus purpuratus*   143
   Yellow bill and circumorbital patch; yellow belly blotched black;
   white wing-patch.

6. **DUCHAILLU'S YELLOW-SPOTTED BARBET**   141
   Buccanodon duchaillui
   Crimson crown; yellow stripe on side of head and neck.

7. **LEMON-RUMPED TINKER-BIRD**   *Pogoniulus bilineatus*   142
   Two white stripes on side of head; white throat.

8. **NAKED-FACED BARBET**   *Gymnobucco calvus*   141
   Naked blackish head; bristly chin, nostrils and gape.

9. **EUROPEAN WRYNECK**   *Jynx torquilla*   147
   Vermiculated grey and brown; whitish throat and breast narrowly
   barred darker.

10. **RED-RUMPED TINKER-BIRD**   *Pogoniulus atroflavus*   143
    Scarlet rump; yellow stripes on side of head.

11. **YELLOW-FRONTED BARBET**   *Pogoniulus chrysoconus*   142
    Golden-yellow forecrown; black and white streaked face.

12. **SPECKLED TINKER-BIRD**   *Pogoniulus scolopaceus*   142
    Dark upperparts speckled with yellow.

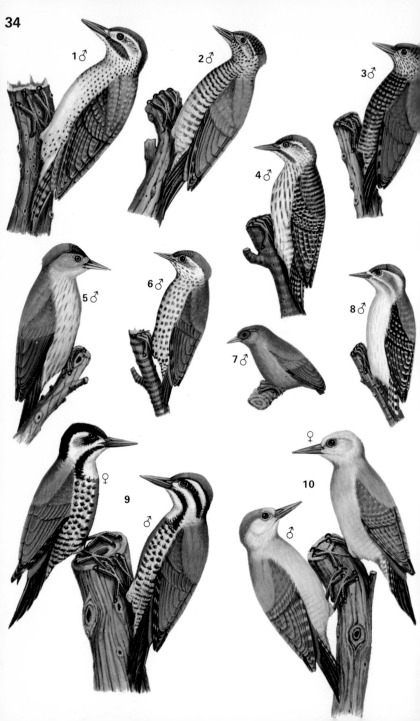

WOODPECKERS

1. **FINE-SPOTTED WOODPECKER** page 148
   Campethera punctuligera
   Crimson malar stripe; pale yellow underparts; spotted chest.

2. **GREEN-BACKED WOODPECKER** *Campethera caillautii* 148
   Heavily barred underparts; no malar stripe.

3. **BUFF-SPOTTED WOODPECKER** *Campethera nivosa* 149
   Streaked ear-coverts; heavily spotted underparts.

4. **CARDINAL WOODPECKER** *Dendropicos fuscescens* 149
   Streaked underparts; brown forehead.

5. **ELLIOT'S WOODPECKER** *Mesopicos ellioti* 151
   Plain olive upperparts; black forecrown; streaked underparts.

6. **GABOON WOODPECKER** *Dendropicos gabonensis* 150
   Plain green mantle; heavily-streaked underparts.

7. **PIGMY WOODPECKER** *Verreauxia africana* 148
   Diminutive; bare red skin round eye.

8. **LESSER WHITE-SPOTTED WOODPECKER** 150
   Dendropicos obsoletus
   Heavily spotted with white on wings and tail; whitish underparts
   very faintly streaked.

9. **FIRE-BELLIED WOODPECKER** *Mesopicos pyrrhogaster* 151
   Golden-olive mantle; crimson rump and mid-line of belly; crimson
   crown (male); black crown (female).

10. **GREY WOODPECKER** *Mesopicos goertae* 150
    Mainly grey; olive-gold mantle; scarlet rump; scarlet crown (male
    only).

varies geographically. In flocks searching the trunks and branches for insects or flying from tree to tree.

Voice: A chattering call frequently uttered and often accompanied by bill snapping.

Distribution and Habitat: Well distributed and locally common north of the forest belt to 15° N. Ranges from Senegal, Gambia and Portuguese Guinea east to southern Chad and the Central African Republic. Frequents orchard bush, open woodland and clearings with crops and scattered small trees.

Nesting: A neat, compact cup of grass bound with spider's web and placed in the fork of a tree. Eggs 3–4, pale bluish-green blotched and spotted with light brown and lilac mainly in a zone near the large end.

RED-BILLED SHRIKE   *Prionops caniceps (Sigmodus caniceps,*
S. rufiventris)   **Pl. 36**

Identification: 8″. Plumage unmistakable. Grey crown and forehead; black cheeks, chin, throat and upperparts; white breast; saffron-buff belly; conspicuous red bill and eyelids. In flight a white patch on the wing. In the very distinct race (*P. caniceps rufiventris*) that occurs in southern Cameroons, Rio Muni and Gaboon, the chin and cheeks are grey and the belly is chestnut. In pairs or parties and sometimes as members of the mixed forest bird parties.

Voice: Various calls, the most frequent a cheerful loud whistle repeated several times.

Distribution and Habitat: The forest from Sierra Leone east to the Central African Republic and south to Rio Muni and Gaboon in virgin growth and also in clearings where some of the tall trees have been spared.

Nesting: Undescribed.

BRUBRU SHRIKE   *Nilaus afer*   **Pl. 36**

Identification: 5½″. Small size, plumage and voice distinguish it. Crown and nape black broadly bordered with white. Upperparts mottled black and white, the wings mainly blackish with a conspicuous buff bar, the tail black tipped and edged white. Underparts white, streaked on the sides with chestnut. In the female the black of the crown and mantle is replaced by brown. Arboreal. Insectivorous.

Voice: A frequently-repeated, drawn-out, soft but carrying 'brruu'. Also a clear flute-like whistle. Birds of a pair sometimes call alternately.

Distribution and Habitat: A Shrike of the small savanna trees commonest in the semi-arid belt penetrating north in the rains to 17° N. in Mauritania and 18° N. in Niger and in the dry season south almost to the forest edge. Ranges from southern Mauritania, Senegal and Portuguese Guinea east to Chad and the Central African Republic. Widespread and locally common.

Nesting: In southern Africa builds a slight inconspicuous nest in a tree fork, laying 2–3 pale greenish-white eggs thickly marked with slate-blue and greenish-brown.

GAMBIAN PUFF-BACK SHRIKE   *Dryoscopus gambensis*   **Pl. 36**

Identification: 7″. Upperparts glossy black but rump mainly white and wing feathers dark brown edged with grey. Underparts whitish. Female has upperparts brown but head grey and wing feathers edged yellowish. Underparts uniformly pale tawny-yellow. In the race occurring in the Central African

Republic the female has a brown head. Usually in pairs; vocal; not shy.

Voice: A variety of calls including a loud, persistent 'cherp-cherp-cherp-cherp . . .' and a harsh chattering.

Distribution and Habitat: A very common and widespread savanna Shrike frequenting leafy trees and shrubs in open woodland, thickets and gardens. Absent from the arid north. Enters the forest clearings and is common in pure mangrove in the Niger delta. From Senegal and Gambia east to southern Chad and the Central African Republic and south to Gaboon and Congo.

Nesting: A compact cup of bark and cobwebs lined with rootlets in the fork of a tree 20 to 70 feet from the ground. Eggs 2, pinkish-white with sepia and stone markings concentrated in a zone near the large end and sparsely distributed over the rest of the shell.

Allied species: The Black-shouldered Puff-back (*Dryoscopus senegalensis*), 6½", is abundant in the Cameroons, Gaboon and Congo rain forest zone and there is one record from southern Nigeria. Male glistening black above except for white rump, white below. Female has a white eye-stripe and the black upperparts are duller in shade. Usually concealed in the foliage of the treetops of the second-growth and the clearings and known by the loud flute-like and other arresting calls of the male. Male closely resembles the male Sabine's Puff-back (*Dryoscopus sabini*), a rarer forest Shrike, the best distinction being the much longer and heavier bill of the latter. Distinguished by its voice and behaviour from the male Shrike Flycatcher (*Megabyas flammulatus*) another forest species of about the same size and with a similar colour pattern.

LITTLE BLACKCAP TCHAGRA   *Tchagra minuta*
(*Antichromus minutus*)   **Pl. 36**

Identification: 7". Chestnut and brown upperparts with a black forehead, crown and nape, and a black shoulder patch; underparts pale buff. Black tail feathers with narrow pale tips. Sexes similar except that female has white eye-stripe. The differently phrased song and the shorter tail and dumpier appearance readily distinguish it from the commoner Black-crowned Tchagra (*Tchagra senegala*). Sometimes perches in full view on a grass stalk or small shrub but usually concealed in rank herbage.

Voice: A brief musical whistling song usually uttered during a short display flight. Also a variety of harsh churring and chucking notes.

Distribution and Habitat: Widely but locally distributed in the savanna from Sierra Leone to the Central African Republic and Gaboon but not in the arid northern parts. In the Cameroons highland savanna ascends to 6,000 feet. Shows a preference for moist pockets where the grass grows rank and tall.

Nesting: Nest usually built a few feet from the ground in rank herbage; an open cup of rootlets and fibre. Eggs 3, white blotched and spotted with warm brown primary markings and a few purplish shellmarks.

Allied species: The Brown-crowned Tchagra (*Tchagra australis*) resembles the Black-crowned Tchagra (*T. senegala*) in size and proportions. In the Brown-crowned Tchagra the crown is brown bordered with black and this distinguishes it from the adult Black-crowned Tchagra and the Little Blackcap Tchagra (*T. minuta*) which have solid black crowns. It ranges from Sierra Leone to Gaboon and Congo and is locally common. It inhabits thick low secondary bush and is to be looked for at the forest savanna edge and in extensive abandoned clearings in the forest.

BLACK-CROWNED TCHAGRA *Tchagra senegala* **Pl. 36**
Identification: 8″. Colour pattern and call diagnostic. Crown black; wide stripe above eye buff; stripe through eye black; back brown; wings rufous; tail long, wide, black tipped and edged white; underparts greyish-white. Usually seen hopping on the ground or flying low from bush to bush with tail spread fanwise. In immature dress crown mixed brown and blackish and confusion with *Tchagra australis* is possible.
Voice: Characteristic. A series of far-carrying, fluting, melodious notes descending the scale and heard especially at dawn and dusk.
Distribution and Habitat: Widespread and very common in all zones except closed forest. Fond of open scrub country and the edges of cultivation.
Nesting: A shallow cup of rootlets and fibre in a shrub or small tree. Eggs 2, white or cream blotched and usually streaked and scrawled with reddish-brown and greyish-purple.

BELL-SHRIKE *Laniarius ferrugineus (L. turatii)* **Pl. 36**
Identification: 9″. Stoutly built. Black above with a conspicuous white wing bar; white below. In the race that occurs in coastal Gaboon and southern Cameroons (*L. f. bicolor*) the white on the wing is greatly reduced and in the very distinct race that occupies Portuguese Guinea and western Sierra Leone (*L. f. turatii*) there is no white on the wing and the breast is pinkish-buff not white. Found in pairs. Skulking in habits, keeping to leafy cover. Duet call characteristic.
Voice: A loud plaintive flute-like duet, the male starting and the female completing each series of whistles.
Distribution and Habitat: Portuguese Guinea and Sierra Leone to Chad and the Central African Republic, Gaboon and Congo. A widely and commonly distributed savanna species frequenting orchard bush and the borders of thickets and gallery woods. In the Cameroons River delta it inhabits mangrove swamp.
Nesting: Nest an open cup of rootlets and fibre lodged in a low fork in a savanna shrub. The two blue-green eggs are speckled, spotted and blotched with light brown and lilac.

BARBARY SHRIKE *Laniarius barbarus (L. erythrogaster)* **Pl. 36**
Identification: 8½″. Sexes similar. Colour pattern unique. Entire upperparts black except for olive-yellow crown and nape. Underparts scarlet. Shy and often skulks in thick cover.
Voice: Usually in duet form, a loud whip-lash, whistling 'whee-oo' answered by a clicking 'tic-tic'. Various other harsh calls.
Distribution and Habitat: Widely but locally distributed in the savanna where there are thickets. Commoner in the thorn scrub. Senegal, Gambia and Portuguese Guinea east to northern Cameroons and southern Chad.
Nesting: A slight shallow cup of plant stems and rootlets in a tree or shrub. Eggs 2, pale green with reddish-brown and purplish-grey spots and blotches forming a cap at the large end and evenly distributed elsewhere.

YELLOW-BREASTED SHRIKE *Laniarius atroflavus* **Pl. 36**
Identification: 7″. Distinguished by glossy black upperparts and yellow underparts. A typical *Laniarius*, usually in pairs exploring the foliage of the forest trees and undershrubs, the pair keeping in touch with loud cries.
Voice: Duet type. A loud swishing 'whee-oo' from one bird of a pair answered immediately by 'chook' from the other. A variety of other loud calls.

Distribution and Habitat: The Obudu Pleateau of eastern Nigeria and the Cameroon highlands where it is abundant in the montane forests of the Cameroon Mountain, Manenguba and the Bamenda uplands.

Nesting: Nest a flimsy shallow cup of roots and fibre built near the ground in undergrowth on the forest edges. Eggs pale green speckled with brown.

Allied species: The Black Mountain Boubou (*Laniarius fulleborni*), 7″, is distinguished by its uniformly black plumage, bill and feet, and its montane habitat. A typical *Laniarius* in appearance and habits, usually in pairs exploring the thick undergrowth for insects and uttering a variety of loud guttural and whistling calls. An abundant resident in the forest of the Cameroon Mountain and the other mountain forests of the Cameroon highlands and the Obudu Plateau of Nigeria. Also in Fernando Po. It is distinguished by its smaller size from the Sooty Boubou (*Laniarius leucorhynchus*) of the lowland forest. The two species occur alongside each other at the base of the Cameroon Mountain.

SOOTY BOUBOU *Laniarius leucorhynchus* Pl. 36

Identification: 9″. A stoutly built Shrike. Entire plumage blackish. Bill black in the adult, whitish in the immature. Found in pairs, skulking near the ground in thick cover, shy, vocal.

Voice: A duet, the male uttering a series of clear mellow whistles and the female interposing a single drawn-out swishing 'hweee'.

Distribution and Habitat: Locally common in the lowland forest from Sierra Leone to Gaboon and Congo. It occurs in thick shrubbery or dense herbage in secondary forest or choked abandoned clearings.

Nesting: A slight nest of twigs lined with fine roots, built in the fork of a forest sapling or shrub. Eggs two, greenish-white with reddish-brown markings.

MANY-COLOURED BUSH-SHRIKE *Malaconotus multicolor*
(*Chlorophoneus multicolor*) Pl. 36

Identification: 9″. Voice distinctive. Difficult to observe in the foliage despite its bright colours. Occurs in three colour phases, a scarlet-breasted, an orange-breasted, and a black-breasted. Head grey, upperparts green, a broad black frontal band passing through the eye to the side of the neck. Female and immature bird less highly coloured and lack the black frontal band. Smaller and slimmer than the Fiery-breasted Bush-Shrike (*Malaconotus cruentus*) and having a quite different call.

Voice: A characteristic whistling 'whoop', rather melancholy in tone, frequently uttered especially by the male. Also harsh rasping calls.

Distribution and Habitat: The main body and the larger gallery extensions of the lowland forest from Sierra Leone to Gaboon. Usually in the leafy canopy in primary forest or less often in old secondary forest, singly or in pairs.

Nesting: Not known.

Allied species: The Orange-breasted Bush-Shrike (*Malaconotus sulfureopectus*), 7½″, is a locally common savanna species which ranges from Senegal to Chad and the Central African Republic. Usually alone, quietly searching the foliage for insects, skulking, and easily overlooked were it not for its full-throated cheerful whistling call of three or four syllables. Brightly coloured. Forehead and stripe over eye yellow; head and nape grey; a broad black band passing through the eye; back, wings and tail mainly green; underparts yellow with a splash of orange-red on the breast.

FIERY-BREASTED BUSH-SHRIKE   *Malaconotus cruentus*   **Pl. 36**
Identification: 10″. Call and bright colours distinctive. Head, nape and sides of face blue-grey; upperparts green, the tail and wing feathers tipped yellow. Underparts yellow washed with crimson, the extent of the crimson wash varying and sometimes absent. Shy, occurring in pairs or small parties.
Voice: Call a characteristic hollow 'hoo-hoo'. Also a variety of harsh cries.
Distribution and Habitat: The lowland forest and its gallery extensions from Sierra Leone east to the Central African Republic and south to Gaboon. Frequents the thick cover of second-growth or of climax forest.
Nesting: The shallow nest is built in a forest thicket and is loosely constructed of dry vines, small twigs and leaf stems with a lining of black rootlets. Eggs 3, pinkish-white spotted and blotched with rich maroon and pale purple especially near the large end where the markings form a zone.
Allied species: The Grey-headed Bush-Shrike (*Malaconotus blanchoti*), 11″, sexes similar, is a very large savanna Shrike with a conspicuous, heavy, hooked, black bill. Head and nape grey; remainder upperparts including wings and tail green, the tail feathers tipped yellow; underparts bright yellow, the breast washed orange. Widely but evenly distributed in the savanna south of 14° N. and north of the forest ranging from Senegal and Gambia east to southern Chad and the Central African Republic.

LONG-TAILED SHRIKE   *Corvinella corvina*   **Pl. 36**
Identification: 12″. Sexes similar. The 7″ long narrow, ragged tail, yellow bill, and in flight the rounded dark-tipped rufous wings identify it. At close range upperparts brown with dark streaks, underparts white or cream finely streaked on breast and flanks. Flight feeble and seldom sustained. Usually in small parties. Hunts from bare branch, telegraph wire or other perch with an open view and swoops down to earth on its prey.
Voice: Various harsh, rasping and chattering cries usually uttered in concert.
Distribution and Habitat: Well distributed and rather common in the northern savanna extending in the rains at least as far north as 16° N. in Senegal and 14° N. in Niger. Absent from the forest and the moist adjoining savanna. From Senegal, Gambia and Portuguese Guinea east to southern Chad and the Central African Republic. Open grass woodland and scattered trees.
Nesting: In an open site in the fork of a tree. A substantial cup of grass, twigs and rootlets. Eggs 3–4, yellowish-buff rather sparsely marked with yellowish-brown and grey, usually with a ring at the large end.

GREAT GREY SHRIKE   *Lanius excubitor*   **Pl. 36**
Identification: 9½″, sexes similar. A large Shrike with a distinctive black, white and grey plumage pattern. Upperparts pale grey but rump whitish; underparts pure white; a conspicuous black patch behind the eye; conspicuous black and white wings; inner tail feathers black, outer tail feathers mainly white. Flight rapid and low with terminal upward glide to perch. Perches prominently on thorn trees.
Voice: Call a harsh 'chak-chak'.
Distribution and Habitat: The borders of the desert where there are bushes from southern Mauritania and Senegal through Mali, Niger and northernmost Nigeria to Chad. Sedentary, but numbers in winter augmented perhaps by Palaearctic immigrants.
Nesting: Nest an open cup in a thorny acacia bush. Eggs 2–3, creamy white spotted with pale brown and pale mauve.

FISCAL SHRIKE *Lanius collaris* (*L. newtoni*) **Pl. 36**
Identification: 9″. A slimly built, long-tailed, black and white Shrike, bold, aggressive and conspicuous, perching prominently in open places. Head, mantle and wings black; prominent white shoulder and wing patches; rump grey; graduated tail black with white tips; entire underparts white. Barred immature plumage.
Voice: At the breeding season a short unpretentious but pleasing song. A rasping call-note.
Distribution and Habitat: The savanna north of the forest from Guinea and Sierra Leone to the Cameroons, reappearing south of the forest in the grasslands of Gaboon and Congo. Widespread but local. Absent from the arid northernmost zone. Often in the vicinity of towns and villages. Partial to extensive areas of well-cleared ground.
Nesting: Nest an open cup built in a tree or shrub. Eggs 3–4, white tinged with green faintly and sparingly sprinkled with pale brown primary and ashy secondary marks mainly concentrated in a wreath near the large end.
Allied species: The Red-backed Shrike (*Lanius collurio*), 7″, is a winter visitor to West Africa known from a few localities in Nigeria, northern Cameroons and Chad, in which last territory it is locally common. The species is divided into two groups of races both of which occur in our area. In the nominate *collurio* group in the male the back is chestnut, the tail blackish, the head and rump grey, and a band through the eye to the ear-coverts black. The dull-coloured female is mainly rufous-brown above and buffish below barred with brown. In the very different *isabellinus* group in the male the back is isabelline-buffish, the tail reddish, the head and rump pale rufous and the band through the eye black. The female is duller and lacks the blackish band. The very small Emin's Red-backed Shrike (*Lanius gubernator*), 6″, has a chestnut mantle and rump and a grey crown and nape; forehead and broad streak through eye black; conspicuous white throat and white wing patch. Sexes almost alike. It occurs sparingly in open country north of the forest in Portuguese Guinea, Ghana, Nigeria, the Cameroons and the Central African Republic. The Grey-backed Shrike (*Lanius excubitorius*), 10″, is locally resident in our area recorded so far only from the arid country near Lake Chad in Nigeria, northern Cameroons and Chad. A large stoutly built Shrike. Upperparts grey; underparts white; forehead and broad black streak through eye black; wings black with a conspicuous white bar.

WOODCHAT SHRIKE *Lanius senator* **Pl. 36**
Identification: 7″. Plumage distinctive. In adult male forecrown and dark band through eye black; crown and nape rich chestnut; back black; scapulars white; rump grey; throat white; remainder underparts buffish-white; wings black with large white patch on quills very conspicuous in flight. The female is duller and browner and lacks the black forecrown and eyeband. In the Corsican race (*Lanius s. badius*) which occurs in West Africa alongside the nominate race the white wing patch is almost entirely absent. A typical Shrike usually discovered on a commanding perch on shrub, tree, fence or telegraph wire, from which it flies down to the ground to capture insects. Solitary, silent.
Distribution and Habitat: A widely distributed and common winter visitor (September–April) to the West African savannas and forest clearings, showing a preference for open cultivated areas. Senegal and Gambia east through arid and moist savanna belts to N. Nigeria, Cameroons, Chad.

Plate 35

SWALLOWS, BROADBILL AND PITTA

1. **EUROPEAN SWALLOW** *Hirundo rustica* page 156
Forked tail; dark blue pectoral band.

2. **WIRE-TAILED SWALLOW** *Hirundo smithii* 156
Long attenuated outer rectrices; chestnut-red crown; pure white underparts.

3. **WHITE-THROATED BLUE SWALLOW** *Hirundo nigrita* 156
White chin spot; white patches on rectrices.

4. **AFRICAN SAND MARTIN** *Riparia paludicola* 155
Pale brown throat and breast; white belly.

5. **FANTI ROUGH-WINGED SWALLOW** 158
Psalidoprocne obscura
Deeply-forked tail; unicoloured, dark, with oily-green or bluish gloss.

6. **LESSER STRIPED SWALLOW** *Hirundo abyssinica* 157
Rufous-chestnut head and rump; streaked underparts.

7. **MOSQUE SWALLOW** *Hirundo senegalensis* 157
Large; rufous rump; pale rufous cheeks.

8. **EUROPEAN HOUSE MARTIN** *Delichon urbica* 158
Pure white rump and underparts.

9. **PIED-WINGED SWALLOW** *Hirundo leucosoma* 157
Large white wing-patch.

10. **BLACK-CAPPED BROADBILL** *Smithornis capensis* 151
Broad heavy bill; black crown; streaked breast.

11. **ANGOLA PITTA** *Pitta angolensis* 152
Bright blue rump and wing spots; red belly and under tail-coverts.

35

Plate 36

SHRIKES

1. **LONG-CRESTED HELMET-SHRIKE**   page 163
   Prionops plumata   White crest; white wing-bar and tail feather tips.

2. **RED-BILLED SHRIKE**   *Prionops caniceps*   166
   Red bill and eyelids; grey crown; black cheeks and throat.

3. **MANY-COLOURED BUSH-SHRIKE**   169
   Malaconotus multicolor   Grey head; green mantle.
   a. Scarlet-breasted phase.
   b. Orange-breasted phase.
   c. Black-breasted phase.

4. **GAMBIAN PUFF-BACK SHRIKE**   *Dryoscopus gambensis*   166
   Glossy black upperparts; whitish rump.

5. **BLACK-CROWNED TCHAGRA**   *Tchagra senegala*   168
   Black crown and stripe through eye; broad buff stripe above eye.

6. **LITTLE BLACKCAP TCHAGRA**   *Tchagra minuta*   167
   Black head; no head stripes; black shoulder patch.

7. **SOOTY BOUBOU**   *Laniarius leucorhynchus*   169
   Entirely blackish.

8. **BRUBRU SHRIKE**   *Nilaus afer*   166
   Broad white stripe over eye; buff wing-bar.

9. **LONG-TAILED SHRIKE**   *Corvinella corvina*   170
   Long tail; yellow bill; rounded dark-tipped rufous wings.

10. **BELL-SHRIKE**   *Laniarius ferrugineus*   168
    Black upperparts; white underparts; usually conspicuous white wing-bar.

11. **BARBARY SHRIKE**   *Laniarius barbarus*   168
    Olive-yellow crown; black upperparts; scarlet underparts.

12. **YELLOW-BREASTED SHRIKE**   *Laniarius atroflavus*   168
    Black upperparts; yellow underparts.

13. **FIERY-BREASTED BUSH-SHRIKE**   170
    Malaconotus cruentus
    Grey head; green mantle; yellow underparts often washed crimson.

14. **GREAT GREY SHRIKE**   *Lanius excubitor*   170
    Mainly pale grey upperparts; white underparts; conspicuous black and white wings; white outer tail feathers.

15. **WOODCHAT SHRIKE**   *Lanius senator*   171
    Chestnut crown and nape.

16. **FISCAL SHRIKE**   *Lanius collaris*   171
    White shoulder and wing patches; long black white-tipped tail.

ORIOLES: Oriolidae

A small group of arboreal birds, about the size of a Song Thrush, with curved, usually pinkish bills. Shy and often difficult to locate in the thick foliage of the tree tops in spite of their bright plumage and loud, melodious, whistling calls.

AFRICAN GOLDEN ORIOLE *Oriolus auratus* **Pl. 37**
Identification: 9″. Male brilliant yellow but wings and tail black margined with yellow and a broad black band from the base of the bill through and beyond the eye. Bill pink. Female duller, especially on the mantle, and the band through the eye dusky not jet black. Immature bird resembles female but lacks the eye band and has underparts heavily streaked blackish. Fast undulating flight. Often hidden in foliage of tree tops.
Voice: A loud, clear, flute-like 'fee-yoo fee-yoo' and other melodious, mewing or squawking notes.
Distribution and Habitat: Widespread and locally common in the wooded savanna where there are large trees. Absent from closed forest. From Senegal (to 16° N. in rains), Gambia and Portuguese Guinea east to southern Chad and the Central African Republic.
Nesting: In a tree. A shallow cup of twigs slung by gossamer from a slender horizontal fork. Eggs 2, buff-pink sparingly spotted and streaked dark red-brown with deep rose suffusions round the markings.
Allied species: The European Golden Oriole (*Oriolus oriolus*), 10″, resembles the African Golden Oriole but lacks the broad black (in the female dusky) band through the eye to the ear-coverts, the black being limited to a spot in front of the eye. Also the wings show less yellow. Its status in West Africa is that of a rather uncommon spring and autumn migrant. Recorded from Senegal, Gambia, Portuguese Guinea, Guinea, Ivory Coast, Ghana, Nigeria, the Cameroons and Chad.

BLACK-HEADED ORIOLE *Oriolus brachyrhynchus* **Pl. 37**
Identification: 10″. Entire head and throat black; collar yellow; upperparts yellowish-green; underparts yellow; wings black with a small white patch visible when perched and in flight; middle pair of tail feathers green, remainder black tipped with yellow. Sexes similar. In pairs in the tree tops and usually located by call.
Voice: A variety of far-carrying liquid melodious calls characteristically 'Oriole' in quality.
Distribution and Habitat: The lowland evergreen forest from Sierra Leone to Gaboon and Congo. The habitat is the interior of the forest and also its clearings where some high trees have been left standing.
Nesting: The nest, of lichen and cobwebs, is slung between two horizontal twigs. Eggs unknown.
Allied species: The Black-winged Oriole (*Oriolus nigripennis*), 10″, resembles the Black-headed Oriole but it lacks the white patch on the wing and the central tail feathers are black not green. Habits and melodious liquid calls similar. It ranges in the forest from Sierra Leone to Gaboon, Congo and Fernando Po. In the Cameroon highlands it ascends to over 7,000 feet.

DRONGOS: Dicruridae

Black plumage. Rather Shrike-like with hooked bill, but differ in their hunting habits, usually flying out from some vantage point to capture their insect prey on the wing. Bold, aggressive and noisy.

GLOSSY-BACKED DRONGO   *Dicrurus adsimilis*
(*D. modestus*)   **Pl. 31**
Identification: 9½". Sexes similar. An arboreal, black, shrike-like bird with a forked tail. The shade and gloss of the upperparts varies geographically. From a high branch, telegraph wire or other commanding perch makes circuit flights to capture insects. Pugnacious and quarrelsome often harrying birds much larger than itself. A little like the Black Flycatcher (*Melaenornis edolioides*) but the latter is not a circuit flier and has a relatively longer tail with a square end. The males of certain Cuckoo-Shrike species also resemble the Drongo, but they have square tails and in behaviour are quite unlike the aggressive, conspicuous Drongo.
Voice: Various loud, harsh, grating calls interspersed with occasional flute-like melodious notes.
Distribution and Habitat: Very widely and commonly distributed in the savanna throughout wherever there are trees, and also in the high forest where it frequents the tree tops and the edges of clearings. Also Fernando Po and Principe.
Nesting: A small, shallow cup of open construction slung in the fork of a small horizontal branch high up. Eggs 2–3, variable, white, cream or pinkish, unmarked or blotched, smeared, or spotted with dark reddish and lilac.
Allied species: The Shining Drongo (*Dicrurus atripennis*), 9", ranges in the lowland forest from Sierra Leone to Gaboon. It is difficult to distinguish in the field from the two West African forest races of the Glossy-backed Drongo (*Dicrurus adsimilis atactus*) and *Dicrurus a. coracinus*. The entire plumage of the Shining Drongo is strongly glossed with steel-blue and at close range this serves to distinguish it from the race *atactus* in which the gloss is less strong and from *coracinus* which is glossy except for the mantle which is unglossed velvet-black. The Shining Drongo is more given to joining the mixed bird parties of the forest than is the Glossy-backed Drongo, and also it prefers the sunlight of the high treetops and the edge of forest clearings, whereas the Glossy-backed Drongo prefers the shade of the forest at moderate heights. But these are not absolute distinctions. Often the specific identification in the field of a fish-tailed forest Drongo is impossible. The Square-tailed Drongo (*Dicrurus ludwigii*), 7", is fairly easily distinguished by its smaller size and its square not forked tail. It is essentially a Drongo of the borders of the main body of the forest and of the gallery extensions and outlying forest patches in the savanna. In such places it ranges from Gambia along the northern edge of the forest to the Cameroons and it reappears south of the forest in Gaboon and Congo. Generally in pairs. It has the aggressive noisy habits and the swooping flight characteristic of the family.

Plate 37

ORIOLES, STARLINGS AND CUCKOO-SHRIKES

BULBULS

STARLINGS: Sturnidae

A numerous family of medium-sized, arboreal, fruit-eating birds of the forest and savanna. Specific identity often difficult. Many species have brilliantly coloured plumage with blue, green and purple reflections. Often gregarious. Noisy. Calls usually raucous and unmusical.

CRAG CHESTNUT-WINGED STARLING   *Onychognathus morio*
Pl. 37

Identification: 12″. Large size, stout build, long graduated tail and fondness of crags distinguish it. Male glossy purplish-blue with an extensive chestnut wing patch conspicuous in flight. Female similar but with a greyish head and throat. The long graduated tail when fanned in flight is quite distinctive. Occurs in pairs or flocks. Vocal, restive and conspicuous.

Voice: The usual call is a frequent loud prolonged plaintive whistle.

Distribution and Habitat: In West Africa locally common north of the forest where there are crags in hilly or mountainous country, in Mali, the Ivory Coast, Nigeria, the Cameroons, Chad and the Central African Republic.

Nesting: Nest built in a hole in a cleft in a rock face. Clutch 3. In South Africa the eggs are described as pale greenish-blue sparingly spotted with reddish.

Allied species: The Forest Chestnut-winged Starling (*Onychognathus fulgidus*), 11″, is rather similar but differs in its forest habitat. From other forest Glossy Starlings it is readily distinguished in good light by its colour, size and long tail. In the male the glossy green of the head and throat is sharply demarcated from the glossy purple of the mantle and breast. In the female the grey streaks on the head and throat are apparent. In both sexes the red iris is conspicuous. As they preen and spread their wings the chestnut patch shows up well, as do the graduated tail feathers when the tail is spread. The range is the forest from Sierra Leone and Guinea to the Central African Republic, Gaboon and Congo and the islands of Fernando Po and Sao Tome. The Narrow-tailed Starling (*Poeoptera lugubris*), 9″, is another lowland forest Starling. It ranges from Sierra Leone to the Cameroons and Congo and the island of Fernando Po. Seen, black against the sky, at forest-canopy level, flighting at dusk to their roost, in close formation, a flock of this species cannot be confused with any other, with their slim cigar-shaped bodies, attenuated tails and direct purposeful flight. At close range, in flight, the chestnut wing-patches of the female show up. The male is known by his dark glossy body plumage. When the tail is spread in flight the long central rectrices are seen. The call is musical, high-pitched and explosive.

PURPLE-HEADED GLOSSY STARLING
Lamprotornis purpureiceps (*Lamprocolius purpureiceps*)   Pl. 37

Identification: 8″. A rather small square-tailed forest Glossy Starling without any arresting plumage characters. In good light the dark purplish head and metallic blue and green body show up. Iris dark brown. Sexes similar. Usually discovered in small parties feeding on fruiting trees in the forest or the forest clearings.

Voice: Call a metallic 'twink'.

Distribution and Habitat: The evergreen lowland forest of the Ivory Coast, southern Nigeria, the Cameroons, Gaboon and Congo.

Nesting: The nest is built in a knot-hole in a forest tree. Clutch 3. An egg taken in Zaïre was described as blue spotted with brown.

Allied species: The Copper-tailed Glossy Starling (*Lamprotornis cupreocauda*), 8″, resembles the Purple-headed Glossy Starling in habits and appearance but the crown and belly usually appear glossy blue and the tail is washed with gold. It is a forest Starling of Sierra Leone, Liberia, Ivory Coast and Ghana.

SPLENDID GLOSSY STARLING   *Lamprotornis splendidus*
(*Lamprocolius splendidus*)   **Pl. 37**

Identification: 12″. A common large Glossy Starling of the forest. Brilliant metallic green, blue and purple. A broad blackish band across the tail and a blackish band across the wing. A conspicuous creamy-yellow eye. Occurs in flocks and huge numbers congregate at evening roosts. Fruit-eater. Garrulous. Wing beats very noisy.

Voice: A variety of loud, piping, rasping and harsh calls that compel attention. The babel of calls at a roost is audible over a quarter of a mile away.

Distribution and Habitat: Commonly and widely distributed in the forest and gallery extensions and outlying woods of the savanna from Gambia and Senegal to the Central African Republic, Gaboon and Congo. Also the islands of Fernando Po and Principe. Subject to local movements.

Nesting: Nest in a hole in a tree, usually high up. Eggs 2–3, pale greenish-blue sparingly spotted and blotched reddish-brown and mauve.

PURPLE GLOSSY STARLING *Lamprotornis purpureus*
(*Lamprocolius purpureus*)   **Pl. 37**

Identification: 9½″. Sexes similar. One of the larger Glossy Starlings. Rather flat-crowned with a large conspicuous orange eye. Head, tail and underparts glossy purple but in certain lights lower breast and belly appear glossy blue. Back and wings glossy golden-green. From below in flight rather thick-set due to the relatively short tail and broad wings. Except in good light at close range difficult to distinguish from certain other Glossy Starlings. Gregarious except when breeding. Fruit-eating and particularly partial to wild figs.

Voice: Noisy. Various chattering, whistling and raucous notes.

Distribution and Habitat: Widely and commonly distributed in the savanna from Senegal (to 15° N.), Gambia and Portuguese Guinea through Guinea, Ivory Coast, southern Mali, Upper Volta, Ghana, Nigeria and northern Cameroons to southern Chad and the Central African Republic.

Nesting: Nest in a hole in a tree. Eggs 3, blue, blotched and spotted with rufous.

BLUE-EARED GLOSSY STARLING   *Lamprotornis chalybaeus*
(*Lamprocolius chalybaeus*)   **Pl. 37**

Identification: 9½″. Sexes similar but female smaller. Another large Glossy Starling. Crown slightly concave. Eye yellow. Glossy metallic green with blue reflections according to the angle of light, but ear-coverts bright blue and belly purple. In the hand indented second to fifth primaries a character. Except when breeding gregarious. Feeds on fruit trees and also on the ground.

Voice: Noisy. A great variety of whistling, mewing, chirping and clicking calls.

Distribution and Habitat: The thorn scrub to the very edge of the desert provided there are trees. Extends southwards to about 12° N. Widely distributed and recorded from Mauritania, Senegal, Gambia, Guinea, Ivory Coast, Mali, Niger, northern Nigeria, northern Cameroons and Chad. Moves northwards in the rains.

Nesting: Nest in a hollow in a tree at no great height. Eggs 2–3, pale blue, immaculate or spotted with rufous.

Allied species: The Lesser Blue-eared Glossy Starling (*Lamprotornis chloropterus*), 8″, closely resembles the Blue-eared Glossy Starling in plumage, but is distinctly smaller. In the hand distinguished by the absence of indentations in the primaries, the shorter, slender tarsus and the sharply defined deep-blue ear-coverts. Though the ranges partly overlap, *L. chloropterus* has a more southerly distribution roughly between 9° N. to 10° N. and 14° N. to 15° N. in a zone extending from Gambia and Senegal through Portuguese Guinea, Sierra Leone, Ivory Coast, Ghana, Nigeria and southern Chad to the Central African Republic. The Short-tailed Glossy Starling (*Lamprotornis chalcurus*), 9″, also resembles the Blue-eared Glossy Starling, but has a much shorter tail, and the tail when closed is purple not blue-green. The second to fifth primaries are indented. It inhabits a fairly narrow zone in the savanna in Senegal, Gambia, Portuguese Guinea, Ivory Coast, Ghana, Nigeria, northern Cameroons and the Central African Republic.

LONG-TAILED GLOSSY STARLING *Lamprotornis caudatus*
Pl. 37

Identification: 21″ (tail 13″). Female like male but smaller. Easily distinguished from other Starlings by its very long graduated supple tail which often moves about in the wind. In the air the slow, laborious flight, short rounded wings and long tail characteristic. Head and throat greenish-bronze; remainder plumage mainly glossy oily-green but rump and tail purple with blue reflections. Eye creamy-white and conspicuous. Gregarious. Often feeds on the ground, where it walks and hops nimbly. Fond of millet.

Voice: Noisy. Various shrill and raucous cries.

Distribution and Habitat: Widely but locally distributed in the semi-arid belt, in places where there are cultivated fields for feeding and large trees for roosting and breeding. Southern limit about 11° N. Inhabits Senegal, Gambia, Portuguese Guinea, Guinea, Ivory Coast, Mali, northern Ghana, Togo, northern Nigeria, northern Cameroons, Niger, Chad and the Central African Republic. Northward movement in rains.

Nesting: Breeds singly or in a loose colony. Nest of leaves in a hole in a baobab or other tree. Eggs 3–4, pale blue unmarked.

AMETHYST STARLING *Cinnyricinclus leucogaster* Pl. 37
Identification: 7″. Plumage the best distinction from other Starlings. Male brilliant metallic violet but breast and belly white. Female and juvenile dark brown upperparts and dark-streaked white underparts. In pairs at the breeding season; usually in flocks at other times. Migratory but pattern of movements not clear.

Voice: Rather silent for a Starling. A monosyllabic call-note. Male on breeding territory utters a simple whistling song.

Distribution and Habitat: Widely, commonly, but irregularly distributed in

the savanna ànd the forest edge from Senegal and Gambia to Chad, the Central African Republic, Gaboon and Congo.
Nesting: Eggs laid in a natural hole in the bole of a small tree. Nest of drying green leaves. Clutch 3. South African eggs are pale blue blotched and spotted with brown and blue.

CHESTNUT-BELLIED STARLING   *Spreo pulcher*   Pl. 37
Identification: 8½″. Sexes similar. Glossy green except for greyish-brown head, glossy blue tail and rufous-chestnut belly, flanks and under tail-coverts. In flight the cream-coloured wings edged with brown are evident. Large whitish eye conspicuous. On the ground squat build and upright stance. Gregarious except when breeding. Mainly a ground feeder.
Voice: Call a resonant 'trrr'. A song of weak liquid notes.
Distribution and Habitat: A Starling of the thorn scrub, reaching to the edge of the desert provided there are bushes, and southwards just reaching 11° N. Recorded from southern Mauritania, Senegal, Gambia, Portuguese Guinea, Guinea, Upper Volta, Mali, Ghana, Niger, northern Nigeria, northern Cameroons and Chad. A shift northwards in the rains.
Nesting: A conspicuous large round domed nest of dried grass lined with feathers, in a thick thorny bush at no great height. Eggs 3–5, blue or greenish-blue sparingly blotched and spotted with rust-brown and lilac, the markings sometimes forming a ring or cap at the large end.

YELLOW-BILLED OXPECKER   *Buphagus africanus*   Pl. 37
Identification: 9″. Sexes similar. Often perched on or climbing over wild or domestic *Herbivora*, particularly the domestic humped ox and the donkey, searching for the parasites on which it feeds. Grey-brown with a creamy-buff rump and buff underparts below the breast. A long stiff tail and a conspicuous red-tipped yellow bill. Eye orange. Gregarious.
Voice: A hard, ringing cry, particularly when disturbed.
Distribution and Habitat: Widespread but local and determined largely by the distribution of the domestic ox. In the savanna from southern Mauritania and Senegal east to Chad and the Central African Republic, and south to Gaboon and Congo. Rarely in the forest.
Nesting: A cup of grass, straw or trash lined with hair, in a hole in a tree. Eggs 3, pinkish-white blotched and spotted with rust-brown and lilac.

CROWS: Corvidae

Large birds with strong bills and feet and, except for the aberrant *Picathartes*, black or black-and-white plumage. Loud voice and omnivorous feeding habits.

BLACK MAGPIE   *Ptilostomus afer*   Pl. 31
Identification: 18″. Sexes similar. Glossy black with brown primaries and a very long (11″), stiff, graduated, dark brown tail. Bill black in adult and mainly pink in juvenile. The Long-tailed Glossy Starling which it slightly resembles has a supple tail coloured purple with blue reflections. Except when breeding usually in flocks. Slow and ungainly in flight but agile on the ground and in

trees, running and hopping. Often on the backs of grazing cattle, goats or donkeys, dropping from its perch to capture the insects raised by the beasts.
Voice: Loquacious. Short, high-pitched, Jackdaw-like cries.
Distribution and Habitat: A savanna species showing a preference for cultivated land with Borassus or other palms. Widely but locally distributed from southern Mauritania, Gambia, Senegal and Portuguese Guinea east to southern Chad and the Central African Republic.
Nesting: In a hollow or niche in the top of a tree, usually a palm. A substantial cup of twigs and grasses thickly lined with fibres. Eggs 3–7, pale greenish-blue, unmarked or sparingly blotched and spotted with brown and greyish-lilac.

PIED CROW *Corvus albus*   **Pl. 31**
Identification: 18″. Sexes similar. A black Crow with a white breast and a white collar that surrounds the neck. Often near towns and villages scavenging with Vultures and Kites. Feeds and roosts gregariously.
Voice: A rather deep croak.
Distribution and Habitat: Throughout the area very common and widespread, yet local, occurring in all vegetation zones but absent from closed forest and most abundant in the arid northern zone. Usually about towns and farmland.
Nesting: A substantial stick nest built in a high tree or pylon and lined with grass, mud, rags and matted hair. Eggs 4–6, typically corvine, pale green blotched, spotted, and streaked with brown and ashy-violet.
Allied species: The Brown-necked Raven (*Corvus ruficollis*), 20″, is only slightly larger than the Pied Crow. Glossy black with a chocolate-brown head, neck and underparts. In the field the brown is often difficult to distinguish, particularly in immature plumage and in bad light. Common and resident in the Cape Verde Islands and on the West African mainland in the desert and near-desert regions in Mauritania, northern Senegal, Mali, Niger, northern Nigeria and northern Chad.

BARE-HEADED ROCK-FOWL *Picathartes gymnocephalus*
(*P. oreas*)   **Pl. 31**
Identification: A strange-looking lanky bird with a crow-like bill, a long neck and tail, long legs and stout feet. The bare brightly coloured head is diagnostic. Progresses on the ground with long springing hops. Nests and roosts in colonies on cliffs or in caves in the forest. Two very differently coloured races (often regarded as full species) occur. In *P. g. gymnocephalus* (Sierra Leone to Togo) the upperparts are grey, the underparts white, and the naked skin of the head is bright yellow with two large circular black patches on the hind crown at either side. In *P. g. oreas* (Cameroons) the upperparts and throat are grey and the rest of the underparts apricot; forepart of crown violet-blue, hind-part carmine-red, and sides of head black.
Voice: A harsh 'chirr', a prolonged 'kaaa', a low 'ow ow ow' and other notes are described, but the bird is often silent.
Distribution and Habitat: Locally distributed in the rain forest in Sierra Leone, Liberia, Ivory Coast, Ghana, Togo, the Cameroons and Gaboon, in broken or mountainous terrain where there are cliffs or large boulders. In such places not uncommon. In the mountain forests of the Cameroons ascends to 7,000 feet.

Nesting: Breeds in colonies. The massive nest of mud bound with roots and grasses is firmly attached to the roof of a cave or to a vertical rock face on a cliff. Clutch two, rarely one. Egg profusely spotted, blotched and mottled with various shades of brown and grey.

CUCKOO-SHRIKES: Campephagidae

A distinct, rather Shrike-like group of the forest and wooded savanna. Often solitary and unobtrusive; quietly searching the foliage for insects.

WHITE-BREASTED CUCKOO-SHRIKE *Coracina pectoralis*
Pl. 37

Identification: 10″. Upperparts dove-grey; underparts white, except that the male has a dark grey and the female a pale grey throat. Usually in pairs, perched quietly in a tree or searching the branches or pursuing an insect in the air.
Voice: A high-pitched, querulous, squeaking whistle, not loud. Usually silent.
Distribution and Habitat: Nowhere abundant but widely distributed in the savanna north of the forest, especially in the orchard bush from Senegal and Gambia to the Cameroons and Central African Republic.
Nesting: In southern Africa builds a saucer-shaped nest high up in the fork of a tree. Eggs 2, pale green, freckled with brown and grey.
Allied species: The Mountain Grey Cuckoo-Shrike (*Coracina caesia*), 9″, is grey all over except that the male has black lores and usually a varying amount of black on the throat. Well distributed in the mountain forests of Fernando Po, the Cameroons, and the Obudu Plateau of eastern Nigeria, living in pairs in the tree tops. Display considerable agility as they hop and fly about the forest roof picking insects off the branches or catching them in the air.

BLUE CUCKOO-SHRIKE *Coracina azurea (Cyanograucalus azureus)*
Pl. 37

Identification: 8½″. An all bright-blue Cuckoo-Shrike. The male shows some black on the throat. Unobtrusive. Inhabits the forest tree tops occurring singly, in pairs, or in small parties, and occasionally joining the mixed bird parties.
Voice: Usually silent. The call is a series of loud whistles, and creaking and grating noises are also described.
Distribution and Habitat: Primary and old secondary forest from Sierra Leone to Gaboon and Congo. Rather uncommon.
Nesting: Not known.

RED-SHOULDERED CUCKOO-SHRIKE *Campephaga phoenicea*
(*C. petiti*)   **Pl. 37**
Identification: 8″. Male glossy black with a diagnostic conspicuous large scarlet (occasionally yellow) shoulder patch. Female brown above with blackish bars on the rump and yellow wing tips; underparts white barred with black; yellow under the wing and on sides of breast. A very distinct race (*C. phoenicea petiti*), often regarded as a separate species, occurs in the Cameroons and Gaboon. In it the male is entirely glossy black and in the field is virtually indistinguishable from *Campephaga quiscalina*. The female *C. phoenicea petiti* is yellow barred black above, with an olive-brown crown; bright yellow below;

wings and tail mixed yellow and black. Singly or in pairs in trees or shrubs searching the foliage or flying out or dropping to the ground to capture insects. **Voice:** A soft whistling disyllabic call.

Distribution and Habitat: Widely distributed but nowhere plentiful from Gambia and Senegal east to southern Chad and the Central African Republic and south to Gaboon and Congo.

Nesting: The cup-shaped nest is built in the fork of a tree. In southern Africa lays 2–3 eggs, yellowish-green with brown and purplish-slate markings.

Allied species: The Purple-throated Cuckoo-Shrike (*Campephaga quiscalina*), 8″, is a rather uncommon species whose range is the forest from Sierra Leone and Guinea to Gaboon. The dark glossy male is virtually indistinguishable in the field from the male of the forest race of the Red-shouldered Cuckoo-Shrike (*Campephaga phoenicea petiti*) except that the underparts are glossed with purplish not greenish. In the hand it resembles also the Shining Drongo (*Dicrurus atripennis*) but in the field its attitude when perched and its appearance and action in flight are quite unlike those of a *Dicrurus*. The female has a grey head, olive-yellow upperparts and bright yellow underparts.

BULBULS: Pycnonotidae

An abundant family in Africa with many species, especially in the forest. Specific field identification difficult in some cases. Plumage inconspicuous, shades of green or brown predominating. Arboreal, eating fruit and sometimes also insects. Many species have resonant, characteristic songs or calls.

COMMON GARDEN BULBUL *Pycnonotus barbatus*   Pl. 38
Identification: 7″. Sexes similar. Head and throat dull brown, upperparts earth-brown, breast pale brown, belly whitish. The shade of the plumage varies geographically. Crown feathers often raised in a short crest. A familiar, lively, noisy pugnacious Bulbul that is conspicuous in spite of its dull plumage. Very common in gardens.

Voice: A short, hard, piping 'tooee-tee-tee-teeo'. Pleasant and ringing and often followed by some harsh chattering notes. Sings all day and especially at dawn and dusk. Wings sometimes raised when singing.

Distribution and Habitat: Common and widely distributed throughout the area in all zones where there are trees or bushes. Fond of gardens and farmland near habitations. Absent from closed forest.

Nesting: A small, light, open, shallow cup built in a tree or shrub. Eggs 2–3, white tinged with violet or pink marked with reddish-brown and ashy-violet either in the form of evenly distributed spots and speckles or of well-scattered blotches, lines and scrolls.

SLENDER-BILLED BULBUL *Andropadus gracilirostris*   Pl. 38
Identification: Olive-green above and pale olive-grey below with a greyish-white throat. A quiet inconspicuous bird most often seen in the higher branches of forest trees, particularly on the edges of clearings and occurring singly or in small parties.

Voice: A high-pitched plaintive 'wheep' reiterated in measured time for long periods and resembling the call of *Andropadus tephrolaemus*. Other calls have been described.

Distribution and Habitat: The main forest and the gallery forests of the savanna from Senegal to Gaboon and Congo; also Fernando Po. Ascends the Cameroon forested highlands at least to 5,500 feet. It occurs in primary and old second-growth and also in the trees left standing in clearings in the forest.
Nesting: Undescribed.

LITTLE GREEN BULBUL *Andropadus virens* Pl. 38

Identification: A small olive-green Bulbul with no distinctive plumage characters. The commonest forest Bulbul in our area, seldom seen but often heard in the thick leafy growth it affects.
Voice: A jumble of guttural chuckling notes followed by a vigorous rich warbling song and ending with a loud characteristic tri-syllabic phrase; repeated over and over again and heard even in the heat of the day.
Distribution and Habitat: Senegal and Gambia to Central African Republic, Chad, Gaboon and Congo; also Fernando Po. In the forest and in the gallery forests and outliers of the savanna. It inhabits the dense leafy second-growth.
Nesting: Nest an open cup of leaves and twigs lined with fibre, placed near the ground in the fork of a shrub or forest sapling. Eggs 2, pinkish-white thickly marked with reddish-brown and purplish-grey.
Allied species: The Yellow-whiskered Bulbul (*Andropadus latirostris*) resembles the Little Green Bulbul but has on either side of the throat a bright yellow stripe which is diagnostic. The distinctive, prolonged vigorous chirruping warble is less varied than that of the latter species. Adept at concealing itself in the dense foliage. It ranges through the forest and gallery forests from Senegal to Gaboon and Congo, and is found in Fernando Po. The Little Grey Bulbul (*Andropadus gracilis*) has the same appearance as the Little Green Bulbul. It prefers the more open parts of the trees and not infrequently seeks the higher branches on the edge of forest clearings. It is much more silent than *virens*. The song is a succession of whistles in a monotone. It occurs from Sierra Leone to Gaboon and Congo. Other forest Bulbuls virtually indistinguishable from *virens*, except perhaps by their voice, occur in our area. Their identification, short of examination in the hand, is rarely possible.

GREY-THROATED BULBUL *Andropadus tephrolaemus*
(*Arizelocichla tephrolaema*) Pl. 38

Identification: Its colour pattern – bright olive-green with a grey head and throat, its montane habitat, and its distinctive call, identify it. It occurs singly or in pairs and occasionally in small parties.
Voice: A very distinctive, rather plaintive, far-reaching 'weep-weep-weep . . .' repeated in a high-pitched monotone for several seconds.
Distribution and Habitat: The Cameroon highlands including Cameroon Mountain, the Obudu Plateau of eastern Nigeria and Fernando Po. One of the commonest birds of the mountain forests of the Cameroon highlands from 3,000 to 8,000 feet. May be found in almost any type of leafy environment from the highest tree-tops to the lowest undergrowth, in primary forest or in small copses on the open hillside.
Nesting: Nest a light but strong well-knit cup of moss, tendrils and plant-stems lined with fine grasses and well-concealed near the ground in a forest under-shrub. The two cream-coloured eggs are blotched, spotted and streaked with shades of brown and grey.

HONEY-GUIDE BULBUL   *Baeopogon indicator*   **Pl. 38**
Identification: A rather large squat Bulbul with conspicuous white outer tail feathers tipped with black. Olive-green above and greyish below except for the abdomen and under tail-coverts which are buff. Frequents the tops of high trees. Call and song characteristic.
Voice: The call has been well described as 'a drawn-out and somewhat slurred "tee-i-ew" ' and the song as 'a wild and fluty jumble of slurred notes, reminiscent of the song of *Turdus viscivorus*'.
Distribution and Habitat: Ranges from Sierra Leone to Gaboon and Congo in the forest and in its gallery extensions and outliers in the savanna. In the main body of the forest fairly common in tall second-growth and on the edges of clearings.
Nesting: Little known. One record of a nest in the slender outer branches near the top of a lower canopy tree in the forest.
Allied species: Sjöstedt's Honey-Guide Bulbul (*Baeopogon clamans*) whose range is limited to the forest country of the Cameroons and Gaboon closely resembles the Honey-Guide Bulbul. It shows more buff on the underparts and the white outer tail feathers have no black tips, but these characters are difficult to spot in a tree-top high-forest species. A better diagnostic is the voice which is harsh and unmusical and quite unlike the sweet voice of *Baeopogon indicator*.

SPOTTED BULBUL   *Ixonotus guttatus*   **Pl. 38**
Identification: Easily recognised by its mainly white tail and underparts and conspicuous white-spotted upperparts. Closely gregarious; usually in parties of six to twelve or more individuals, flying restlessly about the treetops calling cheerfully. At rest it has a habit of raising one wing over its back.
Voice: Cheerful concerted chirping cries.
Distribution and Habitat: The forest from Liberia to Gaboon. Not uncommon in the primary and tall secondary trees.
Nesting: The nest, built in a second-growth tree, is a slight shallow cup of leaf petioles and rootlets. The two highly glossed eggs are yellowish, boldly blotched and spotted in different shades of brown and grey.

SIMPLE LEAF-LOVE   *Chlorocichla simplex* (*Pyrrhurus simplex*)   **Pl. 38**
Identification: Brown above, mainly buffish below, with a white throat and a white eyelid, this last being quite a useful field character. Usually in pairs, not given to associating with other species, restless, adept at concealing itself in the foliage, but constantly disclosing its presence by its loud chatter.
Voice: A frequent throaty chattering. A soft, sweet song has also been recorded.
Distribution and Habitat: The forest zone and its gallery extensions from Portuguese Guinea to Gaboon and Congo. Widely and commonly distributed in low second-growth forest and farm clearings where there is leafy cover.
Nesting: The nest is a slight shallow cup of plant stems and tendrils, built near the ground in the fork of a sapling or plant. The two glossy stone-coloured eggs are handsomely marked with blotches, scrolls and twisted lines of brown and grey.
Allied species: The Yellow-throated Leaf-love (*Chlorocichla flavicollis*) inhabits the fringing forest and the dense thickets of the savanna from Gambia and Senegal to the Central African Republic, Gaboon and Congo. It does not penetrate the forest zone. Widely distributed and locally common, occurring in

pairs and parties, and discovered by its loud throaty babbling. A brown bird with a noticeable yellow or white throat. From Nigeria westwards the throat is bright yellow; from the west Cameroon highlands eastwards and southwards it is white or white tinged with sulphur.

SWAMP PALM BULBUL   *Thescelocichla leucopleurus*   **Pl. 38**

Identification: A large Bulbul, brown above, mainly white tinged yellow below, with a conspicuous white-tipped tail and a strong predilection for raphia palms in swamp forest. Gregarious, noisy and restless.

Voice: Frequent bursts of excited throaty babbling.

Distribution and Habitat: The range is the forest zone from Portuguese Guinea to Gaboon and Congo. Well-distributed in freshwater swamp forest. At times visits the dry forest, planted clearings in the forest, and gardens, in search of fruit.

Nesting: There is a record of a nest with two young in a swamp-palm tree.

LEAF-LOVE   *Phyllastrephus scandens* (*Pyrrhurus scandens*)   **Pl. 38**

Identification: The colour pattern is distinctive – grey crown, rich fawn tail, white throat and creamy-buff breast and belly. Active, noisy, associating in insect-hunting parties of its own kind.

Voice: A concerted throaty babbling.

Distribution and Habitat: Senegal east to Chad and the Central African Republic and south to Gaboon and Congo in the fringing forests and savanna woods and thickets outside the main body of the West African rain forest. Widely distributed but local.

Nesting: The cup-shaped nest is slung between the forks of a twig of a forest tree near water. The two creamy-white eggs are spotted and scrawled with brown and the shellmarks are greyish.

LESSER ICTERINE GREENBUL   *Phyllastrephus icterinus*   **Pl. 38**

Identification: The Lesser Icterine Greenbul is olive-green above, yellow below, and has a rufous-brown tail. In the field it is indistinguishable in appearance and behaviour from the Greater Icterine Greenbul (*Phyllastrephus xavieri*) (see Checklist, p. 283), with which it often associates. Active and agile, sometimes picking insects off the twigs and leaves, sometimes pursuing them on the wing.

Voice: A frequently repeated 'tirrrrr-it-it-it'.

Distribution and Habitat: The interior of lowland forest from Sierra Leone to Gaboon and Congo; also Fernando Po. Its habitat is the foliage of the primary forest or mixed primary and second-growth at any height from ground level to the tree-tops.

Nesting: The nest is a slight cup slung in a horizontal fork of a forest under-shrub. The eggs are pinkish-brown profusely and finely speckled with grey and brown, the markings condensing to form a dark zone at the widest diameter. They are highly glossed.

YELLOW-BELLIED GREENBUL   *Phyllastrephus flavostriatus*
(*Phyllastrephus poliocephalus*)   **Pl. 38**

Identification: A large easily identified Bulbul, olive-green above with a grey head, the throat white and the rest of the underparts bright yellow. Its loud call and montane habitat are further diagnostics. Consorts in foraging parties with other species of the montane forest.

Voice: The call is a loud rich 'churp' frequently uttered, and there is a scolding note which can be represented as 'prit-it-it-it . . .'.

Distribution and Habitat: Locally common in the Cameroons in the mountain forests of Mount Cameroon, Kupe, the Rumpi Hills and the Bangwa District; also in the Obudu Plateau of Nigeria. Usually in the tree tops; occasionally descending to the lower branches and undershrubs. A Bulbul with a wide but discontinuous, mainly highland distribution in East and South Africa. The very distinct and isolated West African race (*P. f. poliocephalus*) is sometimes treated as a full species.

Nesting: No West African records. In southern Africa the nest is a cup of twigs, rootlets and moss, placed in an undershrub or creeper. The two eggs are pink marked with different shades of brown.

BRISTLE-BILL   *Bleda syndactyla*   Pl. 38

Identification: One of the group of insectivorous terrestrial forest Bulbuls that are given to hunting on the fringe of the driver ant columns. Olive-brown above, sulphur-yellow below. Its long rufous tail which is often flicked is a field mark and distinguishes it from the Green-tailed and the Grey-headed Bristlebills which have green tails tipped with yellow.

Voice: A series of plaintive, wavering, unevenly spaced notes of descending pitch, and a variety of other melodious or chattering calls.

Distribution and Habitat: Its range is the rain forest from Sierra Leone to Gaboon and Congo.

Nesting: Nest a shallow cup of leaves and sticks lined with rootlets and tendrils placed in a small forest tree. The two eggs are pale buff heavily marked with different shades of brown.

GREEN-TAILED BRISTLE-BILL   *Bleda eximia*   Pl. 38

Identification: Bright olive-green above, bright yellow below. The tail is green, the outer rectrices tipped with yellow, this last an excellent field mark. In the Lower Guinea race there is a conspicuous yellow spot in front of the eye. A predominantly terrestrial Bulbul often attracted by the driver ant columns and a frequent member of the mixed bird parties of the forest. Vocal.

Voice: Call a loud explosive repeated 'chook'. The song is mellow and thrush-like.

Distribution and Habitat: Widespread in the forest from Sierra Leone to Gaboon and Congo; also Fernando Po. In places, for instance the Cameroons, abundant; in other parts of its range, for instance Nigeria, rather scarce. Frequents primary forest and old second-growth.

Nesting: Nest a few feet from the ground in a small isolated forest shrub. A very slight structure of dry leaves bound to the supporting twigs with vegetable fibre and lined with fibre. Eggs 2, the green, buff or brown ground heavily and variously marked with reddish-brown, blackish-brown, dark olive or purplish marblings and blotches.

Allied species: The Grey-headed Bristle-bill (*Bleda canicapilla*) at first glance recalls the Green-tailed Bristle-bill; its outer tail feathers are similarly tipped with yellow. But the head is grey not olive-green and the spot before the eye is grey not yellow. It ranges from southern Senegal and Sierra Leone to Nigeria. Usually discovered searching for insects on or near the ground in high rain forest or swamp forest or old second-growth. Rather shy but betrayed by its loud clear 'chooeek-choo' whistle, frequently repeated.

BEARDED BULBUL   *Criniger barbatus* (*Trichophorus barbatus*)   **Pl. 38**
Identification: A rather dull, olive-green, grey and brown bird. The throat feathers which are often puffed out are helpful in identification. They are yellow in the races occurring from Nigeria westwards and white in the very distinct race (*chloronotus*) found in the Cameroons and Gaboon. The rather similar White-bearded Bulbul is smaller and has yellow underparts. A gregarious Bulbul not infrequently consorting with other forest species. The call is arresting.
Voice: A fine melodious whistling call; also a loud throaty concerted babbling.
Distribution and Habitat: The forest from Sierra Leone to Gaboon. Often found in the lower strata of primary rain forest and occasionally in the tree tops or on the ground.
Nesting: Nest a few feet from the ground in the primary forest. An open cup of dead leaves, decayed wood and fibre set on top of the leaves of an undershrub and firmly bound to them by *Mycelium*. Characteristically some green-leaved sprigs of an epiphyte are woven into the rim of the nest. Eggs 1–2, greyish-brown or reddish-brown usually boldly marbled with olive-brown or blackish-brown.

WHITE-BEARDED BULBUL   *Criniger calurus*
(*Trichophorus calurus*)   **Pl. 38**
Identification: The crown is dark brown, the mantle olive-green, the tail rufous-brown or olive-green according to locality. The long white throat feathers are conspicuous; the underparts are rather bright yellow. A common forest species and a frequent member of the mixed bird parties.
Voice: Very similar to that of the Bearded Bulbul though the practised ear can detect minor differences.
Distribution and Habitat: The main body of the evergreen forest and its larger gallery extensions from Portuguese Guinea to Gaboon and Congo; also Fernando Po. A common Bulbul of the forest undergrowth.
Nesting: The nest is placed in a forest shrub and is made of twigs and moss lined with black fibres. The two glossy eggs have a pinkish ground very heavily and densely marked with chocolate-brown.

WEST AFRICAN NICATOR   *Nicator chloris*   **Pl. 38**
Identification: The song and calls attract attention. On the rare occasions that it leaves the thick cover of the forest the olive-green upperparts, conspicuous pale grey underparts, yellow under the tail, and yellow spots on the wing, taken together, are diagnostic. An insect hunter that does not join the mixed forest bird parties.
Voice: A full-throated rich song usually delivered at a considerable height in the forest foliage and a variety of harsh, wheezy or whistling calls.
Distribution and Habitat: The forest and gallery forests from Senegal to Gaboon and Congo, nearly always in thick foliage in high second-growth or in the lower strata of the primary forest.
Nesting: A very slight flat structure of twigs and tendrils placed on a leaf or in the fork of a tree a few feet from the ground. One egg only. Markings vary from evenly distributed light reddish-brown spots on a pale ochraceous ground to dense brown and greyish-violet marblings on an olive ground.

THRUSHES AND CHATS: Turdidae

Except for some of the Chats a mainly arboreal family that nevertheless characteristically find their food on the ground. Bill usually rather long, slender and slightly compressed. Legs sturdy. Spotted juvenile plumage. Many are fine songsters.

WHINCHAT   *Saxicola rubetra*   **Pl. 39**
Identification: 5″. A compact, alert, active Chat, usually seen perched conspicuously on a corn stalk, telegraph wire, stump or other vantage point in open country from which it swoops down to the ground to capture insects. The broad white eye-stripe and, in flight, the white patch on the wing and on either side of the base of the tail are the outstanding plumage field characters in the male. In the female they are duller and smaller yet still conspicuous. In West Africa usually in abraded winter plumage with inconspicuous indistinctly streaked br ownish upperparts and buffish underparts. Territorial and solitary. Silent, but the 'tic-tac' note and the song sometimes uttered in spring before its departure.
Distribution and Habitat: An extremely common and widespread winter visitor to the West African savanna. In the dry zone bordering the Sahara from northern Senegal to northernmost Nigeria and Chad a passage migrant only (September–November and March–May). Farther south resident. Unrecorded so far from the Gaboon and Congo savanna.

STONECHAT   *Saxicola torquata*   **Pl. 39**
Identification: 5″. Male easily identified by jet-black head and throat, conspicuous broad white collar, dark mantle, wings and tail, white wing stripe and rump, chestnut breast and white belly. Female duller and browner with reduced white on wing and rump. Alert, active, restless, vocal. Usually perched when the frequent flicks of wing and tail attract attention; in pairs or, after breeding, in family parties.
Voice: Note a frequent harsh 'wee-tuc-tuc'. Song a pleasant unpretentious jingle.
Distribution and Habitat: Resident and sedentary in West Africa. Its headquarters in West Africa are the grasslands of the Cameroon highlands and Fernando Po from 3,000 to 13,000 feet, with isolated populations in the Gaboon and Congo savanna bordering the middle and lower Congo River, on the Djebel Abougoudam, Chad, on the grasslands of the high Sierra Leone, Guinea and Ivory Coast mountains, and near the desert on the Upper Niger at Mopti in Mali.
Nesting: Nest on the ground well-concealed in a tussock of grass. A small cup of grass and moss lined with wool. Eggs 3–4, pale greenish-blue, either immaculate or faintly marked with reddish-brown.

WHEATEAR   *Oenanthe oenanthe*   **Pl. 39**
Identification: 6″. At all seasons the white rump and the white tail with black centre and tips are conspicuous, especially in flight. In winter plumage crown and mantle buffish-grey in male, brown in female, light eye-stripe and dark

ear-coverts, buff and cream underparts. Restless, alert, given to bobbing and flirting its tail, and often perching on stones and ant-hills. Territorial. Silent.
Distribution and Habitat: A common passage migrant and winter visitor (October–April) to West Africa from the Palaearctic and Nearctic regions. It winters in the dry northern zone of the savanna in Senegal, Gambia, Sierra Leone, northern Ghana, northern Nigeria, northern Cameroons and Chad. Absent from the moister savanna zone adjoining the forest, and on passage only in the desert zone and a vagrant in the Cape Verde Islands. It frequents bare, burnt or stony ground, closely cropped pasture, stubble fields and highland grasslands.

SPANISH WHEATEAR   *Oenanthe hispanica*   Pl. 39
Identification: 6″. Rump and tail pattern rather similar to the Wheatear (*Oenanthe oenanthe*) from which species the male is distinguished by its sandy upperparts and, if of the black-throated phase, by its black throat. Female not certainly distinguishable in the field.
Distribution and Habitat: A rather uncommon winter visitor (September–April) to West Africa occurring in the country bordering the desert and recorded from Mauritania, Senegal, Mali, Niger, northern Nigeria (rarely) and Chad.

RED-BREASTED CHAT   *Oenanthe bottae* (*O. heuglini*)   Pl. 39
Identification: 5½″. Sexes alike. A small Chat, dark brown above, rufous below. The upper tail-coverts and the basal part of the tail white contrasting with the black distal portion of the tail. Perches on trees, rocks, termite mounds and grass stems, and usually seen flitting actively about its territory. At the nesting season the song and song flight are characteristic.
Voice: Song a short pleasing warble with sometimes fine mellow notes. Call-note a' harsh 'chack'.
Distribution and Habitat: Locally distributed in the savanna from Mali and Upper Volta through Niger, Nigeria and the Cameroons to Chad and the Central African Republic. Partial to boulder-strewn grassy hillsides and bare recently burnt ground and relatively numerous in the Cameroon highlands and the Jos Plateau. Migratory, shifting north during the rains after breeding.
Nesting: Nest on the ground usually in a hole in an animal's burrow or amongst stones. Materials grasses and fur. Eggs 2–4, pale blue.

RED-TAILED CHAT   *Cercomela familiaris*   Pl. 39
Identification: 5½″. A small brown Chat distinguished by its bright rufous rump and its tail which is rufous tipped black except for the central rectrices which are all black. Easily confused with the female Redstart (*Phoenicurus phoenicurus*) (see p. 195), but the latter lacks the black tips to the tail feathers and is not specially addicted to a rocky habitat as is the Red-tailed Chat. Active, and frequently flirts its tail and wings.
Voice: Usually silent. Whistling, churring and chuckling calls have been described.
Distribution and Habitat: The savanna north of the forest in Ghana, Nigeria, Cameroons and the Central African Republic, in the vicinity of rocky hills. Favours the ravines and tree-dotted uneven rocky ground at the base of the hills and cultivation patches in such terrain. Widespread but local occurring singly or in pairs or small parties.

Plate 39

CHATS, WHEATEARS, ROCK-THRUSH AND REDSTART

1. **RED-TAILED CHAT** *Cercomela familiaris* page 191
   Rufous rump; rufous tail except central rectrices and tips which are black.

2. **WHINCHAT** *Saxicola rubetra* 190
   White eye-stripe; white wing-patch; white tail-patches.

3. **STONECHAT** *Saxicola torquata* 190
   Black head and throat; white collar; chestnut breast.

4. **SPANISH WHEATEAR** *Oenanthe hispanica* 191
   Sandy upperparts; black or light throat; rump and tail pattern like Wheatear.

5. **WHEATEAR** *Oenanthe oenanthe* 190
   Winter: white rump; white tail with black centre and tips; buffish-grey crown and mantle.

6. **RED-BREASTED CHAT** *Oenanthe bottae* 191
   Dark brown upperparts; white upper tail-coverts.

7. **ANT-CHAT** *Myrmecocichla aethiops* 194
   Sooty-brown except for large white wing-patch seen in flight.

8. **WHITE-CROWNED CLIFF-CHAT** 194
   Myrmecocichla cinnamomeiventris
   Female: chestnut rump and belly.
   Male: white shoulder-patch.

9. **ROCK-THRUSH** *Monticola saxatilis* 195
   Winter: bluish-grey head, throat, and mantle; chestnut-orange tail and breast.

10. **WHITE-FRONTED BLACK CHAT** 194
    Myrmecocichla albifrons
    Female: dark all over.
    Male: dark with white forecrown.

11. **REDSTART** *Phoenicurus phoenicurus* 195
    Winter: black throat; rump and tail (except central rectrices) reddish-chestnut.

Plate 40

SCRUB-ROBINS, ROBIN-CHATS ETC.

1. **RUFOUS SCRUB-ROBIN** *Cercotrichas galactotes*   page 196
Rufous upperparts; black and white tipped chestnut tail.

2. **BLACK SCRUB-ROBIN** *Cercotrichas podobe*   196
Sooty-black; long white-tipped tail.

3. **FOREST SCRUB-ROBIN** *Cercotrichas leucosticta*   196
Rufous rump; white-tipped dark tail.

4. **FIRE-CREST ALETHE** *Alethe diademata*   196
Broad orange streak on crown.

5. **FOREST ROBIN** *Stiphrornis erythrothorax*   197
White spot in front of eye; orange throat and breast.

6. **BLUE-SHOULDERED ROBIN-CHAT**   198
    Cossypha cyanocampter
Broad white superciliary streak; blue shoulder-patch.

7. **SNOWY-CROWNED ROBIN-CHAT** *Cossypha niveicapilla* 198
Like White-crowned Robin-Chat but smaller and white on head
more restricted.

8. **WHITE-CROWNED ROBIN-CHAT** *Cossypha albicapilla*   198
White crown and nape.

9. **MOUNTAIN ROBIN-CHAT** *Cossypha isabellae*   197
White superciliary streak; dark upperparts; orange-rufous underparts.

10. **WHITE-TAILED ANT-THRUSH** *Neocossyphus poensis*   199
Blackish tail, outer feathers conspicuously tipped white.

11. **WEST AFRICAN THRUSH** *Turdus pelios*   200
Bright yellow bill.

12. **NIGHTINGALE** *Luscinia megarhynchos*   199
Chestnut-brown tail.

13. **FRASER'S RUSTY THRUSH** *Stizorhina fraseri*   199
In colour closely resembles White-tailed Ant-Thrush, but eastern
race distinguished by absence of white on tail.

Nesting: Nest built in a hole under a rock or in a crevice. Eggs three, greenish-blue speckled with rufous mainly in a zone near the large end.

Allied species: The Black-tailed Rock Chat (*Cercomela melanura*), 5½″, resembles the Red-tailed Chat in size, proportions, brownish plumage and tail and wing flirting habits, but its tail and upper tail-coverts are blackish not rufous. Recorded from a few mountainous or rocky localities on the southern border of the Sahara in Mali, Niger and Chad.

ANT-CHAT   *Myrmecocichla aethiops*   Pl. 39

Identification: 8″. Sexes similar. A sooty-brown bird (black from a distance) which in flight shows a large white patch on the wing. In fresh plumage at close range the light margins of the feathers of the throat and breast are apparent. Typical upright carriage of a Chat. Mainly terrestrial but also perches, especially when singing.

Voice: A clear melodious whistling song and various piping calls.

Distribution and Habitat: Widely but locally distributed in the arid belt between 9° N. and 18° N. in Senegal, Gambia, Mali, Niger, northern Ghana, northern Nigeria, northern Cameroons and Chad. Frequents open farmland, villages, clay and laterite quarries, road cuttings and wells.

Nesting: Nest a flat cup of grass at the end of a long burrow excavated by the bird in the side of a well, pit or cutting. Eggs 3–4, white.

Allied species: The Sooty Ant-Chat (*Myrmecocichla nigra*), 6½″, resembles the Ant-Chat but it is distinctly smaller and the adult male has a conspicuous large white shoulder patch. Irregularly distributed in the savanna occurring in Guinea, Nigeria, the Cameroons, the Central African Republic, Gaboon and Congo. Locally common in the Cameroon highlands grasslands.

WHITE-CROWNED CLIFF-CHAT   *Myrmecocichla cinnamomeiventris* (*Thamnolaea cinnamomeiventris*, *T. coronata*)   Pl. 39

Identification: 8″. Colour pattern diagnostic. The male is glossy black with a white crown and shoulder patches and a chestnut rump and belly. The female is brownish with the rump and belly chestnut and shows no white. In the very distinct races that occur in Senegal and Mali the male lacks the white crown. The loud call, rocky habitat and persistent raising and lowering of the tail are all distinctive.

Voice: Loud melodious whistling calls. Also a sweet warbling song.

Distribution and Habitat: Bare granite kopjes, cliffs and escarpments attract it. Locally common in the Cameroon highlands and northern Nigeria and recorded from the Central African Republic, northern Togo, northern Ghana, Mali and Ivory Coast. Occurs in pairs.

Nesting: Builds its nest in a hole in a rock or rock crevice or utilises an old Swallow's nest beneath a rocky overhang or below the eaves of a house. Eggs 2–3, light blue blotched with pale brown.

WHITE-FRONTED BLACK CHAT   *Myrmecocichla albifrons* (*Pentholaea albifrons*)   Pl. 39

Identification: 6″. A small slimly-built Chat, the adult male slate-black except for a conspicuous white forecrown, the female and immature bird slate-black without the white frontal patch. In the race occurring in eastern Cameroons and the Central African Republic the males have a white shoulder patch in addition to the white forehead. Occurs singly or in pairs. Finds its insect prey on the ground swooping down to retrieve it from a tree stump or other vantage point. Rather silent.

Voice: A short vehement clear sweet song. Also a chattering note.

Distribution and Habitat: Ranges widely through the savanna north of the forest from Senegal, Gambia and Portuguese Guinea to Chad and the Central African Republic. Also in some of the more extensive clearings in the forest. Fond of recently burnt bare stony savanna and of cultivated patches with pollarded stumps for hunting posts. Locally common.

Nesting: Builds on the ground under a boulder or near the ground in a hollow tree stump. Nest of grass and cobwebs. Eggs 2–3, pale green spotted with light rufous.

ROCK-THRUSH *Monticola saxatilis* Pl. 39

Identification: 8″. Stocky build, short tail, upright stance and solitary and shy disposition characterise it. In winter plumage adult male has bluish-grey head, throat and mantle, dark brown and whitish rump, dark brown wings, and chestnut-orange tail, breast and belly. The sharpness of the colours is obscured by numerous buffish feather tips. Female mottled brown above, orange-chestnut below barred brown, upper tail-coverts and tail orange-chestnut.

Distribution and Habitat: A winter visitor (November–March) to West Africa from the Palaearctic Region thinly but widely distributed in the savanna and recorded from Senegal, Portuguese Guinea, Sierra Leone, Liberia, northern Ghana, northern Nigeria and Chad, and occurring on passage in the desert on the northern border of our area in March–April and September–October. In winter frequents stony gullies, recently burnt savanna, and bare cultivation clearings.

Allied species: The male of the Blue Rock-Thrush (*Monticola solitaria*), 8″, in winter is blue-grey mottled with dark brown, and the wings and tail are blackish. In the field it appears almost black. The female has the upperparts brown and the underparts buff closely barred with grey-brown. Sparingly distributed in winter in the West African savanna and recorded from Senegal, Gambia, Liberia, Mali, Ghana, northern Nigeria and Chad, in which last territory it is common.

REDSTART *Phoenicurus phoenicurus* Pl. 39

Identification: 5½″. In both sexes the reddish-chestnut rump and tail is a good field character. Male has white forehead, grey crown and mantle, blackish throat and face, reddish chest, whitish belly. In winter white forehead very narrow, feathers of crown and mantle tipped brown, and feathers of throat and breast tipped white. Female brown above and buffish below and rather similar to the widespread indigenous Red-tailed Chat (*Cercomela familiaris*), except that the rufous tail of the latter is tipped with black. Alert and active and given to flicking its red tail. Silent in winter quarters but occasionally sings or utters alarm call.

Distribution and Habitat: A widespread and rather common passage migrant (September–November and February–May) and winter visitor (September–April) to West Africa from the Palaearctic Region ranging in the savanna north of the forest from Gambia and Senegal to Chad, especially in the arid northern zone. Catholic in choice of habitat.

BLACK SCRUB-ROBIN *Cercotrichas podobe* **Pl. 40**

Identification: 9″. Sexes similar. A long, slimly-built, black-billed, sooty-black bird, with a long, graduated, white-tipped tail. In flight wings mainly pale rufous. Feeds on the ground foraging under the bushes, frequently raising and spreading its long tail. Often sings.

Voice: A short melodious song delivered from the top of a shrub.

Distribution and Habitat: Widespread and locally common in the arid thorn belt between the 13th and 16th parallels penetrating to the edge of the desert where there are bushes and trees. Occurs in Mauritania, Senegal, Portuguese Guinea, Mali, Niger, northern Nigeria, northern Cameroons and Chad.

Nesting: A rather ragged cup of leaves, roots, twigs and trash variously located in the roof of a building, or a crevice or fork of a tree, or between palm fronds. Eggs 2–3, pale green spotted with brown.

RUFOUS SCRUB-ROBIN *Cercotrichas galactotes*
(*Agrobates galactotes*) **Pl. 40**

Identification: 6″. Sexes similar. Rufous above, creamy-white below, with a long, broad, chestnut tail conspicuously tipped with black and white. Whitish eye-stripe. Behaves rather like the Black Scrub-Robin. Terrestrial but also perches, especially when singing. Tail frequently fanned and cocked.

Voice: Song melodious but rather shrill and disjointed.

Distribution and Habitat: Widespread and locally common in the semi-arid belt to the desert edge in Senegal, Mali, Niger, northern Nigeria, northern Cameroons and Chad. Resident but numbers increased in winter by immigrants of the Palaearctic race.

Nesting: In a fork in a thick, thorny tree. A deep cup of twigs, leaves and cotton lined with hair. Eggs 3–5, greyish-white or bluish-white heavily spotted and speckled with brown and lilac.

FOREST SCRUB-ROBIN *Cercotrichas leucosticta*
(*Erythropygia leucosticta*) **Pl. 40**

Identification: 6½″. In our area the only Scrub-Robin of the true forest. Excessively shy. A notable songster. Brown mantle, rufous rump, buffish-white underparts. White eye-stripe, double white wing-bar, and white-tipped dark tail distinctive. Bobs its tail like a Chat.

Voice: A prolonged melodious warbling song of great sweetness. Harsh alarm calls also recorded.

Distribution and Habitat: A rare species of the lowland forest recorded from Sierra Leone, Liberia, Ivory Coast and Ghana. Inhabits the forest floor and the undergrowth of virgin forest.

Nesting: No local records. In the Ituri a nest with a single nestling was built in a small natural cavity in the bole of a forest tree about five feet from the ground.

FIRE-CREST ALETHE *Alethe diademata* (*A. castanea*) **Pl. 40**

Identification: 8″. Slimly built. Chestnut above, mainly whitish below. A broad orange streak on the middle of the crown easily visible at short range. Tail feathers blackish, the three outer pairs conspicuously tipped white. Juvenile heavily spotted. The race occurring from Nigeria eastwards (*Alethe d. castanea*) lacks the white tips to the tail feathers and the upperparts are olive-brown not chestnut. A mainly terrestrial forest bird; a frequent, active, pugnacious member of the bird parties often catching insects disturbed by the driver ants.

Voice: The song consists of a few sweet high-pitched notes. Various harsh calls also recorded.

Distribution and Habitat: The undergrowth of the virgin lowland forest from Portuguese Guinea and Sierra Leone to Gaboon. Also Fernando Po.

Nesting: Builds on the ground or low down in a hole in a forest stump. Nest of rootlets and moss. Eggs 2–3, pinkish-white blotched and spotted with maroon and lilac.

Allied species: The Brown-chested Alethe (*Alethe poliocephala*) often associates with the Fire-crest Alethe at the driver ant columns and its habits and general appearance are similar. It lacks the orange streak on the crown and the white tail tips. As in the Fire-crest Alethe the mantle is chestnut, but the crown is blackish and there is a white stripe above the eye. The pale brown chest is not easily observed in the field. Ranges in the forest from Sierra Leone to Gaboon and Fernando Po. Mainly a lowland species but in the Cameroons montane forests it is common and ascends to 7,000 feet at least.

FOREST ROBIN   *Stiphrornis erythrothorax*   Pl. 40

Identification: 5″. Olive-green or slate-grey upperparts; bright orange throat and breast, rest of underparts white. A conspicuous white spot in front of the eye. In the race that occurs in the interior of south-eastern Cameroons the underparts are golden-yellow. A quiet unobtrusive forest species generally on the ground or in low undergrowth. Adults occur singly or two together and they are occasional members of mixed bird parties gathered round moving driver ants.

Voice· Generally silent. An unpretentious but sweet melodious song.

Distribution and Habitat: The lowland forest from Sierra Leone and Guinea to Gaboon and Fernando Po. Mainly in the tall virgin forest but occasionally in thick second-growth. Not uncommon.

Nesting: Nest a cup of moss lined with fibre built near the ground in a niche in the bole of a forest tree. Clutch 2. Eggs green thickly and indistinctly marked with reddish-brown and orange-brown.

MOUNTAIN ROBIN-CHAT   *Cossypha isabellae*   Pl. 40

Identification: 6″. Quiet, unobtrusive and solitary, a bird of the forest shade, usually on the ground or perched near the ground on a stump, fallen tree, or undershrub, and less commonly in the higher branches up to thirty feet. A prominent white superciliary streak, dark upperparts and orange-rufous underparts. Tail chestnut tipped black but the middle pair of rectrices all black.

Voice: Usually silent. A harsh scolding note recorded.

Distribution and Habitat: The montane forests of the Cameroons and the Obudu Plateau of Nigeria and a common resident within this restricted range.

Nesting: Nest built in a niche in a forest tree. A bulky cup of moss and leaf skeletons lined with roots and fine grasses. The two eggs are pale greenish-blue with or without faint rusty speckling about the large end.

Allied species: The White-browed Robin-Chat (*Cossypha polioptera*) resembles the Mountain Robin-Chat in size, build and plumage except that the tail is entirely chestnut, the crown blacker, and the white superciliary streak longer and broader, but the habitat and distribution of the two species differ. The

White-browed Robin-Chat ranges rather locally north of the forest from Sierra Leone to the Central African Republic, usually in upland areas. It lives in the gallery forests and is usually discovered quietly searching for insects on or near the ground.

BLUE-SHOULDERED ROBIN-CHAT   *Cossypha cyanocampter*
Pl. 40

Identification: 7″. Shy and difficult to see in the thick undergrowth it affects. Fine songster and notable mimic. At short range the blue shoulder patch and the broad white stripe over the eye are characteristic. Head black, mantle brown, underparts orange, tail rufous except the middle tail feathers which are black.
Voice: Song melodious, plaintive and distinctive. It also mimics the cries and songs of other species, mingling their calls with its own.
Distribution and Habitat: The dense undergrowth of the lowland forest from Sierra Leone and Liberia to Gaboon.
Nesting: Builds in thickets in the forest making an open cup of twigs, leaves and moss, lined with roots. Eggs 2, glossy green or greenish-blue thickly and obscurely marked with brown and pale violet.

WHITE-CROWNED ROBIN-CHAT   *Cossypha albicapilla*   **Pl. 40**
Identification: 11″. Sexes similar. A large Robin-Chat with a conspicuous white crown and nape. Cheeks black. Upperparts blackish, but rump and tail orange-rufous except for black central rectrices. Underparts orange-rufous. The race that occurs from Ghana eastwards has the crown feathers black tipped white giving the crown a scaly appearance.
Voice: A melodious song. Also a harsh monosyllabic call.
Distribution and Habitat: Widely but locally distributed in a rather narrow zone in the savanna from Senegal (13° 30′ N.), Gambia and Portuguese Guinea through Sierra Leone, Ivory Coast, southern Mali, Ghana, Nigeria and Cameroons to the Central African Republic. Frequents thick places in fringing forest and kurimis and also gardens with dense shrubbery.
Nesting: A slight cup of rootlets, tendrils and leaves low down in the hollowed-out top of a small tree-stump. Eggs 2, pale grey-green profusely blotched, spotted and suffused with reddish-brown and ashy-violet.

SNOWY-CROWNED ROBIN-CHAT   *Cossypha niveicapilla*   **Pl. 40**
Identification: 8″. Sexes similar. Resembles the White-crowned Robin-Chat but smaller with a shorter tail and having only the centre of the crown white, the sides being black like the cheeks. The colour pattern of the mantle, tail and underparts is similar in the two species. The shade of black on the mantle varies geographically. Nearly always concealed in dense thicket or leafy cover, but voice betrays it.
Voice: A pleasing, sustained, full-throated song of melodious notes interspersed with the calls of other species which it mimics. Also a frequent, soft, musical 'hu-hu' (the second note two tones higher than the first).
Distribution and Habitat: Widespread and locally common in the savanna where there is thick cover and in forest second growth in Senegal, Gambia, Portuguese Guinea, Sierra Leone, Liberia, Ivory Coast, southern Mali, Ghana, Nigeria, Cameroons, southern Chad, the Central African Republic, Gaboon and Congo.

Nesting: Nest variously sited in the branches of a tree, in a hollow in a tree trunk, in a creeper, or in a stem of bananas. Usually well-concealed. A shallow cup of grass, leaves and mud lined with rootlets and tendrils. Eggs 2–3, olive-brown or olive-green and resembling the eggs of the Nightingale.

WHITE-TAILED ANT-THRUSH *Neocossyphus poensis* **Pl. 40**
Identification: 8½″. Usually on the ground or in the undergrowth, occasionally in the higher branches. Occurs singly or two or three together, frequently near driver ants and sometimes joining the mixed flocks of roving insectivorous forest birds. Slate-brown upperparts; cinnamon-rufous underparts; tail blackish, the three outer feathers broadly and conspicuously tipped with white. In the western part of its range (from Nigeria westwards) easily confused with Fraser's Rusty Thrush (*Stizorhina fraseri finschi*), but the White-tailed Ant-Thrush is mainly terrestrial not arboreal, has a different voice, and has a habit when perched of slowly raising and depressing the tail.
Voice: A high-pitched whistle; also various squeaking and ticking calls.
Distribution and Habitat: The lowland forest from Sierra Leone and Guinea to Gaboon and Fernando Po. Frequents both primary and second-growth.
Nesting: Habits unknown.

FRASER'S RUSTY THRUSH *Stizorhina fraseri*
(*S. finschi*) **Pl. 40**
Identification: 8″. A forest and oil palm farmland species, a frequent member of the mixed bird parties but more often alone or two together perched on a high branch or flitting from branch to branch catching insects. Unlike the similar White-tailed Ant-Thrush, seldom seen on the forest floor. Dark olive-brown above; rich rufous below. The races on Fernando Po and on the mainland in the Cameroons, Gaboon and Congo have inconspicuous brown and rufous tails, but that occurring from Nigeria westwards (*S.fraseri finschi*) has conspicuous white-tipped outer tail feathers and is almost indistinguishable in the field on plumage characters from the White-tailed Ant-Thrush (see that species).
Voice: Loud characteristic whistling calls; also harsh croaking cries; often silent.
Distribution and Habitat: Ranges in the forest from Sierra Leone and Liberia to Gaboon and Congo; also Fernando Po. Locally common, frequenting high forest, old second-growth and oil palm farmland.
Nesting: Habits unknown.

NIGHTINGALE *Luscinia megarhynchos* **Pl. 40**
Identification: 6½″. Sexes similar. Upperparts uniform rufous-brown, breast pale greyish-brown, remaining underparts whitish, tail chestnut-brown. Skulks near the ground usually in thick cover, easily located by its song, but difficult to see.
Voice: The fine musical notes are unmistakable although they lack the full-throated exuberant quality of the summer song.
Distribution and Habitat: Widespread and locally common in winter (September–May) in the West African savanna from Senegal and Gambia to the Cameroons, Chad and the Central African Republic in the humid zone near the forest and less common in the arid north where it occurs mainly as a passage migrant. Fond of low second-growth shrubbery and the tangle of rank herbage, bushes and small trees fringing water courses.

WEST AFRICAN THRUSH   *Turdus pelios* (*T. libonyanus*)   **Pl. 40**
Identification: 9″. A typical Thrush in appearance and habits. Brown above,
pale brown below, with the chin whitish streaked dark brown. Under wing-
coverts and, in part of its range, the flanks also, orange-chestnut. Bright yellow
conspicuous bill. Sexes similar. Young spotted below. Mainly a ground feeder.
Voice: Song a loud melodious varied warbling. Call a rich 'churp'.
Distribution and Habitat: Widespread and abundant in West Africa in
savanna and forest. Partial to cultivated land and human habitation. Usually
absent from true forest. Sedentary. Ranges from Senegal and Gambia to Chad,
the Central African Republic, Gaboon and Congo. Mountain races inhabit the
Cameroon Mountain and the wooded highlands of Fernando Po.
Nesting: Nest usually in a farmland or garden tree or shrub. A substantial cup
of grass, roots and earth, lined with fibre. Eggs 2–3, pale greenish-blue spotted
and blotched with brown primary and lavender secondary markings.
Allied species: The Grey Ground-Thrush (*Turdus princei*) is a rare and shy
species recorded from a few localities in the lowland rain forest of Liberia, Ivory
Coast, Ghana, Nigeria and the Cameroons. The upperparts are brown, the
underparts pale brown, and a distinct double white wing-bar is the best field
mark.

BABBLERS: Timaliidae

A group of Thrush-like birds of the savanna and forest. Long legs and stout
feet. Plumage mainly sombre shades of brown, rufous or grey. Several species
are gregarious and noisy with harsh, chattering voices.

HILL-BABBLER   *Alcippe abyssinica* (*Pseudoalcippe abyssinicus*,
P. atriceps)   **Pl. 31**
Identification: A small compact Babbler, reddish-brown above, grey below,
the head black or grey according to locality. The song and habitat help to identify
it.
Voice: A rich melodious sustained song somewhat resembling that of the
Garden-Warbler (*Sylvia borin*) of Europe. A perennial singer.
Distribution and Habitat: A montane species with a wide but discontinuous
distribution in tropical Africa. The grey and black-headed forms are sometimes
regarded as specifically distinct: they are readily distinguishable in the field. In
West Africa it is locally abundant in the forests of the Bamenda highlands, the
Cameroon Mountain and the peak of Fernando Po. Catholic in its choice of
habitat.
Nesting: The nest is a neat open cup made of plant stems and lined with grass
tops, built near the ground in a shrub in the forest undergrowth. The two eggs
are thickly spotted and speckled with brown and lilac on a creamy ground.

BROWN AKALAT   *Malacocincla fulvescens* (*Illadopsis fulvescens*,
I. moloneyanus)   **Pl. 31**
Identification: The various species of lowland forest Babblers found in West
Africa are difficult to distinguish in the field. Their plumage is sombre; they
are often shy; and they are difficult to see in the forest gloom and in the thick
undergrowth where they skulk. The Brown Akalat is olive-brown or rufous-
brown above and brownish or tawny-brown below, the shade varying locally,

some races being colder and others warmer in tone. It occurs in pairs or small parties and is a member sometimes of the bird parties attracted by the driver ant columns.

Voice: A variety of loud harsh notes. A plaintive whistle also recorded.

Distribution and Habitat: Ranging from Portuguese Guinea through the lowland forests bordering the Gulf of Guinea to Gaboon and Congo. A common forest bird affecting the foliage of primary and second-growth but absent from cleared areas.

Nesting: The nest is a shallow cup, mainly of leaves, built near the ground in a forest shrub. The two eggs are spotted with maroon and purplish-grey on a white or cream ground.

WHITE-BREASTED AKALAT *Malacocincla rufipennis*
(*Illdopsis rufipennis*)   Pl. 31

Identification: A rather inconspicuously coloured forest Babbler. Mainly olive-brown and rufous-brown. The throat and the middle of the belly are whitish but these parts are difficult to see in the forest. A quiet, unobtrusive bird, usually on or near the forest floor and occurring in pairs or small parties.

Voice: A fine melodious whistling call; but usually silent.

Distribution and Habitat: In the forest from Guinea and Sierra Leone in the west to Gaboon in the south and east. Also on the island of Fernando Po. Locally rather common.

Nesting: The nest is built near the ground in a fork of an undershrub and is a slight cup of leaves lined with tendrils and fibres. The two eggs are evenly blotched and spotted in different shades of brown and grey.

Allied species: The Rufous-winged Akalat (*Malacocincla rufescens*) and Puvel's Akalat (*Malacocincla puveli*) are so similar in size and colour to each other and to the White-breasted Akalat as to be virtually indistinguishable in the field. Both are Akalats of the forest undergrowth, the former ranging from Sierra Leone to Ghana, and the latter, which frequents the forest outliers and gallery strips, ranging from Portuguese Guinea to the Cameroons.

BLACKCAP AKALAT *Mlacocincla cleaveri* (*Illadopsis cleaveri*) Pl. 31

Identification: In the field distinguished from other forest Babblers in our area by its black cap and the broad white or grey stripe over the eye. In the race that occurs in the lowland forest of eastern Nigeria, however, the head is dark grey, not black.

Voice: A sweet plaintive whistling song.

Distribution and Habitat: Found from Sierra Leone in the west to Gaboon in the south and east. Also on Fernando Po. Not uncommon, in pairs or parties, but difficult to see as it forages on or near the ground in thick forest shrubbery.

Nesting: A shallow loose nest of dead leaves placed low in the forest under-growth. Eggs 2, whitish spotted with dull maroon and purplish-grey.

GILBERT'S BABBLER *Kupeornis gilberti*   page 160

Identification: A stoutly built plump Babbler, brown with the sides of the face and the chin and throat white. The white mask and bib is an excellent field mark. Gregarious, noisy, active, often associating with other forest birds, especially the Yellow-bellied Greenbul (*Phyllastrephus flavostriatus*).

Voice: A frequent explosive 'chook', usually a single note, but sometimes two, three or four in rapid succession. At times a harsh concerted chatter.

Distribution and Habitat: Found only in certain mountain forests in the west Cameroon highlands and the Obudu Plateau of Nigeria. Locally common especially on Kupe Mountain above 4,500 feet. The boles and large upper branches of primary forest trees attract it particularly.
Nesting: Habits unknown.

CAPUCHIN BABBLER *Phyllanthus atripennis*   **Pl. 31**
Identification: 9½″. Sexes similar. A rather squat Babbler with short, rounded wings. Deep maroon-brown (blackish in the field) but head, throat and chest grey. Bill greenish-yellow. In the race found from Ghana eastwards the body plumage is reddish-chestnut, the crown is blackish, and the grey is restricted to the supercilium, cheeks and upper throat. Noisy. Gregarious. Usually near the ground in thick cover. Occasionally in tree tops.
Voice: A loud excited concerted chattering.
Distribution and Habitat: Fairly widespread but local in the second-growth of the forest and its gallery extensions in Portuguese Guinea, Sierra Leone, Liberia, Ghana, Togo, Nigeria and Cameroons. In these last two territories distinctly local.
Nesting: Not known.

BROWN BABBLER *Turdoides plebejus*   **Pl. 31**
Identification: 9″. Sexes similar. A common, gregarious, sedentary savanna Babbler. Except when breeding usually in bands of 6–12 individuals. Not shy though usually hidden in thick leafy cover, and easily located by its frequent noisy babbling. Plumage without distinctive characters, mainly light brown, paler on the cheeks and underside and obscurely flecked or squamated with whitish on the breast. Shade of plumage varies geographically. Eye bright orange. Usually on or near the ground in thickets.
Voice: An almost endless, clamorous, concerted babbling, and various guttural and scolding calls.
Distribution and Habitat: Widely and commonly distributed in the savanna, in woods, shrubbery, or farmland with trees from Senegal, Gambia and Portuguese Guinea east to Chad and the Central African Republic, and south to Congo. Avoids bare, open country.
Nesting: A substantial cup of grass lined with rootlets placed in a bush or a tree fork. Eggs 3–4, glossy, immaculate blue, grey-blue, mauve or pink.

BLACKCAP BABBLER *Turdoides reinwardii*   **Pl. 31**
Identification: 10″. Sexes similar. Similar in build and proportions to the Brown Babbler but slightly larger. The plumage also is similar but the Blackcap Babbler has a conspicuous black head and cheeks and a contrasting whitish throat. Creamy-white eye noticeable. Habits like those of the Brown Babbler. Gregarious even when breeding.
Voice: Rather like that of the Brown Babbler.
Distribution and Habitat: From Senegal, Gambia and Portuguese Guinea east to south-west Chad and the Central African Republic. Widely distributed but less common and more local than the Brown Babbler. Habitat similar but almost entirely restricted to thickets, especially by river banks.
Nesting: A cup of leaves and twigs lined with roots and tendrils. At no great height; well-concealed in the foliage of a tree. Eggs 2, glossy dark blue.

WARBLERS: Sylviidae

A large rather ill-defined family of small, slimly-built, mainly dull-coloured birds that usually lack distinctive markings. Juvenile plumage unspotted. Mainly insectivorous picking their food off the twigs, leaves and grasses. Wide variety of habitats but seldom descend to the ground. Distribution, habitat, behaviour and voice often help identification.

FAN-TAILED SWAMP-WARBLER *Schoenicola platyura*
(*S. brevirostris*)

Pl. 41

Identification: 7″. Very long broad tail serves to distinguish it from other dull-coloured Warblers. The fluttering or jerky flight and the habitat are also characteristic.

Voice: A variety of whistling and other calls uttered by the male, especially during display over his breeding territory.

Distribution and Habitat: Locally distributed in Sierra Leone, Guinea, eastern Nigeria, the Cameroons and Gaboon. Usually in marshy terrain with lush or tussocky grass and in West Africa mainly in mountainous country such as the Cameroon and Sierra Leone highlands. Absent from the forest.

Nesting: In South Africa the loosely woven grass-strip nest is built near the ground in a tuft of coarse grass. Eggs 2, pale cream finely spotted with red-brown and ash-grey.

RUFOUS CANE-WARBLER *Acrocephalus rufescens*
(*Calamoecetor rufescens*)

Pl. 41

Identification: 7″. A large, sturdy, sombre-coloured Warbler with fulvous-brown upperparts and pale grey-brown underparts. Frequents reed-beds and tall herbage near water. Vocal. Furtive. Sometimes glimpsed climbing among or clinging firmly to the vertical reed stalks with its strong legs. Closely resembles the migrant Great Reed Warbler but smaller, has a different voice, and in the hand can be readily distinguished by different wing formula. The Great Reed Warbler has a pointed wing (2nd and 3rd primaries the longest) whilst the Rufous Cane-Warbler has a rounded wing (4th and 5th primaries the longest).

Voice: Both sexes sing. A short phrase of loud, rich, rather harsh contralto notes. Also a loud deep-toned churring.

Distribution and Habitat: Reed-beds, rushes or tall grass by marshes or streams. Recorded from several scattered localities providing this habitat in Senegal, Ghana, Nigeria, Cameroons, Chad, the Central African Republic, Congo and Fernando Po.

Nesting: A substantial, deep, grass cup, often over water, attached by entwining grass blades to one or more stout reed or grass stalks, at a height of a few feet. Eggs 2–3, greyish-white, rather heavily spotted with black, grey and dark yellowish-brown, and with ashy shell-marks.

Allied species: The Sedge Warbler (*Acrocephalus schoenobaenus*), 5″, sexes similar, is a passage migrant (April–May and September–October) and winter visitor (September–May) to West Africa from the Palaearctic region. Very common on passage on the lower Senegal River, on the western shore of Lake Chad, and at Kano, and no doubt in other localities with grassy swamps or reed-beds, and recorded in winter or on passage from several widespread savanna or forest clearing localities in Senegal, Gambia, Liberia, Nigeria, Cameroons, Chad, Gaboon and Congo. The heavily streaked upperparts, the conspicuous broad cream eye-stripe, and the marshy habitat help to identify it and even in its winter quarters it occasionally utters its characteristic harsh chattering song and explosive alarm croak. The Great Reed Warbler (*Acrocephalus arundinaceus*), 7½", sexes similar, is distinguished by its large size and stout build. Upperparts uniform brown, underparts buffish-white. A rather indistinct narrow eye-stripe. Habitat includes swamp, thick herbage by streams, and tall grass and shrubbery in dry places. Characteristic loud vibrant call frequently uttered in winter. Solitary. Recorded in winter or on passage from Senegal, Sierra Leone, Liberia, Ivory Coast, Ghana, Nigeria, Cameroons, Chad, Gaboon and Congo from savanna localities (mainly) and from forest clearings.

MOUSTACHED SCRUB-WARBLER *Sphenoeacus mentalis*
(*Melocichla mentalis*)   **Pl. 41**
Identification: 8". Sexes similar. A very large Warbler with a long and broad dark tail. Skulks in dense vegetation but is betrayed by song or alarm note. Forehead chestnut, eye-stripe white, crown and upperparts earth-brown, throat white, conspicuous black moustachial streak, breast buff, belly white.
Voice: A simple, melodious song and a scolding chatter.
Distribution and Habitat: Widely distributed and locally common in the savanna where there is rank herbage, usually but not always near water. Absent from the forest and from the arid northern regions. Ranges from Senegal and Portuguese Guinea east to Chad and the Central African Republic and south to Gaboon and Congo.
Nesting: An open grassy cup built near the ground in rank herbage. Eggs 2–3, with a rich red-brown or puce ground thickly freckled and clouded with various shades of lilac and brown.

MELODIOUS WARBLER *Hippolais polyglotta*   **Pl. 41**
Identification: 5". Sexes similar. Olive-brown upperparts, bright yellow underparts, yellow eye-stripe. Distinguished from the Leaf-Warbler species by its stouter build, but virtually indistinguishable in the field from the Icterine Warbler (*Hippolais icterina*) (see Checklist, p. 286), which also occurs in West Africa.
Voice: The rich warbling song is sometimes uttered in winter quarters.
Distribution and Habitat: A winter visitor and passage migrant (August–November and February–June) in West Africa from the Palaearctic Region. Widespread throughout the savanna north of the rain forest from Senegal to the Cameroons, resident in the moist zone but mainly on passage only in the arid north. Occurs singly or as a member of mixed bird parties and affects the gallery woods and the trees and shrubs of the orchard bush.

OLIVACEOUS WARBLER *Hippolais pallida*   **Pl. 41**
Identification: 5". Sexes similar. Size, build and pose recall the Icterine and Melodious Warblers. Dull-coloured, uniform pale brown above, whitish below. Whitish eye-stripe. At close range long and broad bill a field character, particularly of the migrant race. Arboreal. Insectivorous.
Voice: A loud churring, vigorous song, uttered by wintering as well as by breeding residents.

Distribution and Habitat: A breeding resident in Niger, Chad and on the Nigerian shore of Lake Chad. A widespread winter visitor and passage migrant from the Palaearctic in Senegal, Gambia, Portuguese Guinea, Ivory Coast, Mali, Ghana, Niger, Nigeria and Chad, especially in the arid parts of these territories. Frequents groves of trees, riparian woodland, and swamp forest.
Nesting: Nest a solid deep cup built in a small tree or shrub. Eggs 2.

GARDEN WARBLER   *Sylvia borin*   Pl. 32
Identification: 5½″. Sexes similar. Light brown above, buffish-white below, without any arresting plumage characters. Plumply built. Arboreal. Occurs singly or as a member of savanna mixed bird parties.
Distribution and Habitat: Widely distributed in winter (September–May) in West Africa, though only on passage in the northernmost arid zone. Recorded from nearly all the territories north of the forest and also from the savanna south of the forest in Congo. Frequents outlying woods, fringing forest, and orchard bush in the savanna, and also the second-growth woods and the scattered trees of extensive farm clearings in the forest.

BLACKCAP   *Sylvia atricapilla*   Pl. 32
Identification: 5½″. In size, proportions and general behaviour similar to the Garden Warbler (*Sylvia borin*), and distinguished from that species by a cap, black in the male and bright reddish-brown in the female, which is sharply demarcated from the grey cheeks at eye level. Occasionally sings in winter quarters before the spring migration. Occurs singly or in small flocks.
Voice: In the Cape Verde Islands a rich bubbling mellow warble preceded by a few seconds' confused chattering like that of a Whitethroat. Sometimes sings on the mainland in winter quarters.
Distribution and Habitat: Resident in the Cape Verde Islands and common there in localities with thick leafy vegetation and water. On the mainland of West Africa a rather sparse winter visitor from the Palaearctic Region yet locally common as on the lower Senegal River. Occurs on passage and also winters (October–May). Recorded from Senegal, Gambia, Sierra Leone, Liberia, Ivory Coast, Ghana, Mali, Nigeria and Chad, mainly from localities in the savanna whose fruiting trees attract it.
Nesting: Nest in a tree or bush. A slight cup of moss, grass and fibres, lined with hair. Eggs pale buff blotched and spotted with reddish-brown and purplish-brown.
Allied species: The Orphean Warbler (*Sylvia hortensis*), 6″, somewhat resembles the male Blackcap but its cap is blackish not jet-black, is less clearly defined from the greyish nape, and extends below the eye. The whitish eye, the white not grey throat, and the white on the outer tail feathers are other diagnostic marks. The female Orphean Warbler has a greyish crown almost concolorous with the nape and mantle. A winter visitor from the Palaearctic Region. Most records come from the arid north in Mali, Niger and Chad. It also occurs on passage or as a resident in Senegal, Gambia and northern Nigeria.

EUROPEAN WHITETHROAT   *Sylvia communis*   Pl. 32
Identification: 5½″. The pure white throat, chestnut wing patch and white outer tail feathers are distinctive. The male has a greyish and the female a brownish crown and face. In winter quarters usually solitary and sings occasionally.

Distribution and Habitat: Widely but unevenly distributed in winter (August–May) in the thorn scrub savanna of West Africa in Gambia, Senegal, Mali, Niger, northern Ghana, northern Nigeria and Chad, frequenting thickets and small trees and feeding on insects and berries. Sometimes in great numbers on spring passage (March–April) on the western shores of Lake Chad.

Allied species: The Subalpine Warbler (*Sylvia cantillans*), 4″, is small and inconspicuously coloured. Upperparts greyish; throat and breast pale pinkish-grey; a thin white moustachial streak; belly white. Female browner and duller and sometimes virtually indistinguishable in the field from the female Lesser Whitethroat (*Sylvia curruca*) which is a rarer winter visitor to West Africa. Skulking and secretive frequenting acacia and other thorny bushes and feeding on insects and berries. Widely distributed and locally common in the thorn scrub belt bordering the desert and recorded from Senegal, Gambia, Mali, Ivory Coast, Niger, northern Nigeria and Chad. A passage migrant and winter resident present from August to April.

WILLOW WARBLER *Phylloscopus trochilus*   **Pl. 41**

Identification: 4″. Sexes similar. A small, slim, active, arboreal Warbler usually engaged in searching the leaves for insects. Yellow eye-stripe. Olive-grey above, whitish below lightly washed with yellow on the breast and under the tail. The shade of the upperparts and underparts varies greatly with age and season. Legs usually pale brown, but sometimes dark brown. The musical song, which is heard occasionally in winter, especially from February onwards, identifies it certainly.

Distribution and Habitat: A very abundant and widespread savanna and forest clearing species throughout our area, occurring as a winter resident (September–April) in the forest and the soft-leaved woodland savanna and as a passage migrant in the arid northern zone.

Allied species: In winter in our area are several other species of Palaearctic Leaf Warblers similar to the Willow Warbler in appearance and behaviour and often difficult or impossible to distinguish from it. The Chiffchaff (*Phylloscopus collybita*) usually has blackish legs. Its 'chiff-chaff chiff-chaff . . .' song is diagnostic and is uttered fairly frequently in its winter quarters after the moult from December onwards. It is a common passage migrant and winter resident (September–May) on the lower Senegal River where it frequents the tall acacias near water, and is recorded from a few other arid localities in Senegal, Gambia, Mali, Nigeria and Chad. Bonelli's Warbler (*Phylloscopus bonelli*) has a yellowish rump and below is whitish without any yellow tinge. The distinctive song, a trill on the same note, slower than but recalling the song of the Wood Warbler, is frequently uttered in its winter quarters. Bonelli's Warbler is a common winter resident (September–April) in the dry acacia scrub in northern Senegal and it is recorded on passage or in winter from a few other localities, mainly near the desert in Gambia, Mali, Niger, northern Nigeria, Cameroons and Chad. The Wood Warbler (*Phylloscopus sibilatrix*), 5″, is distinctly larger than the Willow Warbler and has a sulphur-yellow throat and breast which contrasts with the pure white lower breast and belly. The call, a repeated 'chee-u', and the tinkling, trilling song are both at times uttered in its winter quarters. Widespread in winter (September–May) in the moist wooded savanna bordering the forest and in clearings in the forest with scattered trees, or in the canopy on the forest edge, and recorded from Liberia, Guinea, Ivory Coast, Ghana, Nigeria, Cameroons, Gaboon and Congo. Also on passage in the dry north in Mali, Niger, northern Nigeria, northern Cameroons and Chad, and very occasionally as far west as Senegal.

SINGING CISTICOLA *Cisticola cantans* Pl. 32

Identification: A medium-sized Cisticola. Male has rust-brown crown, hind neck and wing edges, dark grey upperparts, whitish underparts, tail feathers tipped with pale grey. Female and juvenile rather similar. In the field winter dress hardly different from summer dress. Habitat, voice, absence of aerial display and tailor-type nest help to identify it. In pairs during the wet season and in parties during the dry season when it sometimes joins other Cisticolas to form roving insect-hunting bands of twenty or more individuals.

Voice: A variety of loud musical and metallic notes, especially during the breeding season when the male sings from a perch on shrub or tree.

Distribution and Habitat: Ranges in the savanna north of the forest from Senegal, Gambia and Portuguese Guinea to northern Cameroons, Chad and the Central African Republic. Frequents rank herbage with shrubs or trees and is locally abundant.

Nesting: Nest near the ground in a shrub. A cup of dry grass lined with plant down contained within a pouch formed by two or more living green leaves of the shrub sewn together with silk. Eggs 3–4, white or palest blue spotted with brown and lilac.

Allied species: The Red-faced Cisticola (*Cisticola erythrops*) resembles the Singing Cisticola in plumage but the forehead and face are strongly tawny-red, a character which is obvious in the field. Also in winter the mantle is rich brown not grey. Nest tailor-type. Call a reiterated series of shrill notes rising in pitch and volume. Ranges in the northern savanna from Senegal and Gambia to the Cameroons and the Central African Republic and reappears south of the forest in the Gaboon and Congo savanna. Inhabits grass savanna, orchard bush, the edges of farmland, and abandoned farm clearings. The Whistling Cisticola (*Cisticola lateralis*) is larger and more robust than the Singing Cisticola. Males in breeding season conspicuous by reason of their loud sustained whistling song delivered from a high perch. Adult male and female upperparts uniform blackish-brown (no red on crown) with conspicuous reddish edging to the wing; white underparts. Ranges in the savanna from Senegal, Gambia and Sierra Leone to the Central African Republic reappearing south of the forest in Congo and especially common in the moist belt adjoining the forest. The Chattering Cisticola (*Cisticola anonyma*) is distinguished by its habitat. It occupies the clearings and edges of the lowland forest in southern Nigeria, the Cameroons and Gaboon. Absent from the savanna belt. Where it occurs usually abundant. A restless, noisy, easily observed Cisticola with a variety of rather harsh calls and an unmelodious trilling song. No diagnostic plumage characters. Upperparts brown, the crown dark reddish; underparts white lightly washed with buff. Tail feathers light-tipped. Sexes similar. The Brown-backed Cisticola (*Cisticola hunteri*) is a wide-ranging African montane Cisticola which in our area occurs only on the Cameroon Mountain and in the Cameroon highlands. Altitudinal range 3,000–9,500 feet. In the forest zone it affects the herbage and shrubbery of the clearings and forest edges; below the forest zone the copses, grasslands and bracken; and above the forest zone, the shrubs and herbage

208

Plate 41

WARBLERS

42

Plate 42

WARBLERS AND FLYCATCHERS

1. GREEN HYLIA *Hylia prasina* page 217
Pale yellow superciliary streak.

2. OLIVE LONGBILL *Macrosphenus concolor* 216
Long straight bill; no distinctive plumage characters.

3. NUTHATCH WARBLER *Sylvietta brachyura* 216
Very short tail; grey upperparts; tawny-buff underparts.

4. TIT-HYLIA *Pholidornis rushiae* 217
Very small; yellow rump; streaked throat.

5. SPOTTED FLYCATCHER *Muscicapa striata* 218
Whitish underparts indistinctly streaked on the breast.

6. DUSKY BLUE FLYCATCHER *Muscicapa comitata* 219
Dark slate-grey but throat and belly white or greyish.

7. CASSIN'S GREY FLYCATCHER *Muscicapa cassini* 218
Blue-grey; throat and belly whitish; flight feathers and tail black.

8. USSHER'S FLYCATCHER *Artomyias ussheri* 219
Appears uniformly dark.

9. GREY TIT-BABBLER *Myioparus plumbeus* 219
White outer rectrices.

10. SWAMP FLYCATCHER *Muscicapa aquatica* 218
Resembles Spotted Flycatcher but smaller and breast pale grey-brown unstreaked.

11. BLACK FLYCATCHER *Melaenornis edolioides* 220
Long slender round-ended tail.

12. FRASER'S FOREST FLYCATCHER *Fraseria ocreata* 220
White underparts, the breast with conspicuous crescent-shaped black bars.

13. PALE FLYCATCHER *Bradornis pallidus* 221
No distinctive plumage characters; breast unstreaked.

bordering the woods and thickets in the ravines and sheltered hollows on the mountainsides. A lively vocal Cisticola with a characteristic display duet. Upperparts rust-brown, more reddish on the crown; underparts mainly rusty-cream, but breast grey. The Rock-loving Cisticola (*Cisticola aberrans*) has a discontinuous range in our area occurring on bare rocky hills in Sierra Leone, Mount Nimba, Mali, Ghana, Nigeria, the Cameroons, Chad and the Central African Republic. Head rusty-brown, mantle ash-brown, underparts rusty-buff, tail feathers tipped with rusty-buff. Non-breeding plumage redder and brighter. Sexes similar. The unusual Cisticola terrain, the restless, ostentatious behaviour, and the characteristic wheezy note all help to identify it.

RUFOUS GRASS WARBLER *Cisticola galactotes* Pl. 32

Identification: 5″–6″. Male larger than female. A medium-sized Cisticola with streaked upperparts found in marshes and rice fields. In nuptial dress head brown, back smoke-grey boldly mottled with black, tail grey tipped white, underparts pale buff. In eclipse dress head reddish, back rusty-buff heavily and conspicuously streaked with black, tail-tips rusty-white, underparts buff.

Voice: Song a monotonous, repeated, long-drawn-out 'zuip'. Also various chirping calls.

Distribution and Habitat: Widely distributed and common where there is suitable habitat in the form of water-logged grassland, reed-beds, marshes and rice fields. Recorded from Senegal, Gambia, Portuguese Guinea, Sierra Leone, Mali, Ivory Coast, Ghana, Nigeria, Cameroons, Chad, the Central African Republic, Gaboon and Congo.

Nesting: A rounded domed nest with a lateral opening. Of grass blades and lined with down. Low down in thick vegetation, some of the supporting grasses being incorporated into the nest. Eggs 3–4, glossy pinkish-white heavily and evenly marked with well-defined spots and speckles of reddish-brown, orange-brown and violet-grey.

STRIPED CISTICOLA *Cisticola natalensis* Pl. 32

Identification: A large stout-billed Cisticola with an unmistakable song-call. Male conspicuously larger than female. Breeding (wet-season, summer) dress differs greatly from non-breeding (dry season, winter) dress. In summer upperparts mottled in two shades of brown; underparts creamy-white; tail feathers tipped white with blackish subterminal spots; wing-edging russet. In winter upperparts buff heavily striped black; underparts strongly washed with rusty-buff; tail conspicuously longer than in summer.

Voice: The male's loud 'klink-klunk' nuptial song and the hesitant display flight at a fair height over its territory are unmistakable and the song is occasionally uttered by long-tailed dark-striped winter birds.

Distribution and Habitat: The grass savanna and the clearings in the orchard bush and grass woodland from Senegal to the Cameroons (where it ascends to over 7,000 feet), Chad, the Central African Republic and Congo. Widespread and common except in the arid northern areas.

Nesting: A domed elliptical nest with a lateral entrance, built low down in rank herbage. Of dry grass blades and lined with grass tops and plant down. Eggs 2–3. Variable, white or pale blue, spotted, usually sparingly, with various shades of brown and with ashy-violet undermarkings.

REDPATE CISTICOLA *Cisticola ruficeps*   **Pl. 32**
Identification: A small Cisticola. Sexes almost alike in plumage. Head and nape rich rust-red; back and rump plain brown; underparts white; tail with conspicuous white tips and dark subterminal spots. In the dry (non-breeding) season the plumage is more russet and the back is conspicuously dark-streaked. This Cisticola has no aerial display.
Voice: An unpretentious soft musical song.
Distribution and Habitat: The savanna from Gambia and Senegal to northern Cameroon, Chad and the Central African Republic. Well distributed, especially in the more arid northern areas.
Nesting: Nest very near the ground in herbage. Ball-shaped, domed, with a small opening in the side. Of grass blades, thickly lined with vegetable down. Eggs 4, pale green blotched and spotted with claret-brown and greyish-purple.

SHORTWING CISTICOLA *Cisticola brachyptera*   **Pl. 32**
Identification: A tiny Cisticola. In the breeding season the male seen occasionally in 'cloud-scraping' display flight but more often perched conspicuously on a tree top commanding his territory. In summer (breeding) dress, brown above, whitish below, tail feathers with pale tips and blackish subterminal smudges. In winter (non-breeding) dress, upperparts brown with conspicuous dark stripes on the mantle. Sexes similar.
Voice: A thin 'see see see see see . . .' uttered from the song perch.
Distribution and Habitat: Widely and commonly distributed in a variety of terrain in the savanna from Senegal and Mali east to Chad and the Central African Republic and reappearing south of the forest in the grasslands of Congo and Gaboon.
Nesting: A small ball-shaped nest with a circular opening in the side, built near the ground in a tussock of grass and made of dry grass blades with a lining of plant down. Clutch 3. Eggs white or white tinged greenish spotted and speckled with pale orange-brown, reddish-brown or dark purple, the markings varying greatly in colour and distribution from set to set.

COMMON FANTAIL WARBLER *Cisticola juncidis*   **Pl. 32**
Identification: 4″. A small Cisticola with upperparts heavily mottled except for a plain reddish-buff rump. Underparts white washed with buff on the breast and flanks. Short blackish tail tipped white. Female and off-season male streaked rather than mottled above and more strongly washed with buff below. On its breeding ground the song and undulating display flight are distinctive.
Voice: Song a sharp high-pitched rasping 'zit-zit-zit . . .' delivered during the undulating display flight, each 'zit' synchronising with a dip in the flight.
Distribution and Habitat: Sedentary. Widely distributed in the drier West African savanna and recorded from Senegal, Gambia, Portuguese Guinea, Ivory Coast, Volta, Mali, Ghana, northern Nigeria, Chad, Central African Republic, Spanish Guinea, Gaboon and Congo.
Nesting: Nest a few inches to two feet from the ground in a tuft of grass. Of growing grass blades bound with fibre and cobweb and fashioned into a deep purse lined plentifully with plant down. The opening of the nest faces skywards. Clutch 3-4. Eggs variable, white or blue, freckled, spotted, or blotched with brown and mauve.

DESERT FANTAIL WARBLER   *Cisticola aridula*   **Pl. 32**
Identification: 4½". A very small dark-streaked yellowish Cisticola found in arid regions. In nuptial dress upperparts sandy and rufous-buff with dark mottling (more marked in the male). Underparts white tinged rusty-buff. Tail viewed from below has black subapical and white apical spots. In eclipse dress the upperparts are striped not mottled. Somewhat resembles the Common Fantail Warbler (*Cisticola juncidis*) but the dry habitat, song and flight distinguish it.
Voice: Song a short, repeated, high-pitched 'ting' given either in flight or from a low perch.
Distribution and Habitat: The open dry short grassland in the arid regions bordering the desert in Senegal, Mali, Niger, northern Nigeria and Chad.
Nesting: Nest of dry grasses built near the ground in grass. Ball-shaped with a side-top opening. Eggs 3. In southern Africa they are white or pale blue, unmarked, or spotted with red and madder.

RED-WINGED WARBLER   *Prinia erythroptera*
(*Heliolais erythroptera*)   **Pl. 32**
Identification: 5". Sexes similar. Distinguished by bright chestnut on the wings which contrasts with the grey upperparts and tawny-buff underparts. Other characters are the long, graduated, white-tipped tail with black subterminal spots and the relatively large black bill. In eclipse plumage the entire upperparts are pale rufous-pink and the bill horn-coloured. Usually in the tall grass or shrubs in small restless parties which can be located by their frequent loud cries.
Voice: Song varied and pleasing. Call a frequent, high, grating 'tseep'.
Distribution and Habitat: In the savanna where there is high grass with shrubs or trees. Widely distributed but local. Common in parts of Nigeria. Recorded from Senegal, Gambia, Portuguese Guinea, Ivory Coast, Ghana, Nigeria, Cameroons, Chad and the Central African Republic.
Nesting: Nest in a low shrub inside two or three growing leaves sewn together to form a pouch. Eggs 2, pale green closely and evenly speckled with pinkish-brown.

WEST AFRICAN PRINIA   *Prinia subflava*   **Pl. 32**
Identification: 5". Sexes similar. No outstanding plumage characters. Crown and mantle brown, rump tinged rufous. Distinct white stripe over eye. Underparts pale fawn. Tail graduated, tipped white with black subterminal marks. Bill black. In the non-breeding dry-season dress which savanna birds assume the tail is much longer, the upperparts are paler brown with a rusty tinge, and the bill is brown. Rather Cisticola-like, especially in short-tailed summer dress. Usually in small parties progressing openly and fearlessly through the shrubs and herbage, with frequent jerks of the tail.
Voice: Song a characteristic clear, shrill 'che-che-che-che-che . . .'. Call a resonant 'chirr'.
Distribution and Habitat: Widely and very commonly distributed throughout the area in savanna and forest in varied habitat but showing a preference for farmland and abandoned clearings. Absent from the closed forest.
Nesting: A domed structure of openly interwoven grass strips attached to growing grass stems. Often enclosed within two or three leaves of a shrub

drawn and sewn together. Eggs 3–4 with a very wide range of colour and markings. Ground white, bluish, greenish, or pinkish, immaculate, or marked with various shades of brown and lilac spots, blotches and pencillings.

GREEN LONGTAIL *Prinia epichlora* (*Urolais epichlora*) Pl. 41
Identification: 6″. Easily known by its montane habitat, its slim build and long tail, and its engaging lively behaviour. Green above, white tinged with cinnamon below. An arboreal Warbler usually in parties seeking insect food amongst the leaves and small branches.
Voice: The song is a repetition of one clear sharp note.
Distribution and Habitat: Abundant in the mountain forests of the Cameroons, the Obudu Plateau of Nigeria and Fernando Po, mainly between 3,000 and 7,000 feet, but on the Cameroon Mountain occurring as low as 1,750 feet.
Nesting: Not known.
Allied species: The White-chinned Longtail (*Prinia leucopogon*), 6″, is easily recognised by its ash-grey colour, conspicuous white throat and black ear-coverts. A very distinct isolated race (*P. l. leontica*) of Sierra Leone, Guinea and Liberia is darker, has a grey not a white throat, and the flanks and lower belly buff. It is a common Warbler of the thick forest second-growth in eastern Nigeria, the Cameroons, Gaboon and Congo, with an isolated population in the wooded highland area of Sierra Leone, Guinea, Liberia and Ivory Coast.

BROWN-HEADED FOREST-WARBLER *Apalis cinerea* Pl. 41
Identification: 5½″. Restricted to montane forest. Mainly grey above and white tinged with buff below. Usually seen searching the leaves and small branches, progressing with agile, graceful movements, and much fanning and flicking of the tail. Even at a great distance it may be recognised by its actions and by the white markings on its long slender tail.
Voice: A variety of notes, the most frequent a high-pitched, rather sweet 'pirrrrrrr pik pik pik . . .'. Also a monotonous, far-reaching Barbet-like 'pink pink pink pink pink . . .' sung in measured time with great vehemence and delivered from a prominent elevated perch on a tree.
Distribution and Habitat: The mountain forests of Fernando Po, the Cameroons, and the Obudu Plateau of Nigeria between 4,000 and 7,000 feet. Rather common, occurring singly, in pairs, and in parties, in the foliage from undershrub to tree top level but usually at a considerable height.
Nesting: No West African records.
Allied species: The Black-collared Forest-warbler (*Apalis pulchra*) is in our area found only in the forests of the Bamenda highlands and there hardly below 5,000 feet. Usually low down in thick shrubby undergrowth. Lively Warblers much given to tail-flicking and readily recognised by their colour pattern. Mainly slate-grey above and white below, the breast crossed by a conspicuous black band and the flanks washed with bright chestnut. The long graduated tail is edged and tipped with white. The Black-capped Yellow Warbler (*Apalis nigriceps*) is an uncommon forest species recorded from Sierra Leone, Liberia, Ivory Coast, Ghana, the Cameroons, the Central African Republic and Fernando Po. A tiny (4½″) brightly coloured Warbler, the male with a jet-black head, a yellow mantle, and a black pectoral band separating the white throat from the

greyish-white breast and belly. In the female the head and pectoral band are grey. Usually seen in small restless parties exploring the foliage of old second-growth or of the creepers which festoon the primary forest trees on the edge of clearings.

MOHO   *Hypergerus atriceps*   **Pl. 41**
Identification: 8″. Slim build, long tail, slender black bill and colour pattern distinguish it. Head, throat and upper breast black, the feathers edged with silvery white; upperparts bright olive-yellow; underparts bright yellow. Sexes similar. Usually discovered singly or in pairs searching the undergrowth for insects.
Voice: Often silent. The song is a loud melodious whistle of three syllables.
Distribution and Habitat: Locally distributed in the savanna from Gambia to the Cameroons, Chad and the Central African Republic, mainly in the zone just north of the forest. The edges of the gallery extensions and outlying patches of dry forest and dense second-growth, and stands of oil palms and bamboo in damp places are favourite terrain.
Nesting: Nest suspended from a palm frond, twig or tendril. A large bulky structure made of dry grasses with an opening at one side. Eggs 2–3, pale blue blotched and spotted with red-brown.

STREAM WARBLER   *Bathmocercus cerviniventris*
(*Bathmedonia rufa, Eminia cerviniventris*)   **Pl. 41**
Identification: 5″. Colour pattern diagnostic. Male bright rufous-chestnut but forehead, face, throat and breast black, and belly grey. In the female the rufous-chestnut is replaced by olive-brown. In the very distinct race (*B. c. cerviniventris*) occurring in Sierra Leone and Ghana the male has the whole head and throat black and the rest of the plumage is brown except for a bright chestnut patch on the lower breast: the female lacks the bright chestnut patch. Usually discovered skulking near the ground in the thickest shrubbery or herbage in partly cut-out forest country. Occurs in pairs or small parties.
Voice: Male has a distinctive high-pitched plaintive whistle. Members of a party utter little nondescript cries as they move about the undergrowth.
Distribution and Habitat: A rather local Warbler of the evergreen forest recorded from Sierra Leone, Liberia, Ivory Coast and Ghana (*B. c. cerviniventris*) and the Cameroons and Gaboon (*B. c. rufus*). Usually in dense thickets in forest clearings near a stream.
Nesting: Nest a bulky pile lined with grass. Eggs unknown.

YELLOW-BROWED CAMAROPTERA   *Camaroptera superciliaris*
                                                                     Pl. 41
Identification: 4½″. A tiny forest Warbler, apple-green above and whitish below but under tail-coverts yellow. Bright yellow superciliary stripe and ear-coverts and black lores are field marks, and the peculiar call is diagnostic. Sexes alike. Usually concealed in thick tangle where it creeps about the branches.
Voice: A curious far-carrying double whining call reminiscent of the cry of a lamb or kid heard a long way off.
Distribution and Habitat: The lowland forest from Sierra Leone to the Cameroons, Gaboon and Congo. Also Fernando Po. The favourite terrain is thick tangled second-growth on the edge of forest clearings.

Nesting: Nest in a shrub, constructed of living leaves sewn together along their edges with spiders' silk to form a pouch which is lined with seed-down and fine fibres. The three pale blue eggs are spotted and speckled with brown.

Allied species: The Green-backed Camaroptera (*Camaroptera chloronota*), 4½″, ranges locally from Senegal to the Cameroons, Congo and Fernando Po. An unobtrusive, short-tailed, dull-coloured Warbler of the undergrowth of the primary forest and the old tangled second-growth. Dark green above, greyish below. The race occurring from Senegal to Ghana has conspicuous rust-coloured ear-coverts. The mewing call-note and the pouch-like nest sewn into the leaves of a forest shrub are characteristic of the *Camaroptera* group.

GREY-BACKED CAMAROPTERA   *Camaroptera brachyura*
(*C. brevicaudata*)   **Pl. 41**

Identification: 5″. Sexes similar. A small grey Warbler with yellowish-olive wings commonly seen in gardens and shrubbery near habitations and cultivation, moving unobtrusively about the foliage uttering a characteristic mewing note. At close range the orange-buff thighs and whitish belly are seen. Juveniles have lemon-yellow underparts. In the savanna in the dry (non-breeding) season the adult is brown not grey above.

Voice: Song a single, loud, vigorous note uttered five or six times and delivered from a song perch. Also various clicking and plaintive calls including the characteristic mewing mentioned above.

Distribution and Habitat: Very common and widespread throughout the area from the desert edge to the sea coast in savanna and forest provided there is leafy cover. Absent from closed forest.

Nesting: Well-concealed nest low down in a shrub. A pouch of three or four growing leaves sewn together with gossamer and lined with fine grasses or down. Eggs 2–3, white or blue, immaculate or sparingly spotted with brown and lilac.

GREEN-BACKED EREMOMELA   *Eremomela pusilla*   **Pl. 41**

Identification: 4″. Sexes similar. A very small savanna Warbler with a diagnostic colour pattern. Pale grey-brown crown and nape, greenish mantle, yellowish-green rump, white throat and bright yellow lower breast and belly. In small parties moving from tree to tree exploring the twigs and leaves for insects, flicking their tails, and conveying the impression of boundless energy, and frequently uttering little thin cries.

Voice: A pleasing, tinkling, silvery song. Call a soft 'chee-chee' or 'chee-chee-chee'.

Distribution and Habitat: Well distributed in the savanna from Senegal, Gambia and Portuguese Guinea east to southern Chad and the Central African Republic. Fond of orchard bush and farmland with small trees. Rare north of 15° N.

Nesting: Nest at no great height in a shrub. A tiny, compact cup of leaf fragments bound with fine but tough silky fibres. Eggs 2, pale greenish-blue with blotches and spots of brown and purplish-grey mainly concentrated in a wreath at the large end.

Allied species: The Grey-backed Eremomela (*Eremomela icteropygialis*) is found in the arid acacia belt just south of the desert in Senegal, Mali, Upper Volta, Niger, northern Nigeria and Chad between 13° N. and 17° N. but mainly north of 15° N. A little like the Green-backed Eremomela but the upperparts are pale grey-brown and the yellow on the underside is restricted to the belly. The Rufous-crowned Eremomela (*Eremomela badiceps*), 4½″, is readily identified when adult by its chestnut crown, grey mantle, white throat and black gorget. Immature birds lack the chestnut crown and black gorget and have bright yellow throats. It ranges in the forest belt from Sierra Leone to Gaboon and Congo and Fernando Po. Occurs in pairs or small parties, in trees of all sizes in the forest and its clearings, usually busily searching the leaves and twigs for insects.

NUTHATCH WARBLER   *Sylvietta brachyura*   Pl. 42

Identification: 3½″. Sexes similar. Like a tiny Nuthatch. Easily distinguished by colour pattern, diminutive size and very short tail. Upperparts grey. Underparts tawny buff. A well-defined cream eye-stripe. The tail is shorter than the wings when they are closed. Always on the move in the trees and shrubs searching the crevices in the bark and the surface of the twigs and leaves. Sometimes hangs upside down. Calls frequently.

Voice: Song a short, sweet, unvarying warble lasting 7–8 seconds and frequently uttered. A relatively loud single or double call-note.

Distribution and Habitat: The whole thorn scrub belt of the savanna from southern Mauritania and Senegal east to Chad and the Central African Republic with a southern extension in the dry season into the orchard bush and soft-leaved savanna.

Nesting: A little deep pouch suspended by gossamer from a low lateral shoot or tree fork. Made of fibre, fine plant stems and gossamer, and lined with rootlets. Eggs 2, white spotted with rufous and grey.

Allied species: The tiny size and short tail of the Green Crombec (*Sylvietta virens*) are characters shared by other members of the genus. In this species the head, chin and foreneck are brown, the mantle olive-green, and the belly white. In the race occurring west of the Niger River (*S. v. flaviventris*) the breast is bright yellow, but from the Niger eastwards and southwards there is no yellow on the underparts. It ranges in the forest and its outliers from Sierra Leone to Gaboon and is usually encountered in second-growth tangle or in the trees of forest clearings. The Lemon-bellied Crombec (*Sylvietta denti*) is rather similar to the Green Crombec but has a yellow not a white belly. It is an uncommon bird recorded from a few localities in the forests of Sierra Leone, Liberia, Ivory Coast, Ghana and the Cameroons.

OLIVE LONGBILL   *Macrosphenus concolor*   Pl. 42

Identification: 4½″. A small olive-green forest Warbler with a long straight bill. No distinctive plumage characters. Sexes alike. Occurs in pairs and also as a member of mixed bird parties, in the primary but chiefly the secondary forest, searching for insects amongst the vines and thick foliage at all heights from forest floor to forest roof. The rich warbling song usually delivered from a high perch in thick foliage is a good diagnostic character.

Voice: Male has a fine warbling song.

Distribution and Habitat: The lowland forest from Sierra Leone to the Cameroons and Fernando Po. Locally not uncommon.

Allied species: In size, general appearance, habits and habitat the Yellow Longbill (*Macrosphenus flavicans*) resembles the Olive Longbill. Song and plumage characters distinguish it. The plaintive and melodious song consists of four notes slowly descending the scale in measured time. In the adult male and female the upperparts are mainly olive-green and the underparts bright olive-yellow except for the greyish throat. But in the race occurring from Sierra Leone to western Nigeria (*M. f. kempi*) the upperparts are brownish, the middle of the breast and belly are grey not yellow, and the flanks are orange not yellow, and the race occurring in south-eastern Nigeria (*M. f. flammeus*) is similar but has deep flame not orange flanks. The range is the forest from Sierra Leone to the Cameroons and Gaboon; also Fernando Po.

GREEN HYLIA   *Hylia prasina*   Pl. 42

Identification: 4½". Dark olive-green above, greyish below. The pale yellow superciliary streak is the only conspicuous plumage character. A forest species of the shaded primary and old second-growth, occurring singly or in pairs, and not associating with other species. Unobtrusive; more often heard than seen as it searches the foliage of the undershrubs or vines for insects.

Voice: Song a full-throated sustained warble, somewhat marred by occasional interspersed harsh phrases. A frequent, loud, high-pitched disyllabic call-note.

Distribution and Habitat: A well distributed and rather common Warbler of the forest from Senegal, Guinea and Sierra Leone to Gaboon and Congo. Also Fernando Po.

Nesting: Nest a few feet from the ground placed in the fork of a forest shrub or young raphia. A domed oval with a side-top opening; made of fine fibrous strips and dead leaves with a plentiful loose lining of plant down. Eggs 1–2, immaculate white.

TIT-HYLIA   *Pholidornis rushiae*   Pl. 42

Identification: 3". Streaked throat, yellow rump and minute size the best field marks. Mantle and wings dark brown, belly yellow. A tiny active bird that moves rapidly about the foliage and smaller branches, sometimes hanging upside down and often flicking its wings. In pairs or small parties and not given to associating with other species.

Voice: A scarcely audible twittering call.

Distribution and Habitat: Ranges in the forest from Sierra Leone to Gaboon and Fernando Po. Locally common. Often high up, showing a preference for secondary forest and trees in clearings.

Nesting: Nest in a tree placed amongst the smaller branches or attached to a bramble. Domed and rounded; made of felted plant down. Eggs 2, pure white.

FLYCATCHERS: Muscicapidae

A widespread rather ill-defined family of small or medium-sized insectivorous birds. Most species have broad flattened bills and a wide gape. Typically Flycatchers use an exposed branch or other vantage point as a base from which to fly out in pursuit of insects, but some species pick their food off the foliage like Warblers and others retrieve it from the ground like Shrikes. The resident tropical species are mostly bright-coloured.

SPOTTED FLYCATCHER   *Muscicapa striata*   **Pl. 42**
Identification: 6″. Sexes similar. No arresting plumage characters, the upper-parts being ashy-brown and the underparts whitish with indistinct dark streaks on the breast. Characteristic silhouette and upright posture when perched. Frequent short circular excursions from its perch in pursuit of insects, light, agile flight and frequent flicks of wing and tail are also characteristic. Silent and solitary.
Distribution and Habitat: An abundant spring (April–May) and autumn (September–October) migrant throughout West Africa in all vegetation zones and a locally common winter visitor in the forest clearings and in the savanna near the forest.

SWAMP FLYCATCHER   *Muscicapa aquatica* (*Alseonax aquatica*)
                                                            Pl. 42
Identification: 5″. Sexes similar. No noticeable plumage characters. Upper-parts ashy-brown, throat and belly whitish, breast pale grey-brown. Resembles the Spotted Flycatcher (*Muscicapa striata*) but is smaller and lacks the streaked breast. Has the same upright alert pose, mannerisms and feeding habits, making circuit flights from a low perch to capture insects. Found near water. Occurs in pairs.
Voice: A melodious short phrase, not very loud.
Distribution and Habitat: Sedentary. The borders of pools, lakes and rivers, provided there are trees or shrubs. Locally distributed in the savanna in Senegal, Gambia, Ghana, southern Mali, Nigeria, southern Chad and the Central African Republic.
Nesting: Not known.

CASSIN'S GREY FLYCATCHER   *Muscicapa cassini*
(*Alseonax cassini*)   **Pl. 42**
Identification: An ashy-grey Flycatcher with dark wings and tail and a whitish throat and belly. Typically seen on a snag or branch over water from which it makes short flights in pursuit of insects. Tame and rather silent.
Voice: Song short and vigorous, of small compass and no great quality. Call note a monosyllabic 'pink'. Alarm note an excited 'tseet-tseet-tseet-tseet-tseet-tseet'.
Distribution and Habitat: River banks and the margins of lakes in the forest region from Liberia east to the Central African Republic and south to Gaboon and Congo. A sedentary species occurring singly or in pairs and not uncommon.
Nesting: Nest usually some yards from the edge of river or lake in a snag projecting from the water. A little open cup in a niche, fork or hole of the snag. Clutch one or two, occasionally three. Eggs pale greenish, blotched and spotted with reddish-brown and ashy-purple.
Allied species: The White-eye Flycatcher (*Muscicapa caerulescens*) except for an inconspicuous white eye-streak is practically indistinguishable in the field from Cassin's Flycatcher. It differs, however, in its habitat for it frequents the trees in and on the edge of forest clearings. It ranges in the forest from Guinea to Gaboon and is rather uncommon.

DUSKY BLUE FLYCATCHER   *Muscicapa comitata*
(*Pedilorhynchus comitatus*)   **Pl. 42**
Identification: A little Flycatcher noticeably dark slate-grey in colour with a
white or greyish or buffish-grey throat and abdomen. Silent and inconspicuous
but not shy; occurring singly or in pairs, occupying a small territory with a
number of favourite perches, usually only a few feet from the ground. These are
look-out posts for its aerial insect prey.
Voice: Usually silent but has a sweet unpretentious song.
Distribution and Habitat: The forest from Sierra Leone to Gaboon and
Congo. In the Cameroons it ascends to at least 5,000 feet. Well-distributed and
locally common. A bird of clearings and plantations found in oil-palm, banana
and cocoa plantations, in native farm patches and recent unplanted clearings.
Also in regenerating second-growth and the edges of primary forest.
Nesting: The little cup-shaped nest of grass and fibre is built inside the old
nest of a Weaver species. The two eggs are pale green thickly spotted with pale
reddish-brown, the markings coalescing to form a solid cap at the large end.

USSHER'S FLYCATCHER   *Artomyias ussheri*   **Pl. 42**
Identification: 5″. In the field usually appears as a small uniformly dark bird
perched, often at a great height, on a dead forest tree from which it flies out in
pursuit of aerial insects in typical Flycatcher manner. In the air the long pointed
wings and slightly forked tail and the flight itself lend it a swallow-like appearance that is distinctive. Silent. Occurs singly, in pairs or in family parties.
Voice: Not recorded.
Distribution and Habitat: The forest zone from Sierra Leone and Guinea to
Ghana. Clearings in the high forest where some tall dead trees are still standing
or the edges of the high forest are its favourite terrain.
Nesting: Habits unknown. The closely related Dusky Flycatcher builds in a
forest tree making a shallow cup-shaped nest of moss and roots, and lays two
eggs.
Allied species: The Dusky Flycatcher (*Artomyias fuliginosa*) ranges through
the lowland forest from Nigeria to Gaboon and Congo. It closely resembles
Ussher's Flycatcher in habits and appearance except that the underparts are
obscurely mottled or streaked and the throat and belly are lighter.

GREY TIT-BABBLER   *Myioparus plumbeus* (*Parisoma plumbeum*)
                                                      Pl. 42
Identification: 5½″. Sexes similar. Main character the white outer rectrices
which are conspicuous in flight and at rest when the bird lifts and spreads its
tail. Upperparts bluish-grey, wings mainly dark brown, underparts pale grey
but belly white. Unobtrusive rather silent bird that explores the foliage for
insects in the manner of a Warbler.
Voice: Usually silent. A short musical song.
Distribution and Habitat: Widely but thinly distributed in the wooded
savanna and occasionally the forest zone from Senegal and Gambia east to
southern Chad (rare) and the Central African Republic and south to Gaboon
and Congo.
Nesting: In southern Africa nests in old Barbet or Woodpecker holes or in a
natural hole in a tree laying 2 eggs, greenish-white thickly speckled with olive
and slate-brown.

Allied species: The Pied Flycatcher (*Ficedula hypoleuca*), 5″, sexes in winter plumage similar, is a passage migrant and winter visitor, widespread in West Africa, yet nowhere common. Most winter records come from the savanna gallery forests north of the main body of the forest. In the arid country farther north only on passage. Occurs from Senegal and Gambia to Chad and the Central African Republic. Wing and tail flicking and flycatching habits recall Spotted Flycatcher, but it changes its perch more frequently and often swoops down to the ground. Solitary and silent. Dull brown upperparts and buffish-white underparts with a conspicuous and distinctive white wing patch. Unfortunately the White-collared Flycatcher (*Ficedula albicollis*), a rarer Palaearctic winter visitor to West Africa, cannot be distinguished in the field in winter dress from the Pied Flycatcher. In summer the male Pied Flycatcher is black above and pure white below with an enlarged white wing patch. Some individuals acquire this plumage before their departure from West Africa.

FRASER'S FOREST FLYCATCHER   *Fraseria ocreata*   **Pl. 42**
Identification: 7″. A stoutly-built, lively, vocal Flycatcher, dark slate above, white below, the breast conspicuously marked with crescent-shaped black bars.
Voice: Call a loud, harsh, buzzing noise. Song a medley of loud sweet notes.
Distribution and Habitat: Widely but rather thinly distributed in the lowland forest from Sierra Leone to Gaboon and Congo and Fernando Po, occurring singly or in small parties of its own kind or in mixed bird parties, in the primary or secondary forest.
Nesting: The cup-shaped nest is built in a knot-hole or in the fork of a tree. The clutch is two. Eggs olive-green heavily blotched and spotted with umber-brown and grey.
Allied species: The White-browed Forest Flycatcher (*Fraseria cinerascens*) is rather like Fraser's Flycatcher but it is recognisably smaller, the crescent-shaped bars on the breast are not so clear, and there is a large white spot above and in front of the eye, easily seen in the field. Its habits are quite different. It is a strictly riverine forest species, silent, unobtrusive, tame and phlegmatic, occurring singly or a pair together. Usually perched on a horizontal bough over the water or near its edge and found day after day in the same circumscribed territory. It inhabits the forested rivers from Portuguese Guinea to Gaboon and Congo.

BLACK FLYCATCHER   *Melaenornis edolioides*   **Pl. 42**
Identification: 8″. Sexes similar. A large Flycatcher, black all over, with a long slender tail. Rounded not forked tail distinguish it from the Glossy-backed Drongo (see p. 175). Immature dress slaty-black spotted chestnut. Unobtrusive. From a perch makes circuit flights or drops to the ground to capture insects.
Voice: A vigorous song of mixed melodious and wheezy notes. Alarm note a harsh 'churr'.
Distribution and Habitat: A common savanna species in orchard bush, open woodland, fringing forest, the edges of thickets and farmland with trees. Absent from the arid north. Widely distributed from Senegal, Gambia and Portuguese Guinea east to southern Chad and the Central African Republic and south to Congo.
Nesting: Uses the old nest of a Thrush or builds a nest of twigs and petioles in an open hole in a tree. Eggs 2–3, pale green spotted and streaked with brown, and with purple shell marks forming a ring at the large end.

PALE FLYCATCHER *Bradornis pallidus* Pl. 42

Identification: 6¼″. Sexes similar. Upperparts brown; underparts pale brown but throat and belly whitish. Young spotted. A rather plump, sombre-coloured, silent, phlegmatic Flycatcher which flies down from a perch to seize its prey on the ground and only occasionally pursues it in the air. Not shy and can be easily seen. Occurs singly or in pairs.

Voice: Silent. Rarely a weak call.

Distribution and Habitat: Ranges widely and commonly through the savanna from Senegal (to 14° N.), Gambia and Portuguese Guinea east to Chad (rare) and the Central African Republic and south to Gaboon and Congo. Frequents cultivated clearings with trees, orchard bush, soft-leaved woods and also the thorn scrub.

Nesting: A slight shallow cup of rootlets and fibre in a tree or shrub from three to twenty feet up. Eggs 2–3, pale greeny-grey thickly covered with speckles, spots and short streaks of brown with pale lilac under-markings.

YELLOW-BELLIED FLYCATCHER *Hyliota flavigaster* Pl. 43

Identification: 5″. Male conspicuous with glossy dark blue upperparts, a large white patch on the wing, and sharply contrasting yellowish-buff underparts. Female duller with sooty-grey slightly glossed upperparts and dull yellowish underparts. Occurs in pairs, family parties and in the roving mixed bands of savanna species. In general behaviour and feeding habits warbler-like, visiting the trees in turn and searching the leaves and twigs quietly and thoroughly.

Voice: Usually silent. Call a Tit-like 'kep-kep-kep——kep-pink'.

Distribution and Habitat: Widely distributed in the savanna but nowhere abundant. Prefers open woodland, orchard bush and the trees left standing in native farmland. Absent from the arid thorn scrub. From Senegal (to 14° N.), Gambia and Portuguese Guinea east to Chad (rare) and the Central African Republic and south to Congo.

Nesting: In southern Africa builds a small cup-shaped nest in a tree, laying two eggs, dull white with a zone of brown and lilac markings.

BLACK-AND-WHITE FLYCATCHER *Bias musicus* Pl. 43

Identification: 6½″. In the male the upperside, head, throat and upper breast are black glossed with green and the rest of the underparts white. Head distinctly crested; in flight a prominent white wing bar. Female and immature bird cinnamon or chestnut above, the head darker; below pale cinnamon and whitish. Jerky display flight and noisy call distinctive.

Voice: A loud excited whistling song uttered on the wing and various shrill and harsh calls.

Distribution and Habitat: The main body of the forest and its gallery extensions from Portuguese Guinea to Gaboon and Congo. A tree-top bird of the forest edge and the trees of farms and other clearings in the forest. Distribution uneven; locally common.

Nesting: Nest a small open cup built in a tree in a forest clearing: eggs 2–3; greenish blotched and spotted with brown and grey mainly about the large end in the form of a wide zone.

SENEGAL PUFF-BACK FLYCATCHER *Batis senegalensis* Pl. 43

Identification: 4½″. A small, noticeable, contrasting black and white Flycatcher always moving about and easily spotted. Crown blackish bordered by a white streak from the bill over the eye to the nape; mantle slate-grey; white wing bar; outer tail feathers white-edged. Underparts white with wide black pectoral band. In the female the eye-stripe is rusty and the pectoral band chestnut. Eye bright yellow. No eye wattle. Flight undulating.

Voice: A rather harsh frequently repeated 'yoo-beet' and a scolding 'tsit-tsit-tsit'.

Distribution and Habitat: Widely distributed and locally common in the savanna in Senegal, Gambia, Portuguese Guinea, Sierra Leone, Mali, Ivory Coast, Ghana, Nigeria and Niger from the desert edge in the north to the forest edge in the south. Frequents the small trees of the wooded savanna, orchard bush and farmland, and, in the north, the acacia thickets.

Nesting: A tiny cup of lichen and fine grass shreds placed in a fork or on a small branch and bound in place with gossamer. Eggs 2, pale green spotted with red-brown and violet.

Allied species: The Grey-headed Puff-back (*Batis minima*) is a rare bird recorded from a few localities in Liberia, Ivory Coast, Ghana, Nigeria, the Cameroons, Gaboon and Fernando Po. In the field both sexes closely resemble the male Senegal Puff-back Flycatcher but lack the white line over the eye. But in the race that occurs in Fernando Po the female has a chestnut breast band. This species occurs only in the rain forest belt whilst the Senegal Puff-back occupies the savanna belt. The Black-headed Puff-back Flycatcher (*Batis minor*) also closely resembles the Senegal Puff-back and its habitat is similar. It is found in the savanna country of the Cameroons, the Central African Republic and Gaboon, the range lying to the east and south of the Senegal Puff-back. From the latter species the females are distinguished by the narrower breast band but the males of the two species are indistinguishable in the field.

SCARLET-SPECTACLED WATTLE-EYE *Platysteira cyanea*
Pl. 43

Identification: 5½″. Bright red wattle above eye an excellent field mark visible a long way off. Upperparts including tail glossy blue-black; underparts white with broad blue-black pectoral band. Conspicuous white wing bar visible at rest and in flight. Female has slate-grey upperparts and white underparts except for deep maroon throat and breast. In both sexes the red wattle distinguishes it from the *Batis* Flycatchers. Song diagnostic. Tame and easily observed and behaves more like a Tit than a Flycatcher as it searches the foliage for insects.

Voice: A far-carrying song of four, melodious, flute-like notes the highest and lowest widely separated in pitch, and various whistling calls and also bill-snapping.

Distribution and Habitat: Widespread and very common throughout the area in the savanna and the forest clearings but absent from the arid north (in Nigeria, for example, rare north of 10° N.) and from closed forest. In the Cameroon highlands to 6,500 feet. Varied habitat including pure mangrove. Specially common in gardens, villages and farms with trees.

Nesting: A small, compact cup on a branch at varying heights. Eggs 2, yellowish with a zone of brown and mauve markings at the large end.

CHESTNUT WATTLE-EYE *Platysteira castanea*
(*Dyaphorophyia castanea*)   Pl. 43
Identification: 4″. A tiny short-tailed dumpy Flycatcher, the male black above with a white rump, and white below with a broad black breast band. In the race found from Sierra Leone to Togo a white collar encircles the neck. The female is chestnut above with a grey crown and rump; its throat and chest are chestnut and the rest of the underparts white.
Voice: A loud croaking note is common and other bizarre calls are described: loud wing beats and audible snaps of the bill are also characteristic.
Distribution and Habitat: The forest and its gallery extensions and outlying woods in the savanna from Sierra Leone to Gaboon and Congo and also in Fernando Po. Found in primary and second-growth forest and in clearings planted with cocoa or kola. Common and a frequent member of the insect-hunting bands of forest birds.
Nesting: Nest built on the branch of a forest undershrub: eggs two, bluish-white, spotted with brown and grey, especially about the large end.
Allied species: The White-spotted Wattle-eye (*Platysteira tonsa*) is a rarer bird than the Chestnut Wattle-eye, sometimes occupying exactly the same ground as the latter, but showing a preference for the higher more unspoilt forest, whereas the Chestnut Wattle-eye mainly affects second-growth. It ranges from the Ivory Coast to Gaboon. When adult the male is distinguished from the Chestnut Wattle-eye by a prominent white superciliary stripe and the female by a glossy black head. Otherwise the two species are rather similar.

BLISSETT'S WATTLE-EYE *Platysteira blissetti*
(*Dyaphorophyia blissetti, D. chalybea*)   Pl. 43
Identification: 3½″. Two races of Blissett's Wattle-eye occur in our area. They are very distinct and are often treated as separate species. The Red cheeked Wattle-eye (*P. blissetti blissetti*) ranges from Sierra Leone to the Cameroons. The male is dark glossy green above and on the chin and throat. The rest of the underparts are white. The large pale blue eye-wattle and the bright chestnut on the cheeks and the sides of the neck are field marks. The female resembles the male but is greyer and less glossy above. The other race, the Black-throated Wattle-eye (*P. blissetti chalybea*) ranges from the Cameroons and Fernando Po to Gaboon. The male is glossy bottle-green above and on the chin and throat; the rest of the underparts are creamy-yellow; the eye wattle is green and there is no chestnut cheek patch. Female like male but upperparts duller, greyer.
Voice: A croaking note. Wing and bill snapping are also characteristic.
Distribution and Habitat: The lowland forest and outlying patches in the savanna from Sierra Leone to Gaboon, in the primary and old second-growth where it affects the tangled vines and the undershrubs.
Nesting: Nest a little cup of fibres and cobwebs. Clutch 2, the eggs greenish-white heavily blotched and spotted with brown and grey, mainly in a zone about the large end.
Allied species: The Golden-bellied Wattle-eye (*Platysteira concreta*) is a rather rare Flycatcher found in the forest from Sierra Leone to Gaboon. Readily recognised in the field by the colour of the underparts. In the western part of its range in Sierra Leone these are in the male rufous-chestnut and in the female vivid yellow with a clearly defined chestnut throat patch. In the eastern part of its range from Nigeria to Gaboon the underparts of the male are brilliant orange-yellow and in the female orange-yellow washed with chestnut. The upperparts

Plate 43

FLYCATCHERS

43

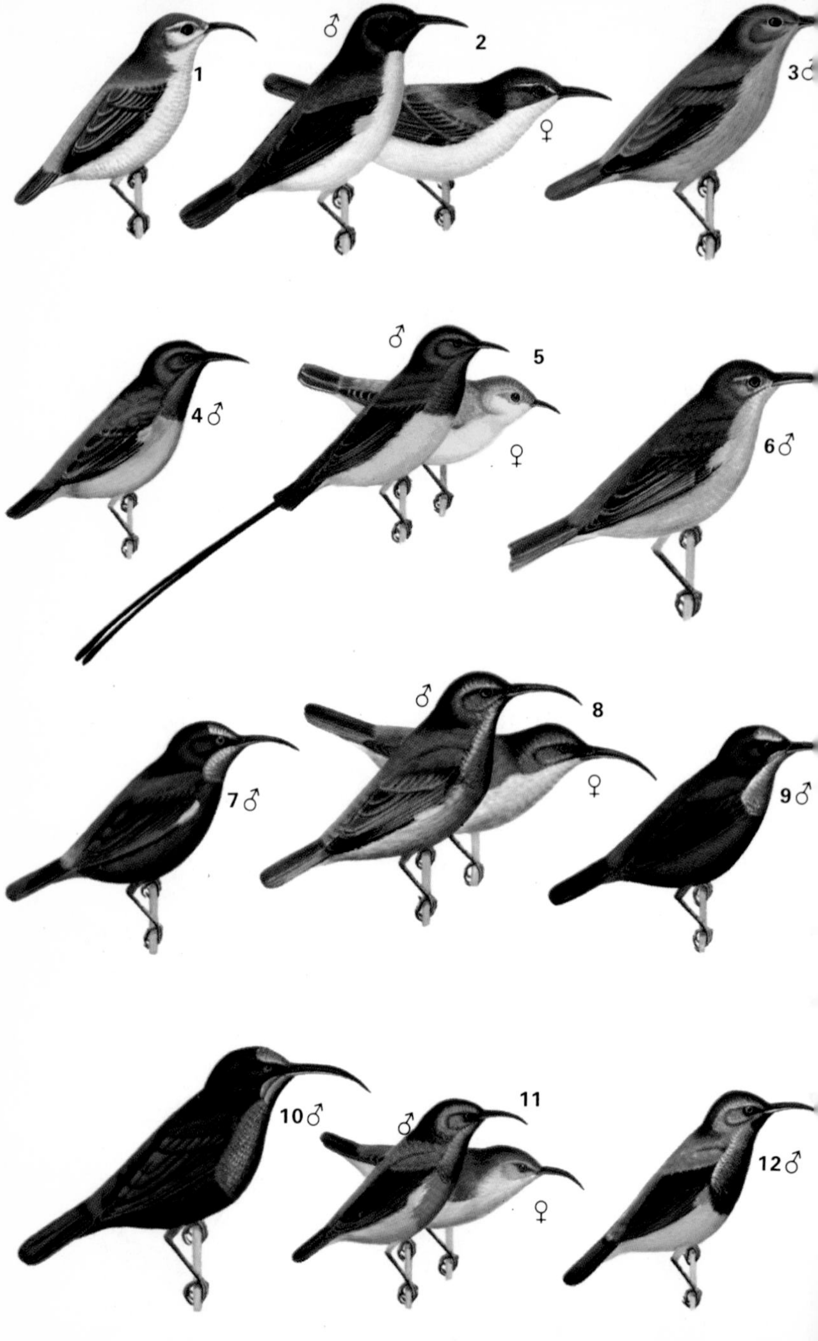
1
♂ 2
♀
3♂
4♂
♂ 5
♀
6♂
7♂
♂ 8
♀
9♂
10♂
11
♂
♀
12♂

Plate 44

SUNBIRDS

1. **MOUSE-BROWN SUNBIRD** *Anthreptes gabonicus*   page 229
White stripes above and below eye.

2. **VIOLET-BACKED SUNBIRD** *Anthreptes longuemarei*   230
Male: metallic violet upperparts and throat: white underparts.
Female: metallic violet tail; yellow belly.

3. **SCARLET TUFTED SUNBIRD** *Anthreptes fraseri*   229
Stout straight bill; scarlet pectoral tufts.

4. **COLLARED SUNBIRD** *Anthreptes collaris*   230
Metallic green upperparts and throat; yellow breast and belly.

5. **PIGMY LONG-TAILED SUNBIRD** *Anthreptes platura*   231
Male: very long central tail feathers; sharply defined golden-yellow
breast and belly.
Female: brown upperparts; sulphur-yellow underparts.

6. **OLIVE SUNBIRD** *Nectarinia olivacea*   231
Large for a Sunbird; long decurved bill; dull greenish plumage.

7. **CARMELITE SUNBIRD** *Nectarinia fuliginosa*   232
Mainly dark chocolate-brown; metallic blue forehead.

8. **OLIVE-BACKED SUNBIRD** *Nectarinia verticalis*   232
Male: metallic head; olive mantle.
Female: olive mantle; pale grey underparts.

9. **GREEN-THROATED SUNBIRD** *Nectarinia rubescens*   233
Appears black in most lights; metallic green forecrown and throat.

10. **SCARLET-BREASTED SUNBIRD** *Nectarinia senegalensis* 233
Metallic red throat and breast.

11. **OLIVE-BELLIED SUNBIRD** *Nectarinia chloropygia*   234
Male: metallic green upperparts and throat; scarlet breast band.
Female: no distinctive plumage characters.

12. **YELLOW-BELLIED SUNBIRD** *Nectarinia venusta*   233
Metallic purple breast; yellow belly.

of the Golden-bellied Wattle-eye are mainly glossy dark green, and the large eye-wattle is apple-green. They occur singly, in pairs, and in family parties, and are usually discovered seeking their insect food in the undershrubs and lower branches of the shaded primary forest or old second-growth.

CHESTNUT-CAPPED FLYCATCHER *Erythrocercus mccalli*
Pl. 43

Identification: 4″. Even at a great height in the forest this tiny Flycatcher can be recognised when it fans its tail, as it often does, and the sun lights up the rufous rectrices. At close quarters the chestnut crown and fawn throat are also good field marks. Active and agile as they hunt the leaves and twigs for insects. They occur in small flocks and sometimes they join the mixed forest bird parties.
Voice: Little nondescript high-pitched cries; song a pleasant warble.
Distribution and Habitat: The primary and old second-growth of the lowland forest from Sierra Leone to Gaboon.
Nesting: A nest in the Cameroons forest was Cisticola-like, being suspended from two small twigs and their leaves to which it was stuck on with cobwebs; made of dry leaves and down. Two eggs are laid.

BLUE FAIRY FLYCATCHER *Trochocercus longicauda*
(*Erannornis longicauda*)   **Pl. 43**
Identification: 7″. Sexes similar. Unmistakable. A trim, slender Flycatcher with a long graduated tail. Light blue all over except for some white on the belly and some black on the wing. Usually in pairs. Not shy. Flits gracefully amongst the foliage searching for insects or pursuing them on the wing. Frequently fans tail.
Voice: A sweet, varied song.
Distribution and Habitat: Widespread geographical range coinciding with that of the Scarlet-spectacled Wattle-eye, though it is less common and in some areas local. Fond of shade in the vicinity of water. In the savanna mainly in the fringing forests and kurimis. In the forest clearings in cocoa and rubber plantations, farms with trees, gardens and open second-growth.
Nesting: An exquisite, tiny, shallow cup decorated outside with lichen; placed on a small branch and attached to it with gossamer. Eggs 2, cream with yellowish-brown and ashy spots and speckles concentrated in a zone about the large end.

BLUE-HEADED CRESTED FLYCATCHER *Trochocercus nitens*
Pl. 43

Identification: 6″. The male is mainly glossy steel-blue with a grey lower breast and belly; in the female the entire underparts are grey. The head is crested. It fans its tail in the manner of the genus. Lively in its actions as it searches for insects amongst the branches and foliage of the undershrubs and small trees of the primary forest.
Voice: A short sharp call represented as 'tii-ti-ti-twit'.
Distribution and Habitat: Sierra Leone to Gaboon in the lowland forest. Its habitat is the foliage of the undershrubs and small trees in the true forest. Rather uncommon.
Nesting: A nest in Uganda was a cup of bark fibres and cobwebs lined with tendrils, built 8 feet up in the upright fork of a sapling. The two cream-coloured eggs were spotted with red-brown and maroon with mauve undermarks at the large end where the markings formed a ring.

WHITE-BELLIED FLYCATCHER *Trochocercus albiventris* **Pl. 43**
Identification: 4½". Sexes alike. Dark grey birds with a black head which is a field mark. The belly is light grey. Lively, flitting about the branches and foliage at all levels in the forest, frequently fanning its tail. Usually in pairs, and frequent members of the mixed bird parties of the montane forest.
Voice: Song a vigorous, melodious, short warble; call note a sharp 'pink'.
Distribution and Habitat: A very common Flycatcher but restricted to the montane forests of Fernando Po, the Cameroon Mountain, the Bamenda highlands and the Obudu Plateau.
Nesting: Nest built near the ground in the fork of a forest sapling. A tiny cup of moss and plant down lined with fine grass stems and bound to the fork by cobwebs. Clutch 2. Eggs creamy-white blotched and spotted with different shades of brown, the markings usually concentrated in a solid wreath near the large end.

RED-BELLIED PARADISE FLYCATCHER *Terpsiphone*
rufiventer (*Tchitrea rufiventer, T. nigriceps, T. smithii, T. tricolor*) **Pl. 43**
Identification: There is great racial and individual variation in plumage in this species. An obvious Paradise Flycatcher with a typical penetrating rasping 'see-see' note that betrays it. Head and throat deep glossy blue or purple, the rest of the underparts orange-rufous, the shade varying according to locality; mantle, back and tail rufous-chestnut or orange-rufous or rufous-brown except that in the race occurring in Fernando Po and on the opposite mainland from the Niger delta to Gaboon these parts are grey. The length of the tail varies with locality as does the presence or absence of white on the wing or a crest on the head. The female resembles the male but is paler and less glossy and has a shorter tail.
Voice: Song a three-note silvery phrase, repeated twice – 'tsisisi-tsisisi'; call a characteristic 'see-see'.
Distribution and Habitat: Senegal and Gambia south to Gaboon and Congo and east to the Central African Republic. Also Fernando Po and Annobon. A common bird in the main body of the forest and its gallery extensions, affecting primary and second-growth, swamp forest and oil-palm groves. Also in the woods and shrubberies of the savanna.
Nesting: Nest a small cup of moss lined with fibre, placed in the fork of a tree or undershrub.

PARADISE FLYCATCHER *Terpsiphone viridis*
(*Tchitrea viridis, T. plumbeiceps, T. melampyra*) **Pl. 43**
Identification: Male 13" (tail 10"). Identified by very long, ribbon-like, supple tail. Plumage dark blue, chestnut and white with a wide pattern range. Head and underparts usually glossy dark blue. Mantle and tail may be dark blue like the underparts or mainly chestnut or mainly white, and there are many other variations due to racial difference or to polymorphism. The females and juveniles of all phases lack the long tail and have a dark blue head, chestnut upperparts and slate underparts. An active, arboreal Flycatcher that searches for insects on the foliage or captures them on the wing.
Voice: Usual call a frequent resonant, rasping 'chwe'. A short, faint but musical song.
Distribution and Habitat: Widespread in savanna and forest from Senegal

and Gambia east to southern Chad and the Central African Republic and south to Gaboon and Congo. Migratory, with a shift north in the rains. In the forest zone common in certain parts and rare, absent or seasonal in others. In the savanna mainly in the gallery forests and open woodland and penetrates in the wet (the breeding) season at least to 16° N. in Senegal and 13° N. in Nigeria. **Nesting:** A compact, shallow, tiny cup in the fork of a twig. Eggs 2, cream with red and lilac spots in a zone at the large end and thinly scattered over the rest of the shell.

TITS: Paridae

WHITE-SHOULDERED BLACK TIT *Parus leucomelas*
(*Melaniparus niger*)   Pl. 45

Identification: 5½″. Sexes similar. Black glossed with blue except for a conspicuous contrasting white patch on the shoulder and white edging to the wing feathers. In flight the contrast is particularly striking. Creamy-white eye. Arboreal. Characteristic acrobatic Tit movements when feeding.

Voice: A sweet, simple song and various calls, a common one a rather harsh, repeated 'teer-teer-zeet'.

Distribution and Habitat: Widespread and rather common in the savanna from Senegal, Gambia and Portuguese Guinea east to Chad and the Central African Republic and south to Gaboon and Congo. Absent from the arid thorn-scrub. Fond of trees with fairly open foliage, especially in the orchard bush and cultivation clearings.

Nesting: In southern Africa builds in a hole in a tree laying 3–4 eggs, white speckled with red, brown or grey.

PENDULINE TITS: Remizidae

WEST AFRICAN PENDULINE TIT *Remiz parvulus*
(*Anthoscopus parvulus*)   Pl. 45

Identification: 3″. A tiny bird, olive-yellow above but forehead yellow with black dots; bright yellow below. A short, tapering, sharp-pointed bill. Actively searches the branches for insects, sometimes in the company of White-eyes or Warblers.

Voice: Not described.

Distribution and Habitat: The savanna, especially the dry northern zone, in Senegal, Portuguese Guinea, Ivory Coast, Mali, Upper Volta, northern Ghana, northern Nigeria, northern Cameroons, Chad and the Central African Republic. Nowhere common.

Nesting: Nest suspended from a high twig. Of closely felted pappus fashioned into an ellipsoidal pouch. Opening near the top end consisting of an upper and lower flap which are in apposition and require to be separated by the bird as it enters or leaves the nest. Eggs two, white.

Allied species: The Sudan Penduline Tit (*Remiz punctifrons*), 3″, sexes similar, ranges across the southern edge of the desert from Senegal, through Mali and Niger to Chad. Frequents the thorn bushes. Its dull colouring distinguishes it from the West African Penduline Tit. Upperparts olive-yellow. Underparts buffish-white.

TREE-CREEPER: Salpornithidae

SPOTTED CREEPER *Salpornis spilonota* **Pl. 45**
Identification: 6″. Plumage brown spotted all over with white. Bill thin and curved. A small arboreal species with the action of a Woodpecker climbing up the bole and branches of trees spirally. Occurs singly or as a member of a savanna mixed bird party.
Voice: Call a high-pitched 'tsee'. Song a rapid series of weak, high-pitched whistles.
Distribution and Habitat: Widely distributed but nowhere abundant in the savanna north of the forest from Gambia and Portuguese Guinea to Chad and the Central African Republic. Partial to the smaller fire-resisting trees of the orchard bush.
Nesting: In southern Africa the nest is described as small, cup-shaped, decorated with lichen and seeds which camouflage it, built in a tree on a horizontal bough or in a fork. Eggs 3, pale blue, zoned with blotches and spots of lavender and brown.

SUNBIRDS: Nectariniidae

A very distinct family of small nectar-loving birds with long, protrusile, hollow tongues for imbibing nectar and elongated, curved, pointed bills for puncturing and probing into flowers. Insects are another source of food and the species that subsist largely on these tend to have shorter, straighter bills. Males of many species have brilliant metallic colouring. Females tend to be dull-coloured and difficult to identify. Rapid, erratic flight. Song and call notes high-pitched and metallic and in some species diagnostic.

MOUSE-BROWN SUNBIRD *Anthreptes gabonicus* **Pl. 44**
Identification: 4″. Sexes alike. Grey-brown upperparts, greyish-white underparts. Distinguished from most male Sunbird species by absence of any metallic plumage and from most female and immature Sunbird species by virtual absence of green or yellowish in plumage. Short straight beak. White stripes above and below eye good field marks at close range. Mangrove and riverine habitat a reliable clue to identification. Usually singly or in pairs searching the leaves and branches for insects.
Voice: Utters little monosyllabic cries whilst feeding.
Distribution and Habitat: Ranges from Gambia to Gaboon. Closely associated with mangroves and locally common in the mangrove bordered coastal waterways and lagoons. Occurs also sparingly on the larger rivers in the forest and savanna zones.
Nesting: Nest usually conspicuous, suspended a few feet above high water level from the sprig of a shrub or a bare pendant mangrove shoot or a projecting stake or snag. A compact domed pouch. Eggs 2, brown or greenish-grey densely clouded and finely streaked with grey and brown.
Allied species: The Scarlet-tufted Sunbird (*Anthreptes fraseri*), **Pl. 44**, 5½″, is readily recognised at close range by its non-metallic green colour, large size (for a Sunbird), and stout straight bill. Sexes alike, but male larger and has

scarlet pectoral tufts. A silent, undemonstrative, rather uncharacteristic Sunbird. Usually in flocks high up in the foliage in primary or partly cut-out primary forest; sometimes a member of the mixed insect-hunting bird parties. Ranges in the rain forest from Sierra Leone to Gaboon and Congo and the island of Fernando Po. *Anthreptes rectirostris*, 4″, is represented in West Africa by two distinct races. *Anthreptes r. rectirostris*, the Yellow-chinned Sunbird, ranges from Sierra Leone to Ghana. The male has metallic green upperparts, a conspicuous yellow throat, a green metallic chest band bordered below with orange, and a greyish breast. *Anthreptes r. tephrolaema*, the Grey-chinned Sunbird, ranges from south-western Nigeria to Gaboon, Congo and Fernando Po. The male has a grey not yellow throat and otherwise rather resembles the Yellow-chinned Sunbird. The females of both races are olive-green above, only faintly metallic, and pale yellow below. A small, straight-and-stout-billed seed-eating Sunbird. Usually discovered quietly and methodically searching the foliage of the secondary forest at all heights from the undershrubs to the high tree-tops. Usually in pairs or small parties and sometimes associates with other Sunbirds especially the Collared Sunbird.

VIOLET-BACKED SUNBIRD *Anthreptes longuemarei* **Pl. 44**
Identification: 5″. Unique colour for a Sunbird. Male has metallic violet (at a distance black) upperparts and throat and vividly contrasting white underparts. Pectoral tufts yellow. Female is brown above with metallic-violet upper tail-coverts and violet-washed tail and white below with a sulphur-yellow belly. At a distance can be confused with the Yellow-bellied Flycatcher (*Hyliota flavigaster*) (p. 221), which, however, has white on the wing. Singly, in pairs, in small parties, or mixed bird parties, searching the foliage for insects and at times pursuing and capturing them on the wing.
Voice: Not known.
Distribution and Habitat: Widespread but not abundant in the savanna and absent from the arid north. Frequents fringing forest, kurimis, open woodland and orchard bush. From Senegal (14° N.), Gambia and Portuguese Guinea east to southern Chad and the Central African Republic and south to Congo.
Nesting: In a tree attached near the end of a twig. A domed pouch of felted cobwebs, fibre and grass lined with fluff and fibre. Eggs 2. In southern Africa they are white or pale blue with blackish-brown and slate-grey scribblings and hair-lines.

COLLARED SUNBIRD *Anthreptes collaris* **Pl. 44**
Identification: 4″. In the male upperparts and throat metallic green, narrow breast band purple, and underparts below the breast band yellow. Female underparts entirely yellowish. A tiny short-tailed Sunbird with a short only slightly curved bill. Usually in small parties actively searching the twigs and foliage.
Voice: Call-note a frequent 'seep'. Song a soft pleasing warble.
Distribution and Habitat: An abundant and widespread species of the forest and the southern zone of the savanna ranging from Senegal and Portuguese Guinea to Gaboon, Congo and Fernando Po. In the forest it frequents the primary and second-growth and farmland clearings with trees. In the savanna it frequents the gallery woods and outliers and the thicker orchard bush.
Nesting: Nest a neat compact 'Sunbird' pouch, suspended from the twig of a

tree or shrub. Eggs 2, very variable in colour and markings. White tinged with blue, green or brown with grey, brown and black markings which are usually concentrated near the large end.

PIGMY LONG-TAILED SUNBIRD *Anthreptes platura*
(*Hedydipna platura*) **Pl. 44**

Identification: Male 7″ (including 3″ tail streamers). Very short bill. In the breeding (dry) season metallic green upperparts, throat and chest. Sharply defined bright golden-yellow lower breast and belly. Conspicuous long narrow tail streamers with racquet-shaped tips. Despite its distinctive colour pattern can be confused at a distance with the Beautiful Long-tailed Sunbird (*Nectarinia pulchella*) (p. 235). Female and male in eclipse (wet season) brown above, pale sulphur-yellow below. Lively and attractive.

Voice: Song of male a pleasing silvery trill. Call-note 'cheek' or 'cheek cheek'.

Distribution and Habitat: Widely and commonly distributed throughout the savanna except in Gaboon and Congo. Penetrates as far north as Mauritania (17° N.), Air and Ennedi. Frequents acacia scrub, open woodland, orchard bush and gardens.

Nesting: Nest 5 to 10 feet up, firmly attached by gossamer to a twig. Oval-shaped, domed, made mainly of felted vegetable down. Eggs 1–2, immaculate white.

OLIVE SUNBIRD *Nectarinia olivacea* (*Cyanomitra olivacea*) **Pl. 44**

Identification: 5½″. A plain-coloured fairly large Sunbird, olive-green above, greyish-olive below, the male with yellow pectoral tufts, which, however, are seldom visible in life. Habits and habitat help to distinguish it. Usually solitary; addicted to the shady depths of the forest; takes nectar but more often searches for insects and spiders in the foliage, examining the leaves and twigs methodically in the manner of a Leaf-warbler. It lacks the grace and spontaneity of most Sunbirds.

Voice: Call a rapid succession of loud metallic notes frequently uttered. Song sweet and clear, slowly descending the scale, the several notes clearly separated from each other. Both sexes sing.

Distribution and Habitat: The forest and its gallery extensions from Senegal and Portuguese Guinea to Gaboon and Congo. Also Fernando Po and Principe. The habitat is the interior of primary and old secondary forest growth; also thick shrubbery in forest clearings and very occasionally sunlit forest clearings and orchard bush savanna.

Nesting: Nest suspended from a twig in the forest. A little pouch with a long trailing 'beard'. Eggs two, pale greenish or greyish, clouded, blotched and spotted with brown and grey.

Allied species: Reichenbach's Sunbird (*Nectarinia reichenbachii*) has a metallic blue head and throat, olive-green upperparts, a grey breast, and on the belly and under tail-coverts a vivid yellow splash which is an excellent fieldmark. The tail is rather long. The flight is undulating. The song is a high-pitched jingle, and the very distinctive call-note is a finch-like 'choo-ee' with the second syllable high-pitched and accentuated. Reichenbach's Sunbird is locally common in the Cameroons and Gaboon mainly in localities near the sea and occurs also sparingly in Ghana and southern Nigeria. Open places with flowering trees and shrubs such as gardens and abandoned farmland are its favourite terrain.

OLIVE-BACKED SUNBIRD   *Nectarinia verticalis*
(*Cyanomitra verticalis*)   **Pl. 44**

Identification: 5½″. Male has metallic blue or metallic green head, nape and throat, olive upperparts and grey underparts. Pectoral tufts yellow. No eclipse plumage. In the female the metallic blue is reduced to the crown, nape and cheeks, and the entire under surface is very pale grey. There is very little contrast in the plumage of this Sunbird, particularly when seen from a distance. Active. Searches the foliage for insects and the blossom for nectar.

Voice: A faint but sweet unpretentious song. Call note a loud 'cheerick'.

Distribution and Habitat: Widespread and locally abundant in the savanna and in clearings in the forest. Absent from the arid north, in Nigeria for example rare north of 10° N. In the savanna in the gallery forests and kurimis. In the forest clearings in young second-growth, farmland trees, gardens, and especially banana plantations. From Senegal and Gambia east to the Central African Republic and south to Gaboon and Congo.

Nesting: An unkempt, domed, globular nest with a long beard, suspended from the twig of a tree or shrub. Eggs 2, pale pink spotted and clouded with chocolate-brown and lilac-grey.

Allied species: The male Blue-headed Sunbird (*Nectarinia oritis*), 5″, is olive-green with a metallic blue head, throat and breast, and yellow pectoral tufts. Female similar but without tufts. Long decurved bill. Restricted to the mountain forests of Fernando Po, the Cameroon Mountain, Kupe, Manenguba, the Bamenda highlands and the Obudu Plateau. Abundant, usually solitary, undemonstrative, often in the shade of the forest interior although a tree in blossom in a sunlit clearing also attracts it. One call is a nondescript Sunbird jingle of metallic notes; a more distinctive call is a long-sustained repetition of one monosyllabic component, the pitch altering slightly every few seconds. The Blue-throated Brown Sunbird (*Nectarinia cyanolaema*), 6″, ranges in the lowland forest from Sierra Leone to Gaboon, Congo and Fernando Po. It frequents the primary and second-growth and is widespread yet nowhere abundant. The male is brownish above and greyish-brown below with a metallic blue or green forecrown and throat. The female is brown above washed with olive-yellow and mainly greyish-white below washed with yellowish-green on the breast and belly. At close range the white eyebrow and whitish throat are field marks.

CARMELITE SUNBIRD   *Nectarinia fuliginosa*
(*Chalcomitra fuliginosa*)   **Pl. 44**

Identification: 6″. In fresh plumage the male is chocolate-brown with a metallic blue forehead and metallic violet throat and upper tail-coverts. With wear the head and mantle fade to light brown sometimes almost to whitish and the birds are then most conspicuous. The female has brown upperparts and mottled underparts. Occurs singly or two together. Given to perching on flowers or hovering in front of them to extract nectar and occasionally reaching up to a low spray from a stance on the ground.

Distribution and Habitat: Coastal areas from Liberia to Gaboon and Congo frequenting mangrove bush, gardens with flowering shrubs, forest clearings and coconut and rubber plantations.

Nesting: Nest a compact domed pouch with a porch above the opening and a short beard. Suspended from a twig. Eggs 2, brownish-white, streaked and longitudinally blotched with brown and lilac-grey, especially about the large end.

GREEN-THROATED SUNBIRD *Nectarinia rubescens*
(*Chalcomitra rubescens*) **Pl. 44**
Identification: 6″. Male dark brown (in the field black in most lights) with a metallic green forecrown and throat. Female brown above, whitish below, heavily streaked with dark brown on the breast. Singly or in parties, and often associating with other Sunbird species searching for insects and nectar.
Distribution and Habitat: The forest and its gallery extensions and outliers in Fernando Po, the Cameroons, Gaboon, Congo and the Central African Republic. Common, frequenting forest second-growth, cocoa and rubber plantations and forest clearings, and gardens with flowering trees and shrubs.
Nesting: Nest suspended from a branch on the edge of a forest clearing. Of the usual Sunbird type, with a small porch but no beard. Eggs two, fairly heavily streaked and spotted with ashy-grey and pale olive-brown.
Allied species: The clearly defined straw-coloured throat is an excellent field mark in the male Buff-throated Sunbird (*Nectarinia adelberti*). At close range the metallic green forehead, dark brown upperparts, and chestnut underparts can be seen. The dull-coloured female lacks distinctive marks. A small (4″) active Sunbird, generally in pairs, often in the tops of tall flowering trees in farm and other clearings in the forest. It ranges widely but locally in the lowland forest belt from Sierra Leone to Nigeria.

SCARLET-BREASTED SUNBIRD *Nectarinia senegalensis*
(*Chalcomitra senegalensis*) **Pl. 44**
Identification: 5½″. Male distinctively coloured. Metallic green crown and chin, brilliant red throat and breast. Remainder upper and underparts including wings and tail dark brown, but wings tend to fade to light brown. Female has upperparts brown, throat mottled dark brown, breast and belly dull yellow. Often seen in blossoming trees.
Voice: A simple song of four notes 'tipp tioo tip tip', the second note pitched lower than the rest. Call a loud musical 'chirp'.
Distribution and Habitat: Widespread and locally abundant in the savanna ranging far north though not as far as *Anthreptes platura*. Absent from the forest and from the savanna close to the forest. Habitat varied. Recorded from Senegal, Gambia, Portuguese Guinea, Guinea, southern Mali, Ivory Coast, Ghana, Nigeria, Cameroons, southern Chad and the Central African Republic.
Nesting: A hanging domed pouch with porch and beard. Often near human habitation and frequently close to the nest of a wasp. Eggs 2, very variable in colour and markings.

YELLOW-BELLIED SUNBIRD *Nectarinia venusta*
(*Cinnyris venustus*) **Pl. 44**
Identification: 4″. Adult male upperparts metallic green except for metallic blue upper tail-coverts; throat metallic green; breast metallic purple; belly yellow. Female dull-coloured, mainly brown above and yellowish below. Occurs in pairs or small parties, often perching on flowers or hovering before them to extract nectar. Also pursues insects on the wing.
Voice: Song short, cheerful, vehement and musical. Also a sustained pleasing warbling subsong. Call-note short and sharp.
Distribution and Habitat: Widespread and locally common in the savanna from Senegal and Gambia to Chad and the Central African Republic, reappearing south of the forest in the Gaboon savanna. A wide variety of terrain including

fringing forest, orchard bush, farmland clearings, gardens and even thorn-scrub.
Nesting: Nest a little pouch suspended from a low twig of a shrub or weed.
Eggs 2, greyish delicately spotted and speckled with grey brown and with
purplish-grey secondary spots and blotches mainly concentrated in a wreath or
cap near the large end.

OLIVE-BELLIED SUNBIRD   *Nectarinia chloropygia*
(*Cinnyris chloropygius*)   **Pl. 44**
Identification: 4″. Male metallic green except for a scarlet breast band,
yellowish pectoral tufts and an olive-brown belly. Female mainly olive-brown
above and olive washed with yellow below and not distinguishable in the field
from certain other Sunbirds. Sprightly, tame, energetic even in the hottest,
sunniest hours. Occurs in pairs or parties and is especially attracted by flowers
and trees in bloom.
Voice: Call a rapid succession of high-pitched metallic notes. Song a thin
unpretentious squeaky warble.
Distribution and Habitat: Abundant and widespread. The forest and the
moist southern savanna from Sierra Leone to the Central African Republic,
Gaboon and Congo. Also Fernando Po. In the forest it frequents flowering
trees in the clearings and second-growth and especially drawn to gardens with
flowers. In the savanna its habitat is the orchard bush, the outlying woods and
second-growth shrubbery.
Nesting: Nest a little domed pouch suspended from a twig of a tree or shrub.
Eggs 2, variable, ground white tinged with blue, green or brown; markings in
various shades of grey, brown or red, and often disposed in the form of a wreath
of confluent blotches and spots near the large end; exceptionally eggs are
immaculate white.
Allied species: Preuss's Double-collared Sunbird (*Nectarinia preussi*), 4½″,
resembles the Olive-bellied Sunbird (*N. chloropygia*) but differs in its montane
habitat, its slightly larger size, and, in the male, its purple not green upper
tail-coverts and its broader scarlet breast band. An abundant mountain forest
species in Fernando Po, on the Cameroon Mountain, and in the Cameroon
highlands north to Genderu. The normal altitudinal range is 3,000 to 10,000 feet,
but in the wet (the non-breeding) season some, perhaps most, of the birds leave
the mountains and occupy temporarily the clearings in the lowland forest. The
Tiny Sunbird (*Nectarinia minulla*), 4″, also closely resembles the Olive-bellied
Sunbird. The bill is slightly shorter and at close range through glasses the male
can be distinguished by the metallic blue barring on the red breast. It is a much
rarer species, its habitat is similar, and its range is the forest from the Ivory
Coast to Fernando Po, Gaboon and Congo.

COPPER SUNBIRD   *Nectarinia cuprea* (*Cinnyris cupreus*)   **Pl. 45**
Identification: 5″. Male at a distance appears quite black. At close range head
and breast metallic copper and back metallic purple. Female olive-brown above,
yellowish-olive below. Wings and tail dark brown. Male in eclipse (dry season)
plumage resembles female but retains a few metallic feathers.
Voice: Song a sharp, repeated, melodious 'chip-chip-chip'.
Distribution and Habitat: Widespread and common in the savanna from
Senegal, Gambia and Portuguese Guinea east to southern Chad and the Central
African Republic and south to Gaboon and Congo. Absent from the arid north.

Frequents orchard bush, abandoned farmland, gallery forest edges, gardens and villages.

Nesting: Attached to a twig. A compact, domed, hanging nest with a beard. Eggs 2, brown blotched, suffused, and scrawled dark purplish-brown and lilac-grey.

SPLENDID SUNBIRD *Nectarinia coccinigaster*
(*Cinnyris coccinigaster*)   **Pl. 45**

Identification: 6″. A rather large Sunbird with a long decurved bill. The brilliant metallic male has a purple head, green mantle and wing-coverts, bluish rump, barred blue and scarlet breast, and blue under tail-coverts. Only the black wings and belly are non-metallic. Female upperparts brown tinged olive. Underparts pale yellow with greyish mottlings on breast. Song readily identifies it. Often in flowering trees seeking nectar and also hunts for insects.

Voice: Song distinctive. Of unvaried pattern, small compass and indifferent tone, yet resonant consisting of eight or nine clearly separated notes.

Distribution and Habitat: Well distributed in the savanna from Senegal to the Central African Republic and south to Gaboon where it is rare. Absent from the arid north and in the forest present only in the larger clearings near the savanna edge.

Nesting: A rather large domed nest without a beard, suspended from the underside of a twig. Eggs 1–2. At least two distinct types, one heavily blotched, scrawled, and suffused with dark brown and ashy, the other evenly sprinkled with fine streaks and speckles of pale grey and brown.

BEAUTIFUL LONG-TAILED SUNBIRD *Nectarinia pulchella*
Pl. 45

Identification: Male 6″ (including 2½″ tail streamers). Easily recognised by long narrow central rectrices and metallic green plumage with a scarlet patch in the middle of the breast. Pectoral tufts yellow. At a distance it can be confused with the very differently coloured *Anthreptes platura*. Female non-metallic, mainly brown above and dull yellowish below. Male in eclipse (dry season) like female but retains tail streamers and metallic wing-coverts.

Voice: A subdued, sweet warble of small compass. Also a persistent rather loud monosyllabic call-note.

Distribution and Habitat: A savanna Sunbird widespread and common, especially in the arid thorn scrub in the north. From southern Mauritania (17° N.), Senegal, Gambia and Portuguese Guinea east to the Cameroons and Chad. In Niger penetrates the desert to Air and Asben.

Nesting: A compact, elongated, domed pouch suspended from a twig at heights varying from 5 to 18 feet. Eggs 2. A great range in the colour of the ground and the colour and character of the markings.

SUPERB SUNBIRD *Nectarinia superba* (*Cinnyris superbus*)   **Pl. 45**

Identification: 6½″. Large size, long decurved bill and plumage distinguish it. Male metallic golden-green upperparts but head metallic blue-green; throat and chest metallic purple; breast and belly non-metallic dark red. Female mainly olive above and yellow below with a conspicuous orange-red wash on the under tail-coverts; breast unstreaked. Occurs singly or in pairs. Flight zigzagging and undulating.

Voice: Call-note a loud chirp. Song a noisy unmelodious jingle.

Distribution and Habitat: Widely dispersed yet nowhere abundant in the forest zone from Sierra Leone to Gaboon and Congo and Central African Republic, affecting mainly trees in blossom on the forest edge and in forest clearings. Also occurs sparingly in the savanna woods and in orchard bush.

Nesting: Nest suspended from the branch of a tree. Of the usual Sunbird type but relatively bulky, loose and untidy. The single egg is bluish-white and is marked with a zone of bold blotches and spots of inky-black and grey near the large end.

Allied species: Johanna's Sunbird (*Nectarinia johannae*), 5½″, is an uncommon forest Sunbird known from Sierra Leone, Liberia, Ivory Coast, Ghana, Dahomey, the Cameroons, Gaboon and Congo. The male resembles the Superb Sunbird but the head and throat are metallic green like the mantle and the red underparts are brighter in shade. Female underparts conspicuously streaked with blackish.

WHITE-EYES: Zosteropidae

YELLOW WHITE-EYE *Zosterops senegalensis* (*Z. virens*)   **Pl. 45**
Identification: 4″. Sexes similar. Upperparts greenish-yellow, olive-yellow or yellowish-green according to locality. Underparts bright yellow. Wing and tail feathers brown with fringes concolorous with the upperparts. Round the eye a ring of white feathers usually easily seen. A fine, straight, black bill. In parties or pairs busily exploring the foliage in the manner of Leaf-warblers.

Voice: Song a beautiful shivering trill. Birds in a party frequently utter little almost inaudible cries.

Distribution and Habitat: Widely but unevenly distributed in the savanna from Senegal, Gambia and Portuguese Guinea east to southern Chad and the Central African Republic frequenting the trees of the thorn scrub, grass woodland and orchard bush. Abundant in the montane forests of the Cameroons. Rare in the lowland rain forest of Cameroons and Gaboon. Also in Fernando Po.

Nesting: A tiny compact cup of bark, gossamer, and grasses, slung between the limbs of a slender fork. Eggs 2–3, pale blue or white, immaculate.

BUNTINGS: Emberizidae

Finch-like birds with short conical bills. Mainly ground-feeders picking up fallen seeds. Often with yellow in the plumage.

CABANIS'S YELLOW BUNTING *Emberiza cabanisi*   **Pl. 45**
Identification: 6½″. Male distinguished by black head, long white eyebrow, white throat and vivid yellow underparts. Upperparts mottled dark grey and black. A double white wing bar. Female plumage duller.

Voice: An unpretentious, low-pitched, pleasing, characteristic song. Call-note a wheezing 'tsee' or 'tsee-tsee'.

Distribution and Habitat: The wooded savanna from Sierra Leone, Guinea and Mali to Chad and the Central African Republic; also in the Congo savanna south of the forest. Sedentary and locally not uncommon in the farm clearings and in the orchard bush.

Nesting: Nest a shallow cup placed in a yam vine or plantain. Eggs 2, white, scrawled and blotched with brown and grey.

Allied species: The Yellow-bellied Bunting (*Emberiza flaviventris*), 6″, has a black head with prominent white stripes above and below the eye and down the middle of the crown, and a prominent white patch on the wing, mantle chestnut, rump grey, underparts mainly yellow. Female duller. The white wing patch distinguishes the Yellow-bellied from the rather similar Nigerian Little Bunting (*Emberiza forbesi*) of the West African savanna. The range of the Yellow-bellied Bunting is the northern arid zone of the savanna in Mali, Upper Volta, Niger, northern Nigeria and Chad, and it reappears south of the forest in the Congo savanna. The Nigerian Little Bunting (*Emberiza forbesi*) closely resembles the Yellow-bellied Bunting but is slightly smaller with a shorter tail and lacks the conspicuous large white patch on the wing-coverts. Distributed in a narrow zone in the semi-arid belt roughly between the 12th and 14th parallels in Senegal, Gambia, Portuguese Guinea, Mali, Upper Volta, northern Ghana, northern Nigeria, northern Cameroons, Chad and the Central African Republic.

ROCK BUNTING   *Emberiza tahapisi* (*Fringillaria tahapisi*)   **Pl. 45**
Identification: $5\frac{1}{2}$″. A trim little Bunting with a black and white striped head, brown upperparts streaked with russet, grey chin and throat, and cinnamon-chestnut underparts. Female has a brown crown with a mesial cinnamon streak and shows less white on the head. Usually on open ground in stony places. In small parties except when breeding. Tame.
Voice: A short, simple warbling song. A wheezy, drawn-out monosyllabic call.
Distribution and Habitat: Migratory. Widely distributed and locally common in the savanna from Mauritania, Senegal and Sierra Leone east to Chad and the Cameroons. Rare or absent from the moist savanna adjoining the forest. Also in the Gaboon and Congo savanna where the male has a black not grey chin and throat. Usually in rocky, hilly country. Occasionally in orchard bush.
Nesting: On the ground usually at the base of a rock. A slight, shallow cup, mainly of grass roots and stems. Eggs 2–3, pale green rather thickly spotted and blotched with chocolate-brown and purplish-grey.

CANARIES AND FINCHES: Fringillidae

Small seed-eating birds with strong, hard, conical bills. Songsters.

YELLOW-FRONTED CANARY   *Serinus mozambicus*   **Pl. 45**
Identification: $4\frac{1}{2}$″. Crown grey; broad yellow frontal band and stripe over eye; dark moustachial streak; olive-green back; yellow rump (conspicuous in flight); brown tail; yellow underparts. Female duller and with a necklace of dark spots on the crop. Considerable geographical variation in the shade of the upper and underparts. Tame. Usually seen perched or else on the ground picking up seeds. A common cage-bird in West Africa.
Voice: A short, loud, simple, melodious song. Call-note a frequent 'swee-eet'.
Distribution and Habitat: Widely distributed and locally abundant in the

savanna from Gambia, Senegal and Portuguese Guinea east to southern Chad and the Central African Republic and south to Gaboon and Congo. Mainly in the tree savanna, farm clearings with pollarded trees, gardens and villages. Rare in the thorn scrub. Occasional in the larger forest clearings. Common in the Cameroons highland savanna. Occurs Sao Tome.

Nesting: A tiny, compact, regular cup bound with gossamer to a small branch or fork at a height of 4 to 20 feet. Eggs 2–3, white, either immaculate or sparingly and faintly marked with orange-brown and pale lilac.

GREY CANARY   *Serinus leucopygius (Poliospiza leucopygia)*   **Pl. 45**
Identification: 4″. Sexes similar. Greyish-brown upperparts but rump white (conspicuous in flight) and head dark-streaked. Underparts mainly white, the chest mottled with light brown. Bill whitish at base. In habits rather resembles the Yellow-fronted Canary. Tame and gregarious.

Voice: A pleasant, varied, resonant song like but superior to that of the Yellow-fronted Canary. Delivered from a high perch. Call 'tooee-eet'.

Distribution and Habitat: The dry northern zone of the savanna in Senegal, Gambia, Mali, Upper Volta, Ghana, northern Nigeria, Niger and Chad. Locally common. Often on farmland, especially millet, in the neighbourhood of villages.

Nesting: A tiny, compact cup built in a slender fork in a soft-leaved or thorny tree. Eggs 2–4, white tinged grey or blue sparingly spotted with brown or speckled with black.

Allied species: The Streaky-headed Seed-eater (*Serinus gularis*), 6″, is brown with white streaks on the crown and a white eye-stripe, blackish cheeks and a white throat. The full-throated sustained song recalls that of the Yellow-fronted Canary (*Serinus mozambicus*) but is superior to it. It ranges in the savanna from the Ivory Coast to the Cameroons and the Central African Republic. Locally common, especially in orchard bush with farm clearings.

ORIOLE FINCH   *Linurgus olivaceus*   **Pl. 45**
Identification: 6″. Distinguished by plumage and montane habitat. Bright yellowish-green upperparts, bright yellow underparts. Head and throat black sharply demarcated from the yellow body. Female less conspicuous being mainly olive-green and lacking the jet-black head of the male. Occurs singly, in pairs, and in parties. Not shy.

Voice: Call-note a wheezy 'tzit tzit'. A sweet, sustained, rather thin, high-pitched song.

Distribution and Habitat: The forested mountains of Fernando Po, the Cameroon highlands, and the Obudu Plateau of Nigeria, ascending to 9,000 feet and descending as low as 1,800 feet (on the Cameroon Mountain). Frequents the trees and shrubs on the edge of the forest and in its clearings.

Nesting: Nest 3 or 4 feet above the ground in a bush on the forest edge. A shallow cup of moss, roots and plant down. Eggs 2–3. White sparingly marked with reddish-brown, some eggs showing a few hair lines.

WEAVERS: Ploceidae

A numerous family of the forest and savanna. Most species are thick-set seed-eating birds with strong short bills and the ability to construct elaborate woven nests. In some the males have a conspicuous breeding plumage whilst the female and non-breeding male plumage is drab and nondescript. Many are highly gregarious. Some forest species are mainly insect eaters and have less robust bills.

WHITE-FRONTED GROSBEAK *Amblyospiza albifrons* **Pl. 46**
Identification: 7″. Stout build, large head, massive bill and erect posture when perched aid identification. Male has chestnut head, mantle and throat, grey breast and belly, and conspicuous white patch on the forehead and the wing. Female, upperparts dark brown, underparts conspicuously creamy-white throughout boldly streaked with brown. Circular flights of male over breeding territory and frequent flicking of wings and tail as he clings to a tall reed draw attention.
Voice: Breeding male has a short simple song uttered with great vehemence. Monosyllabic call-note.
Distribution and Habitat: Widely but locally distributed from Sierra Leone to the Cameroons and Gaboon in extensive forest clearings and in the moister savanna near the forest. Reed beds and other tall aquatic vegetation in marshy places and occasionally tall grass in dry places are its habitat.
Nesting: Breeds usually in small scattered colonies. Large, globular, finely woven nests attached to one or more growing reeds, pale yellow, and very conspicuous. Eggs 2–3. Characteristic: pale pink or rufous, spotted, blotched, suffused, and lined with reddish-brown and orange-brown.

SLENDER-BILLED WEAVER *Ploceus luteolus (Sitagra luteola)*
Pl. 46
Identification: 4½″. The smallest savanna Ploceine Weaver in our area. Male has forecrown, face and throat black sharply demarcated from bright yellow hind crown and side of neck. Upperparts olive-green. Underparts bright yellow. Iris brown. Female yellowish-olive above indistinctly streaked, and dull yellow below. Male in eclipse rather like female. Not usually gregarious. Quiet but not shy. Searches foliage for insects like a Warbler.
Voice: Often silent. A squeaky, vibrant phrase typical of Weavers.
Distribution and Habitat: Widely distributed in the northern arid belt of the savanna where there are trees or shrubs. From Mauritania (17° N.), Senegal, Gambia and Portuguese Guinea east to Chad and the Central African Republic.
Nesting: Usually nests singly, but occasionally in small colonies. Often near a wasp's nest. Small, hanging from the horizontal branch of a thorn tree at a height of 5 to 12 feet. Retort-shaped with spouted opening. A latticework of fine grass strips, sometimes lined with grass heads. Eggs 2–3, white.
Allied species: The Little Weaver (*Ploceus pelzelni*), 4½″, occurs here and there from Ghana to Congo in localities near the sea or along the larger rivers. Usually in small compact breeding colonies overhanging or very near water. Male readily recognised by bright yellow underparts, black mask, small size and fine bill. Female olive-yellow above, yellow below, with the fine bill and a conspicuous yellow supercilium the best field marks.

Plate 45

SUNBIRDS ETC.

1. **COPPER SUNBIRD** *Nectarinia cuprea* page 234
At a distance black; at close range metallic purple and copper.

2. **SPLENDID SUNBIRD** *Nectarinia coccinigaster* 235
Metallic purple head, green back, and blue and scarlet breast.

3. **SUPERB SUNBIRD** *Nectarinia superba* 235
Male: large; long bill; dark red breast and belly.
Female: large; long bill; orange-red under tail-coverts.

4. **BEAUTIFUL LONG-TAILED SUNBIRD** 235
Nectarinia pulchella
Long central rectrices; scarlet breast patch; yellow pectoral tufts.

5. **SPOTTED CREEPER** *Salpornis spilonota* 229
Plumage brown spotted and barred white.

6. **WEST AFRICAN PENDULINE TIT** *Remiz parvulus* 228
Bright yellow forehead and underparts.

7. **WHITE-SHOULDERED BLACK TIT** *Parus leucomelas* 228
White shoulder-patch.

8. **YELLOW WHITE-EYE** *Zosterops senegalensis* 236
White eye-ring.

9. **CABANIS'S YELLOW BUNTING** *Emberiza cabanisi* 236
Black head; long white stripe above and behind eye.

10. **ROCK BUNTING** *Emberiza tahapisi* 237
Black-and-white striped head; cinnamon-rufous underparts.

11. **ORIOLE FINCH** *Linurgus olivaceus* 238
Male: black head; bright yellow underparts.
Female: olive-green.

12. **YELLOW-FRONTED CANARY** *Serinus mozambicus* 237
Yellow stripe over eye; yellow rump.

13. **GREY CANARY** *Serinus leucopygius* 238
White rump.

Plate 46

WEAVERS (MALES IN BREEDING PLUMAGE)

1. SLENDER-BILLED WEAVER *Ploceus luteolus*   page 239
Small; black mask; yellow hind-crown.

2. VITELLINE MASKED WEAVER *Ploceus velatus*   242
Chestnut forehead; black mask.

3. BLACK-HEADED WEAVER *Ploceus melanocephala*   243
Black head and throat.

4. VILLAGE WEAVER *Ploceus cucullatus*   242
Chestnut collar; black V-shaped mark on mantle.

5. BLACK-FACED DIOCH *Quelea quelea*   246
Red bill; black mask

6. COMPACT WEAVER *Ploceus superciliosus*   244
Short thick bill; black mask; dark upperparts.

7. ORANGE WEAVER *Ploceus aurantius*   242
Golden-yellow head and underparts.

8. SPECTACLED WEAVER *Ploceus nigricollis brachypterus*   244
Black band through eye; black chin and throat.

9. VIEILLOT'S BLACK WEAVER *Ploceus nigerrimus*   243
a. Eastern race *P. n. nigerrimus*: black.
b. Western race *P. n. castaneofuscus*: black and chestnut.

10. WHITE-FRONTED GROSBEAK *Amblyospiza albifrons*   239
Massive bill; white forehead-patch and wing-patch.

11. RED-VENTED MALIMBE *Malimbus scutatus*   245
Black except for scarlet head, collar, chest, and under tail-coverts.

12. BLUE-BILLED MALIMBE *Malimbus nitens*   245
Bluish bill; crimson throat.

13. CRESTED MALIMBE *Malimbus malimbicus*   245
Red head and crest.

ORANGE WEAVER *Ploceus aurantius* (*Xanthophilus aurantius*) **Pl. 46**
Identification: 6″. Male identified by olive mantle and conspicuous golden-yellow head and underparts, the throat washed with chestnut. Female olive-green above, mainly white below. A typical sociable Ploceine Weaver occurring in noisy breeding colonies in the vicinity of water.
Voice: A noisy concerted chattering at the breeding colony.
Distribution and Habitat: A water-frequenting species partial to coastal waterways and the banks of large rivers. Ranges rather locally from Liberia to Gaboon, Congo and the Central African Republic.
Nesting: The nests are in colonies and are suspended from the branches of a tree or from a grass stalk and usually overhang water. Domed globes of woven grass. Eggs 2, variable, green or blue spotted and blotched with various shades of brown.

VITELLINE MASKED WEAVER *Ploceus velatus*
(*P. vitellinus*) **Pl. 46**
Identification: 6″. Male has forehead chestnut, crown golden-chestnut, nape yellow, remainder upperparts olive-yellow. A conspicuous black mask with clear-cut edges enclosing lores, ear-coverts, cheeks, chin and upper throat. Underparts bright yellow, the lower throat washed with chestnut. Iris orange. Bill black. Males of Heuglin's Masked Weaver and Black-headed Weaver (p. 243) rather similar but Heuglin's Masked Weaver has a yellow forehead and crown, lacks the chestnut wash on the throat, and the black on the upper throat extends on to the bib. The Black-headed Weaver has the entire head black. Female and male in eclipse lack the black mask. Upperparts mainly brown streaked darker. Underparts white, washed with yellow on the throat and breast. In this dress indistinguishable in the field from certain other Ploceine Weavers.
Voice: Typical Weaver wheezy chattering and a sharp 'tssp' call.
Distribution and Habitat: Ranges widely and commonly through the arid northern savanna from Mauritania, Senegal and Gambia to Chad and northern Central African Republic. Mainly north of 12° N. Frequents open thorn scrub. Usually remote from human habitation.
Nesting: Singly or in small colonies. Typical retort-shaped Ploceine nest of woven grass strips with a lining of grass heads. No visible spout. Suspended from branch of thorny or soft-leaved tree. Eggs 2–3, variable, usually pinkish or pale greenish-blue spotted and blotched with different shades of brown and lilac.
Allied species: Heuglin's Masked Weaver (*Ploceus heuglini*), 6″, in male breeding plumage rather resembles the Vitelline Masked Weaver but has a yellow forehead and crown. The black on the upper throat extends on to the bib and the throat lacks the strong chestnut wash. Eye pale yellow. Females and off-season males are virtually indistinguishable in the field from allied species. The nest is rounded like that of the Village Weaver not retort-shaped. Locally distributed in the semi-arid belt with a more southerly range than the Vitelline Masked Weaver. Occurs in Senegal, Gambia, Ivory Coast, Ghana, Nigeria, the Central African Republic and Congo.

VILLAGE WEAVER *Ploceus cucullatus* (*Plesiositagra cucullatus*,
P. collaris) **Pl. 46**
Identification: 6½″. A large conspicuous Weaver abundant especially in towns

and villages and thus the best known of the family. Male has black head, nape, throat and bib, a broad chestnut collar, a mainly yellow mantle with a conspicuous large V-shaped black mark, a yellow rump and green tail. Underparts yellow. In the female and the male in eclipse the head is olive-green, mantle olive-brown, rump olive, and underparts mainly pale yellow. In the very distinctive race *Ploceus cucullatus collaris* found in west Gaboon the broad chestnut collar is absent and the breast is chestnut. Bold, aggressive, gregarious. Very noisy. Life centres on breeding colony and the work of building and repairing their nests.

Voice: Noisy shrill chattering and twittering.

Distribution and Habitat: Very widely and commonly distributed throughout the area in forest and savanna showing a preference for towns, villages and cultivated land. Rare in the extreme north.

Nesting: Breeds in close colonies sometimes of many hundreds of pairs. Nest suspended from the branch of a tree. A thick, strongly woven, lined, ball-shaped nest usually with a short funnel. Eggs 2–3, very diverse, white or of various shades of blue or pink, unmarked or blotched and spotted with brown and lavender.

VIEILLOT'S BLACK WEAVER   *Ploceus nigerrimus*
(*Melanopteryx nigerrimus, Cinnamopteryx castaneofuscus*)   **Pl. 46**

Identification: 7″. Two races occur, the males of which are readily distinguishable in the field. *Ploceus n. nigerrimus* of south-eastern Nigeria, Cameroons, Gaboon and Congo is uniformly black. *Ploceus n. castaneofuscus* (Chestnut-and-Black Weaver) of Gambia to south-eastern Nigeria is black with a chestnut mantle, rump and belly. The sparrowy females of both races are mottled brown and blackish above and mainly olive below. The stout bill, bright yellow eye, gregarious habits, frequent association with the Village Weaver (*Ploceus cucullatus*) and habitat aid identification.

Voice: A shrill and rasping sustained chattering, especially at the nest.

Distribution and Habitat: The forest and the adjoining savanna from Gambia to Gaboon and Congo, in the cultivated clearings and often near villages. Widespread and common.

Nesting: Breeds in close colonies, often alongside the Village Weaver. The globular, domed, woven, unspouted nests are attached to the branches of a tree or shrub or to a tall grass or reed. Village palms are a favourite site. Eggs two, immaculate blue, the depth of shade varying in different parts of the egg.

BLACK-HEADED WEAVER   *Ploceus melanocephalus*
(*Sitagra melanocephala, S. capitalis*)   **Pl. 46**

Identification: 6″. Male has black head and throat, a bright yellow collar on the nape and sides of the neck, and olive-yellow upperparts. Breast and belly yellow in the race (*P. m. melanocephalus*) occupying Gambia and Portuguese Guinea. Breast dark golden-orange and belly yellow in the race (*P. m. capitalis*) occupying the rest of the West African savanna. Iris dark brown. Female has upperparts brownish, the mantle streaked with dark brown, and the wing feathers edged yellowish. Underparts whitish, washed with brown on breast and flanks. Male in eclipse rather similar. Tame. Gregarious. Found near waterways.

Voice: Discordant twitterings and a 'tsssp' call.

Distribution and Habitat: The margins of lakes, rivers and marshes with overhanging trees or bushes. In the semi-arid belt of the savanna from Mauritania, Senegal, Gambia and Portuguese Guinea east to Nigeria, Chad and the Central African Republic, being relatively uncommon in the two last-named territories. Also the Congo savanna.

Nesting: In scattered colonies near water. Nest attached to branch of tree or tall grass stalk. Ball-shaped, without funnel, strongly woven, and lined with grass tops. Eggs 2–3. They exhibit a very wide range in colour and markings.

COMPACT WEAVER *Ploceus superciliosus*
(*Pachyphantes pachyrhynchus*) **Pl. 46**

Identification: 6″. Short thick bill. Male recognised by chestnut forehead, yellow crown, and black mask covering face and upper throat; upperparts mottled and streaked dark brown and olive; underparts yellow. Female similar but forehead and centre of crown black. In non-breeding dress both sexes are tawny-brown with streaked upperparts and a distinctive broad pale cinnamon supercilium. In pairs in the breeding season and flocks in the off-season.

Voice: A musical 'cheewery-cheewery-cheewery'. Call-note a short abrupt 'chee'.

Distribution and Habitat: The grass savanna belt next to the forest from Senegal to the Central African Republic, Gaboon and Congo. Locally not uncommon in moist terrain with rank grass.

Nesting: Single nests, typical round ploceine structures, attached, usually at a fair height, to a stout grass stalk, and very conspicuous. Eggs 3–4, variable, usually grey or brown thickly spotted and stippled with grey.

Allied species: The Yellow-mantled Weaver (*Ploceus tricolor*), 7″, is jet-black with a yellow mantle and a chestnut breast and belly. Sexes similar. It ranges in the lowland forest from Sierra Leone to Gaboon, is local and nowhere common. Usually in the tree tops in the interior or on the edge of the primary forest. Maxwell's Black Weaver (*Ploceus albinucha*) is known from a few localities in Sierra Leone, Liberia, Ivory Coast, Ghana and Gaboon, and is locally common in Fernando Po and southern Cameroons. A forest Weaver, resembling the Village Weaver (*Ploceus cucullatus*) in habits and like it a colonial nester. Plumage in male and female black. Iris creamy-white. The male Vieillot's Black Weaver (*P. nigerrimus*) and the females of certain rare *Malimbus* species are almost indistinguishable in the field except that Vieillot's Black Weaver has a bright yellow eye and the *Malimbus* Weavers have a brown eye. The Black Mountain Weaver (*Ploceus melanogaster*), 5½″, is restricted to the mountain forests of Fernando Po, the Cameroons and the Obudu Plateau of Nigeria. A slimly built Weaver with a slender pointed bill, usually encountered in pairs or parties searching for insects in thick shrubbery or dense creepers. The male is black with a yellow head and a narrow yellow necklace below the black throat. Female similar except that the whole throat is yellow.

SPECTACLED WEAVER *Ploceus nigricollis*
(*Hyphanturgus nigricollis*, *H. brachypterus*) **Pl. 46**

Identification: 6½″. Two very distinct races. From Cameroons eastwards (*P. n. nigricollis*) male has chestnut forecrown, black band through eye, golden-yellow crown, cheeks and nape, black collar behind nape, and remaining upperparts mainly sepia-brown. Chin and throat black, and remaining underparts golden-yellow. From Cameroons westwards (*P. n. brachypterus*) male has no black nuchal collar and the upperparts are mainly bright olive-green not sepia-brown. Female *P. n. nigricollis* has black crown and nape, yellow super-cilium, black band through eye, and bright yellow underparts. In female *P. n. brachypterus* crown and upperparts are olive-green. Common. Not gregarious. Quiet and skulking. Mainly arboreal and insectivorous.

Voice: Rather silent. Occasional soft twittering and also harsh calls.

Distribution and Habitat: Widespread and common in the forest and the moister zone of the savanna from Gambia, Senegal and Portuguese Guinea east to the Central African Republic and south to Gaboon and Congo. Also Fernando Po. Found in high forest, second growth, mangrove, riparian woodland, orchard bush, and farmland with trees.

Nesting: Usually solitary. A round woven nest of palm or grass strips with a tubular entrance 4 to 12 inches long. Suspended from the twig of a tree or bush at various heights and frequently well hidden. Eggs 1–2, varying greatly in colour and markings.

RED-VENTED MALIMBE   *Malimbus scutatus*   Pl. 46

Identification: 7″. Black, with scarlet head, collar, upper breast and under tail-coverts. Female lacks the scarlet head. Noisy and tame. Often in small flocks in the forest, sometimes in the company of other insectivorous birds: or at their conspicuous long-spouted nests.

Voice: Cry a frequent loud harsh 'chirp'. Low soft notes also described.

Distribution and Habitat: The forest from Sierra Leone to the Cameroons. Frequents oil and raphia palms in swamp forest, second-growth and extensive forest clearings. Not uncommon.

Nesting: The very long-spouted woven nest is suspended from the fronds of a palm. Usually several nests together but only one is used for breeding. Eggs 2, pure white.

BLUE-BILLED MALIMBE   *Malimbus nitens*   Pl. 46

Identification: 7″. Sexes similar. Black with a bright crimson throat and upper breast. Bill bluish. Occurs singly or in parties and is a frequent member of the mixed bird-parties of the forest.

Voice: A long-drawn-out 'ze-e-e-e-e'. Also harsh chirping, screeching or churring calls.

Distribution and Habitat: Senegal and Portuguese Guinea to Gaboon and Congo in the forest and its gallery extensions. Widespread and common. Frequents both primary and second-growth and is partial to thick tangled vines where it hunts for insects.

Nesting: Nest typically overhangs a forest pool or stream. Suspended from a palm tree or shrub. A rather untidy globular woven nest with the opening over-hung by a long and wide porch. Eggs 2, variable, usually whitish blotched and spotted with brown and lilac.

CRESTED MALIMBE   *Malimbus malimbicus*   Pl. 46

Identification: 7″. Black with a crested crimson crown and scarlet cheeks and throat. Female similar but crown uncrested. Occurs on its own in pairs or oftener as a member of the mixed bird parties.

Voice: Song consists of a few sweet notes.

Distribution and Habitat: The lowland forest from Sierra Leone to Gaboon and Congo affecting virgin forest and also second-growth with raphia and oil-palm. Locally common.

Nesting: Nest globular, roughly woven, with a short ragged spout, usually suspended from a palm frond. Eggs 2, greenish-white profusely marked with brown and grey.

Allied species: The Red-headed Malimbe (*Malimbus rubricollis*), $7\frac{1}{2}''$, is black with a crimson or scarlet crown and nape. The female differs in having the forecrown black. Occurs locally in the forest belt including the gallery extensions from Portuguese Guinea to Gaboon, Congo and Fernando Po. The Red-winged Malimbe (*Malimbus rubriceps*), $7''$, is an atypical *Malimbus* often placed in the genus *Anaplectes*. A dry-country species locally and sparingly distributed in the savanna from Gambia and Senegal east to the Central African Republic. Distinguished by conspicuous red bill and crimson head, throat, breast and wing feather margins, black cheeks, brown mantle and white belly. Female duller and has brown not red head and breast.

BLACK-FACED DIOCH   *Quelea quelea*   Pl. 46

Identification: $4\frac{1}{2}''$. Male identified by strong, conical, bright red bill and black mask covering forehead, cheeks and throat. Some males have a rufous head and no black mask. Rest of plumage variable: pink or buff crown, light brown mantle marked with blackish, yellow-edged primaries, buff or pinkish underparts. Female plumage sparrowy and lacks black mask. Bill yellow when breeding, red during off-season. Off-season male resembles female. Strongly gregarious, sometimes in flocks of millions. Feeds on seeds and grain.

Voice: Squeaky twittering song at nest. Various cries and noisy chattering when congregated.

Distribution and Habitat: Locally distributed in the semi-arid zone from Senegal and Gambia east to Chad reaching to the desert edge (in the rains at least). Uncommon south of 14° N. Occurs in Congo. Abundant in some areas. Frequents grassy places and open shrubby savanna.

Nesting: In vast closely packed colonies in thorn trees or, less often, in reed beds. A small round nest of grass strips with large lateral opening. Eggs 2–4, immaculate pale blue.

Allied species: The Red-headed Dioch (*Quelea erythrops*), $4\frac{1}{2}''$, inhabits the moist savanna zone and the grassy clearings in the forest and ranges widely but locally from Gambia east to Nigeria, the Cameroons and Chad, and south to Gaboon and Congo. Fond of tall vegetation in both dry and wet places. Male in breeding dress easily distinguished by crimson head and dark red throat sharply demarcated from the sparrowy upperparts and buff and whitish underparts. Bill black. Female and off-season male sparrowy-plumaged with horn-coloured bill and virtually indistinguishable in the field from certain *Euplectes* species.

YELLOW-CROWNED BISHOP   *Euplectes afer*   Pl. 47

Identification: $4\frac{1}{2}''$. Polygamous. Male during nuptial display flight leaps in the air over his territory, the yellow feathers of the rump ruffled. Flight like a butterfly's. Black mask and throat; yellow crown and back except for a blackish collar; brown wings; yellow breast with a touch of chestnut; black belly. Bill black. Female resembles female *Quelea quelea* but has a horn-coloured bill and a pale eye-stripe that the *Quelea* lacks. Male in eclipse resembles female. Common and easy to observe, but local. In the off-season often in flocks with *Quelea quelea*.

Voice: A series of ringing, jingling cries.

Distribution and Habitat: Widespread in our area particularly in the savanna but local because of its marshy habitat. Rice fields, marshes and swampy ground by rivers and lakes. From Senegal and Gambia east to southern Chad and the Central African Republic and south to Gaboon and Congo.

Nesting: A woven ball-shaped nest with lateral opening. Made of dry grasses lined with grass tops and attached to tall plants, sometimes rice, particularly above water. Eggs 2–4, greyish-white with a few small, well-defined, intense black specks and spots and a few obscure grey specks.

LONG-TAILED BLACK WHYDAH   *Euplectes ardens*
(*Coliuspasser ardens*)   **Pl. 47**

Identification: Male in breeding plumage easily recognised by all-black plumage and remarkable plumed tail, 9–10 inches long, especially during the slow flapping display flight when the tail is spread. Females and non-breeding males (5″) are dark-striped and sparrowy and not certainly distinguishable in the field from allied species. In the non-breeding season occurs in flocks feeding mainly on the ground on fallen seeds.

Voice: Characteristically silent.

Distribution and Habitat: The savanna north of the forest from Gambia to the Central African Republic reappearing south of the forest in the Gaboon and Congo savanna. Common in Sierra Leone and in the high grasslands of the Cameroons but rather local elsewhere in its West African range. Grassy hillsides or plains with few or no trees are its favourite terrain.

Nesting: A small spherical woven nest with a lateral opening overhung by a porch. Attached near the ground to growing grass stems. Eggs three, greenish-blue heavily marked with brown and purplish.

FIRE-CROWNED BISHOP   *Euplectes hordeaceus*   **Pl. 47**

Identification: 5½″. Male in breeding dress scarlet and black, conspicuous, but can be confused with the Red Bishop. Crown, nape, breast and rump scarlet; mantle reddish-chestnut; mask enclosing ear-coverts and throat black; wings, tail and belly black. Scarlet colour sometimes replaced by orange. Female and male in eclipse sparrowy and virtually indistinguishable in the field from the Red Bishop and the Yellow-crowned Bishop. Characteristic, slow, fluttering display flight over breeding terrain with nuptial plumes puffed out. Polygamous and strongly territorial.

Voice: Rather nondescript chirps and twitters.

Distribution and Habitat: Throughout our area abundant and widespread in the grasslands of the savanna and the forest clearings and particularly partial to the rank herbage of fallow farmland. Absent from the arid north.

Nesting: Globular nest with lateral opening attached to stout grass stems. Of woven strips of grass and lined with grass tops. Eggs 2–3, pale blue, immaculate or rarely sparingly spotted.

YELLOW-MANTLED WHYDAH   *Euplectes macrourus*
(*Coliuspasser macrourus*)   **Pl. 47**

Identification: Long-tailed breeding male unmistakable. Plumage jet-black with bright yellow mantle and shoulders. Sparrowy non-breeding male retains the diagnostic yellow shoulder patches, but female cannot certainly be identified in the field. Very conspicuous in the breeding season when the males are displaying on their territory. In the non-breeding season in large mixed flocks of Euplectine Weavers.

Voice: The call of the male is a thin 'chee-ee' delivered from its perch on a grass stalk.

Distribution and Habitat: A common Weaver well distributed in the savanna and in the larger grassy clearings in the forest from Senegal east to Chad and the Central African Republic and south to Gaboon and Congo. Affects especially wet grassy areas and fallow arable land overgrown with rank herbage.

Nesting: Nest usually near the ground in thick herbage attached to growing grass stems. A little woven pouch lined inside with grass tops some of which project through the lateral opening to form a ragged porch. Eggs 2–3, grey-green profusely spotted and streaked with dark brown or blackish.

RED BISHOP *Euplectes orix*

Identification: 5″. Male in breeding plumage scarlet and black. Black crown and sides of head. Scarlet upperparts. Brown (not black as in the Fire-crowned Bishop) wings and tail. Tail short and concealed by long scarlet upper and under coverts. Scarlet throat and chest. Black breast and belly. Orange sometimes replaces scarlet. Female and male in eclipse sparrowy and indistinguishable from certain other Bishops. Males display conspicuously over territory with slow, jerky, bouncing flight, puffed-out plumes and wing-clapping. Polygamous.

Voice: Twittering or wheezy calls delivered from a perch or in nuptial flight.

Distribution and Habitat: Widely distributed and common in the grasslands north of the forest from Senegal (to 16° N.), Gambia and Portuguese Guinea east to Chad and the Central African Republic. Fond of millet fields, elephant grass and other rank tall grasses, and swampy grassland.

Nesting: A woven, globular nest of grass strips lined with grass tops. Lateral opening. Attached to stout grass stems or occasionally to the twig of a tree. Eggs 2–4, deep blue, usually immaculate, occasionally sparsely marked.

BUFFALO WEAVER *Bubalornis albirostris*   Pl. 47

Identification: 9″. A large black Weaver of the savanna, highly gregarious at all seasons. A few white patches (the bases of the feathers) usually visible on back and a white patch on the flanks when wings are raised. A large black bill which in the breeding male turns to whitish tipped black and is then very conspicuous. Huge communal nests a focal point (nesting and roosting) throughout the year. Feeds on the ground.

Voice: Very noisy when breeding but not at other times. At the nest utters a variety of harsh, guttural and explosive high-pitched cries.

Distribution and Habitat: Locally common in the semi-arid belt of the savanna in southern Mauritania, Senegal, Gambia, Portuguese Guinea, Mali, Upper Volta, northern Nigeria and Chad.

Nesting: Polygamous, each male the owner of a massive stick nest with several chambers lined with grasses and leaves and each occupied by a female. Usually several such nests in a tree, often a large tree in or near a village. Eggs 1–3, greenish-white thickly and evenly blotched and spotted with grey and brown.

SPARROW-WEAVER   *Plocepasser superciliosus*   **Pl. 47**
Identification: 7″. Sexes similar. A large dull-coloured 'Sparrow' whose best field marks are the long broad white stripe over the eye and the black stripes on the pure white throat. Earth-brown upperparts but crown and cheeks chestnut and two bars on the wing white. Dirty white underparts. Arboreal. In small parties. Not shy but easily overlooked.
Voice: A short ringing cry.
Distribution and Habitat: Fairly common but local in the thorn scrub and the soft-leaved wooded savanna from Senegal, Gambia and Portuguese Guinea to Chad and the Central African Republic.
Nesting: In colonies or singly. A bulky, roofed, untidy structure of dry, stiff grass stems placed in a tree at the end of a branch. Eggs 2, cream or pinkish, profusely blotched and spotted with mauve-brown or brownish-pink with lilac shell-marks.

GREY-HEADED SPARROW   *Passer griseus*   **Pl. 47**
Identification: 5½″. Sexes similar. A typical Sparrow, familiar, impudent and wary; often about human habitation. Head grey, back brown, rump cinnamon, wings and tail brown. Underparts light grey but throat and belly white.
Voice: A loud 'cheerp' or succession of 'cheerps'.
Distribution and Habitat: In towns and villages in the savanna and forest. Also widely dispersed yet local in the savanna in many other habitats up to the border of the desert. Absent from closed forest.
Nesting: In a hole in a building or tree or placed among the branches of a tree. An untidy accumulation mainly of grasses, plentifully lined with feathers. Eggs 3–4, white, profusely blotched, spotted, and suffused with brown and grey.
Allied species: The Golden Sparrow (*Passer luteus*), 5″, ranges in the thorn scrub, mainly between the 15th and 18th parallels from Mauritania and Senegal through Mali, Niger and northernmost Nigeria to Chad. A rather slim, small Sparrow, the male with a sulphur-yellow head, nape and underparts, a chestnut back, and dark brown wings with two whitish wing bars. Bill black. Female and immature male brown above, cream below, and with pale bill. Gregarious at all seasons. Often with *Quelea quelea*. Nests in large scattered colonies in low thorn trees.

BUSH-SPARROW   *Petronia dentata (Gymnoris dentata)*   **Pl. 47**
Identification: 5¼″. A dull-coloured Sparrow. The lemon-yellow throat patch is distinctive but is difficult to detect in the field. The gently curved contour of the tail is a good field mark. Male has grey crown, rufous-brown supercilium, brown upperparts, and mainly ashy-white underparts. In the female the crown is brown, the supercilium pale buff, and the back is striped with dark brown. Occurs in small parties, feeding on the ground on fallen seeds or searching the trees for insects. Frequent noisy chirping an aid to identification.
Voice: Song a short simple twitter. Call a loud Sparrow-like chirp.
Distribution and Habitat: Frequents fallow land and cultivated clearings with scattered trees, and also orchard bush and rocky kopjes. Widely distributed and locally common in the savanna from Senegal, Gambia and Portuguese Guinea east to northern Cameroons and Chad.
Nesting: Nest in a hole in a tree. A pad of feathers, fur, grass and fibres. Eggs 3.

SCALY-FRONTED WEAVER *Sporopipes frontalis* **Pl. 47**
Identification: 4½″. Sexes similar. A small Sparrow-like bird with a characteristic hopping gait. Rufous nape a field mark. Forehead, forecrown and moustach-
ial streak bordering pale grey cheeks, black speckled with white; nape and collar
cinnamon-rufous; remainder upperparts pale brown. Underparts whitish.
Occurs in small flocks, usually on the ground picking up seeds.
Voice: A little trilling song uttered particularly when taking flight.
Distribution and Habitat: Fairly widespread but local in the arid savanna
from the desert edge to about 11° N. and from Mauritania and Senegal east to
Niger and Chad. Frequents the thickets and shrubs in the thorn scrub. Sometimes around villages.
Nesting: A Sparrow-like ball of grass lined with feathers placed a few feet
from the ground in a tree or shrub. Eggs 3–4, whitish, and so heavily clouded
and speckled with brown as to appear uni-coloured.

PIN-TAILED WHYDAH *Vidua macroura* **Pl. 47**
Identification: 5″, excluding the 7½″ long tail of the nuptial male. Male in
breeding dress unmistakable. Upperparts mainly glossy black; white patch on
nape and wings; face and underparts mainly white. Bill red. Very long ribbon-
like streamers black. Female and male in eclipse sparrowy, head and upperparts
striped sandy and blackish; wing and tail feathers blackish with light edges;
underparts whitish tinged buff on breast. No tail streamers. Bill pinkish. Male
in breeding season very conspicuous, singing and displaying over territory
with hovering flight. In off-season in large flocks on the ground in open places
with short grass, feeding on fallen seeds.
Voice: A little twittering song. Call 'tseet tseet'.
Distribution and Habitat: Common throughout the area except in the desert
and in closed forest. From southern Mauritania, Gambia and Senegal, east to
Chad and the Central African Republic and south to Gaboon and Congo. Also
in the Cameroons savanna up to 9,500 feet and on Fernando Po and Sao Tome.
Nesting: Parasitic. In other parts of Africa victimises Waxbill species. Eggs
pure white.

SENEGAL INDIGO FINCH *Vidua chalybeata*
(*Hypochera. c. chalybeata, H. c. neumanni*) **Pl. 47**
Identification: 4½″. Breeding male shining blue-black or shining deep blue
body plumage; black flight feathers. Bright orange feet. Pinkish-white bill.
Female and non-breeding male: crown with broad pale central streak bordered
dark brown; upperparts streaked dark and light brown; underparts buffish-
white. Feet orange. In breeding season male hovers over female in display flight.
Voice: Mimics the song of the Senegal Fire-Finch (*Lagonosticta senegala*).
Distribution and Habitat: The dry northern belt of the savanna in southern
Mauritania, Senegal, Gambia, Portuguese Guinea, Mali, northern Ghana,
Niger, northern Nigeria and Chad. Rather common, especially in villages and
on farmland.
Nesting: Parasitic, victimising the Senegal Fire-Finch (*Lagonosticta senegala*).
Eggs pure white.
Allied species: Three other species of Indigo Finch occur in the less arid parts
of the savanna. Breeding males are distinguished from *V. chalybeata* and from
each other only with difficulty and the sparrowy females and eclipse plumage

males cannot be specifically identified in the field. The male Cameroon Indigo Finch (*Vidua camerunensis*) (**Pl. 47**), 4½″, is distinguished by the dull blue gloss of the body plumage, brown flight feathers and light purplish feet. Frequents farmland with trees, orchard bush, road verges and the vicinity of villages, and is recorded from Portuguese Guinea, Sierra Leone, Ghana, Nigeria, Cameroons and the Central African Republic. The male mimics the song of the Black-faced Fire-Finch (*Estrilda larvata*). The Nigerian Indigo Finch (*Vidua funerea nigeriae*), 4½″, is distinguished in the breeding male by the bright green-glossed body plumage, brown flight feathers and whitish feet. Recorded from Portuguese Guinea, Sierra Leone, Ivory Coast, Ghana, Nigeria and the Cameroons. The male mimics the song of the Black-billed Fire-Finch (*Lagonosticta rubricata*). Wilson's Indigo Finch (*Vidua wilsoni*), 4½″, is distinguished in the breeding male by its glossy purplish body plumage, light brown flight feathers, and pinkish-white feet. Recorded from Senegal, Gambia, Portuguese Guinea, Ghana, Nigeria, Cameroons and the Central African Republic.

BROAD-TAILED PARADISE WHYDAH *Vidua orientalis*
(*Steganura orientalis*) **Pl. 47**

Identification: Male unmistakable, 5½″, excluding the long, broad nuptial tail feathers. Central rectrices up to 14″ long, varying geographically in length and breadth. Upperparts and throat black but nuchal collar tawny-rufous; chest chestnut; breast golden-rufous; belly cream. Female and male in eclipse sparrowy; on the crown a broad pale central stripe bordered with blackish. Bill black. Rather resembles the female Pin-tailed Whydah (*Vidua macroura*). Male has characteristic high undulating flight and often perches conspicuously on a tree top.

Voice: Call a sharp 'chip'.

Distribution and Habitat: Nowhere abundant yet widespread throughout the savanna north of the forest from the desert edge to the forest edge and from Senegal and Portuguese Guinea in the west to Chad and the Central African Republic in the east. Fond of the open grass savanna provided there are some high trees.

Nesting: Parasitic, in West Africa laying its eggs in the nest of *Pytilia melba* and also almost certainly in the nest of *Pytilia hypogrammica*. Egg white, immaculate.

ESTRILDINE WEAVERS: Estrildidae

A numerous family of small seed-eating birds which differ from the ploceid Weavers in the form of their nest which is not woven but is usually a domed structure of compacted grass tops. The nestlings have characteristic conspicuous dark markings on the palate and tongue arranged in a pattern.

SEED-CRACKER *Pirenestes ostrinus* (*P. sanguineus*) **Pl. 48**

Identification: 5½″. Massive bill and crimson head, neck, breast and upper tail-coverts identify it. Back and belly in the male black and in the female brown but in the races occurring west of Ghana both male and female have these parts

brown. Shy and elusive. Usually on or near the ground in pairs or small parties.
Voice: Song a short pleasing warble. Call note a sharp 'zeet'.

Distribution and Habitat: The forest and its gallery extensions in the savanna from Gambia and Portuguese Guinea east to the Central African Republic and south to Gaboon and Congo. Partial to swamps and the vicinity of forest streams and thickets in old forest clearings. Widely distributed yet nowhere abundant.

Nesting: Nest built near the ground in a shrub or tree. A large globular mass of grass or leaf strips lined with finer grasses. Eggs 3, white.

GREY-CROWNED NEGRO-FINCH *Nigrita canicapilla* **Pl. 48**
Identification: 6″. Forehead, face and entire underparts black; hind-crown, nape and mantle grey, a white streak separating the black forehead and face from the grey crown and nape; rump pale grey or whitish; wings and tail black, the upper surface of the wing conspicuously spotted with white in the race occurring from Nigeria eastwards. Sexes similar. Far-carrying song diagnostic. Arboreal. Usually solitary.

Voice: Song short, persistent, perennial, very distinctive consisting of half a dozen clear whistling notes and delivered from a favourite perch in a tree.

Distribution and Habitat: Common and widespread. The range is the lowland forest from Guinea and Sierra Leone to Gaboon and Congo. Also Fernando Po. Inhabits the trees of the clearings and second-growth but not of the primary forest. Often in the vicinity of oil-palms to whose fruit it is partial.

Nesting: Nests in a tree or shrub. A bulky domed structure of grass and leaves lined with fresh grass-heads. Eggs 5–7, white.

Allied species: The Pale-fronted Negro-Finch (*Nigrita luteifrons*) ranges in the forest belt from Ghana to Gaboon and Fernando Po. The male has black underparts and a light grey rump and somewhat resembles the Grey-crowned Negro-Finch but is considerably smaller (4½″) and has a golden-buff not a black forehead and lacks the white spots on the wing. Female similar but grey not black below. Song and call-note distinctive, the former a simple sweet phrase that descends the scale, the latter a faint musical whistling 'choo' repeated every few seconds. Singly or in pairs quietly searching the foliage in the forest and its clearings.

CHESTNUT-BREASTED NEGRO-FINCH *Nigrita bicolor* **Pl. 48**
Identification: 4½″. Plumage pattern distinctive. Forehead, face and entire underparts chestnut; crown and back slate. In the race occurring from southern Nigeria eastwards and on the island of Principe (*N. b. brunnescens*) the crown and back are earth-brown not slate. Female differs slightly in shade. Often solitary but sometimes joins the insect-hunting forest bird parties. Song distinctive.

Voice: A low, sweet, plaintive song of several modulated notes.

Distribution and Habitat: The forest, particularly the trees in its clearings and on its edges. Ranges from Senegal and Portuguese Guinea to Gaboon, Congo and Principe in the Gulf of Guinea. Widespread but nowhere abundant.

Nesting: Nest lined in the fork of a forest tree, globular with a side entrance, made of skeleton leaves, moss and grass stems, and lined with grass tops. Eggs 4, white.

WHITE-BREASTED NEGRO-FINCH *Nigrita fusconota* **Pl. 48**
Identification: 4″. Sexes similar. Plumage distinctive, the dark upperparts contrasting with the light underparts. Head, nape and tail blackish; back, rump and wings brown; entire underparts whitish. In the race occurring from Ghana westwards (*N. f. uropygialis*) the back and rump are noticeably paler in shade. Usually solitary. Draws attention to itself by distinctive song delivered from a tree-top perch or as it moves about the branches and foliage foraging for food.
Voice: Song a simple, sweet, stereotyped phrase, with only a brief pause after each delivery.
Distribution and Habitat: Range the forest from Guinea to Gaboon and Fernando Po. Frequents the trees of old clearings and the forest edges and stands of oil palms.
Nesting: Loose globular nest placed in the angle of the stub of a palm frond. Eggs 3–6, pure white.

BLUE-BILLED WEAVER *Spermophaga haematina* **Pl. 48**
Identification: 6″. Distinctively coloured. Male glossy black but throat, chest and flanks scarlet. Conspicuous heavy bill, pearly-blue in colour with a red tip. Female mainly slate-grey above but face and upper tail-coverts red mainly scarlet below but belly blackish marked with conspicuous large white spots. In the race occurring from Togo eastwards the upper tail-coverts are red in both sexes. Usually singly or in pairs, on or near the ground, skulking or quietly feeding.
Voice: A sweet desultory little song which first increases in pitch and becomes louder and then dies away. Call a metallic 'swink-swink-swink'.
Distribution and Habitat: From Gambia and Portuguese Guinea through the forest and its gallery extensions east to the Central African Republic and south to Gaboon and Congo. Widespread and locally common. Habitat includes second-growth thicket and the rank herbage and shrubbery of forest clearings and abandoned farmland. Often in swampy places.
Nesting: Large loose globular nest with side entrance built near the ground in a shrub. Eggs 3, white.

WHITE-CHEEKED OLIVE WEAVER *Nesocharis capistrata* **Pl. 48**
Identification: 5½″. Sexes similar. Olive-yellow upperparts, black chin and throat, and white cheeks the best field marks. Crown, nape, breast and belly grey. Mainly an insect-eater, rather Tit-like in action, occurring singly or in pairs and fond of exploring the foliage of trees and shrubs on the borders of woods.
Voice: The song consists of a few pleasant notes in descending pitch.
Distribution and Habitat: From Gambia and Portuguese Guinea to the Central African Republic in the savanna, especially in the outlying woods and riparian thickets of the moist belt just north of the forest. Local and nowhere abundant.
Nesting: A nest in Uganda was typically estrildine, ball-shaped with rather a long spout, made of grass stems, and lodged in the fork of a young Acacia. Eggs 4, plain matt white.

CUT-THROAT WEAVER   *Amadina fasciata*   **Pl. 48**

Identification: 4½″. Male readily identified by crimson band across throat and sandy-brown upperparts barred with black. Underparts below throat fawn lightly barred and with a chestnut patch on belly. Female paler, less prominently barred, and lacks crimson throat and chestnut belly. Tail in both sexes white-tipped. Strong stumpy bill. Gregarious in off-season. Feeds on the ground on fallen seeds.

Voice: Sparrow-like chirps.

Distribution and Habitat: Widespread yet local in the savanna, mainly in the northern arid parts. Found in cultivated land near villages and in open thorn scrub. Occurs in southern Mauritania, Senegal, Gambia, Mali, Ivory Coast, northern Ghana, northern Nigeria, Niger and Chad.

Nesting: Nests in a hole in a building, or utilises an old Weaver's nest, or builds a ball-shaped nest of grass and feathers in a tree or bush. Eggs 5, pure white.

MELBA FINCH   *Pytilia melba*   **Pl. 48**

Identification: 5″. Vividly coloured contrasting plumage. Male has scarlet face and throat, grey crown and neck, yellowish-olive back and wings, red tail, yellow chest, and brown and white barred lower breast and belly. The female lacks the scarlet on the face and throat and the yellow on the chest. Usually out of sight on the ground in thick scrub searching for fallen seeds. Shy.

Voice: A sweet subdued song and a monosyllabic call.

Distribution and Habitat: A local and generally an uncommon savanna species yet frequent in Senegal and Chad. Mainly in the dry semi-arid belt where it frequents the denser thickets in the thorn scrub. Recorded from southern Mauritania, Senegal, Gambia, Portuguese Guinea, Mali, Upper Volta, Niger, Nigeria, Chad and Congo.

Nesting: Low down in a shrub in a thicket. A globular nest with a side entrance. Made of grass lined with grass tops. Eggs 3–4, pure white.

Allied species: The Red-winged Pytilia (*Pytilia phoenicoptera*), 5″, is grey with crimson rump and tail, and also much crimson on the wing. Female resembles male but is browner and the underparts are barred buffish-brown and whitish. A savanna species that is widespread but nowhere abundant and is rare in or absent from the arid north. Occurs in Gambia, southern Senegal, Portuguese Guinea, Mali, Ivory Coast, Ghana, Nigeria, Cameroons and Chad. Usually in pairs. Often perches in trees. Frequents open orchard bush and the herbage of old farm patches.

ORANGE-CHEEKED WAXBILL   *Estrilda melpoda*   **Pl. 48**

Identification: 4″. Sexes similar. Orange cheeks and red rump are field marks. Crown grey, cheeks orange, back earth-brown, rump crimson, tail blackish, underparts pale grey, the belly washed yellow. Bill orange-red. When not breeding usually in flocks. Feeds on grass seeds. Mainly terrestrial.

Voice: Song a shrill 'zee-wheezee-whee'. Call a high-pitched squeak.

Distribution and Habitat: Abundant and widespread throughout the area in the savanna and in the grassy clearings in the forest.

Nesting: Well-concealed on the ground in herbage. Pear-shaped with a short tubular opening in one side. Made of grass stems and grass tops. Eggs 5–6, white.

BLACK-CROWNED WAXBILL *Estrilda nonnula* **Pl. 48**
Identification: 4½″. Sexes in the field virtually indistinguishable. The black cap sharply demarcated from the white cheeks and throat, the closely barred black and grey back, the red rump, and the black tail are the field marks of this Waxbill. The underparts are whitish and the bill red and black. In pairs at the breeding season. At other times in small compact flocks feeding on fallen seeds in open grassy places. Tame. Sociable.
Voice: A rather faint concerted twittering.
Distribution and Habitat: Fernando Po, the Cameroons and the Central African Republic. In the Cameroons where it is abundant and widespread its varied habitat includes grassy forest clearings, gardens, the foliage of forest edges, farm and grassland in the savanna, and grass and bracken mountain slopes.
Nesting: The typical Waxbill nest is made of *Panicum* grasstops and is placed in tree, shrub or hedge, or on the ground in a tuft of grass. Sometimes a super-imposed 'cock-nest'. Eggs 5–6, pure white.
Allied species: The Black-headed Waxbill (*Estrilda atricapilla*) closely resembles the Black-crowned Waxbill but has predominantly grey not white underparts. When, as is common, the Waxbills are feeding on the ground and the underparts are obscured or in shade, this is an uncertain field mark. In the Black-headed Waxbill the upper mandible is black and the red patch on the lower mandible much reduced. Also the red patch on the flanks is more con-spicuous than that of the Black-crowned Waxbill. The habits of the two species are similar and often they consort in close flocks. The Black-headed Waxbill frequents the grassy clearings in the forest belt of lowland Cameroons, Gaboon, and Congo and is locally abundant.

BLACK-RUMPED WAXBILL *Estrilda troglodytes* **Pl. 48**
Identification: 4″. Sexes similar. Upperparts grey-brown but rump black and tail blackish. A conspicuous broad crimson stripe through eye. Underparts mainly grey washed with pink. Bill dark red. Gregarious. Has the habit of agitating the tail rhythmically from side to side.
Voice: A characteristic drawn-out 'tsooeet' frequently uttered.
Distribution and Habitat: Irregularly distributed in the savanna, especially in the arid northern zone. Common locally. Frequents the edges of woods and the borders of thickets in cultivated areas. Occurs in Senegal, Gambia, Guinea, Mali, Upper Volta, Ghana, Niger, Nigeria, Chad and the Central African Republic.
Nesting: On the ground at the base of a small bush or grass tuft. Pear-shaped with a lateral entrance. Made of dry grass tops. Eggs 5–6, white.

COMMON WAXBILL *Estrilda astrild* **Pl. 48**
Identification: 4½″. Sexes virtually alike. A tiny Waxbill with closely gregarious habits in the non-breeding season. In flight the relatively long tail distinguishes it from allied species. Red bill and red stripe through the eye good field marks. Upperparts grey-brown with fine dark barring; underparts whitish washed with rosy-pink and lightly barred with brown, especially on the flanks. Tail blackish. Feeds in compact flocks on the ground on fallen grass seeds or on low-growing seeding grasses. Lively, restless and tame.
Voice: A concerted twittering.
Distribution and Habitat: Widespread but local. Where it occurs often

Plate 47

WEAVERS AND SPARROWS

48

Plate 48

ESTRILDINE WEAVERS

abundant. Ranges in the forest and the adjoining savanna zone from Sierra Leone to Gaboon, Congo and Fernando Po. Common in the Cameroons highlands grasslands. Also Cape Verde Islands, Sao Tome and Principe, where probably introduced. A species of grassy clearings, especially in damp localities where the vegetation is rank.

Nesting: A pear-shaped nest of *Panicum* grass tops with a tubular entrance. Nest near the ground in high grass. Eggs 4–5, white.

LAVENDER FIRE-FINCH   *Estrilda caerulescens*   Pl. 48
Identification: 4″. Sexes similar. Totally grey except for crimson rump, tail and under tail-coverts. Bill reddish-brown tipped black. Tame. Occurs in small parties, sometimes with other Waxbills. Feeds on fallen grass seeds and also searches shrubs for insects.

Distribution and Habitat: Frequents the edges of thickets, grass verges of roads, and open places where the grass is short. Widely, unevenly and rather sparsely distributed in the savanna, especially in its arid parts from Senegal, Gambia and Portuguese Guinea east to southern Chad and the Central African Republic.

Nesting and Voice: Unknown.

RED-CHEEKED CORDON-BLEU   *Estrilda bengala*
(*Uraeginthus bengalus*)   Pl. 48
Identification: 5″. Unmistakable. Pale brown crown, mantle and wings; turquoise-blue rump, tail and underparts except for pale brown belly. A large vivid crimson patch on the blue cheek. Female paler and lacks crimson cheek-patch. Tail relatively long, graduated and tapered. Usually on the ground picking up seeds. Occurs in parties and associates with other Estrildine Weavers.

Voice: Little sharp cries.

Distribution and Habitat: An abundant savanna species, widespread, especially in the drier zones and ranging from southern Mauritania, Senegal, Gambia and Portuguese Guinea east to Chad and the Central African Republic. Fond of villages and farmland but also frequents orchard bush and open woodland.

Nesting: In a bush or tree. A spherical domed nest of grass tops often enclosed in a layer of rootlets and lined inside with feathers. May appropriate a Ploceine Weaver's nest. Frequently near a wasp's nest. Sometimes colonial. Eggs 4–5, white.

BLACK-FACED FIRE-FINCH   *Estrilda larvata*
(*Lagonosticta nigricollis, L. vinacea*)   Pl. 48
Identification: 4″. The male's mask formed by the black cheeks and throat is a field mark. Upperparts grey but rump and tail dull crimson. Underparts grey, with white dots on the sides of the breast. Female has dull brown upperparts and buffish underparts, lacks the black mask but has the crimson tail. A very distinct race, *E. larvata vinacea*, formerly considered a species, occupies Senegal, Gambia and Portuguese Guinea. In this form the mantle, wings and underparts of the male and the underparts of the female are strongly washed with pink.

Voice: Distinctive. A series of two clear whistled notes sung together, the first one low and slurred down and the second high and slurred up.

Distribution and Habitat: A savanna species. Widespread but local and nowhere abundant, frequenting the edges of thickets and woods and abandoned farm patches choked with herbage. Recorded from Senegal, Gambia, Portuguese Guinea, Ivory Coast, Mali, Ghana, Nigeria, Chad and the Central African Republic.

Nesting: Near the ground in a small bush or pile of brushwood. A round nest of grass with a side opening and lined with grass tops and a few feathers. Eggs 3–4, white.

SENEGAL FIRE-FINCH *Lagonosticta senegala* Pl. 48

Identification: 4″. Male mainly red. Head, rump, throat and breast crimson. Female brown above, pale brown below with a crimson spot in front of the eye and crimson upper tail-coverts. Bill red with blackish culmen. Unusually tame and fond of human habitations.

Voice: A simple sweet short song without trills.

Distribution and Habitat: Abundant and widespread in the drier parts of the savanna mainly in towns and villages and less commonly in farmland and in thickets by streams. Ranges from Mauritania, Senegal, Gambia and Portuguese Guinea east to Chad and the Central African Republic.

Nesting: Usually in dwellings and especially in the grass walls and roofs of African huts. Sometimes in a hole in the ground or a bush. Loosely constructed of grass or rootlets and liberally lined with feathers. Eggs 3–5, white.

Allied species: The Bar-breasted Fire-Finch (*Lagonosticta rufopicta*), 4″, sexes similar, rather resembles the male Senegal Fire-Finch with rose-pink replacing the crimson. Crown, back and wings grey-brown; face, upper tail-coverts, outer webs of tail feathers, throat and breast rose-pink; belly pinkish-grey; under tail-coverts cream. Bill red, ridge of culmen black. Ranges in the savanna mainly between 5° N. and 14° N. in Senegal, Gambia, Portuguese Guinea, Sierra Leone, Ivory Coast, Ghana, Nigeria, Cameroons and the Central African Republic. The Blue-billed Fire-Finch (*Lagonosticta rubricata*), 4″, has a grey crown, brown back, crimson upper tail-coverts and blackish tail. The face and underparts are crimson and the under tail-coverts black. The female is paler, especially on the underparts, which are rose-pink not crimson. Bluish bill an aid to identification. A savanna species with a wide habitat range. Found from Portuguese Guinea, Guinea and Sierra Leone east to the Central African Republic and south to Gaboon and Congo.

ZEBRA WAXBILL *Amandava subflava (Estrilda subflava)* Pl. 48

Identification: 3½″. The smallest Waxbill. Vivid orange-scarlet splash on the underparts of the male, seen especially in flight, is diagnostic. Upperparts brown except for crimson rump. Eye-stripe and bill red. Underparts orange-scarlet but flanks barred brownish and yellow. Female lacks red eye-stripe and is mainly pale yellow below. Outside breeding season usually in flocks in rank grass near or growing in water.

Voice: In flight a characteristic concerted metallic twittering. Also a thin squeaky call.

Distribution and Habitat: Widespread but local in the savanna from Senegal, Gambia and Portuguese Guinea east to the Cameroon highlands, Chad and the Central African Republic, and south to Gaboon and Congo. Mainly in tall vegetation in swamps, rice fields and the margins of water-courses. Not a village Waxbill.

Nesting: A pear-shaped nest with opening at top. Made of bundles of grass tops and lined with feathers and placed inside an old Weaver's nest attached to tall grass stems. Eggs 4–5, white.

QUAIL-FINCH   *Ortygospiza atricollis*   **Pl. 48**

Identification: 4″. A tiny, plump, brown Waxbill fond of swampy ground. When flushed rises vertically almost from beneath one's feet and makes off with soaring, swift and erratic flight, uttering a few squeaky cries. Male has earth-brown or dark grey upperparts, a black mask, large chestnut breast-patch, and white-barred flanks and chest. Female is paler and lacks black mask. Terrestrial. Usually in small parties. Feeds on grass seeds.

Voice: A few squeaky vibrant notes uttered in flight. Characteristic.

Distribution and Habitat: Widely but locally distributed in the savanna from Senegal, Gambia and Portuguese Guinea east to Chad and south to Gaboon and Congo. Mainly in short grassy tussocky waterlogged plains.

Nesting: A well-concealed domed nest in the lee of a tussock of grass or cultivation furrow. Made of grasses and lined with feathers. Eggs 2–5, white.

WARBLING SILVERBILL   *Lonchura malabarica*
(*Euodice cantans*)   **Pl. 48**

Identification: 5″. Sexes similar. In flight blackish pointed tail contrasts with pale body plumage. Settled the large blunt bluish bill is a feature. Upperparts grey-brown, wings darker; crown scale-like dark brown and sandy. Underparts mainly cream. Tame. Gregarious. Given to soft sustained warbling.

Voice: Soft twittering warble. Little sharp cries in flight.

Distribution and Habitat: Widespread but local and mainly in the arid northern savanna right to the desert edge in Mauritania, Senegal, Gambia, Mali, Upper Volta, Ghana, Niger, Nigeria, Cameroons and Chad.

Nesting: Either a ball-shaped nest in a thorn tree or else tucked into a hole in a roof or else inside an old Ploceine Weaver's nest. Made of grass and twigs lined with feathers. Eggs 4–6, white.

BRONZE MANNIKIN   *Lonchura cucullata* (*Spermestes cucullatus*)
                                                                       Pl. 48

Identification: 4½″. Sexes similar. At a distance black above and white below. At close range head and throat blackish, back grey-brown, rump barred brown and white, tail black. Underparts below throat white, the flanks barred brownish. Bill black. A common, tame, closely gregarious Mannikin that feeds on grass seeds, stripping them from the growing grass heads or picking them off the ground.

Voice: Soft, concerted chirping or twittering when feeding or in flight.

Distribution and Habitat: Widespread and abundant throughout our area including the islands of the Gulf of Guinea. In the savanna and the forest clearings but absent from closed forest and the arid northern savanna. Fond of gardens and cultivated and waste land near towns and villages.

Nesting: Often colonial. In trees, especially citrus trees, or under house eaves. A globular nest of grass tops with a lateral opening. Eggs 3–6, white.

Allied species: The Magpie Mannikin (*Lonchura fringilloides*), 5″, sexes similar, rather resembles the Bronze Mannikin but is considerably larger. Head, neck and throat glossy black, sharply defined from the white underparts. A conspicuous black patch on each side of breast. Back and rump uniform brown. Tail black. In habits rather like the Bronze Mannikin. Fond of rice fields. Locally common in Sierra Leone and the Cameroons but elsewhere in the savanna and forest clearings only patchily distributed from Senegal to the Cameroons. The Black-and-White Mannikin (*Lonchura bicolor*), $4\frac{1}{2}''$, is a common inhabitant of the rain forest clearings and edges where there is herbage or new secondary growth, ranging from Portuguese Guinea to the Central African Republic, Gaboon, Congo and Fernando Po. Usually in compact flocks by itself or with other Estrildine or Ploceine Weavers. Glossy black except for lower breast, belly and under tail-coverts, which are white. At close range the heavy light-blue bill and barred flanks are field characters.

CHECKLIST OF SPECIES

An asterisk indicates that the species so marked is not dealt with in the body of the text.

STRUTHIONIDAE

Struthio camelus   Linnaeus

PODICIPEDIDAE

Podiceps ruficollis   (Pallas) (Bann. *Poliocephalus ruficollis* (Pallas))
Podiceps cristatus   (Linnaeus)   Rare. Breeds Gaboon.

PROCELLARIIDAE

Daption capensis   Linnaeus   Off coast of Gaboon. Rare.
Procellaria diomedea   Scopoli   (Bann. *Calonectris kuhli* (Boie))   Breeds Cape Verde Islands.
Procellaria gravis   (O'Reilly)   (Bann. *Ardenna gravis*(O'Reilly))   West African seas.
Procellaria grisea   Gmelin   (Bann. *Neonectris griseus* (Gmelin))   West African seas.
Procellaria assimilis boydi   (Mathews)   (Bann. *Puffinus lherminieri* Lesson) Breeds Cape Verde Islands.
Bulweria mollis feae   (Salvadori)   (Bann. *Pterodroma mollis feae* (Salvadori)) Breeds Cape Verde Islands.
Bulweria bulwerii   (Jardine and Selby)   West African seas and breeds Cape Verde Islands.
Oceanites oceanicus   (Kuhl)   Non-breeding visitor from Antarctic to Cape Verde Islands and West African seas.
Oceanites marinus eadesi   (Bourne)   (Bann. *Pelagodroma marina eadesi* Bourne) Breeds Cape Verde Islands.
Fregetta tropica   (Gould)   West African seas.
Hydrobates pelagicus   (Linnaeus)   West African seas.
Hydrobates castro   (Harcourt)   (Bann. *Cymochorea castro* (Harcourt))   Cape Verde Islands (breeding) and Sao Tome.
Hydrobates leucorhoa   (Vieillot) (Bann. *Cymochorea leucorhoa* (Vieillot)) Winter visitor Cape Verde Islands and West African seas.

PHAETHONTIDAE

Phaethon aethereus   Linnaeus   West African seas and breeds Cape Verde Islands and Senegal.
Phaethon lepturus   Daudin   Breeds Gulf of Guinea Islands.

PELECANIDAE

Pelecanus onocrotalus   Linnaeus
Pelecanus rufescens   Gmelin

SULIDAE

* *Sula bassana* (Linnaeus) (Bann. *Morus bassanus* (Linnaeus) and *Morus capensis* (Licht.))   Migrant to West African seas.
* *Sula leucogaster* (Boddaert)   West African seas. Breeds Cape Verde Islands and Gulf of Guinea Islands.

PHALACROCORACIDAE

Phalacrocorax carbo   (Linnaeus) (Bann. *Phalacrocorax lucidus* (Licht.))
* *Phalacrocorax capensis* (Sparrman)   Congo sea-board.
Phalacrocorax africanus   (Gmelin)
Anhinga rufa (Daudin)

FREGATIDAE

* *Fregata magnificens*   Mathews   Cape Verde Islands and Gambian seas.

ARDEIDAE

* *Botaurus stellaris* (Linnaeus)   Rare winter visitor.
Ixobrychus minutus   (Linnaeus)
Ixobrychus sturmii   (Wagler) (Bann. *Ardeirallus sturmii* (Wagler))
Tigriornis leucolopha   (Jardine)
Nycticorax nycticorax   (Linnaeus)
Nycticorax leuconotus   (Wagler)
Ardeola ralloides   (Scopoli)
Ardeola ibis   (Linnaeus) (Bann. *Bubulcus ibis* (Linnaeus))
Butorides striatus   (Linnaeus)
Egretta ardesiaca   (Wagler) (Bann. *Melanophoyx ardesiaca* (Wagler))
Egretta alba   (Linnaeus) (Bann. *Casmerodius albus* (Linnaeus))
Egretta intermedia   (Wagler) (Bann. *Mesophoyx intermedius* (Wagler))
Egretta garzetta   (Linnaeus)
Egretta gularis   (Bosc.) (Bann. *Demigretta gularis* (Bosc.))
Ardea cinerea   Linnaeus
Ardea melanocephala   Vigors and Children
Ardea goliath   Cretzschmar (Bann. *Typhon goliath* (Cretzschmar))
Ardea purpurea   Linnaeus (Bann. *Pyrrherodia purpurea* (Linnaeus))

BALAENICIPITIDAE

* *Balaeniceps rex*   Gould   Scarce resident Central African Republic and Cameroons.

SCOPIDAE

Scopus umbretta   Gmelin

CICONIIDAE

Ciconia ciconia   (Linnaeus)
*Ciconia nigra   (Linnaeus)   Uncommon winter visitor from Palaearctic.
Ciconia abdimii   Licht.   (Bann. *Sphenorynchus abdimii* (Licht.))
Ciconia episcopus   (Boddaert)   (Bann. *Dissoura episcopus* (Boddaert))
Ephippiorhynchus senegalensis   (Shaw)
Anastomus lamelligerus   Temminck
Leptoptilos crumeniferus   (Lesson)
Ibis ibis   (Linnaeus)

THRESKIORNITHIDAE

Threskiornis aethiopica   (Latham)
**Geronticus eremitus*   (Linnaeus)   Rare visitor Cape Verde Islands and southern
   Mauritania.
Bostrychia hagedash   (Latham)   (Bann. *Hagedashia hagedash* (Latham))
Bostrychia rara   (Rothschild)   (Bann. *Lampribis rara* Rothschild)
Bostrychia olivacea   Dubus   (Bann. *Lampribis olivacea* (Dubus))
Plegadis falcinellus   (Linnaeus)
Platalea alba   Scopoli
**Platalea leucorodia*   Linnaeus   Cape Verde Islands, Mauritania (breeding),
   Senegal, Gambia, Nigeria and Chad.

PHOENICOPTERIDAE

Phoenicopterus ruber   Linnaeus
Phoenicopterus minor   Geoffroy   (Bann. *Phoeniconais minor* (Geoffroy))

ANATIDAE

Dendrocygna bicolor   (Vieillot)   (Bann. *Dendrocygna fulva* (Gmelin))
Dendrocygna viduata   (Linnaeus)
Alopochen aegyptiaca   (Linnaeus)
Plectropterus gambensis   (Linnaeus)
Pteronetta hartlaubii   (Cassin)
Sarkidiornis melanota   (Pennant)
Nettapus auritus   (Boddaert)
Anas sparsa   Eyton
*Anas penelope   Linnaeus   Winter visitor. Uncommon except in Chad.
*Anas strepera   Linnaeus   Uncommon winter visitor.
Anas crecca   Linnaeus
*Anas capensis   Gmelin   Uncommon and local.
*Anas undulata   Dubois   Western Cameroons. Rare.
**Anas platyrhynchos*   Linnaeus   Uncommon winter visitor.

Anas acuta   Linnaeus   (Bann. *Dafila acuta* (Linnaeus))
Anas hottentota   Eyton   (Bann. *Anas punctata* Burchell)
Anas angustirostris   Ménétries   Rare.
Anas querquedula   Linnaeus
Anas clypeata   Linnaeus   (Bann. *Spatula clypeata* (Linnaeus))
Aythya ferina   (Linnaeus)   (Bann. *Nyroca ferina* (Linnaeus))   Winter visitor.
  Uncommon except in Chad.
Aythya nyroca   (Guldenstadt)   (Bann. *Nyroca nyroca* (Guldenstadt))
Aythya fuligula   (Linnaeus)   (Bann. *Nyroca fuligula* (Linnaeus))   Winter
  visitor.
Thalassornis leuconotus   Eyton

ACCIPITRIDAE

Aegypius tracheliotus   (Forster)   (Bann. *Torgos tracheliotus* (Forster))
Trigonoceps occipitalis   (Burchell)
Gyps fulvus   (Hablizl)   Uncommon visitor from Palaearctic.
Gyps rüppellii   (Brehm)
Gyps bengalensis   (Gmelin)   (Bann. *Pseudogyps africanus* (Salvadori))
Neophron percnopterus   (Linnaeus)
Neophron monachus   (Temminck)   (Bann. *Necrosyrtes monachus* (Temminck))
Gypohierax angolensis   (Gmelin)
Circus macrourus   (Gmelin)
Circus pygargus   (Linnaeus)
Circus aeruginosus   (Linnaeus)
Polyboroides radiatus   (Scopoli)   (Bann. *Gymnogenys typicus* (Sharpe))
Terathopius ecaudatus   (Daudin)
Circaetus gallicus   (Gmelin)
Circaetus beaudouini   Verreaux and Des Murs
Circaetus pectoralis   Smith   Congo.
Circaetus cinereus   Vieillot
Circaetus cinerascens   Müller
Dryotriorchis spectabilis   (Schlegel)
Accipiter melanoleucus   Smith
Accipiter toussenelii   (Verreaux)
Accipiter castanilius   Bonaparte
Accipiter badius   (Gmelin)
Accipiter nisus   (Linnaeus)   Uncommon winter visitor from Palaearctic.
Accipiter erythropus   (Hartlaub)   (Bann. *Accipiter minullus* (Daudin))
Accipiter ovampensis   Gurney
Melierax metabates   Heuglin
Melierax gabar   (Daudin)   (Bann. *Micronisus gabar* (Daudin))
Urotriorchis macrourus   (Hartlaub)
Kaupifalco monogrammicus   (Temminck)
Butastur rufipennis   (Sundevall)
Buteo rufinus   (Cretzschmar)   Uncommon Palaearctic winter migrant.
Buteo auguralis   Salvadori
Buteo buteo   (Linnaeus)   Breeds Cape Verde Islands. Also rare Palaearctic
  migrant (race *B. b. vulpinus*) to West African mainland.
Lophaetus occipitalis   (Daudin)

Stephanoaetus coronatus (Linnaeus)
Polemaetus bellicosus (Daudin)
Hieraaetus africanus (Cassin) (Bann. *Cassinaetus africanus* (Cassin))
Hieraaetus spilogaster Bonaparte (Bann. *Hieraaetus fasciatus* (Vieillot))
Hieraaetus pennatus (Gmelin) Rare Palaearctic migrant.
Hieraaetus dubius (Smith) (Bann. *Hieraetus ayresi* (Gurney))
Aquila rapax Temminck
Aquila clanga Pallas Uncommon Palaearctic migrant.
Aquila verreauxii Lesson Chad. Local.
Aquila wahlbergi Sundevall
Haliaetus vocifer (Daudin) (Bann. *Cuncuma vocifer* (Daudin))
Milvus migrans (Boddaert)
Pernis apivorus (Linnaeus)
Aviceda cuculoides Swainson
Elanus caeruleus (Desfontaines)
Elanus riocourii (Vieillot) (Bann. *Chelictinia riocourii* (Vieillot))
Macheirhamphus alcinus Westerman
Pandion haliaetus (Linnaeus)

FALCONIDAE

Falco biarmicus Temminck
Falco cherrug Gray Palaearctic migrant.
Falco peregrinus Tunstall
Falco cuvieri Smith
Falco subbuteo Linnaeus Uncommon Palaearctic migrant.
Falco concolor Temminck Rare. Northern Chad.
Falco chicquera Daudin
Falco ardosiaceus Bonnaterre and Vieillot
Falco vespertinus Linnaeus Palaearctic migrant.
Falco naumanni Fleischer
Falco tinnunculus Linnaeus
Falco alopex (Heuglin)

SAGITTARIIDAE

Sagittarius serpentarius (Miller)

PHASIANIDAE

Francolinus lathami Hartlaub
Francolinus albogularis Hartlaub
Francolinus schlegelii Heuglin Chad, Central African Republic and eastern
Cameroons. Local.
Francolinus coqui (Smith)
Francolinus streptophorus Ogilvie-Grant Cameroons. Rare.
Francolinus finschi Bocage Congo. Local.
Francolinus bicalcaratus (Linnaeus)
Francolinus icterorhynchus Heuglin Central African Republic.
Francolinus clappertoni Children

Francolinus afer (Müller)   Gaboon and Congo.
Francolinus camerunensis Alexander   Cameroon Mountain.
Francolinus ahantensis Temminck
Francolinus squamatus Cassin
Coturnix coturnix (Linnaeus)
Coturnix delegorguei Delegorgue
Coturnix chinensis (Linnaeus)   (Bann. *Excalfactoria adansoni* (Verreaux))
Ptilopachus petrosus (Gmelin)
Agelastes meleagrides Bonaparte
Agelastes niger (Cassin)   (Bann. *Phasidus niger* (Cassin))
Numida meleagris (Linnaeus)
Guttera edouardi (Hartlaub)
Guttera plumifera (Cassin)

RALLIDAE

Rallus caerulescens Gmelin   Sierra Leone and Sao Tome.
Canirallus oculeus (Hartlaub)
Crex crex (Linnaeus)
Crex egregia (Peters)   (Bann. *Crecopsis egregia* (Peters))
Porzana parva (Scopoli)   Palaearctic migrant to Senegal.
Porzana pusilla (Hermann)   Palaearctic migrant to Senegal.
Porzana porzana (Linnaeus)   Uncommon Palaearctic migrant.
Porzana marginalis Hartlaub
Limnocorax flavirostra (Swainson)
Sarothrura rufa (Vieillot)
Sarothrura lugens (Böhm)   Cameroons. Rare.
Sarothrura bohmi (Reichenow)   Guinea and Cameroons. Rare.
Sarothrura elegans (Smith)
Sarothrura pulchra (Gray)
Himantornis haematopus Hartlaub
Gallinula angulata Sundevall
Gallinula chloropus (Linnaeus)
Porphyrio porphyrio (Linnaeus)   (Bann. *Porphyrio madagascariensis* (Latham))
Porphyrio alleni Thomson   (Bann. *Porphyrula alleni* (Thomson))
Fulica atra Linnaeus

HELIORNITHIDAE

Podica senegalensis (Vieillot)

GRUIDAE

Grus carunculatus (Gmelin)   Portuguese Guinea.
Anthropoides virgo (Linnaeus)   Palaearctic migrant to Chad and northern Nigeria.
Balearica pavonina Linnaeus

OTIDIDAE

Otis arabs Linnaeus   (Bann. *Ardeotis arabs* (Linnaeus))
Neotis denhami (Children)

Neotis nuba (Cretzschmar)
Eupodotis ruficrista Smith (Bann. *Lophotis savilei* Lynes)
Eupodotis senegalensis (Vieillot)
Eupodotis melanogaster (Rüppell) (Bann. *Lissotis melanogaster* (Rüppell))

JACANIDAE

Actophilornis africana (Gmelin)
Microparra capensis (Smith)

BURHINIDAE

*Burhinis oedicnemus (Linnaeus) (Bann. *Oedicnemus oedicnemus* (Linnaeus))
    Palaearctic migrant to Mali and Senegal.
Burhinus senegalensis (Swainson) (Bann. *Oedicnemus senegalensis* Swainson)
Burhinus capensis (Lichtenstein) (Bann. *Oedicnemus capensis* Lichtenstein)
Burhinus vermiculatus (Cabanis) (Bann. *Oedicnemus vermiculatus* Cabanis)

HAEMATOPODIDAE

Haematopus ostralegus Linnaeus

CHARADRIIDAE

*Vanellus vanellus Linnaeus Vagrant to Senegal.
Vanellus crassirostris (Hartlaub) (Bann. *Hemiparra crassirostris* (Hartlaub))
Vanellus spinosus (Linnaeus) (Bann. *Hoplopterus spinosus* (Linnaeus))
Vanellus tectus (Boddaert) (Bann. *Sarciophorus tectus* (Boddaert))
Vanellus albiceps Gould (Bann. *Xiphidiopterus albiceps* (Gould))
Vanellus lugubris (Lesson) (Bann. *Stephanibyx lugubris* (Lesson))
Vanellus senegallus (Linnaeus) (Bann. *Afribyx senegallus* (Linnaeus))
Vanellus superciliosus (Reichenow) (Bann. *Anomalophrys superciliosus* (Reich.))
*Vanellus leucurus (Lichtenstein) Vagrant to Nigeria and Chad.
*Pluvialis apricarius (Linnaeus) Rare Palaearctic migrant.
*Pluvialis dominica (Müller) Rare arctic visitor.
Pluvialis squatarola (Linnaeus) (Bann. *Squatarola squatarola* (Linnaeus))
Charadrius hiaticula Linnaeus
Charadrius dubius Scopoli
Charadrius pecuarius Temminck (Bann. *Leucopolius pecuarius* (Temminck))
*Charadrius tricollaris Vieillot (Bann. *Afroxyechus tricollaris* (Vieillot))
    Chad, Cameroons, Nigeria and Ghana. Uncommon.
Charadrius forbesi (Shelley) (Bann. *Afroxyechus forbesi* (Shelley))
Charadrius alexandrinus Linnaeus (Bann. *Leucopolius alexandrinus* (Linnaeus))
Charadrius marginatus (Vieillot) (Bann. *Leucopolius marginatus* (Vieillot))
*Charadrius leschenaulti Lesson Palaearctic migrant to Nigeria. Rare.
*Charadrius asiaticus Pallas (Bann. *Eupoda asiatica* (Pallas)) Palaearctic
    migrant to Cameroons and Nigeria.

Numenius phaeopus (Linnaeus)
Numenius arquata (Linnaeus)
Limosa limosa (Linnaeus)
Limosa lapponica (Linnaeus)
Tringa nebularia (Gunnerus) (Bann. *Glottis nebularius* (Gunnerus))
Tringa stagnatilis (Bechstein) (Bann. *Glottis stagnatilis* (Bechstein))
*Tringa flavipes (Gmelin) Rare Nearctic migrant.
Tringa glareola Linnaeus
Tringa ochropus Linnaeus
Tringa hypoleucos Linnaeus (Bann. *Actitis hypoleucos* (Linnaeus))
Tringa totanus (Linnaeus)
Tringa erythropus (Pallas)
*Tringa terek (Latham) (Bann. *Xenus cinereus* (Güldenstädt)) Uncommon
  Palaearctic migrant.
Arenaria interpres (Linnaeus)
Gallinago media (Latham) (Bann. *Capella media* (Latham))
Gallinago gallinago (Linnaeus) (Bann. *Capella gallinago* (Linnaeus))
Gallinago minima (Brünnich) (Bann. *Lymnocryptes minima* (Brünnich))
Calidris canutus (Linnaeus)
Calidris alpina (Linnaeus) (Bann. *Erolia alpina* Linnaeus)
Calidris ferruginea (Pontoppidan) (Bann. *Erolia testacea* (Pallas))
*Calidris melanotos (Vieillot) Rare Nearctic vagrant.
Calidris minuta (Leisler) (Bann. *Erolia minuta* (Leisler))
Calidris temminckii (Leisler) (Bann. *Erolia temminckii* (Leisler))
Calidris alba (Pallas) (Bann. *Crocethia alba* (Pallas))
*Limicola falcinellus (Pontoppidan) Rare Palaearctic migrant.
Philomachus pugnax (Linnaeus)
*Phalaropus fulicarius (Linnaeus) Palaearctic migrant. West African seas
  mainly in area of Guinea Current.
Himantopus himantopus (Linnaeus)
Recurvirostra avosetta Linnaeus Palaearctic migrant. Local.
Rostratula benghalensis (Linnaeus)

GLAREOLIDAE

Pluvianus aegyptius (Linnaeus)
Cursorius cursor (Latham)
Cursorius temminckii Swainson
Cursorius chalcopterus Temminck (Bann. *Rhinoptilus chalcopterus* (Temminck))
Glareola pratincola (Linnaeus)
*Glareola nordmanni Fischer Palaearctic migrant. Local.
Glareola nuchalis Gray (Bann. *Galachrysia nuchalis* (Gray))
Glareola cinerea Fraser (Bann. *Galachrysia cinerea* (Fraser))

LARIDAE

*Stercorarius skua (Brünnich) West African seaboard. Uncommon.
*Stercorarius pomarinus (Temminck) West African seas.

Stercorarius parasiticus (Linnaeus) West African seas.

Stercorarius longicaudus Vieillot West African seas. Uncommon.

Larus tridactylus (Linnaeus) (Bann. *Rissa tridactyla* (Linnaeus)) Uncommon Palaearctic migrant to Cape Verde Islands and seaboard of Senegal and Gambia.

Larus melanocephalus Temminck Vagrant to Senegal.

Larus minutus Pallas Rare Palaearctic migrant.

Larus ridibundus Linnaeus

Larus genei Brème

Larus cirrhocephalus Vieillot

Larus sabini Sabine Arctic migrant to West African seas.

Larus audouinii Payrandeau Palaearctic migrant. Rare.

Larus argentatus Pontoppidan (Bann. *Larus atlantis* (Dwight))

Larus fuscus Linnaeus

Rynchops flavirostris Vieillot

Anous stolidus (Linnaeus) Breeds Gulf of Guinea islands. Non-breeding visitor West African coasts.

Anous tenuirostris (Temminck) (Bann. *Megalopterus minutus* (Boie)) Breeds Gulf of Guinea islands. Non-breeding visitor West African coasts.

Sterna nilotica Gmelin (Bann. *Gelochelidon nilotica* (Gmelin))

Sterna caspia Pallas (Bann. *Hydroprogne caspia* (Pallas))

Sterna maxima Boddaert

Sterna sandvicensis Latham

Sterna dougalii Montagu Migrant to West African coasts.

Sterna hirundo Linnaeus

Sterna paradisea Pontoppidan (Bann. *Sterna macrura* Naumann)

Sterna balaenarum (Strickland) Migrant from southern Africa to West African coasts. Local.

Sterna anaethetus Scopoli West African coast. Breeds Mauritania and Gulf of Guinea islands.

Sterna fuscata Linnaeus West African coast. Breeds Principe.

Sterna hybrida Pallas (Bann. *Chlidonias leucopareia* (Temminck))

Sterna leucoptera Temminck (Bann. *Chlidonias leucoptera* (Temminck))

Sterna nigra Linnaeus (Bann. *Chlidonias nigra* (Linnaeus))

Sterna albifrons Pallas

PTEROCLIDIDAE

Pterocles senegallus (Linnaeus) Southern border of Sahara in Niger and Chad.

Pterocles exustus Temminck

Pterocles lichtensteinii Temminck Southern edge of Sahara in Niger and Chad.

Pterocles quadricinctus Temminck

Pterocles coronatus Lichtenstein Southern edge of Sahara in Niger and Chad.

TURNICIDAE

Turnix sylvatica (Desfontaines)

Turnix hottentotta Temminck (Bann. *Turnix nana* (Sundevall))

Ortyxelos meiffrenii Vieillot

COLUMBIDAE

Columba livia   Gmelin   Resident in Cape Verde Islands and locally in West Africa.
Columba unicincta   Cassin
Columba guinea   Linnaeus
Columba arquatrix   Temminck
Columba albinucha   Sassi   Cameroons. Rare.
Columba malherbii   Verreaux   (Bann. *Turturoena malherbii* (Verreaux) and *Turturoena iriditorques* (Cassin))
Streptopelia turtur   (Linnaeus)
Streptopelia lugens   (Rüppell)   (Bann. *Streptopelia hypopyrrhus* (Reichenow))
Streptopelia semitorquata   (Rüppell)
Streptopelia decipiens   (Hartlaub and Finsch)
Streptopelia vinacea   (Gmelin)
Streptopelia capicola   (Sundevall)   Congo.
Streptopelia roseogrisea   (Sundevall)
Streptopelia senegalensis   (Linnaeus)   (Bann. *Stigmatopelia senegalensis* (Linn.))
Oena capensis   (Linnaeus)
Turtur tympanistria   (Temminck)   (Bann. *Tympanistria tympanistria* (Temminck))
Turtur afer   (Linnaeus)
Turtur chalcospilos   (Wagler)   Gaboon. Rare.
Turtur abyssinicus   (Sharpe)
Turtur brehmeri   (Hartlaub)   (Bann. *Calopelia puella* (Schlegel))
Aplopelia larvata   (Temminck)   (Bann. *Aplopelia simplex* (Hartlaub))
Treron australis   (Linnaeus)   (Bann. *Vinago australis* (Linnaeus))
Treron waalia   (Meyer)   (Bann. *Vinago waalia* (Meyer))

PSITTACIDAE

Poicephalus robustus   (Gmelin)
Poicephalus gulielmi   (Jardine)
Poicephalus crassus   (Sharpe)   Cameroons, Chad and Central African Republic.
Poicephalus senegalus   (Linnaeus)
Poicephalus meyeri   (Cretzschmar)   Cameroons, Chad and Central African Republic.
Psittacus erithacus   Linnaeus
Psittacula krameri   Scopoli
Agapornis pullaria   (Linnaeus)
Agapornis swinderniana   (Kuhl)

MUSOPHAGIDAE

Tauraco persa   (Linnaeus)   (Bann. *Turacus persa* (Linnaeus))
Tauraco schutti   (Cabanis)   (Bann. *Turacus schutti* (Cabanis))   Central African Republic and Congo.
Tauraco bannermani   (Bates)   (Bann. *Proturacus bannermani* Bates)

Tauraco macrorhynchus (Fraser) (Bann. *Turacus macrorhynchus* (Fraser) and
  Turacus verreauxi (Schlegel))
Tauraco leucolophus (Heuglin) (Bann. *Turacus leucolophus* (Heuglin))
Musophaga violacea Isert
Musophaga rossae Gould
Crinifer piscator (Boddaert)
Crinifer zonurus (Rüppell)
Corythaeola cristata (Vieillot)

CUCULIDAE

Clamator glandarius (Linnaeus)
Clamator jacobinus (Boddaert)
Clamator levaillantii (Swainson)
Cuculus solitarius Stephens
Cuculus clamosus Latham
Cuculus canorus Linnaeus (Bann. *Cuculus canorus* Linnaeus and *Cuculus
  gularis* Stephens)
*Pachycoccyx audeberti (Schlegel) (Bann. *Pachycoccyx validus* (Reichenow))
  Guinea to Cameroons and Gaboon. Rare and local.
*Cercococcyx mechowi Cabanis West African rain forest. Local.
*Cercococcyx olivinus Sassi West African rain forest. Local.
*Chrysococcyx flavigularis Shelley (Bann. *Lampromorpha flavigularis*
  (Shelley)) West African rain forest and occasionally wooded savanna. Local.
Chrysococcyx klaas (Stephens) (Bann. *Lampromorpha klaasi* (Stephens))
Chrysococcyx caprius (Boddaert) (Bann. *Lampromorpha caprius* (Boddaert))
Chrysococcyx cupreus (Shaw)
Ceuthmochares aereus (Vieillot)
Centropus grillii Hartlaub
Centropus leucogaster (Leach)
*Centropus anselli Sharpe Cameroons, Gaboon and Congo.
Centropus monachus Rüppell
Centropus senegalensis (Linnaeus)

STRIGIDAE

Tyto alba (Scopoli)
*Tyto capensis (Smith) Cameroon highlands. Rare.
*Otus icterorhynchus (Shelley) West African rain forest. Rare and local.
Otus scops (Linnaeus) (Bann. *Otus scops* (Linnaeus) and *Otus senegalensis*
  (Swainson) and *Otus leucopsis* (Hartlaub))
Otus leucotis (Temminck) (Bann. *Ptilopsis leucotis* (Temminck))
Lophostrix letti (Büttikofer) (Bann. *Jubula lettii* Büttikofer)
*Bubo bubo (Linnaeus) (Bann. *Bubo ascalaphus* Savigny) Edge of Sahara
  in Mauritania, Mali, Niger and Chad.
Bubo africanus (Temminck)
Bubo poensis Fraser
*Bubo shelleyi Sharpe and Ussher West African rain forest. Local.
Bubo lacteus (Temminck)
Bubo leucostictus Hartlaub

Scotopelia peli   (Bonaparte)

*_Scotopelia ussheri_   Sharpe   Rain forest of Sierra Leone, Liberia and Ghana. Rare.

*_Scotopelia bouvieri_   Sharpe   West African rain forest. Local.

Glaucidium perlatum   (Vieillot)

Glaucidium tephronotum   Sharpe

*_Glaucidium capense_   (Smith)   Ivory Coast. Rare.

Glaucidium sjöstedti   Reichenow

*_Athene noctua_   (Scopoli)   (Bann. *Carine noctua* (Scopoli))   Edge of Sahara in Mali, Niger and Chad.

Ciccaba woodfordi   (Smith)   (Bann. *Strix woodfordi* (Smith))

Asio flammeus   (Pontoppidan)

Asio capensis   (Smith)

CAPRIMULGIDAE

*_Caprimulgus binotatus_   Bonaparte   West African rain forest. Rare and local.

*_Caprimulgus ruficollis_   Temminck   Palaearctic migrant. Local.

*_Caprimulgus europaeus_   Linnaeus   Uncommon Palaearctic migrant.

*_Caprimulgus aegyptius_   Lichtenstein   Rather uncommon Palaearctic migrant.

Caprimulgus eximius   Temminck

Caprimulgus pectoralis   Cuvier   (Bann. *Caprimulgus nigriscapularis* Reich.)

*_Caprimulgus rufigena_   Smith   Local, wet season, non-breeding migrant from southern Africa.

Caprimulgus natalensis   Smith

Caprimulgus inornatus   Heuglin

Caprimulgus tristigma   Rüppell

*_Caprimulgus batesi_   Sharpe   Cameroons and Gaboon rain forest.

*_Caprimulgus fossii_   Hartlaub   Savanna of Ivory Coast, Ghana, Cameroons, Gaboon and Rio Muni. Local.

Caprimulgus climacurus   Vieillot   (Bann. *Scotornis climacurus* (Vieillot))

Macrodipteryx longipennis   (Shaw)

Macrodipteryx vexillarius   (Gould)   (Bann. *Cosmetornis vexillarius* Gould)

APODIDAE

Apus melba   (Linnaeus)

Apus aequatorialis   (von Müller)

Apus apus   (Linnaeus)   (Bann. *Micropus apus* (Linnaeus))

*_Apus pallidus_   (Shelley)   Palaearctic migrant.

*_Apus niansae_   (Reichenow)   Congo. Rare.

*_Apus barbatus_   (Sclater)   (Bann. *Micropus sladeniae* (Ogilvie-Grant))   Sierra Leone, Nigeria, Cameroons and Fernando Po. Local.

*_Apus myoptilus_   (Salvadori)   (Bann. *Micropus unicolor* (Jardine))   Fernando Po.

*_Apus alexanderi_   Hartert   (Bann. *Micropus unicolor* (Jardine))   Cape Verde Islands.

Apus batesi   (Sharpe)   (Bann. *Micropus batesi* (Sharpe))

*_Apus horus_   (Salvadori and Antinori)   Chad.

Apus caffer   (Lichtenstein)   (Bann. *Micropus caffer* (Lichtenstein))

Apus affinis (Gray) (Bann. *Colletoptera affinis* (Gray))
Cypsiurus parvus (Lichtenstein)
Chaetura sabini Gray
Chaetura thomensis Hartert Sao Tome.
Chaetura ussheri Sharpe
Chaetura melanopygia Chapin Cameroons and Gaboon. Rather rare.
Chaetura cassini Sclater

COLIIDAE

Colius striatus Gmelin
Colius macrourus (Linnaeus)

TROGONIDAE

Apaloderma narina (Stephens)
Apaloderma aequatoriale Sharpe Cameroons and Gaboon.
Apaloderma vittatum Shelley (Bann. *Heterotrogon vittatum* (Shelley))

ALCEDINIDAE

Ceryle maxima (Pallas) (Bann. *Megaceryle maxima* (Pallas))
Ceryle rudis (Linnaeus)
Alcedo quadribrachys (Bonaparte)
Alcedo cristata Pallas (Bann. *Corythornis cristata* (Pallas))
Alcedo leucogaster (Fraser) (Bann. *Corythornis leucogaster* (Fraser))
Ceyx picta (Boddaert) (Bann. *Ispidina picta* (Boddaert))
Ceyx lecontei (Cassin) (Bann. *Myioceyx lecontei* (Cassin))
Halcyon senegalensis (Linnaeus)
Halcyon malimbica (Shaw)
Halcyon badia Verreaux
Halcyon chelicuti (Stanley)
Halcyon albiventris (Scopoli) Southern Gaboon and Congo.
Halcyon leucocephala (Müller)

MEROPIDAE

Merops apiaster Linnaeus
Merops superciliosus Linnaeus (Bann. *Merops persicus* Pallas)
Merops orientalis Latham
Merops malimbicus Shaw
Merops nubicus Gmelin
Merops albicollis Vieillot (Bann. *Aerops albicollis* (Vieillot))
Merops pusillus Müller (Bann. *Melittophagus pusillus* (Müller))
Merops variegatus Vieillot (Bann. *Melittophagus variegatus* (Vieillot))
   Cameroons, Gaboon and Congo.
Merops bulocki Vieillot (Bann. *Melittophagus bullocki* (Vieillot))
Merops bullockoides Smith Gaboon and Congo. Rare.
Merops gularis Shaw
Merops muelleri (Cassin) (Bann. *Melittophagus muelleri* (Cassin))

Merops hirundineus Lichtenstein (Bann. *Dicrocercus hirundineus* (Lichtenstein))

*Bombylonax breweri (Cassin) Eastern Nigeria, Cameroons, Gaboon and Congo. Local.

CORACIIDAE

Coracias garrulus Linnaeus
Coracias abyssinica Hermann
Coracias naevia Daudin
Coracias cyanogaster Cuvier
Eurystomus glaucurus (Müller) (Bann. *Eurystomus afer* (Latham))
Eurystomus gularis Vieillot

UPUPIDAE

Upupa epops Linnaeus (Bann. *Upupa epops* Linnaeus and *Upupa senegalensis* Swainson)
Phoeniculus purpureus (Miller) (Bann. *Phoeniculus erythrorhynchus* (Latham) and *Phoeniculus senegalensis* (Vieillot))
Phoeniculus bollei (Hartlaub)
Phoeniculus castaneiceps (Sharpe) (Bann. *Scoptelus castaneiceps* (Sharpe) and *Scoptelus brunneiceps* Sharpe)
Phoeniculus aterrimus (Stephens) (Bann. *Scoptelus aterrimus* (Stephens))

BUCEROTIDAE

Tockus nasutus (Linnaeus) (Bann. *Lophoceros nasutus* (Linnaeus))
Tockus erythrorhynchus (Temminck) (Bann. *Lophoceros erythrorhynchus* (Temminck))
Tockus camurus Cassin (Bann. *Lophoceros camurus* (Cassin))
Tockus hartlaubi Gould (Bann. *Lophoceros hartlaubi* (Gould))
Tockus fasciatus (Shaw) (Bann. *Lophoceros fasciatus* (Shaw) and *Lophoceros semifasciatus* (Hartlaub))
*Tockus alboterminatus (Buttikofer) Congo.
Tropicranus albocristatus (Cassin)
Ceratogymna elata (Temminck)
Ceratogymna atrata (Temminck)
Bycanistes fistulator (Cassin) (Bann. *Bycanistes fistulator* (Cassin) and *Bycanistes sharpii* (Elliott))
Bycanistes cylindricus (Temminck) (Bann. *Bycanistes cylindricus* (Temminck) and *Bycanistes albotibialis* (Cabanis and Reichenow))
Bycanistes subcylindricus (Sclater)
Bucorvus abyssinicus (Boddaert)

CAPITONIDAE

Lybius dubius (Gmelin) (Bann. *Pogonornis dubius* (Gmelin))
*Lybius rolleti (Defilippi) Central African Republic and Chad.
Lybius bidentatus (Shaw) (Bann. *Pogonornis bidentatus* (Shaw))

Lybius minor (Cuvier) Gaboon and Congo.
Lybius leucocephalus (Defilippi)
Lybius vieilloti (Leach)
Lybius hirsutus (Swainson) (Bann. *Tricholaema hirsutum* (Swainson) and *Tricholaema flavipunctata* Verreaux)
Gymnobucco calvus (Lafresnaye)
Gymnobucco peli Hartlaub
Gymnobucco bonapartei Hartlaub
Buccanodon duchaillui (Cassin)
Pogoniulus scolopaceus (Bonaparte)
Pogoniulus coryphaeus (Reichenow) (Bann. *Viridibucco coryphaea* (Reichenow))
Pogoniulus chrysoconus (Temminck)
Pogoniulus bilineatus (Sundevall) (Bann. *Pogoniulus leucolaima* (Verreaux))
Pogoniulus subsulphureus (Fraser)
Pogoniulus atro-flavus (Sparrman) (Bann. *Pogoniulus erythronotos* (Cuvier))
Trachyphonus purpuratus (Verreaux) (Bann. *Trachylaemus purpuratus* (Verreaux))
Trachyphonus margaritatus (Cretzschmar)

INDICATORIDAE

Indicator maculatus Gray
Indicator indicator (Sparrman)
Indicator minor Stephens (Bann. *Indicator minor* Stephens and *Indicator conirostris* (Cassin))
Indicator exilis (Cassin)
Indicator willcocksi Alexander
Melichneutes robustus (Bates)
Melignomon zenkeri Reichenow Rain forest in Cameroons and Rio Muni.
Prodotiscus insignis (Cassin)
Prodotiscus regulus Sundevall Savanna woodland in Liberia, Nigeria, Cameroons and Central African Republic.

PICIDAE

Jynx torquilla Linnaeus
Jynx ruficollis Wagler Cameroons, Gaboon, Congo and Central African Republic.
Verreauxia africana (Verreaux)
Campethera punctuligera (Wagler)
Campethera nubica (Boddaert) Chad.
Campethera abingoni (Smith)
Campethera maculosa (Valenciennes)
Campethera cailliautii (Reichenow) (Bann. *Campethera permista* Reichenow)
Campethera caroli (Malherbe)
Campethera nivosa (Swainson)
Campethera tullbergi Sjöstedt
Dendropicos fuscescens (Vieillot)
Dendropicos elachus Oberholser

Dendropicos poecilolaemus Reichenow Savanna woodland in Nigeria, Cameroons, Chad and Central African Republic.
Dendropicos gabonensis (Verreaux)
Dendrocopos obsoletus (Wagler) (Bann. *Dendropicos obsoletus* (Wagler))
Mesopicos goertae (Müller)
Mesopicos xantholophus (Hargitt)
Mesopicos pyrrhogaster (Malherbe)
Mesopicos ellioti (Cassin)
Thripias namaquus (Lichtenstein) Chad and Central African Republic.

EURYLAEMIDAE

Smithornis capensis (Smith)
Smithornis rufolateralis Gray
Smithornis sharpei Alexander Lowland forest in Cameroons, Rio Muni and Fernando Po.

PITTIDAE

Pitta angolensis Vieillot
Pitta reichenowi Madarasz

ALAUDIDAE

Mirafra javanica Horsfield (Bann. *Mirafra cantillans* Blyth)
Mirafra albicauda Reichenow Central African Republic and vicinity of Lake Chad.
Mirafra cordofanica Strickland Edge of desert in Senegal, Mali and Chad.
Mirafra africana Smith
Mirafra rufocinnamomea (Salvadori) (Bann. *Mirafra buckleyi* (Shelley))
Mirafra rufa Lynes Mali, Niger and Chad.
Mirafra nigricans (Sundevall) (Bann. *Pinarocorys erythropygia* (Strickland))
Alaemon alaudipes (Desfontaines) Cape Verde Islands, Niger and Chad.
Ammomanes cincturus (Gould) Cape Verde Islands, Mali, Niger and Chad.
Ammomanes deserti (Lichtenstein) Niger, northern Nigeria and Chad.
Calandrella brachydactyla (Leisler) Palaearctic migrant to Senegal, Mali, Niger, Nigeria and Chad.
Calandrella cinerea (Gmelin)
Eremalauda dunni (Shelley) Southern edge of Sahara from Mali to Chad.
Eremopterix nigriceps (Gould)
Eremopterix leucotis (Stanley)
Galerida cristata (Linnaeus)
Galerida modesta Heuglin (Bann. *Heliocorys modesta* (Heuglin))
Alauda arvensis Linnaeus Palaearctic vagrant to Chad.
Razocorys razae Alexander Cape Verde Islands.

HIRUNDINIDAE

Riparia riparia (Linnaeus)
Riparia congica (Reichenow) Ubangi River, Congo.
Riparia cincta (Boddaert) Non-breeding migrant to Principe, Gambia, Ivory

Coast, Ghana, Nigeria, Chad, Cameroons, Gaboon and Congo. Probably also resident in last three territories.

Riparia paludicola (Vieillot)

Hirundo rustica Linnaeus (Bann. *Hirundo rustica* Linnaeus and *Hirundo lucida* Hartlaub)

*Hirundo angolensis Bocage Gaboon.

Hirundo nigrita Gray

Hirundo smithii Leach

Hirundo aethiopica Blanford

Hirundo leucosoma Swainson

Hirundo semirufa Sundevall

Hirundo senegalensis Linnaeus

Hirundo daurica Linnaeus (Bann. *Hirundo rufula* Temminck)

Hirundo abyssinica Guerin

*Hirundo griseopyga Sundevall (Bann. *Pseudohirundo griseopyga* (Sundevall))
Wide but local range in the savanna from Gambia to Cameroons, Gaboon and Congo.

*Hirundo spilodera Sundevall (Bann. *Lecythoplastes preussi* Reichenow)
Local in Portuguese Guinea, Mali, Ivory Coast, Ghana, Nigeria, Cameroons and Chad.

*Hirundo fuliginosa (Chapin) (Bann. *Lecythoplastes fuliginosa* Chapin)
Lowland forest in Cameroons and Gaboon.

*Hirundo rupestris Scopoli Rare Palaearctic migrant to Senegal.

*Hirundo fuligula Lichtenstein (Bann. *Ptyonoprogne rufigula* (Fischer and Reichenow)) Rocky open terrain in Mali, Niger, Chad, Sierra Leone, Liberia, Ivory Coast, Ghana, Nigeria, Cameroons, Central African Republic and Congo.

Delichon urbica (Linnaeus)

*Phedina brazzae Oustalet Congo. Local.

Psalidoprocne nitens (Cassin)

*Psalidoprocne pristoptera (Rüppell) (Bann. *Psalidoprocne chalybea* Reich. and *Psalidoprocne petiti* Sharpe) Obudu Plateau, Cameroons, Central African Republic, Gaboon and Congo.

Psalidoprocne obscura (Hartlaub)

*Psalidoprocne fuliginosa Shelley Cameroon Mountain and Fernando Po.

*Pseudochelidon eurystomina Hartlaub Gaboon and Congo.

MOTACILLIDAE

Motacilla flava Linnaeus (Bann. *Budytes flavus* (Linnaeus))

*Motacilla cinerea Tunstall Palaearctic migrant to Gambia and Senegal.

Motacilla clara Sharpe

Motacilla alba Linnaeus

Motacilla aguimp Dumont

Anthus campestris Linnaeus

*Anthus godlewskii (Taczanowski) Rare Palaearctic migrant.

Anthus novaeseelandiae (Gmelin) (Bann. *Anthus richardi* (Vieillot))

Anthus leucophrys Vieillot

*Anthus pallidiventris Sharpe Rio Muni, Gaboon and Congo in open grassy areas.

Anthus similis Jerdon (Bann. *Anthus similis* Jerdon and *Anthus bannermani* Bates) Congo savanna, and highland areas in Sierra Leone, Liberia, Guinea, Niger, Nigeria, Cameroons and Chad.

Anthus brachyurus Sundevall Gaboon and Congo.

Anthus trivialis Linnaeus

Anthus cervinus (Pallas)

Macronyx croceus (Vieillot)

LANIIDAE

Prionops plumata (Shaw)

Prionops caniceps (Bonaparte) (Bann. *Sigmodus caniceps* Bonaparte and *Sigmodus rufiventris* Bonaparte)

Nilaus afer (Latham)

Dryoscopus gambensis (Lichtenstein)

Dryoscopus senegalensis (Hartlaub)

Dryoscopus angolensis Hartlaub Montane forests of Cameroons. Also Congo.

Dryoscopus sabini (Gray) (Bann. *Chaunonotus sabini* (Gray)) Lowland forest from Sierra Leone to Gaboon. Local.

Tchagra minuta (Hartlaub) (Bann. *Antichromus minutus* (Hartlaub))

Tchagra australis (Smith)

Tchagra senegala (Linnaeus)

Laniarius lühderi Reichenow Rain forest second-growth in Cameroons, Gaboon and Congo.

Laniarius ferrugineus (Gmelin) (Bann. *Laniarius ferrugineus* (Gmelin) and *Laniarius turatii* (Verreaux))

Laniarius barbarus (Linnaeus) (Bann. *Laniarius barbarus* (Linnaeus) and *Laniarius erythrogaster* (Cretzschmar))

Laniarius atroflavus Shelley

Laniarius fülleborni (Reichenow) (Bann. *Laniarius poensis* (Alexander))

Laniarius leucorhynchus (Hartlaub)

Malaconotus bocagei (Reichenow) (Bann. *Dryoscopus bocagei* (Reichenow)) Cameroons, Rio Muni and Gaboon.

Malaconotus sulfureopectus (Lesson) (Bann. *Chlorophoneus sulfureopectus* (Lesson))

Malaconotus multicolor (Gray) (Bann. *Chlorophoneus multicolor* (Gray))

Malaconotus kupeensis (Serle) (Bann. *Chlorophoneus kupeensis* Serle) Kupe Mountain, Cameroons.

Malaconotus cruentus (Lesson)

Malaconotus lagdeni (Sharpe) Ghana and Liberia. Rare.

Malaconotus gladiator (Reichenow) (Bann. *Malaconotus poliocephalus gladiator* (Reichenow)) Montane forests of Cameroons and Obudu Plateau.

Malaconotus blanchoti Stephens (Bann. *Malaconotus poliocephalus* (Lichtenstein))

Corvinella corvina (Shaw)

Lanius souzae Bocage Congo.

Lanius collurio Linnaeus (Bann. *Lanius collurio* Linnaeus and *Lanius isabellinus* Hemprich and Ehrenberg)

Lanius gubernator Hartert

Lanius mackinnoni Sharpe Cameroons, Gaboon and Obudu Plateau.
Lanius minor Gmelin Palaearctic migrant to Chad, Niger, Nigeria, Congo and Principe.
Lanius excubitor Linnaeus
Lanius excubitorius Prévost and Des Murs
Lanius collaris Linnaeus (Bann. *Lanius collaris* Linnaeus and *Lanius newtoni* Bocage)
Lanius senator Linnaeus
Lanius nubicus Lichtenstein Palaearctic migrant to Niger, Chad, Cameroons and Nigeria.

ORIOLIDAE

Oriolus oriolus (Linnaeus)
Oriolus auratus Vieillot
Oriolus brachyrhynchus Swainson
Oriolus nigripennis J. and E. Verreaux
Oriolus crassirostris Hartlaub Sao Tome.

DICRURIDAE

Dicrurus ludwigii (Smith) (Bann. *Dicrurus sharpei* Oustalet)
Dicrurus atripennis Swainson
Dicrurus adsimilis Bechstein (Bann. *Dicrurus adsimilis* Bechstein and *Dicrurus modestus* Hartlaub)

STURNIDAE

Poeoptera lugubris Bonaparte
Grafisia torquata (Reichenow) Cameroons and Central African Republic. Local.
Onychognathus walleri (Shelley) Montane forests of Fernando Po and the Cameroons.
Onychognathus morio (Linnaeus)
Onychognathus fulgidus Hartlaub
Lamprotornis purpureiceps (J. and E. Verreaux) (Bann. *Lamprocolius purpureiceps* J. and E. Verreaux)
Lamprotornis cupreocauda (Hartlaub) (Bann. *Lamprocolius cupreocauda* Hartlaub)
Lamprotornis splendidus (Vieillot) (Bann. *Lamprocolius splendidus* (Vieillot))
Lamprotornis ornatus (Daudin) (Bann. *Lamprocolius ornatus* (Daudin)) Principe.
Lamprotornis purpureus (Müller) (Bann. *Lamprocolius purpureus* (Müller))
Lamprotornis chloropterus Swainson (Bann. *Lamprocolius chloropterus* (Swainson))
Lamprotornis chalcurus Nordmann (Bann. *Lamprocolius chalcurus* (Nordmann))
Lamprotornis chalybaeus Hemprich and Ehrenberg (Bann. *Lamprocolius chalybaeus* (Hemprich and Ehrenberg))
Lamprotornis nitens (Linnaeus) (Bann. *Lamprocolius nitens* (Linnaeus)) Gaboon.

Lamprotornis caudatus (Müller)

*_Lamprotornis iris_ (Oustalet) (Bann. *Coccycolius iris* (Oustalet)) Wooded savanna in Guinea, Sierra Leone and Ivory Coast.

Cinnyricinclus leucogaster (Gmelin)

*_Creatophora cinerea_ Menschen Eastern Central African Republic.

Spreo pulcher (Müller)

Buphagus africanus Linnaeus

CORVIDAE

Ptilostomus afer (Linnaeus)

Corvus albus Müller

Corvus ruficollis Lesson

*_Corvus rhipidurus_ Hartert (Bann. *Rhinocorax rhipidurus* (Hartert)) Niger and Chad.

Picathartes gymnocephalus (Temminck) (Bann. *Picathartes gymnocephalus* (Temminck) and *Picathartes oreas* Reichenow)

CAMPEPHAGIDAE

Coracina pectoralis (Jardine and Selby)

Coracina caesia (Lichtenstein)

Coracina azurea (Cassin) (Bann. *Cyanograucalus azureus* Cassin)

Campephaga quiscalina Finsch

Campephaga phoenicea (Latham) (Bann. *Campephaga phoenicea* (Latham) and *Campephaga petiti* (Oustalet))

*_Campephaga lobata_ (Temminck) (Bann. *Lobotos lobatus* (Temminck) and *Lobotos oriolinus* Bates) Lowland forest in Liberia, Ghana, Cameroons and Gaboon.

PYCNONOTIDAE

Pycnonotus barbatus (Desfontaines)

*_Andropadus curvirostris_ Cassin Lowland forest from Sierra Leone to Gaboon. Also Fernando Po.

Andropadus gracilis Cabanis

*_Andropadus ansorgei_ Hartert (Bann. *Andropadus gracilis ansorgei* Hartert) Lowland forest in Sierra Leone, Liberia, Nigeria, Cameroons, Rio Muni and Gaboon.

Andropadus gracilirostris Strickland

Andropadus virens Cassin

Andropadus latirostris Strickland

*_Andropadus montanus_ Reichenow (Bann. *Arizelocichla montana* (Reichenow)) Montane forests of Cameroons and Obudu Plateau.

Andropadus tephrolaemus (Gray) (Bann. *Arizelocichla tephrolaema* (Gray))

*_Calyptocichla serina_ (J. and E. Verreaux) Sierra Leone to Gaboon. Also Fernando Po.

Baeopogon indicator (Cassin).

Baeopogon clamans (Sjöstedt)

Ixonotus guttatus J. and E. Verreaux

Chlorocichla falkensteini (Reichenow) (Bann. *Arizelocichla falkensteini* (Reich.)) Lowland forest second-growth in Cameroons, Gaboon and Congo.

Chlorocichla flavicollis (Swainson) (Bann. *Pyrrhurus flavicollis* (Swainson))

Chlorocichla simplex (Hartlaub) (Bann. *Pyrrhurus simplex* (Hartlaub))

Thescelocichla leucopleurus Cassin

Phyllastrephus scandens Swainson (Bann. *Pyrrhurus scandens* (Swainson))

Phyllastrephus baumanni Reichenow Lowland forest from Sierra Leone to Nigeria.

Phyllastrephus poensis Alexander Montane forests of Cameroons, Obudu Plateau and Fernando Po.

Phyllastrephus xavieri (Oustalet) Lowland forest in Cameroons, Gaboon, Congo and Central African Republic.

Phyllastrephus icterinus (Bonaparte)

Phyllastrephus albigularis (Sharpe) Sierra Leone to Gaboon in lowland forest.

Phyllastrephus flavostriatus (Sharpe) (Bann. *Phyllastrephus poliocephalus* (Reichenow))

Neolestes torquatus Cabanis Wooded savanna in Gaboon and Congo.

Bleda syndactyla (Swainson)

Bleda eximia (Hartlaub)

Bleda canicapilla (Hartlaub)

Criniger barbatus (Temminck) (Bann. *Trichophorus barbatus* Temminck)

Criniger calurus (Cassin) (Bann. *Trichophorus calurus* Cassin)

Criniger olivaceus (Swainson) (Bann. *Trichophorus olivaceus* Swainson) Lowland forest. Senegal to Ghana.

Nicator chloris (Valenciennes)

Nicator vireo Cabanis Lowland forest in Cameroons and Gaboon.

TURDIDAE

Saxicola rubetra (Linnaeus)

Saxicola torquata (Linnaeus)

Oenanthe oenanthe (Linnaeus)

Oenanthe pleschanka (Lepechin) Rare Palaearctic migrant to Chad.

Oenanthe hispanica (Linnaeus)

Oenanthe deserti (Temminck) Palaearctic migrant to Mali, Niger and Chad.

Oenanthe isabellina (Temminck) Palaearctic migrant to southern Mauritania, Senegal, Mali and Chad.

Oenanthe leucopyga (Brehm) Niger and Mali.

Oenanthe bottae (Bonaparte) (Bann. *Oenanthe heuglini* (Finsch and Hartlaub))

Cercomela melanura (Temminck)

Cercomela scotocerca (Heuglin) Eastern Chad.

Cercomela familiaris (Stephens)

Myrmecocichla aethiops Cabanis

Myrmecocichla nigra (Vieillot)

Myrmecocichla tholloni (Oustalet) Congo grasslands.

Myrmecocichla cinnamomeiventris (Lafresnaye) (Bann. *Thamnolaea cinnamomeiventris* (Lafresnaye) and *Thamnolaea coronata* Reich.)

Myrmecocichla albifrons (Rüppell) (Bann. *Pentholaea albifrons* (Rüppell))

Monticola saxatilis (Linnaeus)

Monticola solitaria (Linnaeus)

Phoenicurus phoenicurus (Linnaeus)

**Phoenicurus ochruros* (Gmelin)   Rare Palaearctic migrant to Chad.

Cercotrichas podobe (Müller)

Cercotrichas galactotes (Temminck)   (Bann. *Agrobates galactotes* (Temminck))

**Cercotrichas leucophrys* (Vieillot)   (Bann. *Erythropygia leucophrys* (Vieillot))   Gaboon and Congo.

**Cercotrichas hartlaubi* (Reichenow)   (Bann. *Erythropygia hartlaubi* Reichenow   Cameroons. Local. Savanna near forest edge.

Cercotrichas leucosticta (Sharpe)   (Bann. *Erythropygia leucosticta* (Sharpe))

**Cichladusa ruficauda* (Hartlaub)   Gaboon and Congo.

Alethe diademata (Bonaparte)   (Bann. *Alethe castanea* (Cassin))

Alethe poliocephala (Bonaparte)

**Sheppardia cyornithopsis* (Sharpe)   Lowland forest in Sierra Leone, Liberia, Ivory Coast, Cameroons and Gaboon.

Stiphrornis erythrothorax Hartlaub

*Cossypha bocagei Finsch and Hartlaub   (Bann. *Cossypha insulana* Grote)   Montane forest of Fernando Po and Kupe Mountain and at Muambong.

Cossypha isabellae Gray

Cossypha polioptera Reichenow

**Cossypha natalensis* Smith   Cameroons, Central African Republic, Gaboon and Congo.

Cossypha cyanocampter (Bonaparte)

**Cossypha heuglini* Hartlaub   Chad, Central African Republic, Gaboon and Congo.

Cossypha albicapilla (Vieillot)

Cossypha niveicapilla (Lafresnaye)

*Cossypha roberti (Alexander)   (Bann. *Cossyphicula roberti* (Alexander))   Montane forests of the Cameroons and Fernando Po.

**Neocossyphus rufus* (Fischer and Reichenow)   Lowland forest of Cameroons and Gaboon.

Neocossyphus poensis (Strickland)

Stizorhina fraseri (Strickland)   (Bann. *Stizorhina fraseri* (Strickland) and *Stizorhina finschi* (Sharpe))

Luscinia megarhynchos Brehm

*Luscinia svecica (Linnaeus)   Palaearctic migrant to Senegal, Mali, Nigeria and Chad.

**Turdus philomelos* Brehm   Uncommon Palaearctic migrant to Senegal and Chad.

Turdus pelios Bonaparte   (Bann. *Turdus libonyanus* (Smith))

**Turdus olivaceofuscus* Hartlaub   Sao Tome and Principe.

**Turdus camaronensis* (Sharpe)   (Bann. *Geokichla camaronensis* Sharpe)   Lowland forests of Cameroons. Rare.

Turdus princei Sharpe   (Bann. *Geokichla princei* (Sharpe))

*Turdus gurneyi Hartlaub   (Bann. *Geokichla gurneyi* (Hartlaub))   Montane forests of Cameroons and Obudu Plateau.

TIMALIIDAE

Alcippe abyssinica (Rüppell)   (Bann. *Pseudoalcippe abyssinicus* (Rüppell) and *Pseudoalcippe atriceps* (Sharpe))

*_Malacocincla poliothorax_ (Reichenow) (Bann. _Illadopsis poliothorax_ (Reiche-now)) Montane forests of the Cameroons, Obudu Plateau and Fernando Po.
Malacocincla fulvescens (Cassin) (Bann. _Illadopsis fulvescens_ (Cassin) and _Illadopsis moloneyanus_ (Sharpe))
Malacocincla rufipennis (Sharpe) (Bann. _Illadopsis rufipennis_ (Sharpe))
Malacocincla cleaveri (Shelley) (Bann. _Illadopsis cleaveri_ (Shelley))
Malacocincla rufescens (Reichenow) (Bann. _Illadopsis rufescens_ (Reichenow))
Malacocincla puveli ' (Salvadori) (Bann. _Illadopsis puveli_ (Salvadori))
*_Ptyrticus turdinus_ Hartlaub Gallery forests in northern and eastern Cameroons.
Kupeornis gilberti Serle
Phyllanthus atripennis (Swainson)
Turdoides plebejus (Cretzschmar)
*_Turdoides jardinei_ (Smith) Congo. Local.
Turdoides reinwardii (Swainson)
*_Turdoides fulvus_ (Desfontaines) (Bann. _Argya fulva_ (Desfontaines)) Southern fringe of the Sahara in Mali, Niger and Chad.

SYLVIIDAE

*_Cettia cetti_ (Temminck) Rare Palaearctic migrant to Nigeria.
*_Bradypterus baboecala_ (Vieillot) (Bann. _Bradypterus brachypterus_ (Vieillot)) Vicinity of Lake Chad, Cameroons and Nigeria. Local.
*_Bradypterus graueri_ Neumann (Bann. _Bradypterus grandis_ Ogilvie-Grant) Cameroons and Gaboon. Rare and local.
*_Bradypterus barratti_ Sharpe (Bann. _Bradypterus manengubae_ Serle, _Bradypterus mariae_ Madarasz, _Bradypterus camerunensis_ Alexander and _Bradypterus lopezi_ (Alexander)) Montane forest in Cameroons and Obudu Plateau.
*_Bradypterus cinnamomeus_ (Rüppell) (Bann. _Bradypterus castaneus_ Reichenow Edges of montane forest in Cameroons and Obudu Plateau.
Schoenicola platyura (Jerdon) (Bann. _Schoenicola brevirostris_ (Sundevall))
*_Locustella luscinioides_ (Savi) Palaearctic migrant to Senegal, Nigeria, Cameroons and Chad.
*_Locustella fluviatilis_ (Wolf) Rare Palaearctic migrant.
*_Locustella naevia_ (Boddaert) Palaearctic migrant to Senegal.
*_Lusciniola melanopogon_ (Temminck) Rare Palaearctic migrant to Lake Chad and Chad.
Acrocephalus schoenobaenus (Linnaeus)
*_Acrocephalus paludicola_ (Vieillot) Rare Palaearctic migrant to Mali.
*_Acrocephalus scirpaceus_ (Hermann) Palaearctic migrant to Senegal, Gambia, Liberia, Ivory Coast, Ghana, Niger, Chad, Nigeria and Cameroons.
Acrocephalus arundinaceus (Linnaeus)
*_Acrocephalus boeticatus_ (Vieillot) Senegal, Lake Chad, Chad and Cameroons. Local.
Acrocephalus rufescens (Sharpe and Bouvier) (Bann. _Calamoecetor rufescens_ Sharpe and Bouvier)
*_Acrocephalus brevipennis_ Keulemans (Bann. _Calamoecetor brevipennis_ (Keulemans)) Cape Verde Islands.
*_Acrocephalus gracilirostris_ (Hartlaub) (Bann. _Calamoecetor leptorhyncha_ (Reich.)) Lake Chad.

Chloropeta natalensis Smith   Upland savanna of Obudu Plateau and Cameroon highlands and lowland savanna of Cameroons and Gaboon.

Sphenoeacus mentalis (Fraser)   (Bann. *Melocichla mentalis* (Fraser))

Hippolais icterina (Vieillot)   Palaearctic migrant to Ivory Coast, Ghana, Nigeria, Cameroons, Chad, Gaboon and Congo.

Hippolais polyglotta (Vieillot)

Hippolais olivetorum (Strickland)   Rare Palaearctic migrant to Nigeria.

Hippolais pallida Hemprich and Ehrenberg

Sylvia nisoria (Bechstein)   Rare Palaearctic migrant to Nigeria.

Sylvia hortensis (Gmelin)

Sylvia borin (Boddaert)

Sylvia atricapilla (Linnaeus)

Sylvia communis Latham

Sylvia curruca (Linnaeus)   Palaearctic migrant to Mali, Niger, Chad and northern Nigeria.

Sylvia nana (Hemprich and Ehrenberg)   Cape Verde Islands. Vagrant.

Sylvia ruppelli Temminck   Palaearctic migrant to northern Chad.

Sylvia melanocephala (Gmelin)   Palaearctic migrant to Senegal and Mauritania.

Sylvia cantillans (Pallas)

Sylvia conspicillata Temminck   Cape Verde Islands.

Phylloscopus trochilus (Linnaeus)

Phylloscopus collybita (Vieillot)

Phylloscopus bonelli (Vieillot)

Phylloscopus sibilatrix (Bechstein)

Phylloscopus herberti (Alexander) (Bann. *Seicercus herberti* (Alexander)) Montane forests of Fernando Po, Cameroons and Obudu Plateau.

Cisticola erythrops (Hartlaub)

Cisticola cantans (Heuglin)

Cisticola lateralis (Fraser)

Cisticola anonyma (Müller)

Cisticola bulliens Lynes   Gaboon.

Cisticola hunteri Shelley   (Bann. *Cisticola discolor* (Sjöstedt))

Cisticola aberrans Smith   (Bann. *Cisticola emini* (Reichenow))

Cisticola chiniana Smith   Gaboon and Congo.

Cisticola galactotes (Temminck)

Cisticola robusta (Rüppell)   Cameroon highlands and Congo.

Cisticola natalensis (Smith)

Cisticola fulvicapilla (Vieillot)   Gaboon and Congo.

Cisticola ruficeps (Cretzschmar)

Cisticola brachyptera (Sharpe)

Cisticola rufa (Fraser)   Gambia, Mali, Upper Volta, Nigeria, Central African Republic and Chad.

Cisticola troglodytes (Antinori)   Nigeria, Cameroons and Central African Republic.

Cisticola juncidis (Rafinesque)

Cisticola aridula Witherby

Cisticola eximia (Heuglin)   Portuguese Guinea to Central African Republic.

Cisticola brunnescens Heuglin   Cameroon highlands and Congo.

Cisticola ayresi Hartlaub   Gaboon and Congo.

Prinia clamans (Temminck) (Bann. *Spiloptila clamans* (Temminck))   Senegal, Mali, Niger, northern Nigeria and Chad.

Prinia erythroptera (Jardine) (Bann. *Heliolais erythroptera* (Jardine))

Prinia subflava (Gmelin)

*Prinia molleri Bocage Sao Tome.

Prinia epichlora (Reichenow) (Bann. *Urolais epichlora* (Reichenow))

Prinia leucopogon (Cabanis) (Bann. *Prinia leucopogon* (Cabanis) and *Prinia leontica* Bates)

*Prinia bairdii Cassin (Bann. *Herpystera bairdii* (Cassin)) Cameroons and Gaboon.

Apalis pulchra Sharpe

Apalis nigriceps (Shelley)

*Apalis jacksoni Sharpe Forests in Cameroons highlands and lowlands. Local.

*Apalis binotata Reichenow Lowland forests of Cameroons and Gaboon. Local.

*Apalis flavida (Strickland) (Bann. *Apalis caniceps* (Cassin)) Savanna in Ivory Coast, Ghana, Nigeria, Cameroons, Gaboon and Congo. Local.

*Apalis sharpii Shelley (Bann. *Apalis sharpii* Shelley, *Apalis goslingi* Alexander and *Apalis bamendae* Bannerman) Sierra Leone, Liberia, Ivory Coast, Ghana, Bamenda highlands and Cameroons lowland forest. Local.

Apalis cinerea Sharpe

*Apalis rufogularis (Fraser) Lowland forest in Nigeria, Cameroons, Gaboon and Fernando Po. Local.

*Apalis rufifrons (Rüppell) Eastern Chad.

*Apalis pulchella (Cretzschmar) (Bann. *Phyllolais pulchella* (Cretzschmar)) Northern Nigeria and Central African Republic.

*Drymocichla incana Hartlaub Northern Cameroons and Central African Republic.

Hypergerus atriceps (Lesson)

Bathmocercus cerviniventris Sharpe (Bann. *Bathmedonia rufa* (Reichenow) and *Eminia cerviniventris* (Sharpe))

Camaroptera superciliaris (Fraser)

Camaroptera chloronota Reichenow

Camaroptera brachyura (Vieillot) (Bann. *Camaroptera brevicaudata* (Cretzschmar))

*Camaroptera lopezi (Alexander) (Bann. *Poliolais lopezi* (Alexander)) Montane forests of Fernando Po, Cameroons and Obudu Plateau.

Eremomela icteropygialis (Lafresnaye) (Bann. *Eremomela griseoflava* Heuglin)

Eremomela pusilla Hartlaub

*Eremomela scotops Sundevall Wooded savanna in Congo.

Eremomela badiceps (Fraser)

Sylvietta virens Cassin (Bann. *Sylvietta virens* Cassin and *Sylvietta flaviventris* (Sharpe))

Sylvietta denti Ogilvie-Grant

Sylvietta brachyura Lafresnaye

Macrosphenus concolor Hartlaub

Macrosphenus flavicans Cassin (Bann. *Macrosphenus flavicans* Cassin and *Macrosphenus kempi* (Sharpe))

*Amaurocichla bocagei Sharpe Sao Tome.

Hylia prasina (Cassin)

Pholidornis rushiae (Cassin)

MUSCICAPIDAE

Muscicapa striata (Pallas)

*Muscicapa gambagae (Alexander) Wooded savanna in Liberia, Ghana, Nigeria, Cameroons and Chad.

*Muscicapa adusta (Boie) (Bann. *Alseonax minimus* (Heuglin)) Montane forests of Fernando Po and the Cameroons. Also Central African Republic. Local.

Muscicapa aquatica Heuglin (Bann. *Alseonax aquatica* (Heuglin))

Muscicapa cassini Heine (Bann. *Alseonax cassini* (Heine))

*Muscicapa seth-smithi (van Someren) (Bann. *Alseonax seth-smithi* (van Someren)) Lowland forest of Fernando Po, Cameroons and Gaboon.

*Muscicapa epulata (Cassin) (Bann. *Alseonax epulatus* (Cassin)) Lowland forest in Liberia, Ivory Coast, Ghana, Cameroons, Rio Muni and Gaboon.

*Muscicapa olivascens (Cassin) (Bann. *Alseonax olivascens* (Cassin)) Lowland forest in Liberia, Ivory Coast, Ghana, Cameroons and Gaboon.

Muscicapa caerulescens (Hartlaub) (Bann. *Alseonax cinereus* Cassin)

*Muscicapa griseigularis (Jackson) (Bann. *Parisoma griseigularis* (Jackson)) Lowland forest in Liberia, Ivory Coast, Nigeria, Cameroons and Gaboon.

Muscicapa comitata (Cassin) (Bann. *Pedilorhynchus comitatus* Cassin)

*Muscicapa tessmanni (Reichenow) (Bann. *Pedilorhynchus tessmanni* Reichenow Ivory Coast to Cameroons in lowland forest. Rather uncommon.

Artomyias fuliginosa (J. and E. Verreaux)

Artomyias ussheri Sharpe

Myioparus plumbeus (Hartlaub) (Bann. *Parisoma plumbeum* (Hartlaub))

Ficedula hypoleuca (Pallas)

*Ficedula albicollis (Temminck) Palaearctic migrant to Niger, Chad, Ghana, Nigeria and Central African Republic.

*Horizorhinus dohrni (Hartlaub) Principe.

Fraseria ocreata (Strickland)

Fraseria cinerascens Hartlaub

Melaenornis edolioides (Swainson)

*Melaenornis annamarulae Forbes-Watson Lowland forest in Liberia.

Bradornis pallidus (Müller)

Hyliota flavigaster Swainson

*Hyliota violacea Verreaux (Bann. *Hyliota violacea* Verreaux and *Hyliota nehrkorni* Hartlaub) Lowland forest. Liberia and Ivory Coast to Gaboon.

*Hyliota australis Shelley Cameroons. Uncommon.

*Megabyas flammulata Verreaux Lowland forest from Sierra Leone to Gaboon and Congo. Also Fernando Po.

Bias musicus (Vieillot)

*Batis minulla (Bocage) Cameroons and Congo.

Batis minima (Verreaux) (Bann. *Batis minima* (Verreaux) and *Batis poensis* Alexander)

*Batis molitor (Hahn and Kuster) Congo.

*Batis orientalis (Heuglin) (Bann. *Batis minor chadensis* Alexander) Nigeria in vicinity of Lake Chad.

Batis senegalensis (Linnaeus)

Batis minor Erlanger

Platysteira cyanea (Müller)
*Platysteira peltata Sundevall (Bann. *Platysteira laticincta* (Bates)) Montane forest in Bamenda highlands.
Platysteira castanea Fraser (Bann. *Dyaphorophyia castanea* (Fraser))
Platysteira tonsa (Bates) (Bann. *Dyaphorophyia tonsa* Bates)
Platysteira blissetti (Sharpe) (Bann. *Dyaphorophyia blissetti* Sharpe and *Dyaphorophyia chalybea* Reichenow)
Platysteira concreta Hartlaub (Bann. *Dyaphorophyia concreta* (Hartlaub) and *Dyaphorophyia ansorgei* Hartert)
Erythrocercus mccalli (Cassin)
Trochocercus longicauda (Swainson) (Bann. *Erannornis longicauda* (Swainson))
Trochocercus nitens Cassin
*Trochocercus nigromitratus (Reichenow) Lowland forest in Liberia, Nigeria, Cameroons and Gaboon.
Trochocercus albiventris Sjöstedt
Terpsiphone rufiventer (Swainson) (Bann. *Tchitrea rufiventer* (Swainson), *Tchitrea nigriceps* (Hartlaub), *Tchitrea smithii* (Fraser) and *Tchitrea tricolor* (Fraser).
*Terpsiphone atrochalybeia (Thomson) (Bann. *Tchitrea atrochalybeia* (Thomson)) Sao Tome.
Terpsiphone viridis (Müller) (Bann. *Tchitrea viridis* (Müller), *Tchitrea plumbeiceps* (Reichenow) and *Tchitrea melampyra* Verreaux)
*Terpsiphone batesi Chapin (Bann. *Tchitrea batesi* (Chapin)) Cameroons lowland forest.

PARIDAE

Parus leucomelas Rüppell (Bann. *Melaniparus niger* (Vieillot))
*Parus albiventris Shelley (Bann. *Melaniparus albiventris* (Shelley)) Cameroon highlands savanna.
*Parus funereus (Verreaux) (Bann. *Melaniparus funereus* Verreaux) Lowland forest in Liberia, Ghana, Cameroons and Gaboon.
*Parus rufiventris Bocage Congo.

REMIZIDAE

*Remiz caroli (Sharpe) Congo.
Remiz punctifrons (Sundevall) (Bann. *Anthoscopus punctifrons* (Sundevall))
Remiz parvulus (Heuglin) (Bann. *Anthoscopus parvulus* (Heuglin))
*Remiz flavifrons (Cassin) (Bann. *Anthoscopus flavifrons* (Cassin)) Forest clearings in Liberia, Ghana, Nigeria, Cameroons and Gaboon. Uncommon.

SALPORNITHIDAE

Salpornis spilonota (Franklin)

NECTARINIIDAE

Anthreptes gabonicus (Hartlaub)
*Anthreptes pujoli Berlioz Guinea. Rare.
Anthreptes fraseri Jardine

B.W.A.

T

Anthreptes rectirostris (Shaw)

Anthreptes longuemarei (Lesson)

Anthreptes aurantium Verreaux Forested rivers in Nigeria, Cameroons, Gaboon, Congo and Central African Republic.

Anthreptes collaris (Vieillot)

Anthreptes platura (Vieillot) (Bann. *Hedydipna platura* (Vieillot))

Nectarinia seimundi (Ogilvie-Grant) (Bann. *Anthreptes seimundi* (Ogilvie-Grant)) Lowland forest in Sierra Leone to Gaboon. Also Fernando Po.

Nectarinia batesi (Ogilvie-Grant) (Bann. *Cyanomitra batesi* (Ogilvie-Grant)) Forest edges. Ivory Coast to Gaboon and Fernando Po.

Nectarinia olivacea (Smith) (Bann. *Cyanomitra olivacea* (Smith))

Nectarinia ursulae (Alexander) (Bann. *Chalcomitra ursulae* (Alexander)) Montane forest in Cameroons and Fernando Po.

Nectarinia reichenbachii (Hartlaub) (Bann. *Anabathmis reichenbachii* (Hartlaub))

Nectarinia hartlaubii Verreaux (Bann. *Anabathmis hartlaubii* (Verreaux)) Principe.

Nectarinia newtonii Bocage (Bann. *Anabathmis newtonii* (Bocage)) Sao Tome.

Nectarinia thomensis Bocage (Bann. *Dreptes thomensis* (Bocage)) Sao Tome.

Nectarinia oritis (Reichenow) (Bann. *Cyanomitra oritis* (Reichenow))

Nectarinia verticalis (Latham) (Bann. *Cyanomitra verticalis* (Latham))

Nectarinia cyanolaema Jardine (Bann. *Cyanomitra cyanolaema* (Jardine))

Nectarinia fuliginosa (Shaw) (Bann. *Chalcomitra fuliginosa* (Shaw))

Nectarinia rubescens (Vieillot) (Bann. *Chalcomitra rubescens* (Vieillot))

Nectarinia amethystina (Shaw) Congo.

Nectarinia senegalensis (Linnaeus) (Bann. *Chalcomitra senegalensis* (Linnaeus))

Nectarinia adelberti (Gervais) (Bann. *Chalcomitra adelberti* (Gervais))

Nectarinia venusta (Shaw and Nodder) (Bann. *Cinnyris venustus* (Shaw and Nodder))

Nectarinia preussi (Reichenow) (Bann. *Cinnyris reichenowi* Sharpe)

Nectarinia chloropygia Jardine (Bann. *Cinnyris chloropygius* (Jardine))

Nectarinia minulla (Reichenow) (Bann. *Cinnyris minullus* Reichenow)

Nectarinia bifasciata (Shaw) (Bann. *Cinnyris bifasciatus* (Shaw)) Gaboon.

Nectarinia bouvieri (Shelley) (Bann. *Cinnyris bouvieri* Shelley) Obudu Plateau, Cameroons highlands, Central African Republic and Gaboon.

Nectarinia osea (Bonaparte) (Bann. *Cinnyris oseus* Bonaparte) Chad.

Nectarinia cuprea (Shaw) (Bann. *Cinnyris cupreus* (Shaw))

Nectarinia coccinigaster (Latham) (Bann. *Cinnyris coccinigaster* (Latham))

Nectarinia congensis van Oort Congo. Rare.

Nectarinia pulchella (Linnaeus)

Nectarinia johannae (Verreaux) (Bann. *Cinnyris johannae* Verreaux)

Nectarinia superba (Shaw) (Bann. *Cinnyris superbus* (Shaw))

ZOSTEROPIDAE

Zosterops senegalensis Bonaparte (Bann. *Zosterops senegalensis* Bonaparte and *Zosterops virens* Sundevall)

Zosterops ficedulina Hartlaub Principe and Sao Tome.

Zosterops griseovirescens Bocage Annobon.
Speirops brunnea Salvadori Fernando Po.
Speirops leucophaea (Hartlaub) Principe.
Speirops lugubris (Hartlaub) Sao Tome and Cameroon Mountain.

EMBERIZIDAE

Emberiza cia Linnaeus Rare Palaearctic migrant to Chad.
Emberiza hortulana Linnaeus Palaearctic migrant to Senegal, Gambia, Nigeria and Chad.
Emberiza caesia Cretzschmar Rare Palaearctic migrant to Chad.
Emberiza cabanisi (Reichenow)
Emberiza flaviventris Stephens
Emberiza forbesi Hartlaub
Emberiza tahapisi Smith (Bann. *Fringillaria tahapisi* (Smith))
Emberiza striolata Lichtenstein (Bann. *Fringillaria striolata* (Lichtenstein))
  Fringe of Sahara.

FRINGILLIDAE

Serinus mozambicus (Müller)
Serinus leucopygius Sundevall (Bann. *Poliospiza leucopygia* (Sundevall))
Serinus capistratus (Finsch and Hartlaub) Gaboon and Congo.
Serinus burtoni (Gray) (Bann. *Poliospiza burtoni* (Gray)) Montane forests of Cameroons and Obudu Plateau.
Serinus rufobrunneus (Gray) (Bann. *Poliospiza rufobrunnea* (Gray)) Principe and Sao Tome.
Serinus gularis (Smith) (Bann. *Poliospiza gularis* (Smith))
Acanthis cannabina (Linnaeus) Vagrant to Senegal.
Linurgus olivaceus (Fraser)
Rhodopechys githaginea (Lichtenstein) (Bann. *Bucanetes githaginea* (Lichtenstein)) Southern Sahara in Niger and Chad.

PLOCEIDAE

Amblyospiza albifrons (Vigors)
Neospiza concolor (Bocage) Sao Tome.
Ploceus baglafecht (Daudin) (Bann. *Othyphantes baglafecht* (Daudin))
  Cameroon highlands and Ngaundere area.
Ploceus bannermani Chapin (Bann. *Othyphantes bannermani* (Chapin))
  Edges of montane forests in Cameroons.
Ploceus batesi (Sharpe) (Bann. *Othyphantes batesi* Sharpe) Cameroons lowland forest.
Ploceus nigrimentum Reichenow Congo.
Ploceus luteolus (Lichtenstein) (Bann. *Sitagra luteola* (Lichtenstein))
Ploceus subpersonatus (Cabanis) (Bann. *Icteropsis subpersonata* (Cabanis))
  Gaboon.
Ploceus pelzelni (Hartlaub) (Bann. *Sitagra monacha* Sharpe)
Ploceus xanthops (Hartlaub) (*Xanthophilus xanthops* (Hartlaub)) Gaboon and Congo.
Ploceus aurantius (Vieillot) (Bann. *Xanthophilus aurantius* (Vieillot))

Ploceus princeps (Bonaparte) (Bann. *Xanthophilus princeps* (Bonaparte))
Principe.

Ploceus velatus Vieillot (Bann. *Ploceus vitellinus* (Lichtenstein))

Ploceus heuglini Reichenow (Bann. *Plesiositagra heuglini* (Reichenow))

Ploceus cucullatus (Müller) (Bann. *Plesiositagra cucullatus* (Müller) and
Plesiositagra collaris (Vieillot))

Ploceus grandis (Gray) (Bann. *Hyphantornis grandis* Gray) Sao Tome.

Ploceus nigerrimus Vieillot (Bann. *Melanopteryx nigerrimus* (Vieillot) and
Cinnamopteryx castaneofuscus (Lesson))

Ploceus melanocephalus (Linnaeus) (Bann. *Sitagra melanocephala* (Linnaeus)
and *Sitagra capitalis* (Latham))

Ploceus superciliosus (Shelley) (Bann. *Pachyphantes pachyrhynchus* (Reich.))

Ploceus bicolor Vieillot (Bann. *Symplectes amaurocephalus* (Cabanis))
Obudu Plateau, Cameroons, Gaboon and Fernando Po, occurring in highland
and lowland forest.

Ploceus tricolor (Hartlaub) (Bann. *Melanoploceus tricolor* (Hartlaub))

Ploceus albinucha (Bocage) (Bann. *Melanopteryx albinucha* (Bocage))

Ploceus ocularis Smith (Bann. *Hyphanturgus ocularius* (Smith)) Cameroons, Gaboon and Congo.

Ploceus nigricollis (Vieillot) (Bann. *Hyphanturgus brachypterus* (Swainson)
and *Hyphanturgus nigricollis* (Vieillot))

Ploceus melanogaster Shelley (Bann. *Heterhyphantes melanogaster* (Shelley))

Ploceus preussi (Reichenow) (Bann. *Phormoplectes preussi* (Reichenow))
Sierra Leone, Liberia, Ivory Coast, Ghana, Cameroons and Gaboon.

Ploceus dorsomaculatus (Reichenow) (Bann. *Phormoplectes dorsomaculatus*
(Reichenow)) Cameroons lowland forest. Rare.

Ploceus insignis (Sharpe) (Bann. *Phormoplectes insignis* (Sharpe)) Montane
forests of Cameroons, Obudu Plateau and Fernando Po.

Ploceus st.-thomae (Hartlaub) (Bann. *Thomasophantes st-thomae* (Hartlaub))
Sao Tome.

Malimbus coronatus Sharpe Lowland forest in Cameroons, Rio Muni and
Gaboon.

Malimbus cassini (Elliot) Lowland forest in Cameroons and Gaboon.

Malimbus ibadanensis Elgood South-western Nigeria.

Malimbus scutatus (Cassin)

Malimbus racheliae (Cassin) Lowland forest in Nigeria, Cameroons and
Gaboon.

Malimbus nitens (Gray)

Malimbus rubricollis (Swainson)

Malimbus erythrogaster Reichenow Lowland forest in Nigeria, Cameroons
and Gaboon.

Malimbus malimbicus (Daudin)

Malimbus rubriceps (Sundevall) (Bann. *Anaplectes melanotis* (Lafresnaye))

Quelea erythrops (Hartlaub)

Quelea quelea (Linnaeus)

Euplectes afer (Gmelin)

Euplectes albonotatus (Cassin) (Bann. *Coliuspasser albonotatus* (Cassin))
Gaboon and Congo.

Euplectes anomalus (Reichenow) (Bann. *Brachycope anomala* (Reichenow))
Congo and Cameroons.

Euplectes ardens Boddaert (Bann. *Coliuspasser ardens* (Boddaert))
*Euplectes aureus (Gmelin) Sao Tome and Gaboon.
Euplectes axillaris* (Smith) (Bann. *Coliuspasser axillaris* (Smith)) **Mali,
 Niger, Nigeria, Cameroon highlands, Chad and Congo. Local.
**Euplectes capensis* (Linnaeus) Montane grasslands of the Cameroons.
**Euplectes hartlaubi* (Bocage) (Bann. *Coliuspasser hartlaubi* (Bocage)) Camer-
 oon highlands, Gaboon and Congo.
Euplectes hordeaceus (Linnaeus)
Euplectes macrourus (Gmelin) (Bann. *Coliuspasser macrourus* (Gmelin))
Euplectes orix (Linnaeus)
**Anomalospiza imberbis* (Cabanis) Sierra Leone, Mt. Nimba, Ivory Coast,
 Nigeria and Cameroons. Local.
Bubalornis albirostris (Vieillot)
Plocepasser superciliosus (Cretzschmar)
**Passer domesticus* Linnaeus Ennedi Mountains, Chad.
**Passer motitensis* (Smith) (Bann. *Passer iagoensis* (Gould)) Cape Verde
 Islands and eastern Chad.
**Passer hispaniolensis* (Temminck) Cape Verde Islands (resident) and Chad
 (migrant).
*Passer simplex (Lichtenstein) Southern edge of Sahara in Mali, Niger and
 Chad.
Passer griseus (Vieillot)
Passer luteus (Lichtenstein) (Bann. *Auripasser luteus* (Lichtenstein))
**Petronia xanthocollis* (Burton) (Bann. *Gymnoris pyrgita* (Heuglin)) Senegal,
 Mauritania, Niger and Chad.
**Petronia superciliaris* (Blyth) Congo.
Petronia dentata (Sundevall) (Bann. *Gymnoris dentata* (Sundevall))
Sporopipes frontalis (Daudin)
Vidua macroura (Pallas)
Vidua chalybeata (Müller) (Bann. *Hypochera chalybeata* (Müller))
Vidua wilsoni (Hartert) (Bann. *Hypochera funerea* (de Tarragon))
Vidua funerea nigeriae (Alexander) (Bann. *Hypochera nigeriae* Alexander)
Vidua camerunensis (Grote) (Bann. *Hypochera camerunensis* Grote)
Vidua orientalis Heuglin (Bann. *Steganura orientalis* (Heuglin))

ESTRILDIDAE

**Clytospiza monteiri* (Hartlaub) Cameroons. Chad, Central African Republic,
 Congo and Gaboon.
**Clytospiza dybowskii* (Oustalet) Senegal, Sierra Leone, Nigeria, Cameroons,
 Chad, Central African Republic. Local. Savanna often with rocky hills.
**Hypargos nitidulus* (Hartlaub) (Bann. *Mandingoa nitidula* (Hartlaub))
 Sierra Leone to Gaboon and Fernando Po. Evergreen thickets in forest
 clearings.
**Cryptospiza reichenovii* (Hartlaub) Montane forests of Cameroons, Obudu
 Plateau and Fernando Po.
Pirenestes ostrinus (Vieillot) (Bann. *Pirenestes ostrinus* (Vieillot) and *Pirenestes
 sanguineus* Swainson)
Nigrita canicapilla (Strickland)
Nigrita luteifrons Verreaux

Nigrita bicolor (Hartlaub)

Nigrita fusconota Fraser

Parmoptila woodhousei Cassin (Bann. *Parmoptila woodhousei* Cassin and *Parmoptila rubrifrons* Sharpe and Ussher) Lowland forest in Liberia, Ghana, Nigeria, Cameroons, Central African Republic, Gaboon and Congo.

Spermophaga haematina (Vieillot)

Nesocharis capistrata (Hartlaub)

Nesocharis ansorgei (Hartert) (Bann. *Nesocharis shelleyi* Alexander) Montane forests of the Cameroons and Fernando Po.

Amadina fasciata (Gmelin)

Pytilia melba (Linnaeus)

Pytilia afra (Gmelin) Congo.

Pytilia hypogrammica Sharpe In the savanna from Sierra Leone east to Central African Republic and Chad.

Pytilia phoenicoptera Swainson

Estrilda poliopareia Reichenow (Bann. *Estrilda paludicola anambrae* Kemp) Vicinity of Onitsha, Nigeria.

Estrilda paludicola Heuglin Congo.

Estrilda melpoda (Vieillot)

Estrilda nonnula Hartlaub

Estrilda atricapilla J. and E. Verreaux

Estrilda troglodytes (Lichtenstein)

Estrilda astrild (Linnaeus)

Estrilda caerulescens (Vieillot)

Estrilda perreini (Vieillot) Gaboon and Congo.

Estrilda bengala (Linnaeus) (Bann. *Uraeginthus bengalus* (Linnaeus))

Estrilda larvata (Rüppell) (Bann. *Lagonosticta nigricollis* Heuglin and *Lagonosticta vinacea* (Hartlaub))

Lagonosticta rufopicta (Fraser)

Lagonosticta senegala (Linnaeus)

Lagonosticta rhodopareia Heuglin Mali.

Lagonosticta rubricata (Lichtenstein)

Lagonosticta rara Antinori The savanna from Senegal to Central African Republic.

Amandava subflava (Vieillot) (Bann. *Estrilda subflava* (Vieillot))

Ortygospiza locustella (Neave) Congo.

Ortygospiza atricollis (Vieillot)

Lonchura malabarica (Linnaeus) (Bann. *Euodice cantans* (Gmelin))

Lonchura fringilloides (Lafresnaye) (Bann. *Amauresthes fringilloides* (Lafresnaye))

Lonchura bicolor (Fraser) (Bann. *Spermestes poensis* (Fraser))

Lonchura cucullata (Swainson) (Bann. *Spermestes cucullatus* Swainson)

page	Latin	English	Spanish	French	German
	STRUTHIONIDAE				
15	*Struthio camelus*	Ostrich	Avestruz	Autruche	Strauss
	PODICIPEDIDAE				
15	*Podiceps ruficollis*	Dabchick	Zampullin Chico	Grèbe Castagneux	Zwergtaucher
	PELECANIDAE				
15	*Pelecanus rufescens*	Pink-backed or Grey Pelican	Pelicano Africano Gris	Pélican Gris	Rötelpelikan
18	*P. onocrotalus*	White Pelican	Pelicano Vulgar	Pélican Blanc	Rosapelikan
	PHALACROCORACIDAE				
18	*Phalacrocorax africanus*	Long-tailed Shag	Cormoran Africano Chico	Cormoran Africain	Riedscharbe
18	*P. carbo lucidus*	White-breasted Cormorant	Cormoran Grande	Grand Cormoran	Kormoran
18	*Anhinga rufa*	African Darter	Marbella	Anhinga d'Afrique	Afrikanischer Schlangenhalsvogel
	ARDEIDAE				
19	*Ixobrychus minutus*	Little Bittern	Avetorillo Europeo	Butor Blongios	Zwergdommel
19	*I. sturmii (Ardeirallus sturmii)*	Dwarf Bittern	Avetorillo Etiópico	Blongios de Stúrm	Graurückendommel (Schieferdommel)
19	*Tigriornis leucolopha*	Tiger Bittern	Avetigre de Calabar	Butor à Crête Blanche	Weissschopfreiher
19	*Nycticorax nycticorax*	Night Heron	Martinete Europeo	éron Bihoreau	Nachtreiher
20	*N. leuconotus*	White-backed Night Heron	Martinete Dorsiblanco	Bihoreau à Dos Blanc	Weissrückenreiher
20	*Ardeola ralloides*	Squacco Heron	Garcilla Cangrejera	Héron Crabier	Rallenreiher
20	*A. ibis (Bubulcus ibis)*	Cattle Egret	Garcilla Bueyera	Héron Garde-boeufs	Kuhreiher
21	*Butorides striatus*	Green-backed Heron	Garcita Verdosa	Héron à Dos Vert	Mangrovereiher
21	*Egretta alba (Casmerodius albus)*	Great White Egret	Garceta Grande	Grande Aigrette	Silberreiher
21	*E. intermedia*	Yellow-billed Egret	Garcilla Intermedia	Aigrette Intermédiaire	Mittelreiher
21	*E. ardesiaca*	Black Heron	Garcita Negra Africana	Héron Noir	Glockenreiher

page	Latin	English	Spanish	French	German
	ARDEIDAE (cont.)				
21	E. garzetta	Little Egret	Garceta Común	Aigrette Garzette	Seidenreiher
22	E. gularis	Reef Heron	Garceta Sombria	Aigrette Dimorphe	Küstenreiher
	(Demigretta gularis)				
22	Ardea cinerea	Grey Heron	Garza Real	Héron Cendré	Fischreiher (Graureiher)
22	A. melanocephala	Black-headed Heron	Garza Cuellinegra	Héron Mélanocéphale	Schwarzhalsreiher
22	A. goliath	Goliath Heron	Garza Goliat	Héron Goliath	Goliathreiher
	(Typhon goliath)				
23	A. purpurea	Purple Heron	Garza Purpúrea	Héron Pourpré	Purpurreiher
	(Pyrrherodia purpurea)				
	SCOPIDAE				
23	Scopus umbretta	Hammerkop	Ave Martillo	Ombrette	Hammerkopf (Schattenvogel)
	CICONIIDAE				
23	Ciconia abdimii	Abdim's Stork	Gigüeña de Abdim	Cigogne d'Abdim	Abdimstorch
	(Sphenorynchus abdimii)				
24	C. episcopus	White-necked Stork	Gigüeña Lanuda	Cigogne Episcopale	Wollhalsstorch
	(Dissoura episcopus)				
24	C. ciconia	White Stork	Gigüeña Comúa	Cigogne Blanche	Weisstorch
24	Ephippiorhynchus senegalensis	Saddlebill Stork	Gigüeña Ensillada	Jabiru du Sénégal	Sartelstorch
25	Anastomus lamelligerus	Openbill	Picotijera	Bec-ouvert	Schwarzer Klaffschnabel
25	Leptoptilos crumeniferus	Marabou Stork	Marabú Africano	Marabout	Marabu
25	Ibis ibis	Wood Ibis	Tántalo Africano	Tantale Ibis	Nimmersart
	THRESKIORNITHIDAE				
26	Threskiornis aethiopica	Sacred Ibis	Ibis Sagrado	Ibis Sacré	Heiliger Ibis
26	Bostrychia hagedash	Hadada Ibis	Ibis Hadada	Ibis Hagedash	Hagedasch
	(Hagedashia hagedash)				
26	B. rara	Spotted-breasted Ibis	Ibis Rara	Ibis Vermiculé	Fleckenibis
26	B. olivacea	Olive Ibis	Ibis Oliváceo	Ibis Olivâtre	Guinea-Ibis
26	Plegadis falcinellus	Glossy Ibis	Morito	Ibis Falcinelle	Braunsichler

page	Latin	English	Spanish	French	German
	THRESKIORNITHIDAE (cont.)				
27	Platalea alba	African Spoonbill	Espátl Africanula	Spatule d'Afrique	Afrikanischer Löffler
27	P. leucorodia	European Spoonbill		Spatule Blanche	(Rosenfusslöffler)
	PHOENICOPTERIDAE				
27	Phoenicopterus ruber	Greater Flamingo	Flamenco Común	Flamant Rose	Flamingo
27	P. minor	Lesser Flamingo	Flamenco Enano	Petit Flamant	Zwergflamingo (Kleiner Flamingo)
	ANATIDAE				
28	Dendrocygna bicolor (Dendrocygna fulva)	Fulvous Tree-duck	Suiriri Leonado	Dendrocygne Fauve	Gelbbrust-pfeifgans
28	D. viduata	White-faced Tree-duck	Suiriri Cariblanco	Dendrocygne Veuf	Witwenpfeifgans (Witwenente)
28	Alopochen aegyptiaca	Egyptian Goose	Ganso Del Nilo	Oie d'Egypte	Nilgans
29	Plectropterus gambensis	Spur-winged Goose	Ganso Del Gambia	Canard Armé	Sporengans
29	Pteronetta hartlaubii	Hartlaub's Duck	Pato de Hartlaub	Canard de Hartlaub	Hartlaubente
29	Sarkidiornis melanota	Knob-billed Goose	Pato Crestón	Canard Casqué	Glanzente
30	Nettapus auritus	Pigmy Goose	Patito Africano	Sarcelle à Oreillons	Rotbrust-Zwerggans
30	Anas sparsa	African Black Duck	Anade Negro Africano	Canard Noir	Schwarzene (Fleckente)
30	A. hottentota	Hottentot Teal	Cerceta Hotentote	Sarcelle Hottentote	Hottentottenente
30	A. acuta (Dafila acuta)	Pintail	Anade Rabudo	Pilet	Spiessente
31	A. querquedula	Garganey	Cerceta Carretona	Sarcelle d'Eté	Krähente
31	A. crecca	European Teal	Cerceta Común	Sarcelle d'Hiver	Krickente
31	A. clypeata (Spatula clypeata)	Shoveler	Pato Cuchara	Souchet	Löffelente
34	Aythya nyroca (Nyroca nyroca)	Ferruginous Duck	Porrón Pard	Fuligule Nyroca	Moorente
34	Thalassornis leuconotus	White-backed Duck	Porrón Dorsiblanco	Canard à Dos Blanc	Weissrücken-pfeifgans (Weissrückenente)
	ACCIPITRIDAE				
35	Aegypius tracheliotus (Torgos tracheliotus)	Nubian or Lappet-faced Vulture	Buitre Orejudo	Oricou	Ohrengeier
35	Trigonoceps occipitalis	White-headed Vulture	Buitre Piquirrojo	Vautour Huppé	Wollkopfgeier

page	Latin	English	Spanish	French	German
	ACCIPITRIDAE (cont.)				
35	*Gyps rüppellii*	Ruppell's Griffon Vulture	Buitre Moteado	Vautour de Rüppell	Sperbergeier
35	*G. bengalensis* (*Pseudogyps africanus*)	White-backed Vulture	Buitre Leonado Bengalés	Gyps Africain	Weissrückengeier
38	*Neophron monachus* (*Necrosyrtes monachus*)	Hooded Vulture	Alimoche Sombrío	Percnoptère Brun	Kappengeier
38	*N. percnopterus*	Egyptian Vulture	Alimoche Común	Percnoptère d'Egypte	Schmutzgeier
38	*Gypohierax angolensis*	Palm-nut Vulture	Aguila Vulturina	Vautour Palmiste	Palmgeier (Geierseeadler)
39	*Circus macrourus*	Pallid Harrier	Aguilucho Papialbo	Busard Pâle	Steppenweihe
39	*C. pygargus*	Montagu's Harrier	Aguilucho Cenizo	Busard Cendré	Wiesenweihe
39	*C. aeruginosus*	Marsh Harrier	Aguilucho Lagunero	Busard des Roseaux	Rohrweihe
39	*Polyboroides radiatus* (*Gymnogenys typicus*)	Harrier Hawk	Azor Culebrero	Petit Serpentaire	Höhlenweihe
40	*Terathopius ecaudatus*	Bateleur	Aguila Volantinera	Bateleur	Gaukler
40	*Circaetus gallicus*	Short-toed Eagle or Snake Eagle	Aguila Culebrera	Circaète Jean-le-Blanc	Schlangenadler
40	*C. beaudouini*	Beaudouin's Harrier-Eagle	Aguila Culebrera de Beaudouin	Circaète de Beaudouin	Senegalschlangenadler
40	*C. cinereus*	Brown Harrier-Eagle	Aguila Culebrera de Brown	Circaète Brun	Einfarb-schlangenadler
41	*C. cinerascens*	Banded Harrier-Eagle	Aguila Culebrera Culiblanca	Circaète Cendré	Band-schlangenadler
41	*Dryotriorchis spectabilis*	Serpent Eagle	Aguila Culebrera Colilarga	Aigle Serpentaire	Schlangenbussard
41	*Accipiter melanoleucus*	Great Sparrowhawk	Azor Blanquinegro	Epervier Pie	Mohrenhabicht
41	*A. toussenlii*	West African Goshawk	Gavilán Pechirroseo	Autour Tachiro	Guineahabicht
42	*A. castanilius*	Chestnut-flanked Goshawk	Gavilán Pechirrojo	Autour à Flancs Roux	Rotflankenhabicht
42	*A. badius*	Shikra	Gavilán Chikra	Epervier Shikra	Schikra
42	*A. ovampensis*	Ovampo Sparrowhawk	Gavilán de Ovampo	Epervier de l'Ovampo	Ovambospherber
42	*A. erythropus* (*A. minullus*)	West African Little Sparrowhawk	Gavilancito de Hartlaub	Autour Minulle	Waldsperber

page	Latin	English	Spanish	French	German
	ACCIPITRIDAE (cont.)				
42	*Melierax metabates*	Chanting Goshawk	Azor Lagartijero	Autour Chanteur	Graubürzel-singhabicht
43	*M. gabar* (*Micronisus gabar*)	Gabar Goshawk	Gavilán Gabar	Autour Gabar	Gabarhabicht
43	*Urotriorchis macrourus*	Long-tailed Hawk	Azor Rabilargo	Autour à Longue Queue	Langschwanzhabicht
43	*Kaupifalco monogrammicus*	Lizard Buzzard	Azor Barbiluengo	Buse Unibande	Sperberbussard (Kehlstreifbussard)
46	*Butastur rufipennis*	Grasshopper Buzzard	Aguililla Langostera	Busard des Sauterelles	Heuschreckenteesa
46	*Buteo auguralis*	Red-tailed Buzzard	Ratonero Cueliirojo	Buse à Queue Rousse	Salvadoribussard (Argusbussard)
46	*Lophaetus occipitalis*	Long-crested Hawk-Eagle	Aguila Copetuda Africana	Aigle Huppard	Schopfadler
46	*Stephanoaetus coronatus*	Crowned Hawk-Eagle	Aguila Coronada Rabuda	Aigle Blanchard	Kronenadler
47	*Hieraaetus africanus*	Cassin's Hawk-Eagle	Aguila de Cassin	Aigle-autour Africain	Schwarzachseladler
47	*H. dubius*	Ayres' Hawk-Eagle	Aguila de Ayres	Aigle-autour d'Ayres	Fleckenadler
47	*H. spilogaster*	African Hawk-Eagle	Aguila Perdicera Africana	Aigle-autour Fascié	Afrikanischer habichtsadler
47	*Polemaetus bellicosus*	Martial Eagle	Aguila Lidiadora	Aigle Martial	Kampfadler
47	*Aquila rapax*	Tawny Eagle	Aguila Rapaz	Aigle Ravisseur	Raubadler
50	*A. wahlbergi*	Wahlberg's Eagle	Aguila de Wahlberg	Aigle de Wahlberg	Wahlbergadler (Silberadler)
50	*Haliaeetus vocifer* (*Cuncuma vocifer*)	West African River Eagle	Pigargo Vocinglero	Aigle Pêcheur	Schreiseeadler
50	*Milvus migrans*	Black Kite	Milano Negro	Milan Noir	Schwarzmilan
51	*Pernis apivorus*	Honey Buzzard	Nalcón Abejero	Bondrée Apivore	Wespenbussard
51	*Aviceda cuculoides*	West African Cuckoo Falcon	Baza Africano	Faucon-coucou	Kuckucksweih
51	*Elanus caeruleus*	Black-shouldered Kite	Elanio Azul	Elanion Blanc	Gleitaar
51	*E. riocourii* (*Chelictinia riocourii*)	Swallow-tailed Kite	Elanio Tijereta Africano	Naucler d' Afrique	Schwalbens Chwanzaar
52	*Macheirhamphus alcinus*	Bat Hawk	Aguila Murcielaguera	Faucon des Chauves-souris	Fledermausaar
52	*Pandion haliaetus*	Osprey	Aguila Pescadora	Balbuzard Pêcheur	Fischadler

page	Latin	English	Spanish	French	German
FALCONIDAE					
52	*Falco biarmicus*	Lanner Falcon	Halcón Borni	Faucon Lanier	Lannerfalke
53	*F. peregrinus*	Peregrine Falcon	Halcón Peregrino	Faucon Pèlerin	Wanderfalke
53	*F. cuvieri*	African Hobby	Alcotán de Cuvier	Hobereau Africain	Afrikanischer Baumfalke
53	*F. chicquera*	Red-necked Kestrel	Alcotán Cuellirrojo	Faucon à Cou Roux	Rothalsfalke
53	*F. ardosiaceus*	Grey Kestrel	Cernícalo Pizarroso	Faucon Ardoisé	Graufalke
54	*F. tinnunculus*	Kestrel	Cernícalo Vulgar	Crécerelle	Turmfalke
54	*F. naumanni*	Lesser Kestrel	Cernícalo Primilla	Crécerellette	Rötelfalke
54	*F. alopex*	Fox Kestrel	Cernícalo Zorruno	Faucon-renard	Fuchsfalke
SAGITTARIIDAE					
54	*Sagittarius serpentarius*	Secretary-bird	Secretatio	Serpentaire	Sekretär
PHASIANIDAE					
55	*Francolinus lathami*	Latham's Francolin	Francolin de Latham	Francolin de Latham	Waldfrankolin
55	*F. albogularis*	White-throated Francolin	Francolin Gorgiblanco	Francolin à Gorge Blanche	Weisskehlfrankolin
55	*F. coqui*	Coqui Francolin	Francolin Coqui	Francolin à Poitrine Barrée	Coquifrankolin
56	*F. bicalcaratus*	Double-spurred Francolin	Francolin Biespolado	Francolin Commun	Doppelspornfrankolin
56	*F. clappertoni*	Clapperton's Francolin	Francolin de Clapperton	Francolin de Clapperton	Clappertonfrankolin
56	*F. squamatus*	Scaly Francolin	Francolin Escamoso	Francolin Ecailleux	Schuppenfrankolin
57	*F. ahantensis*	Ahanta Francolin	Francolin Ahanta	Francolin d' Ahanta	Ahantafrankolin
57	*Coturnix delegorguei*	Harlequin Quail		Caille Arlequin	Harlekinwachtel
57	*C. coturnix*	Common Quail	Codorniz Europea	Caille des Blés	Wachtel
57	*C. chinensis*	African Blue Quail	Codorniz China	Caille Bleue	Zwergwachtel
	(*Excalfactoria adansoni*)				
58	*Ptilopachus petrosus*	Stone-partridge	Perdicilla Roquera	Poule de Rocher	Felsenrebhuhn
58	*Numida meleagris*	Grey-breasted Helmet Guinea-fowl	Pintade Común	Pintade Commune	Helmperlhuhn
58	*Guttera edouardi*	Crested Guinea-fowl	Pintade Moñuda de Eduardo	Pintade Huppée	Kräuselhauben-perlhuhn

page	Latin	English	Spanish	French	German
	PHASIANIDAE (cont.)				
58	*G. plumifera*	Plumed Guinea-fowl	Pintada Plumi Fera	Pintade à Crête	Schlichthauben-perlhuhn
59	*Agelastes meleagrides*	White-breasted Guinea-fowl	Pintada Pechiblanca	Pintade à Poitrine blanche	Weissbrust-perlhuhn
59	*A. niger*	Black Guinea-fowl	Pintada Unicolor	Pintade Noire	Schwarzperlhuhn
	RALLIDAE				
59	*Canirallus oculeus*	Grey-throated Rail	Rascón Cariris	Râle à Gorge Grise	Augenralle
59	*Himantornis haematopus*	Nkulengu Rail	Polla Nkulenga	Râle à Pattes Rouges	Rotfussralle
59	*Crex egregia* (*Crecopsis egregia*)	African Crake	Guión Egregio	Râle Africain	Steppenralle
60	*C. crex*	European Corn Crake	Guión de Codornices	Râle de Genêts	Wachtelkönig
60	*Porzana marginalis*	Striped Crake	Polluela Listada	Marouette d' Afrique	Graukehl–Sumpfhuhn
60	*Limnocorax flavirostra*	Black Crake	Polluela Negra	Râle Noir	Mohrenralle
60	*Sarothrura pulchra*	White-spotted Pigmy Rail	Rallícula Pulcra	Râle Pygmée	Perlenschmuckralle
61	*S. rufa*	Red-chested Pigmy Rail	Rallícula de Vieillot	Râle Nain à Poitrine Châtaine	Rotbrust-schmuckralle
61	*S. elegans*	Buff-spotted Pigmy Rail	Rallícula Elegante	Râle Nain Elégant	Tropfenschmuckralle
61	*Gallinula chloropus*	Moorhen	Polla de Agua	Poule d'Eau	Teichhuhn
61	*G. angulata*	Lesser Moorhen	Polla de Sundevall	Petite Poule d'Eau	Zwergteichhuhn
61	*Porphyrio porphyrio* (*Porphyrio madagascariensis*)	King Reed-hen	Calamón Común	Poule Sultane	Purpurhuhn
62	*P. alleni* (*Porphyrulla alleni*)	Allen's Reed-hen	Calamón de Allen	Poule d'Allen	Afrikanisches sultanshuhn
62	*Fulica atra*	European Coot	Focha Común	Foulque Macroule	Blässhuhn
	HELIORNITHIDAE				
62	*Podica senegalensis*	Finfoot	Gallifocha	Grébifoulque	Afrikanische Binsenralle
	GRUIDAE				
63	*Balearica pavonina*	Crowned Crane	Grulla Coronada	Grue Couronnée	Kronenkranich

page	Latin	English	Spanish	French	German
OTIDIDAE					
63	*Otis arabs*	Sudan Bustard	Avutatda Árabe	Grande Outarde	Arabertrappe
	(*Ardeotis arabs*)			Arabe	
66	*Neotis denhami*	Denham's Bustard	Avutarda de Denham	Outarde de Denham	Stanleytrappe
66	*N. nuba*	Nubian Bustard	Avutarda Nubica	Outarde de Nubie	Nubiertrappe
66	*Eupodotis senegalensis*	Senegal Bustard	Avutarda Senegalesa	Poule de Pharaon	Senegaltrappe
66	*E. ruficrista*	Savile's Pigmy Bustard	Sisón Moñirrojo	Outarde Naine	
66	*E. melanogaster*	Black-bellied Bustard	Sisón Ventrinegro	Outarde à Ventre Noir	Schwarzbauchtrappe
	(*Lissotis melanogaster*)				
JACANIDAE					
67	*Actophilornis africana*	Lily-trotter	Jacana Africana	Jacana	Blaustirn-blatthühnchen
67	*Microparra capensis*	Lesser Lily-trotter	Jacanita del Cabo	Petit Jacana	Zwergblatthühnchen
BURHINIDAE					
70	*Burhinus senegalensis*	Senegal Thick-knee	Alcaraván Senegalés	Oedicnème du Sénégal	Senegaltriel
	(*Oedicnemus senegalensis*)				
70	*B. vermiculatus*	Water Thick-knee	Alcaraván Acuatico	Oedicnème Vermiculé	Wassertriel
70	*B. capensis*	Spotted Thick-knee	Alcaraván del Cabo	Oedicnème du Cap	Kaptriel
	(*Oedicnemus capensis*)				
HAEMATOPODIDAE					
84	*Haematopus ostralegus*	Oyster-catcher	Ostrero	Huitrier Pie	Austernfischer
CHARADRIIDAE					
71	*Vanellus spinosus*	Spur-winged Plover	Avefria Espolada	Vanneau Armé	Spornkiebitz
	(*Hoplopterus spinosus*)				
71	*V. crassirostris*	White-faced Lapwing	Avefría Palustre	Vanneau à Face Blanche	Langzehenkiebitz
71	*V. tectus*	Black-headed Plover	Avefría de Babero	Vanneau à Tête Noire	Schwarzkopfkiebitz
	(*Sarciophorus tectus*)				
71	*V. albiceps*	White-headed Plover	Chorlito Espolado	Vanneau à Tête Blanche	Langspornkiebitz
	(*Xiphidiopterus albiceps*)		Cariblanco		
72	*V. lugubris*	Senegal Plover	Chorlito Lúgubre	Vanneau Terne	Trauerkiebitz
	(*Stephanibyx lugubris*)				

page	Latin	English	Spanish	French	German
	CHARADRIIDAE (cont.)				
72	V. senegallus (Afribyx senegallus)	Senegal Wattled Plover	Chorlito Carunculado senegalés	Vanneau Caronculé	Senegalkiebitz
72	V. superciliosus (Anomalophrys superciliosus)	Brown-chested Wattled Plover	Chorlito Supercilioso	Vanneau à Poitrine Châtaine	Rotbrustkiebitz
73	Pluvialis squatarola (Squatarola squatarola)	Grey Plover	Chorlito Gris	Pluvier Argenté	Kiebitzregenpfeifer
73	Charadrius hiaticula	Ringed Plover	Chorlitejo Grande	Grand Gravelot	Sandregenpfeifer
73	C. dubius	Little Ringed Plover	Chorlitejo Chico	Petit Gravelot	Flussregenpfeifer
73	C. pecuarius (Leucopolius pecuarius)	Kittlitz's Sand Plover	Chorlitejo de Kittlitz	Pluvier Pâtre	Hirtenregenpfeifer
74	C. forbesi (Afroxyechus forbesi)	Forbes's Banded Plover	Chorlitejo de Forbes	Pluvier à Triple Collier	Braunstirnregenpfeifer
74	C. marginatus (Leucopolius marginatus)	White-fronted Sand Plover	Chorlitejo Marginado	Pluvier à Front Blanc	Weissstirnregenpfeifer
74	C. alexandrinus	Kentish Plover	Chorlitejo Patinegro	Gravelot à Collier Interrompu	Seeregenpfeifer
75	Numenius phaeopus	Whimbrel	Zarapito Trinador	Courlis Corlieu	Regenbrachvogel
75	N. arquata	Curlew	Zarapito Real	Courlis Cendré	Grosser Brachvogel
75	Limosa limosa	Black-tailed Godwit	Aguja Colinegra	Barge à Queue Noire	Uferschnepfe
75	L. lapponica	Bar-tailed Godwit	Aguja Colipinta	Barge Rousse	Pfuhlschnepfe
75	Tringa nebularia (Glottis nebularius)	Greenshank	Archibebe Claro	Chevalier Aboyeur	Grünschenkel
78	T. stagnatilis (Glottis stagnatilis)	Marsh Sandpiper	Archibebe Fino	Chevalier Stagnatile	Teichwasserläufer
78	T. glareola	Wood Sandpiper	Andarrios Bastardo	Chevalier Sylvain	Bruchwasserläufer
78	T. ochropus	Green Sandpiper	Andarrios Grande	Chevalier Cul-blanc	Waldwasserläufer
78	T. hypoleucos (Actitis hypoleucos)	Common Sandpiper	Andarrios Chico	Chevalier Guignette	Flussuferläufer
79	T. totanus	Redshank	Archibebe Común	Chevalier Gambtete	Rotschenkel
79	T. erythropus	Spotted Redshank	Archibebe Oscuro	Chevalier Arlequin	Dunkler Wasserläufer
79	Arenaria interpres	Turnstone	Vuelbepiedras	Tournepierre à Collier	Steinwälzer
79	Gallinago gallinago (Capella gallinago)	Common Snipe	Agachadiza Común	Bécassine des Marais	Bekassine

page	Latin	English	Spanish	French	German
	CHARADRIIDAE (cont.)				
82	*G. media*	Great Snipe	Agachadiza Real	Bécassine Double	Doppelschnepfe
82	*G. minima*	Jack Snipe	Agachadiza Chica	Bécassine Sourde	Zwergschnepfe
82	*Calidris ferruginea* (*Erolia testacea*)	Curlew Sandpiper	Correlimos Zarapitín	Bécasseau Cocorli	Sichelstrandläufer
82	*C. alpina*	Dunlin	Correlimos Común	Bécasseau Variable	Alpenstrandläufer
82	*C. canutus*	Knot	Correlimos Gordo	Bécasseau Maubêche	Knutt
82	*C. minuta* (*Erolia minuta*)	Little Stint	Correlimos Menudo	Bécasseau Minute	Zwergstrandläufer
83	*C. temmincki*	Temminck's Stint	Correlimos de Temminck	Bécasseau de Temminck	Temminckstrandläufer
83	*C. alba* (*Crocethia alba*)	Sanderling	Correlimos Tridáctilo	Bécasseau Sanderling	Sanderling
83	*Philomachus pugnax*	Ruff	Combatiente	Chevalier Combattant	Kampfläufer
83	*Himantopus himantopus*	Black-winged Stilt	Cigüeñuela Española	Echasse Blanche	Stelzenläufer
84	*Rostratula benghalensis*	Painted Snipe	Rostrátula Bengalesa	Rhynchée	Goldschnepfa
	GLAREOLIDAE				
84	*Pluvianus aegyptius*	Crocodile Bird	Pluvial Egipcio	Pluvian d'Egypte	Krokodilwächter
85	*Cursorius cursor*	Cream-coloured Courser	Corredor Canario	Courvite Isabelle	Rennvogel
85	*C. temmincki*	Temminck's Courser	Corredor de Temminck	Courvite de Temminck	Temminckrennvogel
85	*C. chalcopterus*	Bronze-wing Courser	Corredor Alipúrpura	Courvite à Ailes Bronzées	Amethystrennvogel
86	*Glareola pratincola*	Pratincole	Canastera Española	Glaréole à Collier	Brachschwalbe
86	*G. nuchalis*	Collared Pratincole	Canastera de Collera	Glaréole à Collier Blanc	Halsband-Brachschwalbe
86	*G. cinerea*	Grey Pratincole	Canastera gris	Glaréole Cendrée	Weissachsel- Brachschwalbe
	LARIDAE				
87	*Larus cirrhocephalus*	Grey-headed Gull	Gaviota Carigris	Mouette à Tête Grise	Graukopfmöwe
87	*L. ridibundus*	Black-headed Gull	Gaviota Reidora	Mouette Rieuse	Lachmöwe
87	*L. genei*	Slender-billed Gull	Gaviota Picofina	Goéland Railleur	Dünnschnabelmöwe

page	Latin	English	Spanish	French	German
	LARIDAE (cont.)				
87	L. fuscus	Lesser Black-backed Gull	Gaviota Sombria	Goéland Brun	Heringsmöwe
88	L. argentatus	Herring Gull	Gaviota Argéntea	Goéland Argenté	Silbermöwe
88	Rynchops flavirostris	African Skimmer	Rayador	Bec-en-Ciseau	Braunmantel-Scherenschnabel
88	Sterna nilotica (Gelochelidon nilotica)	Gull-billed Tern	Pagaza Piconegra	Sterne Hansel	Lachseeschwalbe
89	S. caspia (Hydroprogne caspia)	Caspian Tern	Pagaza Piquirroja	Sterne Caspienne	Raubseeschwalbe (Riesenseeschwalbe)
89	S. hirundo	Common Tern	Charrán Común	Sterne Pierregarin	Flusseeschwalbe
89	S. maxima	Royal Tern	Charrán Real	Sterne Royale	Königsseeschwalbe
89	S. sandvicensis	Sandwich Tern	Charrán Patinegro	Sterne Caugek	Brandseeschwalbe
89	S. paradisea	Arctic Tern	Charrán Ártico	Sterne Arctique	Küstenseeschwalbe
90	S. leucoptera (Chlidonias leucoptera)	White-winged Tern	Fumarel Aliblanco	Guifette Leucoptère	Weissflügel-Seeschwalbe
90	S. hybrida	Whiskered Tern	Fumarel Cariblanco	Guifette Moustac	Weissbartseeschwalbe
90	S. nigra	Black Tern	Fumarel Común	Guifette Noire	Trauerseeschwalbe
90	S. albifrons	Little Tern	Charrancito	Sterne Naine	Zwergseeschwalbe
	PTEROCLIDIDAE				
91	Pterocles exustus	Chestnut-bellied Sand-grouse	Ganga Moruna	Ganga Sénégalais	Braunbauch-Flughuhn
91	P. quadricinctus	Four-banded Sand-grouse	Ganga de Collares	Ganga de Gambie	Buschflughuhn
	TURNICIDAE				
92	Turnix sylvatica	African Button-quail	Torillo Común	Turnix d'Afrique	Spitzschwanz-Laufhühnchen
92	T. hottentotta nana	Black-rumped Button-quail	Torillo Hotentote	Turnix Nain	Hottentotten Laufhühnchen
92	Ortyxelos meiffrenii	Quail-Plover	Chorlo Torillo	Turnix de Meiffren	Lerchenlaufhühnchen

B.W.A.

U

page	Latin	English	Spanish	French	German
	COLUMBIDAE				
92	Columba unicincta	Grey Wood Pigeon	Paloma Afep	Pigeon Gris Ecailleux	Kongotaube
93	C. arquatrix	Olive Pigeon	Paloma Rejujú	Pigeon des Montagnes du Cameroun	Oliventaube
93	C. malherbii	Bronze-naped Pigeon	Zurita de Santo Tomé	Pigeon à Nuque Bronzée de Sao Tomé	Malherbetaube
93	C. guinea	Speckled Pigeon	Paloma de Guinea	Pigeon de Guinée	Guineataube
93	Streptopelia semitorquata	Red-eyed Dove	Tórtola Rizum	Tourterelle à Collier	Halbmondtaube
94	S. turtur	European Turtle-dove	Tórtola Común	Tourterelle des Bois	Turteltaube
94	S. lugens hypopyrrhus	Adamawan Turtle-dove	Tórtola Llorona	Tourterelle de l'Adamaoua	Trauerturteltaube
94	S. decipiens	Mourning Dove	Tórtola Engañosa	Tourterelle Pleureuse	Brillentaube
94	S. vinacea	Vinaceous Dove	Tórtola Vinosa	Tourterelle Vineuse	Röteltaube
95	S. roseogrisea	Rose-grey Dove	Tórtola Rosigris	Tourterelle Rieuse	Lachtaube
95	S. senegalensis (Stigmatopelia senegalensis)	Laughing Dove	Tórtola Senegalesa	Tourterelle Maillée	Palmtaube (Senegaltaube)
95	Oena capensis	Long-tailed Dove	Palomita Especulada Capense	Tourterelle du Cap	Kaptäubchen
95	Turtur tympanistria (Tympanistria tympanistria)	Tambourine Dove	Tórtola tamborilera	Tourterelle Tambourette	Tambourintaube
98	T. afer	Red-billed Wood-Dove	Palomita Especulada Africana	Emerauldine à Bec Rouge	Stahlflecktaube
98	T. abyssinica	Black-billed Wood-Dove	Palomita Especulada Abisinica	Emerauldine à Bec Noir	Erzflecktaube
98	T. brehmeri (Calopelia puella)	Blue-headed Dove	Palomita Especulada Cobriza	Tourterelle à Tête Bleue	Maidtaube
98	Aplopelia larvata	Lemon Dove	Palomita Encantada	Tourterelle du Cameroun	Zimttaube
99	Treron australis (Vinago australis)	Green Fruit-pigeon	Vinago Obeng	Pigeon Vert à Front Nu	Grüntaube
99	T. waalia (Vinago waalia)	Yellow-bellied Fruit-Pigeon	Vinago Waalia	Pigeon à Epaulettes Violettes	Waaliataube

page	Latin	English	Spanish	French	German
	PSITTACIDAE				
99	*Poicephalus robustus*	Brown-necked Parrot	Papagayo robusto	Perroquet Robuste	Kappapagei
102	*P. gulielmi*	Red-crowned Parrot	Papagayo de Gulielm	Perroquet Vert à Calotte Rouge	Kongopapagei
102	*P. senegalus*	Senegal Parrot	Papagayo Senegalés	Youyou	Mohrenkopf
102	*Psittacus erithacus*	Grey Parrot	Yaco	Jacko	Graupapagei
102	*Psittacula krameri*	Senegal Long-tailed Parrakeet	Loro Rabudo Collar	Perruche à Collier	Halsbandsittich
103	*Agapornis pullaria*	Red-headed Lovebird	Inseparable Carirrojo	Inséparable à Tête Rouge	Orangeköpfchen
103	*A. swinderniana*	Black-collared Lovebird	Inseparable de Collera	Inséparable à Collier Noir	Grunköpfchen
	MUSOPHAGIDAE				
103	*Tauraco persa* (*Turacus persa*)	Green-crested Touraco	Turaco Capucha-verde de Guinea	Touraco Vert	Hollenturako
103	*T. bannermani*	Bannerman's Touraco	Turaco de Bannerman	Touraco Doré	Bannermanturako
104	*T. macrorhynchus* (*Turacus macrorhynchus*)	Verreaux's Touraco	Turaco Capucha-franjeada	Touraco à Gros Bec	Blaurückenturako
104	*T. leucolophus* (*Turacus leucolophus*)	White-crested Touraco	Turaco Capucha-blanca	Touraco à Huppe Blanche	Weisshaubenturako
104	*Musophaga violacea*	Violet Plantain-eater	Turaco Azul	Touraco Violet	Schildturako
104	*M. rossae*	Lady Ross's Violet Plantain-eater	Turaco Azul de Ross	Touraco Violet du Congo	Rossturako
105	*Crinifer piscator*	Grey Plantain-eater	Turaco de Crin Occidental	Touraco Gris	Schwarzschwanz-Lärmvogel
105	*C. zonurus*	Abyssian Grey Plantain-eater	Turaco de Crin Oriental	Touraco Gris d'Abyssinie	Braunlärmvogel
105	*Corythaeola cristata*	Blue Plantain-eater	Turaco Gigante	Touraco Géant	Riesenturako
	CUCULIDAE				
106	*Clamator glandarius*	Great Spotted Cuckoo	Crialo Español	Coucou-geai	Häherkuckuck
106	*C. jacobinus*	Pied Crested Cuckoo	Crialo Jacobino	Coucou Jacobin	Elsterkuckuck (Jakobinerkuckuck)

page	Latin	English	Spanish	French	German
	CUCULIDAE (cont.)				
106	C. levaillantii	Levaillant's Cuckoo	Crialo de Levaillant	Coucou de Levaillant	Kapkuckuck
107	Cuculus solitarius	Red-chested Cuckoo	Cuco Pechirrojo	Coucou Solitaire	Einsiedlerkuckuck
107	C. clamosus	Black Cuckoo	Cuco Cafre	Coucou Criard	Schwarzkuckuck
107	C. canorus	Common Cuckoo	Cuco Europeo	Coucou Gris	Kuckuck
110	Chrysococcyx klaas	Klaas's Cuckoo	Cuco Klaas	Coucou de Klaas	Klaaskuckuck
	(Lampromorpha klaasi)				
110	C. caprius	Didric Cuckoo	Cuco Verdi-aureo	Coucou Didric	Goldkuckuck (Diderikkuckuck)
	(Lampromorpha caprius)				
110	C. cupreus	Emerald Cuckoo	Cuco Verdi-cúpreo	Foliotocol	Smaragdkuckuck
111	Ceuthmochares aereus	Yellowbill Coucal	Cuco Piquigualdo Africano	Coucal à Bec Jaune	Erzkuckuck
111	Centropus grillii	Black Coucal	Cuco Espolado Tulú	Coucal Noirou	Grillkuckuck
111	C. leucogaster	Black-throated Coucal	Cuco Espolado Gorginegro	Coucal à Ventre Blanc	Weissbauchkuckuck
114	C. monachus	Blue-headed Coucal	Cuco Espolado Monje	Coucal à Nuque Bleue	Mönchskuckuck
114	C. senegalensis	Senegal Coucal	Cuco Espolado Senegalés	Coucal du Sénégal	Spornkuckuck
	STRIGIDAE				
114	Tyto alba	Barn Owl	Lechuza Común	Effraie Africaine	Schleiereule
115	Otus scops	Scops Owl	Autillo Europeo	Petit-duc Africain	Zwergohreule (Afrikanische Zwergohreule)
	(Otus senegalensis				
	O. leucopsis)				
115	O. leucotis	White-faced Owl	Gran Autillo Veliblanco	Petit-duc à Face Blanche	Weissgesichtohreule
	(Ptilopsis leucotis)				
115	Lophostrix letti	Maned Owl	Gran Autillo de Lett	Hibou à Bec Jaune	Mähneneule
115	Bubo africanus	Spotted Eagle-Owl	Buho Africano Chico	Grand-duc Africain	Fleckenuhu
116	B. poensis	Fraser's Eagle-Owl	Buho de Fernando Po	Grand-duc à Aigrettes	Guinea-uhu
116	B. leucostictus	Akun Eagle-Owl	Buho de Akun	Grand-duc Tacheté	Schwachschnabeluhu
116	B. lacteus	Milky Eagle-Owl	Gran Buho Etiópico	Grand-duc de Verreaux	Milchuhu (Blassuhu)
116	Scotopelia peli	Pel's Fishing Owl	Lechuza Pescadora	Chouette Pêcheuse	Bindenfischeule

page	Latin	English	Spanish	French	German
	STRIGIDAE (cont.)				
117	*Glaucidium perlatum*	Pearl-spotted Owlet	Mochuelin Perlado	Chevêchette Perlée	Perlkauz
117	*G. tephronotum*	Yellow-legged Owlet	Mochuelo Flanquirrojo	Chevêchette à Pieds Jaunes	Rotbrustkauz
117	*G. sjöstedti*	Sjöstedt's Barred Owlet	Mochelo de Sjöstedt	Chevêchette à Queue Barrée	Sjöstedtkauz
117	*Ciccaba woodfordi* (*Strix woodfordi*)	West African Wood-Owl	Lechuzón de Woodford	Hulotte Africaine	Woodfordkauz
117	*Asio capensis*	African Marsh-Owl	Lechuza Mora	Hibou du Cap	Kapohreule
118	*A. flammeus*	Short-eared Owl	Lechuza Campestre	Hibou Brachyote	Sumpfohreule
	CAPRIMULGIDAE				
118	*Caprimulgus inornatus*	Plain Nightjar	Chotacabras Modesto	Engoulevent Terne	Marmornachtschwalbe
118	*C. eximius*	Golden Nightjar	Chotacabras Dorado	Engoulevent Doré	Prachtnachtschwalbe
118	*C. tristigma*	West African Freckled Nightjar	Chotacabras Pecoso	Engoulevent Pointillé	Fleckennachtschwalbe
119	*C. pectoralis*	Black-shouldered Nightjar	Chotacabras Pectoral	Engoulevent à Epaulettes Noires	Rotnacken-Nachtschwalbe
119	*C. natalensis*	White-tailed Nightjar	Chotacabras Natalense	Engoulevent à Queue Blanche	Natalnachtschwalbe
119	*C. climacurus* (*Scotornis climacurus*)	Long-tailed Nightjar	Chotacabras Tribandeado	Engoulevent à Longue Queue	Schleppennachtschwalbe (Feennachtschwalbe)
119	*Macrodipteryx longipennis*	Standard-wing Nightjar	Chotacabras Abanderado	Engoulevent à Balanciers	Flaggenflügel
120	*M. vexillarius* (*Cosmetornis vexillarius*)	Pennant-winged Nightjar	Chotacabras Portacintas	Engoulevent Porte-étendard	Ruderflügel (Fahnennachtschwalbe)
	APODIDAE				
120	*Apus aequatorialis*	Mottled Swift	Vencejo Real Agavilanado	Martinet Marbré	Schuppensegler
120	*A. apus* (*Micropus apus*)	European Swift	Vencejo Comun	Martinet Noir	Mauersegler
121	*A. melba*	Alpine Swift	Vencejo Real	Martinet Alpin	Alpensegler

page	Latin	English	Spanish	French	German
	APODIDAE (cont.)				
121	A. batesi (Micropus batesi)	Bates's Black Swift	Vencejillo Negro	Martinet Noir de Bates	Braunkehlsegler
121	A. caffer (Micropus caffer)	White-rumped Swift	Vencejillo Culiblanco Cafre	Martinet à Croupion Blanc	Kaffernsegler
121	A. affinis (Colletoptera affinis)	Little African Swift	Vencejillo Culiblanco moro	Martinet à Dos Blanc	Haussegler (Weissbürzelsegler)
122	Cypsiurus parvus	Palm Swift	Vencejillo Palmero Africano	Martinet des Palmiers	Palmensegler
122	Chaetura ussheri	Ussher's Spine-tailed Swift	Rabitojo de Ussher	Martinet Epineux d'Ussher	Fleckenbrustsegler
122	C. sabini	Sabine's Spine-tailed Swift	Rabitojo de Sabine	Martinet Epineux de Sabine	Graubrustsegler
122	C. cassini	Cassin's Spine-tailed Swift	Rabitojo de Cassin	Martinet Epineux à Ventre Blanc	Stummelschwanzsegler
	COLIIDAE				
123	Colius striatus	Bar-breasted Mousebird	Pájaro-ratón Estriado	Coliou Barré	Braunflügel-Mausvogel
123	C. macrourus	Blue-naped Mousebird	Pájaro-ratón Nuquiazul	Coliou Huppé	Blaunacken-Mausvogel
	TROGONIDAE				
123	Apaloderma narina	Narina Trogon	Trogón Narina	Couroucou à Joues Vertes	Narina-Trogon
124	A. vittatum	Bar-tailed Trogon	Trogón Colirrayado	Couroucou à Queue Barrée	Bergtrogon
	ALCEDINIDAE				
124	Ceryle maxima (Megaceryle maxima)	Giant Kingfisher	Martín-Pescador Gigante	Martin-pêcheur Géant	Riesenfischer
124	C. rudis	Pied Kingfisher	Gran Martín-pescador pío	Martin-pêcheur Pie	Graufischer

page	Latin	English	Spanish	French	German
	ALCEDINIDAE (cont.)				
125	*Alcedo quadribrachys*	Shining-blue Kingfisher	Martín-pescador Ultramaro	Martin-pêcheur Azuré	Schillereisvogel
125	*A. cristata* (*Corythornis cristata*)	Malachite Kingfisher	Martín-pescador Crestado	Martin-pêcheur Huppé	Malachiteisvogel (*Haubenzwergfischer*)
125	*A. leucogaster* (*Corythornis leucogaster*)	White-bellied Kingfisher	Martín-pescador Ventriblanco	Petit Martin-chasseur à Ventre Blanc	Weissbaucheisvogel
126	*Ceyx picta* (*Ispidina picta*)	Pigmy Kingfisher	Martinito-cazador de Natal	Martin-chasseur Pygmée	Zwergfischer
126	*C. lecontei*	Red-headed Dwarf Kingfisher	Martinito-cazador de leconte	Petit Martin-chasseur à Tête Châtaine	Braunkopfzwergfischer
126	*Halcyon senegalensis*	Senegal Kingfisher	Alción Senegalés	Martin-chasseur du Sénégal	Senegalliest
126	*H. malimbica*	Blue-breasted Kingfisher	Alción Pechiazul	Martin-chasseur à Poitrine Bleue	Zügelliest
127	*H. badia*	Chocolate-backed Kingfisher	Alción Chocolate	Martin-chasseur Marron	Kastanienliest
127	*H. chelicuti*	Striped Kingfisher	Alción Listado	Martin-chasseur Strié	Streifenliest
127	*H. leucocephala*	Grey-headed Kingfisher	Alción Cabeciblanco	Martin-chasseur à Tête Grise	Graukopfliest
	MEROPIDAE				
130	*Merops apiaster*	European Bee-eater	Abejaruco Europeo	Guêpier d'Europe	Bienenfresser
130	*M. superciliosus* (*M. persicus*)	Blue-cheeked Bee-eater	Abejaruco Persa	Guêpier de Perse	Blauwangenspint
130	*M. orientalis*	Little Green Bee-eater	Abejaruco Oriental	Petit Guêpier Vert	Smaragdspint
130	*M. nubicus*	Carmine Bee-eater	Abejaruco Escarlata	Guêpier Ecarlate	Scharlachspint
131	*M. malimbicus*	Rosy Bee-eater	Abejaruco Malimbo	Guêpier Gris-rose	Rosenspint
131	*M. albicollis* (*Aerops albicollis*)	White-throated Bee-eater	Abejaruco Gorgiblanco	Guêpier à Gorge Blanche	Weisskehlspint
131	*M. pusillus* (*Melittophagus pusillus*)	Little Bee-eater	Melitófago Pusilo	Guêpier Nain	Zwergspint
132	*M. bullocki* (*Melittophagus bullocki*)	Red-throated Bee-eater	Melitófago de Bullock	Guêpier à Gorge Rouge	Grünstirnspint (*Rotkehlspint*)

page	Latin	English	Spanish	French	German
	MEROPIDAE (cont).				
132	*M. gularis*	Black Bee-eater	Melitófago Dorsinegro	Guêpier Noir	Purpurspint
132	*M. muelleri*	Blue-headed Bee-eater	Melitófago de Müller	Guêpier à Tête Bleue	Saphirspint (*Blauscheitelspint*)
132	*M. hirundineus* (*Dicrocercus hirundineus*)	Swallow-tailed Bee-eater	Abejaruco Ahorquillado	Guêpier à Queue d'Hirondelle	Schwalbenschwanzspint
	CORACIIDAE				
133	*Coracias abyssinica*	Abyssinian Roller	Carraca Abisinica	Rollier d'Abyssinie	Senegalracke
133	*C. garrulus*	European Roller	Carraca Europea	Rollier d'Europe	Blauracke
133	*C. naevia*	Rufous-crowned Roller	Carraca Nuquiblanca	Rollier Varié	Strichelracke
133	*C. cyanogaster*	Blue-bellied Roller	Carraca de Vientre afiil	Rollier à Ventre Bleu	Blaubauchracke
134	*Eurystomus glaucurus*	Broad-billed Roller	Carraca Picogorda Pechilila	Rolle Africain	Zimtroller
134	*E. gularis*	Blue-throated Roller	Carraca Picogorda Gorgiazul	Rolle à Gorge Bleue	Blaukehlroller
	UPUPIDAE				
134	*Upupa epops* (*U. senegalensis*)	Hoopoe	Abubilla	Huppe Fasciée	Wiedehopf
135	*Phoeniculus purpureus,* (*P. erythrorhynchus* *P. senegalensis*)	Senegal Wood-Hoopoe	Irrisor Kakelaar	Moqueur	Baumhopf
135	*P. aterrimus* (*Scoptelus aterrimus*)	Lesser Wood-Hoopoe	Irrisor Negro	Petit Moqueur Noir	Zwergbaumhopf
135	*P. bollei*	Buff-headed Wood-Hoopoe	Irrisor Cariblanco	Moqueur à Tête Claire	Weissmasken-Baumhopf
135	*P. castaneiceps*	Forest Wood-Hoopoe	Irrisor Cabecipardo	Petit Moqueur	Waldbaumhopf
	BUCEROTIDAE				
136	*Tockus nasutus* (*Lophoceros nasutus*)	Grey Hornbill	Toco Gris	Petit Calao à Bec Noir	Grautoko (*Weisschafttoko*)
136	*T. erythrorhynchus* (*Lophoceros erythrorhynchus*)	Red-beaked Hornbill	Toco Piquirrojo Fino	Petit Calao à Bec Rouge	Rotschnabeltoko

page	Latin	English	Spanish	French	German
	BUCEROTIDAE (cont.)				
137	T. camarus (Lophoceros camurus)	Red-billed Dwarf Hornbill	Toco Piquirrojo Menor	Calao Pygmée	Zwergtoko
137	T. hartlaubi	Black Dwarf Hornbill	Toco de Hartlaub	Calao Pygmée à Bec Noir	Hartlaubtoko
137	T. fasciatus (Lophoceros fasciatus, L. semifasciatus)	Black-and-white-tailed Hornbill	Toco Picofajado	Calao Longibande	Elstertoko
137	Tropicranus albocristatus	White-crested Hornbill	Toco Rabilargo	Calao à Huppe Blanche	Weisschopf-Hornvogel
138	Ceratogymna atrata	Black-casqued Hornbill	Calao de Papada	Grand Calao à Casque Noir	Keulenhornvogel
138	C. elata	Yellow-casqued Hornbill	Calao Cascogualdo	Grand Calao à Casque Jaune	Goldhelm-Hornvogel
138	Bycanistes fistulator (B. sharpii)	Piping Hornbill	Niame Flautista	Calao Siffleur	Schreihornvogel
138	B. cylindricus (B. albotibialis)	Brown-cheeked Hornbill	Niame Cilindrico	Calao à Joues Brunes	Babali-Hornvogel
139	B. subcylindricus	Black-and-white-casqued Hornbill	Niame Subcilindrico	Calao à Joues Grises	Grauwangenhornvogel
139	Bucorvus abyssinicus	Ground Hornbill	Abanto-calao Abisinio	Grand Calao d'Abyssinie	Sudanhornrabe
	CAPITONIDAE				
139	Lybius dubius (Pogonornis dubius)	Bearded Barbet	Barbudo Embridado	Barbican à Poitrine Rouge	Sengalfurchenschnabel
140	L. bidentatus (Pogonornis bidentatus)	Tooth-billed Barbet	Barbudo Bidentado	Barbican à Bec Denté	Doppelzahn-Bartvogel
140	L. leucocephalus	White-headed Barbet	Barbudo Cabeciblanco	Barbu à Tête Blanche	Weisskopf-Bartvogel
140	L. vieilloti	Vieillot's Barbet	Barbudo de Vieillot	Barbu de Vieillot	Blutbrust-Bartvogel
141	L. hirsutus (Tricholaema hirsutum, T. flavipunctatum)	Hairy-breasted Toothbill	Barbudo Hirsuto	Barbu Hérissé	Fleckenbartvogel
141	Gymnobucco calvus	Naked-faced Barbet	Barbudo Calvo	Barbu Chauve	Glatzenbartvogel

page	Latin	English	Spanish	French	German
CAPITONIDAE (cont.)					
141	G. peli	Bristle-nosed Barbet	Barbudo de Pel	Barbu Chauve à Narines Emplumées	Pel-Bartvogel
141	G. bonapartei	Grey-throated Barbet	Barbudo de Bonaparte	Barbu à Gorge Grise	Graukopf-Bartvogel
141	Buccanodon duchaillui	Duchaillu's Yellow-spotted Barbet	Barbudo de Duchaillu	Petit Barbu à Taches Jaunes	Gelbfleck-Bartvogel
142	Pogoniulus scolopaceus	Speckled Tinker-bird	Barbudito Ondeado	Petit Barbu Grivelé	Schuppenbartvogel
142	P. coryphaeus	Mountain Barbet	Barbudito Corifeo	Barbu Montagnard	Gelbrücken-Bartvogel
142	P. chrysoconus	Yellow-fronted Barbet	Barbudito Frentiaureo	Petit Barbu à Front Jaune	Gelbstirn-Bartvogel
142	P. bilineatus (Pogoniulus leucolaima)	Lemon-rumped Tinker-bird	Barbudito Bilistado	Petit Barbu à Croupion Jaune	Goldbürzel-Bartvogel
143	P. subsulphureus	Yellow-throated Tinker-bird	Barbudito Subsulfúreo	Petit Barbu à Gorge Jaune	Gelbkehl-Bartvogel
143	P. atroflavus (P. erythronotos)	Red-rumped Tinker-bird	Barbudito Culirrojo	Barbu à Croupion Rouge	Rotbürzel-Bartvogel
143	Trachyphonus purpuratus (Trachylaemus purpuratus)	Yellow-billed Barbet	Barbudo Piquigualdo	Trachyphone Pourpré	Gelbschnabel-Bartvogel
143	T. margaritatus	Yellow-breasted Barbet	Barbudo Carigualdo	Barbu Perlé	Perlenbartvogel
INDICATORIDAE					
146	Indicator indicator	Black-throated Honey-Guide	Indicador Gorginegro	Grand Indicateur	Grosser Honiganzeiger (Schwarzkehl-Honiganzeiger)
146	I. minor (I. conirostris)	Lesser Honey-Guide	Indicador Menor	Petit Indicateur	Kleiner Honiganzeiger
146	I. maculatus	Spotted Honey-Guide	Indicador Moteado	Indicateur Tacheté	Tropfenbrust-Honiganzeiger
146	I. exilis	Least Honey-Guide		Indicateur Minulle	Bart-Honiganzeiger
146	I. willcocksi	Willcock's Honey-Guide	Indicador de Willcock	Indicateur Minulle du Ghana	Guinea-Honiganzeiger

page	Latin	English	Spanish	French	German
INDICATORIDAE (cont.)					
147	*Melichneutes robustus*	Lyre-tailed Honey-Guide	Indicador Lira	Indicateur à Lyre	Leierschwanz-Honiganzeiger
147	*Prodotiscus insignis*	Cassin's Sharp-billed Honey-Guide	Indicador Minimo	Indicateur Pygmée	Liliput-Honiganzeiger
PICIDAE					
147	*Jynx torquilla*	European Wryneck	Torccuello	Torcol Fourmilier	Wendehals
148	*Verreauxia africana*	Pigmy Woodpecker	Carpintero Africano	Picule	Mausspecht
148	*Campethera punctuligera*	Fine-spotted Woodpecker	Campetera Punticulada	Pic à Taches Noires	Pünktchenspecht
148	*C. cailliautii* (*C. permista*)	Green-backed Woodpecker	Campetera de Cailliaut	Pic à Dos Vert	Tüpfelspecht
148	*C. maculosa*	Golden-backed Woodpecker	Campetera Maculosa	Pic Barré à Dos d'Or	Goldmantelspecht
149	*C. nivosa*	Buff-spotted Woodpecker	Campetera Nivosa	Pic Tacheté	Termitenspecht
149	*C. caroli*	Brown-eared Woodpecker	Campetera de Carol	Pic à Oreillons Bruns	Braunohrspecht
149	*C. tullbergi*	Tullberg's Woodpecker	Campetera de Tullberg	Pic de Tullberg	Kehlbindenspecht
149	*C. abingoni*	Golden-tailed Woodpecker	Campetera de Abingon	Pic à Queue Dorée	Goldschwanzspecht
149	*Dendropicos fuscescens*	Cardinal Woodpecker	Dendropico Bandeado	Pic Cardinal	Kardinalspecht
150	*D. elachus*	Least Grey Woodpecker	Dendropico Gris Chico	Petit Pic Gris	Wüstenspecht
150	*D. gabonensis*	Gaboon Woodpecker	Dendropico del Gabon	Pic Vert du Gabon	Gabunspecht
150	*Dendrocopos obsoletus* (*Dendropicos obsoletus*)	Lesser White-spotted Woodpecker	Dendropico Desusado	Petit Pic à Dos Brun	Braunrückenspecht
150	*Mesopicos goertae*	Grey Woodpecker	Mesopico Gris	Pic Gris	Graubrustspecht
151	*M. pyrrhogaster*	Fire-bellied Woodpecker	Mesopico Ventrirrojo	Pic à Ventre Rouge	Rotbauchspecht
151	*M. xantholophus*	Golden-crowned Woodpecker	Mesopico de Hargitt	Pic à Huppe Jaune	Gelbscheitelspecht
151	*M. ellioti*	Elliot's Woodpecker	Mesopico de Elliot	Pic d'Elliot	Elliotspecht

page	Latin	English	Spanish	French	German
EURYLAEMIDAE					
151	*Smithornis capensis*	Black-capped Broadbill	Bocaza Capense	Eurylaime du Cap	Kap-breitrachen
152	*S. rufolateralis*	Rufous-sided Broadbill	Bocaza Rojilateral	Eurylaime à Flancs Roux	Rotbrust-breitrachen
PITTIDAE					
152	*Pitta angolensis*	Angola Pitta	Pita de Angola	Brève à Poitrine Fauve	Angola-pitta
152	*P. reichenowi*	Green-breasted Pitta	Pita de Reichenow	Brève à Poitrine Verte	Kongo-pitta
ALAUDIDAE					
153	*Mirafra javanica*	Singing Bush-Lark	Mirafra Cantarina	Alouette Chanteuse	Buschlerche
	M. africana	Rufous-naped Lark	Mirafra Africana	Alouette à Nuque Rousse	Rotnackenlerche
153	*M. rufocinnamomea* (*M. buckleyi*)	Flappet Lark	Mirafra Aplaudidora	Alouette Bourdonnante	Baum-Klapperlerche
154	*M. nigricans* (*Pinarocorys erythropygia*)	Rufous-rumped Bush-Lark	Mirafra sombria	Alouette à Queue Rousse	Drossellerche
154	*Eremopterix leucotis*	Chestnut-backed Finch-Lark	Gurrio-alondra Acastañada	Alouette-moineau à Oreillons Blancs	Weisswangenlerche
154	*E. nigriceps*	White-fronted Finch-Lark	Gurrio-alondra Frentiblanca	Alouette-moineau à Front Blanc	Weisstirnlerche
154	*Galerida cristata*	Crested Lark	Cogujada Común	Cochevis Huppé	Haubenlerche
155	*G. modesta*	Sun-lark	Alondrita Etiopica	Alouette Modeste	Sonnenlerche
155	*Calandrella cinerea*	Red-capped Lark	Terrera Común	Alouette Calandrelle	Kurzzehenlerche
HIRUNDINIDAE					
155	*Riparia paludicola*	African Sand Martin	Avión Zapador Paludicola	Hirondelle Paludicole	Braunkehl-Uferschwalbe (Afrikanische Uferschwalbe)
155	*R. riparia*	European Sand Martin	Avión Zapador	Hirondelle de Rivage	Uferschwalbe
156	*Hirundo rustica* (*H. lucida*)	European Swallow	Golondrina Común	Hirondelle de Cheminée	Rauchschwalbe

page	Latin	English	Spanish	French	German
	HIRUNDINIDAE (cont.)				
156	*H. nigrita*	White-throated Blue Swallow	Golondrina Negra	Hirondelle Noire	Mohrenschwalbe
156	*H. smithii*	Wire-tailed Swallow	Golondrina de Smith	Hirondelle à Longs Brins	Rotkappenschwalbe
156	*H. aethiopica*	Ethiopian Swallow	Golondrina Etiópica	Hirondelle à Gorge Blanche	Fahlkehlschwalbe
157	*H. leucosoma*	Pied-winged Swallow	Golondrina Aliblanca	Hirondelle à Ailes Tachetées	Scheckflügelschwalbe
157	*H. senegalensis*	Mosque Swallow	Gran Golondrina Senegalesa	Hirondelle à Ventre Roux	Senegalschwalbe
157	*H. daurica*	Red-rumped Swallow	Golondrina Dáurica	Hirondelle Rousseline	Rötelschwalbe
157	*H. abyssinica*	Lesser Striped Swallow	Golondrina Abisínica	Hirondelle à Gorge Striée	Kleine Streifenschwalbe
158	*H. semirufa*	Rufous-breasted Swallow	Golondrina Senegalesa Chica	Petite Hirondelle à Ventre Roux	Rotbauchschwalbe
158	*Delichon urbica*	European House Martin	Avión Común	Hirondelle de Fenêtre	Mehlschwalbe
158	*Psalidoprocne obscura*	Fanti Rough-winged Swallow	Ala-de-Sierra de Hartlaub	Hirondelle Hérissée	Scherenschwanzschwalbe
158	*P. nitens*	Square-tailed Rough-winged Swallow	Ala-de-Sierra de Cassin	Hirondelle Hérissée à Queue Courte	Glanzschwalbe
	MOTACILLIDAE				
159	*Motacilla flava* (*Budytes flavus*)	Yellow Wagtail	Lavandera Boyera	Bergeronnette Printanière	Schafstelze
159	*M. alba*	White Wagtail	Lavandera Blanca	Bergeronnette Grise	Bachstelze
162	*M. aguimp*	African Pied Wagtail	Lavandera Pía	Bergeronnette Pie	Witwenstelze
162	*M. clara*	Mountain Wagtail	Lavandera Clara	Bergeronnette à Longue Queue	Langschwanzstelze
162	*Anthus leucophrys*	Plain-backed Pipit	Bisbita Dorsiliso	Pipit à Dos Roux	Braunrückenpieper
162	*A. campestris*	Tawny Pipit	Bisbita Campestre	Pipit Rousseline	Brachpieper
162	*A. novaeseelandiae*	Richard's Pipit	Bisbita de Richard	Pipit de Richard	Spornpieper

page	Latin	English	Spanish	French	German
	MOTACILLIDAE (cont.)				
163	A. trivialis	Tree-pipit	Bisbita Arbóreo	Pipit des Arbres	Baumpieper
163	A. cervinus	Red-throated Pipit	Bisbita Gorgirrojo	Pipit à Gorge Rousse	Rotkehlpieper
163	Macronyx croceus	Yellow-throated Long-claw	Bisbita Espolado Ventrigualdo	Alouette Sentinelle	Gelbkehlpieper (Safrangrossporn)
	LANIIDAE				
163	Prionops plumata	Long-crested Helmet-shrike	Alcaudón Patirrojo de Shaw	Bagadais Casqué	Brillenwürger
166	P. caniceps (Sigmodus caniceps, S. rufiventris)	Red-billed Shrike	Alcaudón Patirrojo Cariblanco	Bagadais à Bec Rouge	Rostbauchwürger
166	Nilaus afer	Brubru Shrike	Brubrú Norteño	Pie-grièche Bru-bru	Brubru
166	Dryoscopus gambensis	Gambian Puff-back Shrike	Culipompón del Gambia	Pie-grièche Cubla de Gambie	Wald-Schneeballwürger
167	D. senegalensis	Black-shouldered Puff-back	Culipompón Senegalés	Pie-grièche Cubla à Yeux Rouges	Schwarzschulter-Schneeballwürger
167	Tchagra minuta (Antichromus minutus)	Little Blackcap Tchagra	Chagra Capirotado	Petit Téléphone	Sumpftschagra
167	T. australis	Brown-crowned Tchagra	Chagra austral	Tchagra à Tête Brune	Dorntschagra (Damaratschagra)
168	T. senegala	Black-crowned Tchagra	Chagra Senegalés	Téléphone Tchagra	Senegaltschagra
168	Laniarius ferrugineus (L. turatii)	Bell-Shrike	Bubú Etiópico	Gonolek à Ventre Blanc	Flötenwürger
168	L. barbarus (L. erythrogaster)	Barbary Shrike	Bubú Gonolek	Gonolek de Barbarie	Scharlachwürger
168	L. atroflavus	Yellow-breasted Shrike	Bubú Pechigualdo	Gonolek à Ventre Jaune	Gelbbauchwürger
169	L. fulleborni	Black Mountain Boubou	Bubú Negro Chico	Gonolek Noir de Fernando Po	Füllebornwürger
169	L. leucorhynchus	Sooty Boubou	Bubú Negro	Gonolek Noir	Schwarzwürger

page	Latin	English	Spanish	French	German
	LANIIDAE (cont.)				
169	Malaconotus multicolor (Chlorophoneus multicolor)	Many-coloured Bush-shrike		Pie-grièche Variable	Vielfarbenwürger
170	M. sulfureopectus	Orange-breasted Bush-shrike	Gladiadorcito Pechirrojo	Pie-grièche Soufrée	Orangebrustwürger
170	M. cruentus	Fiery-breasted Bush-shrike	Gladiador Cruento	Pie-grièche Verte Ensanglantée	Blutbrustwürger
170	M. blanchoti	Grey-headed Bush-shrike	Gladiador de Blanchot	Pie-grièche de Blanchot	Riesenbuschwürger
170	Corvinella corvina	Long-Tailed Shrike	Alcaudón Piquigualdo	Corvinelle	Gelbschnabelwürger
170	Lanius excubitor	Great Grey Shrike	Alcaudón Real	Pie-grièche Grise	Raubwürger (Grauwürger)
171	L. collaris (L. newtoni)	Fiscal Shrike	Alcaudón Fiscal	Pie-grièche Fiscale	Fiskalwürger (Büttelwürger)
171	L. collurio	Red-backed Shrike	Alcaudón Dorsirrojo	Pie-grièche Ecorcheur	Neuntöter
171	L. gubernator	Emin's Red-backed Shrike	Alcaudón de Emin	Petite Pie-grièche à Dos Roux	Rotbürzelwürger
171	L. excubitorius	Grey-backed Shrike	Alcaudón Real Rabilargo	Pie-grièche Fiscale à Dos Gris	Graumantelwürger
171	L. senator	Woodchat Shrike	Alcaudón Común Ibérico	Pie-grièche à Tête Rousse	Rotkopfwürger
	ORIOLIDAE				
174	Oriolus auratus	African Golden Oriole	Oropéndola Etiópica	Loriot Doré	Schwarzohrpirol
174	O. oriolus	European Golden Oriole	Oropéndola Europea	Loriot d'Europe	Pirol
174	O. brachyrhynchus	Black-headed Oriole	Oropéndola Cabecinegra de Swainson	Loriot à Tête Noire	Blauflügelpirol
174	O. nigripennis	Black-winged Oriole	Oropéndola Cabecinegra de Verreaux	Loriot à Ailes Noires	Gabunpirol

page	Latin	English	Spanish	French	German
	DICRURIDAE				
175	*Dicrurus adsimilis* (*D. modestus*)	Glossy-backed Drongo	Drongo Africano Negro	Drongo Brillant	Trauerdrongo (Gabelschwanzdrongo)
175	*D. atripennis*	Shining Drongo	Drongo Africano Metálico	Drongo de Forêt	Glanzdrongo
175	*D. ludwigii*	Square-tailed Drongo	Drongo Africano Chico	Drongo de Ludwig	Geradschwanzdrongo
	STURNIDAE				
178	*Onychognathus morio*	Crag Chestnut-winged Starling	Estornino Alirrijo Morio	Etourneau Roupenne d'Alexander	Rotschwingenstar
178	*O. fulgidus*	Forest Chestnut-winged Starling	Estornino Alirrojo de Hartlaub	Etourneau Roupenne	Kastanienflügelstar
178	*Poeoptera lugubris*	Narrow-tailed Starling	Estornino Rabilargo Lúgubre	Etourneau à Queue Etroite	Spitzschwanzstar
178	*Lamprotornis purpureiceps* (*Lamprocolius purpureiceps*)	Purple-headed Glossy Starling	Bruñido Caripurpúreo	Merle Métallique à Tête pourprée	Samtglanzstar
179	*L. cupreocauda*	Copper-tailed Glossy Starling	Bruñido Colicupreo	Merle Métallique à Dos Bleu	Kupferglanzstar
179	*L. splendidus* (*Lamprocolius splendidus*)	Splendid Glossy Starling	Bruñido Espléndido	Merle Métallique à Oeil Blanc	Prachtglanzstar
179	*L. purpureus* (*Lamprocolius purpureus*)	Purple Glossy Starling	Bruñido purpúreo	Merle Métallique Pourpré	Purpurglanzstar
179	*L. chalybaeus* (*Lamprocolius chalybaeus*)	Blue-eared Glossy Starling	Bruñido Oído-azul	Merle Métallique Commun	Grünschwanzglanzstar
180	*L. chloropterus*	Lesser Blue-eared Glossy Starling	Bruñido Oído-azul Chico	Merle Métallique de Swainson	Messingglanzstar
180	*L. chalcurus*	Short-tailed Glossy Starling	Bruñido Colibronce	Merle Métallique à Queue Violette	Erzglanzstar
180	*L. caudatus*	Long-tailed Glossy Starling	Bruñido Rabilargo	Merle Métallique à Longue Queue	Langschwanzglanzstar

page . Latin	English	Spanish	French	German
PYCNONOTIDAE (cont.)				
185 *A. virens*	Little Green Bulbul	Bulbulito Verdoso	Bulbul Verdâtre	Grünbülbül
185 *A. latirostris*	Yellow-whiskered Bulbul	Bulbul de Bigote Gualdo	Bulbul à Moustaches Jaunes	Gelbbartbülbül
185 *A. gracilis*	Little Grey Bulbul	Bulbulito Grácil	Bulbul Gracile	Zwergbülbül
185 *A. tephrolaemus* (*Arizelocichla tephrolaema*)	Grey-throated Bulbul	Bulbul Oliva de Montaña	Bulbul à Tête Grise	Graukopfbülbül
186 *Baeopogon indicator*	Honey-Guide Bulbul	Bulbul indicator	Bulbul à Queue Blanche	Weisschwanzbülbül
186 *B. clamans*	Sjöstedt's Honey-Guide Bulbul	Bulbul clamador	Bulbul Bruyant	Sjöstedtbülbül
186 *Ixonotus guttatus*	Spotted Bulbul	Bulbul Moteado	Bulbul Tacheté	Fleckenbülbül
186 *Chlorocichla simplex* (*Pyrrhurus simplex*)	Simple Leaf-love	Bulbul Colirrojo Simple	Bulbul Modeste	Hartlaubbülbül
186 *C. flavicollis*	Yellow-throated Leaf-love	Bulbul Gorgigualdo	Grand Bulbul à Gorge Jaune	Gelbkehlbülbül
187 *Thescelocichla leucopleurus*	Swamp Palm Bulbul	Bulbul Coliblanco	Bulbul à Queue Tachetée	Raphiabülbül
187 *Phyllastrephus scandens* (*Pyrrhurus scandens*)	Leaf-love	Bulbul Colirrojo Trepador	Bulbul à Queue Rousse	Uferbülbül
187 *P. icterinus*	Lesser Icterine Greenbul	Bulbulito Icterino	Bulbul Ictérin	Zeisigbülbül
187 *P. flavostriatus* (*P. poliocephalus*)	Yellow-bellied Greenbul	Bulbul Gualdilistado	Bulbul à Ventre Jaune	Gelbstreifenbülbül
188 *Bleda syndactyla*	Bristle-bill	Bleda Colirroja	Bulbul Moustac à Queue Rousse	Rotschwanz-bleda
188 *B. eximia*	Green-tailed Bristle-bill	Bleda eximia	Bulbul Moustac à Tête Olive	Grünschwanz-bleda
188 *B. canicapilla*	Grey-headed Bristle-bill	Bleda Cabecigris	Bulbul Moustac à Tête Grise	Graukopf-Bleda
189 *Criniger barbatus* (*Trichophorus barbatus*)	Bearded Bulbul	Criniger Barbado	Grand Bulbul Huppé	Haarbülbül
189 *C. calurus* (*Trichophorus calurus*)	White-bearded Bulbul	Criniger Colirrojo	Bulbul Huppé à Barbe Blanche	Cassins Haarbülbül
189 *Nicator chloris*	West African Nicator	Nicator Grande	Pie-grièche Nicator	Graukehlnicator

page	Latin	English	Spanish	French	German
	TURDIDAE				
190	Saxicola rubetra	Whinchat	Tarabilla Norteña	Traquet Tarier	Braunkehlchen
190	S. torquata	Stonechat	Tarabilla Común	Traquet Pâtre	Schwarzkehlchen
190	Oenanthe oenanthe	Wheatear	Collalba Gris	Traquet Motteux	Steinschmätzer
191	O. hispanica	Spanish Wheatear	Collalba Rubia	Traquet Oreillard	Mittelmeerstein-schmätzer
191	O. bottae (O. heuglini)	Red-breasted Chat	Collalba Pechirroja	Traquet à Poitrine Rousse	Rostbrust-steinschmätzer
191	Cercomela familiaris	Red-tailed Chat	Cercomela Colirroja	Traquet de Roche à Queue Rousse	Rostschwanzschmätzer (Rostschwanz)
194	C. melanura	Black-tailed Rock-Chat	Cercomela Colinegra	Traquet de Roche à Queue Noire	Schwarzschwanz-schmätzer
194	Myrmecocichla aethiops	Ant-Chat	Tarabilla Termitera de Cabanis	Traquet-fourmilier Brun	Russchmätzer
194	M. nigra	Sooty Ant-Chat	Tarabilla Termitera Negra	Traquet-fourmilier Noir	Hadesschmätzer
194	M. cinnamomeiventris (Thamnolaea cinnamomeiventris, T. coronata)	White-crowned Cliff-Chat	Roquero Rojinegro	Traquet de Roche à Ventre Roux	Rotbauchschmätzer
194	M. albifrons (Pentholaea albifrons)	White-fronted Black Chat	Tarabilla Negra Frentiblanca	Traquet Noir à Front Blanc	Weisstirnschmätzer
195	Monticola saxatilis	Rock-Thrush	Roquero Rojo	Merle de Roche	Steinrötel
195	M. solitaria	Blue Rock-Thrush	Roquero Solitario	Merle Bleu	Blaumerle
195	Phoenicurus phoenicurus	Redstart	Colirrojo Real	Rouge-queue à Front Blanc	Gartenrotschwanz
196	Cercotrichas podobe	Black Scrub-Robin	Alzacola Negra	Merle Podobé	Russheckensänger
196	C. galactotes (Agrobates galactotes)	Rufous Scrub-Robin	Alzacola Española	Agrobate Rubigineux	Heckensänger
196	C. leucosticta (Erythropygia leucosticta)	Forest Scrub-Robin	Alzacola Bigotuda de Sharpe	Rouge-queue du Ghana	Waldheckensänger
196	Alethe diademata (A. castanea)	Fire-crest Alethe	Alete Coliblanco	Alèthe à Huppe Rousse	Diadem-Alethe
197	A. poliocephala	Brown-chested Alethe	Alete Tarabillino	Alèthe à Poitrine Brune	Braunbrust-Alethe

page	Latin	English	Spanish	French	German
	TURDIDAE (cont.)				
197	Stiphrornis erythrothorax	Forest Robin	Peterrojo del Gabón	Rouge-gorge de Forêt	Rotbrust-Akalat
197	Cossypha isabellae	Mountain Robin-Chat	Cosifa de Isabel	Cossypha d'Isabelle	Kamerunrötel
197	C. polioptera	White-browed Robin-Chat	Cosifa Polióptera	Cossyyphe à Sourcils Blancs	Grauflügelrötel
198	C. cyanocampter	Blue-shouldered Robin-Chat	Cosifa de Hombros Azules	Cossyphe à Ailes Bleues	Blauschulterrötel
198	C. albicapilla	White-crowned Robin-Chat	Gran Cosifa	Grand Cossyphe à Tête Blanche	Schuppenkopfrötel
198	C. niveicapilla	Snowy-crowned Robin-Chat	Cosifa Capirotada	Petit Cossyphe à Tête Blanche	Weisscheitelrötel
199	Neocossyphus poensis	White-tailed Ant-Thrush	Zorzal-cosifa Coliblanco	Grive Fourmilière à Queue Blanche	Weissschwanz-Fuchsdrossel
199	Stizorhina fraseri (S. finschi)	Fraser's Rusty Thrush	Zorzal-cosifa Rojo	Gobe-mouches Roux	Kurzlaufdrossel
199	Luscinia megarhynchos	Nightingale	Ruiseñor Común	Rossignol Philomèle	Nachtigall
200	Turdus pelios (T. libonyanus)	West African Thrush	Zorzal Oliváceo	Grive Kurrichane	Peliosamsel
200	T. princei	Grey Ground-Thrush	Zorzal de Prince	Grive Olivâtre	Grauerdrossel
	TIMALIIDAE				
200	Alcippe abyssinica (Pseudoalcippe abyssinicus, P. atriceps)	Hill-Babbler	Timalí abisinico	Alcippe à Tête Grise	Mönchsalcippe
200	Malococincla fulvescens (Illadopsis fulvescens, I. moloneyanus)	Brown Akalat	Tordinito Pardo Oscuro	Grive Akalat Brune	Brauner buschdrossling (Braune maustimalie)
201	M. rufipennis (Illadopsis rufipennis)	White-breasted Akalat	Tordinito Pardo Claro	Grive Akalat à Poitrine Blanche	Grauwangen-buschdrossling (Grauwangen-maustimalie)
201	M. rufescens	Rufous-winged Akalat	Tordinito Pardo Alirrubio	Grive Akalat du Libéria	Reichennows buschdrossling

page	Latin	English	Spanish	French	German
	SYLVIIDAE (cont.)				
207	C. lateralis	Whistling Cisticola	Buitrón Silbador	Cisticole Siffleuse	Pfeifzistensänger
207	C. anonyma	Chattering Cisticola	Buitrón Anónimo	Cisticole Babillarde	Waldzistensänger
207	C. hunteri	Brown-backed Cisticola	Buitrón de Hunter	Cisticole à Dos Brun	Bergzistensänger
210	C. aberrans	Rock-loving Cisticola	Buitrón Aberrante	Cisticole des Rochers	Smiths zistensänger
210	C. galactotes	Rufous Grass-Warbler	Buitrón Rubita	Cisticole Roussâtre	Schwarzrücken-zistensänger
210	C. natalensis	Striped Cisticola	Buitrón de Natal	Cisticole Striée	Strichelzistensänger
211	C. ruficeps	Redpate Cisticola	Buitrón Cabecirrojo	Cisticole à Tête Rousse	Rotkopf-zistensänger
211	C. brachyptera	Shortwing Cisticola	Buitrón Alicorto	Cisticole à Ailes Courtes	Kurzflügel-zistensänger
211	C. juncidis	Common Fantail Warbler	Buitrón Ibérico	Cisticole des Joncs	Zistensänger
212	C. aridula	Desert Fantail Warbler	Buitrón Desértico	Cisticole du Désert	Kalahari-zistensänger
212	Prinia erythroptera (Heliolais erythroptera)	Red-winged Warbler	Prinia Alirroja	Fauvette à Ailes Rousses	Sonnenprinie
212	P. subflava	West African Prinia	Prinia Chica	Fauvette-roitelet Commune	Rahmbrustprinie
213	P. epichlora (Urolais epichlora)	Green Longtail	Prinia Verde	Fauvette Verte à Longue Queue	Langschwanzprinie
213	P. leucopogon	White-chinned Longtail	Prinia Gorgiblanca	Fauvette-roitelet à Gorge Blanche	Weisskehlprinie
213	Apalis cinerea	Brown-headed Forest-Warbler	Apalis Gris	Fauvette Forestière à Tête Brune	Graurücken-feinsänger
213	A. pulchra	Black-collared Forest-Warbler	Apalis de Collar	Fauvette Forestière à Collier Noir	Schmuckfeinsänger
213	A. nigriceps	Black-capped Yellow Warbler	Apalis Capirotado	Fauvette Forestière à Tête Noire	Kappenfeinsänger
214	Hypergerus atriceps	Moho	Curruca-tordino Buscarla	Timalie à Tête Noire	Pirolsänger
214	Bathmocercus cerviniventris (Bathmedonia rufa, Eminia cerviniventris)	Stream Warbler	Cabecinegra	Fauvette Aquatique à Capuchon	Fuchssänger

page	Latin	English	Spanish	French	German
SYLVIIDAE (cont.)					
214	Camaroptera superciliaris	Yellow-browed Camaroptera	Camaróptera Cejigualda	Camaroptère à Sourcils	Gelbbrauen-Camaroptera
215	C. chloronota	Green-backed Camaroptera	Camaróptera Dorsiverde	Camaroptère à Dos Vert	Olivcamaroptera
215	C. brachyura (C. brevicaudata)	Grey-backed Camaroptera	Camaróptera Colicorta Dorsiverde	Camaroptère à Tête Grise	Meckergrasmücke
215	Eremomela pusilla	Green-backed Eremomela	Eremomela Chica	Erémomèle à Dos Vert	Graukappen-eremomela
215	E. icteropygialis	Grey-backed Eremomela	Eremomela Culigualda	Erémomèle Gris-Jaune	Gelbbauch-eremomela
216	E. badiceps	Rufous-crowned Eremomela	Eremomela Capirotada	Erémomèle à Tête Brune	Rotkopf-eremomela
216	Sylvietta brachyura	Nuthatch Warbler	Crombec de Senegambia	Fauvette Crombec	Braunbauch-sylvietta
216	S. virens	Green Crombec	Crombec Verdoso	Fauvette Crombec Verte	Grünmantel-sylvietta
216	S. denti	Lemon-bellied Crombec	Crombec Ventrigualdo	Fauvette Crombec à Gorge Tachetée	Gelbsteiss-sylvietta
216	Macrosphenus concolor	Olive Longbill	Curruca-chochin Gris	Fauvette Nasique Grise	Einfarb-bülbülgrasmücke
216	M. flavicans	Yellow Longbill	Curruca-chochin Gualda	Fauvette Nasique Jaune	Graukehl-bülbülgrasmücke
217	Hylia prasina	Green Hylia	Hilia Verdosa	Hylia Verte	Hylie
217	Pholidornis rushiae	Tit-Hylia	Hilia Chica	Astrild-mésange	Strichelköpfchen
MUSCICAPIDAE					
218	Muscicapa striata	Spotted Flycatcher	Papamoscas Gris	Gobe-mouches Gris	Grauschnäpper
218	M. aquatica (Alseonax aquatica)	Swamp Flycatcher	Papamoscas Palustre	Gobe-mouches des Marais	Sumpfschnäpper
218	M. cassini (Alseonax cassini)	Cassin's Grey Flycatcher	Papamoscas de Cassin	Gobe-mouches de Cassin	Cassinschnäpper
218	M. caerulescens	White-eye Flycatcher	Papamoscas ceniciento	Gobe-mouches à Lunettes Blanches	Schieferschnäpper

page	Latin	English	Spanish	French	German
	MUSCICAPIDAE (cont.)				
219	M. comitata (Pedilorhynchus comitatus)	Dusky Blue Flycatcher	Papamoscas Pizarroso	Gobe-mouches Ardoisé	Stuhlmannschnäpper
219	Aromyias ussheri	Ussher's Flycatcher	Papamoscas de Ussher	Gobe-mouches d'Ussher	Schwalbenschnäpper
219	A. fuliginosa	Dusky Flycatcher	Papamoscas Fuliginoso	Gobe-mouches Fuligineux	Russchnäpper
219	Myioparus plumbeus (Parisoma plumbeum)	Grey Tit-Babbler	Papamoscas plomizo	Gobe-mouches Mésange	Meisenschnäpper
220	Ficedula hypoleuca	Pied Flycatcher	Papamoscas Cerrojillo	Gobe-mouches Noir	Trauerschnäpper
220	Fraseria ocreata	Fraser's Forest Flycatcher	Gran Papamoscas Gavilano	Gobe-mouches Forestier	Waldschnäpper
220	F. cinerascens	White-browed Forest Flycatcher	Papamoscas Gavilano Chico	Gobe-mouches à Sourcils Blancs	Brauenwaldschnäpper
220	Melaenornis edolioides	Black Flycatcher	Papamoscas Enlutado	Gobe-mouches Drongo	Swainsonschnäpper (Schieferschwarzer drongoschnäpper
221	Bradornis pallidus	Pale Flycatcher	Papamoscas Palido	Gobe-mouches Pâle	Fahlschnäpper (Blasser drosselschnäpper)
221	Hyliota flavigaster	Yellow-bellied Flycatcher	Hiliota Ventrigualdo	Gobe-mouches à Ventre Jaune	Gelbbauch-Hyliota
221	Bias musicus	Black-and-white Flycatcher	Bias Músico	Gobe-mouches Chanteur	Vangaschnäpper
222	Batis senegalensis	Senegal Puff-back Flycatcher	Batis senegalés	Gobe-mouches Soyeux du Sénégal	Senegalschnäpper
222	B. minima	Grey-headed Puff-back	Batis mínimo	Gobe-mouches Soyeux à Tête Grise	Gabunschnäpper
222	B. minor	Black-headed Puff-back Flycatcher	Batis menor	Gobe-mouches Soyeux à Joues Noires	Kongoschnäpper
222	Platysteira cyanea	Scarlet-spectacled Wattle-eye	Batis Carunculado Gorgipardo	Gobe-mouches Caronculé à Collier	Lappenschnäpper
223	P. castanea (Dyaphorophyia castanea)	Chestnut Wattle-eye	Batis Carunculado Castaño	Gobe-mouches Caronculé Châtain	Weissbürzel-lappenschnäpper

page	Latin	English	Spanish	French	German
	MUSCICAPIDAE (cont.)				
223	P. tonsa	White-spotted Wattle-eye	Batis Carunculado Tonsa	Gobes-mouches Caronculé à Taches Blanches	Weissbrauen-lappenschnäpper
223	P. blissetti (Dyaphorophyia blissetti, D. chalybea)	Blissett's Wattle-eye	Batis Carunculado Cuellirrojo	Gobe-mouches Caronculé de Blissett	Glanz-lappenschnäpper
223	P. concreta	Golden-bellied Wattle-eye	Batis carunculado Ventrigualdo	Gobe-mouches Caronculé à Ventre Doré	Gelbbauch-lappenschnäpper
226	Erythrocercus mccalli	Chestnut-capped Flycatcher	Papamoscas Colirrojo de Mccall	Gobe-mouches à Tête Rousse	Braunkappenschnäpper
226	Trochocercus longicauda (Erannornis longicauda)	Blue Fairy Flycatcher	Papamoscas Moñudo Azulino	Gobe-mouches Bleu	Elminie
226	T. nitens	Blue-headed Crested Flycatcher	Papamoscas Moñudo de Cassin	Gobe-mouches Noir Huppé	Glanzhaubenschnäpper
227	T. albiventris	White-bellied Flycatcher	Papamoscas Moñudo Ventriblanco	Gobe-mouches Huppé à Ventre Blanc	Weissbauch-haubenschnäpper
227	Tersiphone rufiventer (Tchitrea rufiventer, T. nigriceps, T. smithii, T. tricolor)	Red-bellied Paradise Flycatcher	Papamoscas del Paraiso Ventrirrojo	Moucherolle à Ventre Roux	Wald-paradiesschnäpper
227	T. viridis (Tchitrea viridis, T. plumbeiceps, T. melampyra),	Paradise Flycatcher	Papamoscas del Paraiso de Müller	Moucherolle de Paradis	Afrikanischer paradiesschnäpper
	PARIDAE				
228	Parus leucomelas (Melaniparus niger)	White-shouldered Black Tit	Carbonero Negro	Mésange Noire à Epaulettes Blanches	Rüppellmeise

page	Latin	English	Spanish	French	German
	REMIZIDAE				
228	*Remix parvulus* (*Anthoscopus parvulus*)	West African Penduline Tit	Pájaro Moscón Amarillo	Rémiz à Ventre Jaune	Senegal-beutelmeise
228	*R. punctifrons*	Sudan Penduline Tit	Pájaro Moscón del Sennar	Rémiz du Soudan	Sudan-beutelmeise
	SALPORNITHIDAE				
229	*Salpornis spilonota*	Spotted Creeper	Salpornis Africano	Grimpereau Tacheté	Stammsteiger (Fleckenbaumläufer)
	NECTARINIDAE				
229	*Anthreptes gabonicus*	Mouse-brown Sunbird	Suimanga Gabónica	Soui-manga Brun	Gabun-nektarvogel
229	*A. fraseri*	Scarlet-tufted Sunbird	Suimanga de Fraser	Soui-manga de Fraser	Laubnektarvogel
230	*A. rectirostris*	Yellow-chinned Sunbird	Suimanga de Pico Recto	Soui-manga à Gorge Jaune	Goldband-nektarvogel
230	*A. longuemarei*	Violet-backed Sunbird	Suimanga de Longuemare	Soui-manga Violet	Violettmantel-nektarvogel
230	*A. collaris*	Collared Sunbird	Suimanga de Collar	Soui-manga à Collier	Stahlnektarvogel
231	*A. platura* (*Hedydipna platura*)	Pigmy Long-tailed Sunbird	Suimanga Pigmeo	Petit Soui-manga à Longue Queue	Erznektarvogel
231	*Nectarinia olivacea* (*Cyanomitra olivacea*)	Olive Sunbird	Suimanga Olivácea	Soui-manga Olivâtre	Olivnektarvogel
231	*N. reichenbachii*	Reichenbach's Sunbird	Suimanga de Reichenbach	Soui-manga de Reichenbach	Kamerun-nektarvogel
232	*N. verticalis* (*Cyanomitra verticalis*)	Olive-backed Sunbird	Suimanga Cabeciverde	Soui-manga Olive à Tête Bleue	Grünkopf-nektarvogel
232	*N. oritis*	Blue-headed Sunbird	Suimanga oritis	Soui-manga à Tête Bleue	Blaukopfnektarvogel
232	*N. cyanolaema*	Blue-throated Brown Sunbird	Suimanga Gorgiazul	Soui-manga à Gorge Bleue	Braunrücken-nektarvogel
232	*N. fuliginosa* (*Chalcomitra fuliginosa*)	Carmelite Sunbird	Suimanga fuliginosa	Soui-manga Carmélite	Karmelglanzköpfchen
233	*N. rubescens* (*Chalcomitra rubescens*)	Green-throated Sunbird	Suimanga Gorgiverde	Soui-manga à Gorge Verte	Grünkehl-glanzköpfchen

page	Latin	English	Spanish	French	German
	NECTARINIDAE (cont.)				
233	N. adelberti	Buff-throated Sunbird	Suimanga de Adalbert	Soui-manga à Gorge Rousse	Fahlkehl-glanzköpfchen
233	N. senegalensis (Chalcomitra senegalensis)	Scarlet-breasted Sunbird	Suimanga Senegalesa	Soui-manga à Poitrine Rouge	Rotbrust-glanzköpfchen
233	N. venusta (Cinnyris venustus)	Yellow-bellied Sunbird	Suimanga Variable	Soui-manga à Ventre Jaune	Gelbbauch-nektarvogel (Ziernektarvogel)
234	N. chloropygia (Cinnyris chloropygius)	Olive-bellied Sunbird	Suimanga Culiverde	Soui-manga à Ventre Olive	Olivbauch-nektravogel
234	N. preussi	Preuss's Double-collared Sunbird	Suimanga de Preuss	Soui-manga de Reichenow	Preussnektarvogel
234	N. minulla	Tiny Sunbird	Suimanga minúscula	Soui-manga Minulle	Zwergnektarvogel
234	N. cuprea (Cinnyris cupreus)	Copper Sunbird	Suimanga Cobriza	Soui-manga Cuivré	Kupfernektarvogel
235	N. coccinigaster (Cinnyris coccinigaster)	Splendid Sunbird	Suimanga Espléndida	Soui-manga Eclatant	Rotbauch-nektarvogel
235	N. pulchella	Beautiful Long-tailed Sunbird	Suimanga Bonita	Soui-manga à Longue Queue	Elfennektarvogel
235	N. superba (Cinnyris superbus)	Superb Sunbird	Suimanga Soberbia	Soui-manga Superbe	Prachtnektarvogel
236	N. johannae	Johanna's Sunbird	Suimanga de Juana	Soui-manga de Jeanne	Grünscheitelnektarvogel
	ZOSTEROPIDAE				
236	Zosterops senegalensis (Z. virens)	Yellow White-eye	Miopito senegalés	Oiseau-lunettes Jaune	Senegalbrillenvogel
	EMBERIZIDAE				
236	Emberiza cabanisi	Cabanis's Yellow Bunting	Escribano de Cabanis	Bruant de Cabanis	Cabanisammer
237	E. flaviventris	Yellow-bellied Bunting	Escribano Ventrigualdo	Bruant à Poitrine Dorée	Gelbbauchammer
237	E. forbesi	Nigerian Little Bunting	Escribano de Forbes	Bruant à Ventre Jaune	Braunbürzelammer

page	Latin	English	Spanish	French	German
EMBERIZIDAE (cont.)					
237	E. tahapisi (Fringillaria tahapisi)	Rock Bunting	Escribano de Tahapis	Bruant Cannelle	Bergammer (Siebenstreifenammer)
FRINGILLIDAE					
237	Serinus mozambicus	Yellow-fronted Canary	Canario de Mozambique	Serin du Mozambique	Moçambique girlitz
238	S. leucopygius (Poliospiza leucopygia)	Grey Canary	Serin Culiblanco	Chanteur d'Afrique	Weissbürzelgirlitz (Grauedelsänger)
238	S. gularis	Streaky-headed Seed-eater	Serin Mofletudo	Serin Gris à Tête Blanche	Brauengirlitz
238	Linurgus olivaceus	Oriole Finch	Lúgano Montañero Africano	Pinson-loriot	Pirolgimpel
PLOCEIDAE					
239	Amblyospiza albifrons	White-fronted Grosbeak	Tejedor picogordo	Gros-bec à Front Blanc	Weisstirnweber
239	Ploceus luteolus (Sitagra luteola)	Slender-billed Weaver	Sitagra Chico Común	Tisserin Minulle	Zwergweber
239	P. pelzelni	Little Weaver	Sitagra de pelzeln	Tisserin Nain	Mönchsweber
242	P. aurantius (Xanthophilus aurantius)	Orange Weaver	Tejedor Naranja	Tisserin Orangé	Königsweber
242	P. velatus (P. vitellinus)	Vitelline Masked Weaver	Tejedor Velado	Tisserin à Tête Rousse	Dotterweber
242	P. heuglini	Heuglin's Masked Weaver	Tejedor de Heuglin	Tisserin Masqué	Heuglinweber
242	P. cucullatus (Plesiositagra cucullatus, P. collaris)	Village Weaver	Tejedor Cogullado	Tisserin Gendarme	Textor (Dorfweber)
243	P. nigerrimus (Melanopteryx nigerrimus, Cinnamopteryx castaneofuscus)	Vieillot's Black Weaver	Tejedor Negro de Vieillot	Tisserin Noir de Vieillot	Mohrenweber
243	P. melanocephalus (Sitagra melanocephala, S. capitalis)	Black-headed Weaver	Tejedor Cabecinegro	Tisserin à tête Noire	Schwarzkopfweber (Kleiner Textor)

page	Latin	English	Spanish	French	German
	PLOCEIDAE (cont.)				
244	P. superciliosus (Pachyphantes pachyrhynchus)	Compact Weaver	Tejedor Rollizo	Tisserin Gros-bec	Braunbürzelweber (Augenbrauenweber)
244	P. tricolor	Yellow-mantled Weaver	Trejedor Tricolor	Tisserin Tricolore	Dreifarbweber
244	P. albinucha	Maxwell's Black Weaver	Tejedor Negro Albinuca	Tisserin Noir de Maxwell	Trauerweber
244	P. melanogaster	Black Mountain Weaver	Tejedor Negro Carigualdo	Tisserin à Tête Jaune	Schwarzbauchweber
244	P. nigricollis (Hyphanturgus nigricollis, H. brachypterus)	Spectacled Weaver	Tejedor Cuellinegro	Tisserin à Lunettes	Kurzflügel weber
245	Malimbus scutatus	Red-vented Malimbe	Malimbo Culirrojo	Malimbe à Queue Rouge	Schildweber (Rotburzel-prachtweber)
245	M. nitens	Blue-billed Malimbe	Malimbo Cabecinegro	Malimbe à Bec Bleu	Rotkehlweber (Rotkopf-prachtweber)
245	M. malimbicus	Crested Malimbe	Malimbo Moñudo	Malimbe Huppé	Haubenweber (Hauben-prachtweber)
246	M. rubricollis	Red-headed Malimbe	Malimbo Cuellirojo	Malimbe à Tête Rouge	Rothalsweber (Kletter-prachtweber)
246	M. rubriceps	Red-winged Malimbe	Malimbo Capirotado	Tisserin à Ailes Rouges	Scharlachweber
246	Quelea quelea	Black-faced Dioch	Laborioso Quelea	Travailleur à Bec Rouge	Blutschnabelweber
246	Q. erythrops	Red-headed Dioch	Laborioso Cabecirrojo	Travailleur à Tête Rouge	Rotkopfweber
246	Euplectes afer	Yellow-crowned Bishop	Euplectes Amarillo	Vorabé	Tahaweber (Napoleonweber)
247	E. ardens (Coliuspasser ardens)	Long-tailed Black Whydah	Falsa Viuda Pechirroja	Veuve Noire	Schildwida
247	E. hordeaceus	Fire-crowned Bishop	Euplectes Alinegro	Monseigneur	Flammenweber
247	E. macrourus (Coliuspasser macrourus)	Yellow-mantled Whydah	Falsa Viuda Dorsigualda	Veuve à Dos d'Or	Gelbschulterwida
248	E. orix	Red Bishop	Euplectes Rojo	Ignicolore	Oryxweber
248	Bubalornis albirostris	Buffalo Weaver	Tejedor de Búfalo	Alecto à Bec Blanc	Büffelweber
249	Plocepasser superciliosus	Sparrow-Weaver	Moineau-tisserin Capirotado	Moineau-tisserin	Braunwangenweber
249	Passer griseus	Grey-headed Sparrow	Gorrión Pardillo	Moineau Gris	Graukopfsperling

page	Latin	English	Spanish	French	German
PLOCEIDAE (cont.)					
249	P. luteus	Golden Sparrow	Gorrioncito Amarillo	Moineau Doré	Goldsperling (Kleinerkehlfleck-sperling)
249	Petronia dentata (Gymnoris dentata)	Bush-Sparrow	Chillón de Sundevall	Petit Moineau Soulcie	Buschsperling
250	Sporopipes frontalis	Scaly-fronted Weaver	Tejedorcito Punteado	Moineau Quadrillé	Schuppenköpfchen
250	Vidua macroura	Pin-tailed Whydah	Viuda Colicinta	Veuve Dominicaine	Dominikanerwitwe
250	V. chalybeata (Hypochera c. chalybeata, H. c. neumanni)	Senegal Indigo Finch	Tejedor Bruñido Verdoso	Combassou du Sénégal	Rotfuss-atlaswitwe
251	V. camerunensis	Cameroon Indigo Finch	Tejedor Brtñído de Alexander	Combassou du Cameroun	Kamerun-atlaswitwe
251	V. funerea nigeriae	Nigerian Indigo Finch	Tejedor Bruñido de Wilson	Combassou du Nigéria	Gongola-atlaswitwe
251	V. wilsoni	Wilson's Indigo Finch		Combassou Noir	Wilson-atlaswitwe
251	V. orientalis (Steganura orientalis)	Broad-tailed Paradise Whydah	Viuda del Paraíso Oriental	Veuve à Collier d'Or	Senegal-paradisswitwe
ESTRILDIDAE					
251	Pirenestes ostrinus (P. sanguineus)	Seed-cracker	Pirenestes Ventrinegro	Gros-bec Ponceau à Ventre Noir	Purpurastrild
252	Nigrita canicapilla	Grey-crowned Negro-Finch	Negrita cana	Sénégali Nègre	Graunacken-schwärzling
252	N. luteifrons	Pale-fronted Negro-Finch	Negrita Frentigualda	Sénégali Nègre à Front Jaune	Blasstirnschwärzling
252	N. bicolor	Chestnut-breasted Negro-Finch	Negrita Pechirroja	Sénégali Brun à Ventre Roux	Zweifarbenschwärzling
253	N. fusconota	White-breasted Negro-Finch	Negrita Pechiblanca	Sénégali Brun à Ventre Blanc	Mantelschwärzling
253	Spermophaga haematina	Blue-billed Weaver	Espermófaga hematina	Gros-bec Sanguin	Rotbrust-samenknacker
253	Nesocharis capistrata	White-cheeked Olive Weaver	Olivino Cariblanco	Sénégali Vert à Joues Blanches	Weisswangenastrild
254	Amadina fasciata	Cut-throat Weaver	Amadina Gorgirroja	Cou-coupé	Bandfink (Bandamadine)

page	Latin	English	Spanish	French	German
	ESTRILDIDAE (cont.)				
254	*Pytilia melba*	Melba Finch	Pitilia de Linneo	Beaumarquet	Buntastrild
254	*P. phoenicoptera*	Red-winged Pytilia	Pitilia Alirroja	Diamant Aurore	Auroraastrild
254	*Estrilda melpoda*	Orange-cheeked Waxbill	Astrilda Carirroja	Joues-oranges	Orangebäckchen
255	*E. nonnula*	Black-crowned Waxbill	Astrilda Monjita	Sénégali à Cape Noire	Nonnenastrild
255	*E. atricapilla*	Black-headed Waxbill	Astrilda Monjita de Verreaux	Astrild à Tête Noire	Kappenastrild
255	*E. troglodytes*	Black-rumped Waxbill	Astrilda Culinegra	Bec de Corail Cendré	Grauastrild
255	*E. astrild*	Common Waxbill	Astrilda Común	Bec de Corail Ondulé	Wellenastrild
258	*E. caerulescens*	Lavender Fire-Finch	Astrilda Ceniza del Senegal	Queue de Vinaigre	Schönbürzel
258	*E. bengala* (*Uraeginthus bengalus*)	Red-cheeked Cordon-bleu	Coliazul Bengali	Cordon Bleu	Schmetterlingsastrild
258	*E. larvata* (*Lagonosticta nigricollis, L. vinacea*)	Black-faced Fire-Finch	Bengali Carinegro	Amarante Masqué	Larvenamarant
259	*Lagonosticta senegala*	Senegal Fire-Finch	Bengali Senegalés	Amarante Commun	Amarant (Senegalamarant)
259	*L. rufopicta*	Bar-breasted Fire-Finch	Bengali de Fraser	Amarante Pointé	Pünktchenamarant
259	*L. rubricata*	Blue-billed Fire-Finch	Bengali de Lichtenstein	Amarante Flambé	Dunkelamarant (Dunkelroter amarant)
259	*Amandava subflava* (*Estrilda subflava*)	Zebra Waxbill	Astrilda Pechigualda	Ventre Orange	Goldbrüstchen
260	*Ortygospiza atricollis*	Quail-Finch	Astrilda aperdizada	Astrild-caille	Wachtelastrild
260	*Lonchura malabarica* (*Euodice cantans*)	Warbling Silverbill	Monjita Pico-de-Plata	Bec d'Argent	Silberschnäbelchen
260	*L. cucullata* (*Spermestes cucullatus*)	Bronze Mannikin	Negrita Bronceada	Spermète Nonnette	Kleinelsterchen
260	*L. fringilloides*	Magpie Mannikin	Negrita Picaza	Spermète Pie	Riesenelsterchen
261	*L. bicolor*	Black-and-white Mannikin		Spermète à Bec Bleu	Glanzelsterchen

INDEX OF SCIENTIFIC NAMES

Families

Genera and Species

INDEX OF ENGLISH NAMES